DESIGN CONTROLS, RISK MANAGEMENT & PROCESS VALIDATION FOR MEDICAL DEVICE PROFESSIONALS

A COMPREHENSIVE HANDBOOK FOR INTERPRETING AND IMPLEMENTING DESIGN CONTROL REGULATION

Vern Geckler

MBA ME PMP

PROCENIUS CONSULTING
www.procenius.com

Publisher: Wasatch Consulting Resources LLC

ISBN 9780692835418

Printed in the United States of America

ABOUT THE AUTHOR

Consulting and Professional Experience

Vern Geckler is president and owner of Procenius Consulting (Procenius.com), a medical device consulting and training firm specializing in medical device regulation compliance and training.

Vern has extensive experience in new product development specializing in design controls, risk management, process validation regulation and project management. He has worked in the medical device field as a new product development design engineer, process validation engineer, project manager, and program manager. Vern has also led numerous development teams through the product development life cycle which has given him invaluable experience with the practical implementation of design control regulation as illustrated in this book. His experience includes but is not limited to developing electromechanical, disposable, implantable, and IVD medical devices.

Vern has significant experience in:

- Design Control:
  - Developing Design Input Requirements
  - Developing Design and Development Plans
  - Developing Validation Master Plans
  - Developing Verification and Validation Protocols/Reports
  - Executing Design Changes
  - Leading and Documenting Design Reviews
  - Planning and Executing Design Transfer
  - Developing Design Control SOP's

- Mechanical Design of Medical Devices
- Development of process validation protocols and reports
- Risk management planning and execution
- Leading numerous cross functional teams in the development of medical devices from concept phase to commercialization

Education and Certifications

- Bachelor of Science (Mechanical Engineering); Brigham Young University
- Masters of Mechanical Engineering (Design Emphasis); University of Utah
- Masters of Business Administration; University of Michigan
- Certified as a Project Management Professional (PMP); Project Management Institute

DISCLAIMER OF WARRANTY/LIMIT OF LIABILITY

While it is the author's intent to provide the readers of this book with the most accurate and up to date information from FDA regulation, international standards, and industry best practices; the accuracy of the contents of this book is not guaranteed or warranted in any way. The author has put forth his best efforts in presenting the content of this book; however, no warranty with respect to the material's accuracy or completeness is made. Also, no warranty is made with respect to applying the recommendations made in this book to any business structure or environments. Businesses should consult regulatory, quality and/or legal professionals prior to deciding on the appropriateness of advice made within this book. The author nor his business shall be held liable for loss of profit or other commercial damages resulting from the implementation of recommendations and/or guidance provided within this book, including special, incidental, consequential, or other damages.

The Purpose of this Book

Over the last two decades since the design control regulation was introduced, the valuable and detailed knowledge for implementing design control systems, outside the walls of the FDA, has only been retained in the minds of a group of medical device industry professionals and consultants that varies greatly depending on the professionals' and consultants' experience.

The purpose of this book is to capture the last two decades of design control expertise from industry experts and to provide detail interpretation of design control regulation and guidance. This book is a download of the author's experience and industry experts' knowledge of design control best practices and practical implementation guidance which is cross referenced with the regulation, design control guidance and quality system preamble.

This book is also intended to provide medical device professionals with one point of reference when trying to understand medical device regulation. There are numerous medical device new product development regulations, standards and guidance documents that are scattered across the FDA website and internet. It can be quite a daunting task to understand them all. This book attempts to bring all of those resources together either by reference or by including the actual document in this book when possible.

This book was also written to provide additional guidance, interpretation, examples and case studies to help medical device professionals solidify their understanding of medical device regulation.

How to Use this Book

This book can be read from cover to cover for those that are interested in becoming an expert in understanding design control or it can be used as a reference manual to research specific design control elements.

The following aspects of the book provide various methods of researching design control topics and also provide regulation and guidance resource references.

Quick Reference Summary

A quick reference summary is located at the beginning of most chapters. These summaries are meant to be used for a high level understanding of the chapter. The summary also contains basic, yet critical information about the design control regulation which the reader can quickly reference as needed.

Design Control Regulation and Guidance

The design control regulation and guidance is contained in each chapter which allows for continuity between regulation, guidance and interpretation provided in the rest of the chapter.

Interpretation, Application and Discussion

The author provides an in-depth interpretation, practical application and expansive discussion for each design control element by breaking down the regulation line by line to ensure the full intent of the regulation is understood.

Quality System Preamble References

Throughout each chapter, the quality system preamble is referenced to provide an understanding of the FDA's initial intent when implementing the design control regulation.

In addition to the preamble references throughout the book, the entire Design Control section of the preamble (subpart C) is contained in Annex B.

Best Practices

Best practices for implementing design controls are included throughout most chapters. The best practices are intended to provide the reader with lessons learned and efficient methods of implementing design controls.

Examples

Many of the chapters contain examples of how design controls are actually implemented. The examples are designed so abstract design control regulations can be more fully understood

Case Studies

Case studies are included in a few chapters to enable the reader a more thorough and concrete understanding of abstract design control principles by using real life scenarios.

Quality System Manual: A Small Entity Guide

Most chapters (3-11) contain applicable sections of the FDA Quality System Manual. Even though this manual was withdrawn from the FDA website in 2014, there are many insightful and detailed suggestions for implementing design controls which readers will find valuable.

MEDICAL DEVICE REGULATION, GUIDANCE AND STANDARDS

	FDA Regulation	Guidance	Standards	Other
Design Controls	*21 CFR 820.30* (FDA QS Regulation, 2015)	*Design Control Guidance for Medical Device Manufacturers* (FDA D.C. Guidance, 2015)	NA	*1) Quality System Preamble (Subpart C)* (FDA Preamble, 2015) *2) Quality Systems Manual* (Med Dev QS Manual, 2014)
	NA	(ISO 14969, 2004)	*ISO 13485 (7.0)* (ISO 13485, 2007)	
Process Validation	*21 CFR 820.75*	1) Quality Management Systems – Process Validation Guidance (GHTF, 2004)	NA	*Quality Systems Manual* (Med Dev QS Manual, 2014)
Risk Management	21 CFR 820.30(g)	IEC/TR 80002-1:2009 (software risk assessments)	ISO 14971 (ISO 14971, 2007)	NA

Software Validation	21 CFR 820.30(g) 21 CFR 820.70(i)	1) General Principles of Software Validation (FDA SW Validation, 2012) 2) IEC/TR 80002-1:2009 (software risk assessments)	IEC 62304 (Software life cycle processes)	NA
Human Factors	NA	1) Applying Human Factors and Usability Engineering to Medical Devices (FDA) 2) Do It By Design – An Introduction to Human Factors in Medical Devices (FDA) 2) Device Use Safety: Incorporating Human Factors in Risk Management (FDA)	AAMI/ANSI HE75:2009 ANSI/AAMI/IEC 62366-1:2015	NA

DESIGN CONTROL CONSULTING AND TRAINING RESOURCES

Procenius Consulting specializes in medical device regulation compliance consulting and training. Visit **Procenius.com** for more details.

Table of Contents

Medical Device Regulation Consulting and Training – www.Procenius.com

Medical Device Regulation Consulting and Training – www.Procenius.com

Medical Device Regulation Consulting and Training – www.Procenius.com

Medical Device Regulation Consulting and Training – www.Procenius.com

Medical Device Regulation Consulting and Training – www.Procenius.com

Medical Device Regulation Consulting and Training – www.Procenius.com

1.0 Design Controls Overview

1.1. <u>The Wonderful World of Design Controls</u>

Welcome to the wonderful world of design controls! Implementing design controls into medical device product development can be a very exciting experience. Design control requirements should be seen as more than just another regulation that needs to be followed; they should become an integral part of an organization's product development process. In other words, design control regulation should not be seen as just another regulatory hoop to jump through, but rather a robust method of developing safe and effective medical devices.

Inherent to any new product development environment there are always technical, business and commercial challenges which introduce unknowns which will often require creative solutions for solving monumental problems. In addition to these traditional challenges, design control requirements add an additional hurdle which must be championed during product development.

Due to the "umbrella" approach the FDA uses to define the regulation, there is significant allowance for interpretation of how the regulation should be implemented. This is where the exciting part comes in to play! Not only do development teams get to figure out how they can overcome their technical problems, they also have to anticipate what development methods will be acceptable to the FDA. As organizations become expert in their devices and work closely with the FDA during device submissions, they will soon be able to effectively anticipate and understand the FDA's expectations.

1.2. <u>History of Design Controls Regulation (21 CFR 820.30)</u>

The design controls regulation (21 CFR 820.30) has its roots in the "Current Good Manufacturing Practices" (CGMP's) as authorized in section 520(f) of the Food and Drug Administration (FDA) Act which became effective December 18, 1978. (FDA CGMP, 2014) The initial intent of these CGMP's was to ensure that commercialized medical devices would experience minimal device failures that may lead to patient injury or death. During the following ten years after 1978, the FDA realized that a significant number of device failures were occurring due to design defects.

Quality Systems Regulation Preamble States:

Subpart C

"Since early 1984, FDA has identified lack of design controls as one of the major causes of device recalls. The intrinsic quality of devices, including their safety and effectiveness, is established during the design phase. Thus, FDA believes that unless appropriate

Medical Device Regulation Consulting and Training – www.Procenius.com

design controls are observed during preproduction stages of development, a finished device may be neither safe nor effective for its intended use. The "Safe Medical Device Act" (SMDA) provided FDA with the authority to add preproduction design controls to the device CGMP regulation. Based on its experience with administering the original CGMP regulation, which did not include preproduction design controls, the agency was concerned that the original regulation provided less than an adequate level of assurance that devices would be safe and effective. Therefore, FDA has added general requirements for design controls to the device CGMP regulation for all class III and II devices and certain class I devices." (FDA Preamble, 2015)

In 1989 FDA published a notice of availability for design control recommendations which was titled, "Preproduction Quality Assurance Planning: Recommendations for Medical Device Manufacturers" (Hooten, 1996). This was an early indication to the industry that controls during the development of medical devices was well on its way to becoming a reality. A year later the "Safe Medical Device Act of 1990" was introduced and became law and section 520(f) was amended which added "preproduction design validation" controls to the device GMP regulation. Over the next six years the design controls regulation was developed and refined. "After an extensive effort, the part 820 revision was published on October 7, 1996 and went into effect June 1, 1997." (FDA CGMP, 2014) Design controls became 21 CFR 820.30 (subpart C) as part of the Quality System Regulation.

1.3. <u>What Is Design Controls and What Is Its Purpose?</u>

The FDA views the purpose of design controls as stated in the following reference from the Design Control Guidance document:

> *"Design controls are an interrelated set of practices and procedures that are incorporated into the design and development process, i.e., a system of checks and balances. Design controls make systematic assessment of the design an integral part of development. As a result, deficiencies in design input requirements, and discrepancies between the proposed designs and requirements, are made evident and corrected earlier in the development process. Design controls increase the likelihood that the design transferred to production will translate into a device that is appropriate for its intended use.*
>
> *In practice, design controls provide managers and designers with improved visibility of the design process. With improved visibility, managers are empowered to more effectively direct the design process-that is, to recognize problems earlier, make corrections, and adjust resource allocations. Designers benefit both by enhanced understanding of the degree of conformance of a design to user and patient needs, and by improved communications and coordination among all participants in the process.*
>
> *The medical device industry encompasses a wide range of technologies and applications, ranging from simple hand tools to complex computer-controlled surgical*

machines, from implantable screws to artificial organs, from blood-glucose test strips to diagnostic imaging systems and laboratory test equipment. These devices are manufactured by companies varying in size and structure, methods of design and development, and methods of management. These factors significantly influence how design controls are actually applied. Given this diversity, this guidance does not suggest particular methods of implementation, and therefore, must not be used to assess compliance with the quality system requirements. Rather, the intent is to expand upon the distilled language of the quality system requirements with practical explanations and examples of design control principles. Armed with this basic knowledge, manufacturers can and should seek out technology-specific guidance on applying design controls to their particular situation.

When using this guidance, there could be a tendency to focus only on the time and effort required in developing and incorporating the controls into the design process. However, readers should keep in mind the intrinsic value of design controls as well. It is a well-established fact that the cost to correct design errors is lower when errors are detected early in the design and development process. Large and small companies that have achieved quality systems certification under ISO 9001 cite improvements in productivity, product quality, customer satisfaction, and company competitiveness. Additional benefits are described in comments received from a quality assurance manager of a medical device firm regarding the value of a properly documented design control system:"

> *"...there are benefits to an organization and the quality improvement of an organization by having a written design control system. By defining this system on paper, a corporation allows all its employees to understand the requirements, the process, and expectations of design and how the quality of design is assured and perceived by the system. It also provides a baseline to review the system periodically for further improvements based on history, problems, and failures of the system (not the product)."*

(FDA D.C. Guidance, 2015)

The Quality Systems Regulation Preamble states:

Subpart C

"With respect to the new regulation, FDA believes that it is reasonable to expect manufacturers who design medical devices to develop the designs in conformance with design control requirements and that adhering to such requirements is necessary to adequately protect the public from potentially harmful devices. The design control requirements are basic controls needed to ensure that the device being designed will perform as intended when produced for commercial distribution." (FDA Preamble, 2015)

1.4. Summary of Design Control Elements

Design controls is a systematic method of developing a product that can potentially maximize the probability of making the "right product" to meet the user's needs while minimizing the probability of exposing the user to harm.

In layman's terms, design controls are comprised of the following concepts and activities. This is intended to be a brief and non-inclusive description of design controls activities. To gain a full understanding of design controls, the proceeding chapters should be researched.

- Planning (Design and Development Plan): The process of establishing who, what, how, when and where the device will be developed. Planning should include the identification of design and development activities. It should also specify how different cross functional groups interface during device development.

- Gathering and Defining Requirements (Inputs): Identification of requirements from potential users about what the device should do, how it should perform and in what environment. Translating the user requirements into design specifications is also performed.

- Design the Device: This step involves transforming design requirements into a detailed design. This may include activities such as creating the design virtually on a CAD system (or drawings), defining design schematics, or writing software code.

- Risk Management: During the design process, a risk analysis should be performed to identify risks that may result in harm to the user or patient while using the device. Unacceptable risks may be identified during the risk assessment which should result in a design change to eliminate or at least minimize the risk.

- Design Reviews: These are formal reviews which are typically comprehensive in nature and involve cross functional team review of the design. Design reviews are a forum where teams can challenge the design and/or identify design problems.

- Design Outputs: The documents, drawings, software code etc. that are generated to define the design that are a result of the design process. Outputs also include the results (reports) of design activities such as verification and validation.

- Design Transfer: Design transfer activities ensure production specifications are created which allow for the device to be produced reliably and repeatable within product and process specifications. This is typically achieved by executing process validations, quality checks and other production support procedures which are implemented in the production environment.

- Design Verification: Design verification is typically performed during the development of the device and just prior to final design validation. It is a confirmation that the design meets the design requirements which can be performed by analysis, inspection or testing.

- <u>Design Validation:</u> Performed on the final device configuration to ensure the device performs as required by the user and also to demonstrate that the device is safe and effective.

- <u>Design Change:</u> Process of ensuring that the impact of making a design change is adequately reviewed controlled and approved prior to making the change.

- <u>Design History File (DHF):</u> This is a compilation of documents that were used during development of the device such as plans, design inputs & outputs, protocols, reports, risk assessments, requirements, design changes, etc.

Figure 1 is the traditional waterfall diagram FDA uses to define the relationship between some of the previously listed design control elements. While this diagram can provide a high level understanding of the process, there is significantly more definition and explanation required when actually implementing the process into a medical device manufacturer's quality system.

(FDA D.C. GUIDANCE, 2015)

FIGURE 1

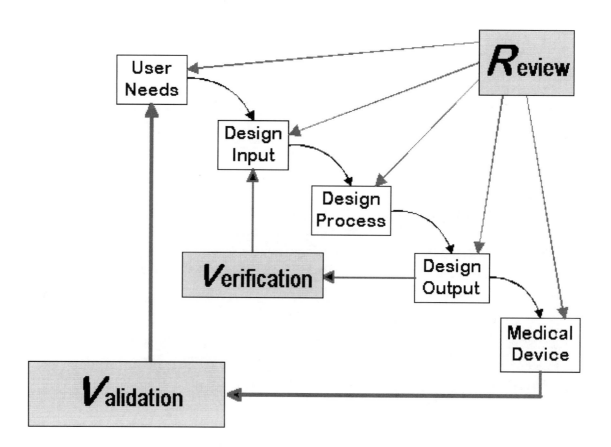

Medical Device Regulation Consulting and Training – www.Procenius.com

1.5. FDA Design Controls (21 CFR 820.30) vs. ISO 13485 (7.3)

The FDA requires all medical device manufacturers that design, produce and sell medical devices in the United States to follow 21 CFR 820.30. In general, the rest of the world follows ISO 13485 (7.3).

For all intents and purposes, ISO 13485 (7.3) and 21 CFR 820.30 are equivalent. One major difference is that ISO 13485 (7.3) does not require a *Design History File* which is required in design controls regulation. Other differences between the regulation and the ISO standard are relatively minor.

1.6. Regulatory Intelligence

The more frequent manufacturers launch products, the better they become at being able to anticipate FDA approval requirements. Over time they increase their "regulatory intelligence" around design controls regulation which allows them to more efficiently launch products relative to competitors which will become a competitive advantage. Manufacturers will begin to better understand the level and type of development activities and documentation the FDA will expect during regulatory submissions. As a natural consequence, the significance and number of delays that may occur during these submission activities will be reduced.

Initially new medical device manufacturers may struggle "getting off the starting blocks", but over time regulatory intelligence will increase and the process of implementing design controls will become a "well-oiled machine".

Medical device startup companies often hire consultants to get through the initial regulatory learning curve quickly and to provide a quick download of regulatory advice which provides these companies with the necessary regulatory intelligence for initial regulatory submissions and quality system inspections.

1.7. Design Controls Regulation Uses the Umbrella Approach

Due to the fact that the medical device industry has such a wide variety of devices, FDA uses an "umbrella" approach for defining the regulation. In other words, the regulation is written very generically and broadly as not to exclude device type or application. In some respects this approach is beneficial for medical device manufacturers because it allows them flexibility of how they want to implement design controls in their organization. On the other hand, even though FDA does not specify details of how each part of the regulation should be implemented, they do have basic expectations that have come to be known as best practices in the industry which FDA inspectors will expect to see during their inspections. To best understand these expectations, manufacturers can tap into various resources such as specialized consultants or other resources such as this book.

1.8. Where Should Design Controls Be Initiated?

Many manufacturers that are new to design controls ask the question, "When should I start design controls?" As with most aspects of the regulation this decision is ultimately up to the manufacturer, but the FDA does give some guidance in the quality systems regulation preamble on this topic:

The Quality Systems Regulation Preamble States:

Comment 62

"The design control requirements are not intended to apply to the development of concepts and feasibility studies. However, once it is decided that a design will be developed, a plan must be established to determine the adequacy of the design requirements and to ensure that the design that will eventually be released to production meets the approved requirements." (FDA Preamble, 2015)

Comment 65

"Clinical evaluation is an important aspect of the design verification and validation process during the design and development of the device. Because some of the device design occurs during the IDE stage, it is logical that manufacturers who intend to commercially produce the device follow design control procedures. Were a manufacturer to wait until all the IDE studies were complete, it would be too late to take advantage of the design control process, and the manufacturer would not be able to fulfill the requirements of the quality system regulation for that device." (FDA Preamble, 2015)

So research scientists and engineers can rest assured that design controls are not required during early research, concept or feasibility phases. In recent decades the term "research and development" (R&D) has frequently been lumped together and is often thought of as primarily one phase of product development when in reality they are different. Research typically has very broad discovery targets while only considering some level of efficacy and will often only narrow concepts down to things that work or don't work without a specific intended use in mind.

Development on the other hand typically begins when the business recognizes a specific market need. From this market need, product scope, plans and requirements can be initiated. The following are indications during development that it is time to begin design controls:

- User needs and design requirements are beginning to be defined
- Management has approved an official project charter to initiate a project to launch the product
- The business begins to form teams which will take the product from feasibility to commercialization

The following graphical models give some clarity as to when design controls typically begin relative to research and development activities.

Medical Device Regulation Consulting and Training – www.Procenius.com

The two humps in Figure 2 depict the relationship and the relative amount of research and development activities which occur during the design and development cycle. The shaded area is the typical time when design controls is initiated. Design controls should continue through development until final design validation and design transfer is completed to support a commercialized product which has been approved/cleared by the FDA.

FIGURE 2

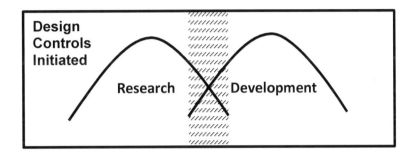

1.9. When Should Design Controls End?

When should design controls end?....design controls never end. As long as device manufacturers have devices in development, in production or in the field, design controls should be followed. Device manufacturers may think that design controls are only used during the development phase when in reality they should be continued to be used even after implemented into the production environment. When the design or manufacturing process is changed or when problems occur in the field that drive a change, many elements of the design control process should be used to address the change or evaluate risk. Or in other words, design controls should be cracked back open to determine if the device should be changed and to determine the necessary design elements that must take place to modify the device such as verification, validation, update inputs & outputs, or update the design history file, etc.

1.10. Various Perspectives of Design Control Regulation

The importance, purpose and understanding of design control principles may not be consistent between the FDA and other roles within the medical device industry such as design engineers, managers and quality assurance representatives.

A design engineer that is new to the medical device industry may typically view design controls as a necessary evil. They take pride in their own engineering judgment, experience, designs and testing strategies. They may often think design controls requires excessive documentation and testing that would otherwise not be required. On the other hand, over the years an experienced medical device engineer will understand the value of implementing the design controls requirements and how it really can increase the probability of developing a safe and effective device.

A quality assurance representative/engineer will use the design control regulation and procedures as a design and development "Bible", as they should. Their job is to make sure that procedures are being strictly followed. They accept design control procedures as the required method of ensuring the device is safe and effective and they tend to think that any deviation from the procedures could lead to user or patient harm. The quality assurance representative is also highly aware that the manufacturer may be at risk of receiving 483 observations or warnings from the FDA if not strictly followed. They are acutely in tune with the manufacturer's compliance to the procedures because they are typically in the hot seat when inspected by the FDA. They are often the one that has to answer questions about why deviations were made or why procedures were not followed.

At times they may appear to only present obstacles of what can't be done by pointing out procedures and regulations that seem to hinder the development process. On the other hand, a savvy quality assurance representative/engineer has the ability to provide guidance during development that will allow design teams to overcome regulatory hurdles yet still be able to stay within the bounds of the regulations and company procedures.

Like design engineers, inexperienced managers in the medical device industry may also see design controls as a necessary evil and will often not understand its intent or purpose. They may only see it as one more regulatory obstacle that must be overcome to launch the product on time. Seasoned managers that have experienced product recalls, consent decrees and potentially even patient deaths as a result of defective devices understand the importance of design controls both from a safety and business investment perspective. Besides the obvious fact that mangers do not want to see their customers harmed, they also realize that defective devices result in product recalls or consent decrees which can be detrimental to a the business's bottom line and to a customer's perception of the company's product quality.

1.11. Design Control Regulation – Compliance and Ethics

Many experienced engineers outside the medical device industry will inherently recognize the principles of design controls previously described. Many of the design control concepts have historically been part of robust design and development procedures for decades. Design controls are simply a proven way that the FDA has formalized the widely accepted practice of development. So some may ask, "if these design and development principles are so common, why do some medical device companies have such trouble following them?" Companies that have a problem following the regulation typically have one or more of the following issues:

1. They don't fully understand the regulation and how to apply its principles
2. The procedures that they have established to apply the design control regulation are inefficient and greatly hinder product development.
3. Management does not provide sufficient resources (people, money, equipment) to support aggressive target development timelines.

Medical Device Regulation Consulting and Training – www.Procenius.com

No matter what the role or position that is held in the medical device industry, design control regulations should be respected and effectively implemented to ensure no harm occurs to patients or users of the medical device. Remembering this charge given to the medical device industry can often be forgotten when companies are under intense pressure to launch new products within budget and under aggressive timelines. Medical device manufacturers may often get lost in the technical development of the device and may lose sight of individuals that may benefit, or in some cases potentially be harmed from the device. It is important to remember that this is not just another commercial product that is targeted to be launched as soon as possible to meet quarterly sales targets. On the contrary, these devices improve, sustain, support or in many cases save lives. Every reasonable effort should be made to make these devices safe and effective.

Unfortunately, in some medical device companies design controls are basically a paper work exercise simply to have the appearance of being compliant to FDA inspectors. There is no doubt that this strategy may work for a time, but sooner or later either the FDA will catch on and issue significant fines or the defective devices can lead to lawsuits against the medical device manufacturer. During the investigation, evidence of following design controls will be scrutinized. Manufacturers are significantly vulnerable to a negligence verdict if compliance to design control regulation cannot be proven. Regardless of the business risk, the ultimate worst case scenario is if ineffective design control implementation leads to patient harm.

Kevin Ong has this to say about why design controls are important in attempts to avoid product liability claims,

> *"Having effective design controls in place can go a long way in preventing and bolstering the defense against products-liability claims alleging a design defect—one of three bases for products liability. The basic allegation behind a design-defect claim is that a safer design exists for the product in question, but that the manufacturer failed to use the safer design. Robust design controls help to ensure that the safest, technologically feasible, design for the product is being used. Further, in the event of litigation, design controls can be used by the manufacturer to demonstrate that the risks associated with alternative designs were weighed and considered.*
>
> *In addition to creating product liability risks for design flaws, failure to institute sufficient design controls is likely to result in regulatory actions. Design controls constitute about a quarter of what the FDA evaluates during a site inspection. This emphasis appears to be appropriate, as the FDA found that approximately 44 percent of the quality problems that led to voluntary recall actions during a six-year period in the 1990's may have been prevented by adequate design controls. As a significant part of the FDA's focus in inspections, it is not surprising that 55 percent of Warning Letters issued in 2010 cited design controls as a deficiency."* (Ong, 2012)

1.12. Design Control Activities, Interfaces, Key Relationships, and Traceability

One of the more difficult aspects to understand about design control regulation is how all of the design control elements should work together. The design control process is anything but linear. The interrelationships between design control elements is not complex, but there are many interactions that must be understood for device manufacturers to effectively execute a design control process. The FDA does not directly explain these relationships in the regulation, guidance or preamble but nevertheless expects them to be correctly implemented.

Figure 3 is a graphical representation of the interfaces between all design control elements. Each tie between the design control elements is labeled with a relationship ID#.

FIGURE 3

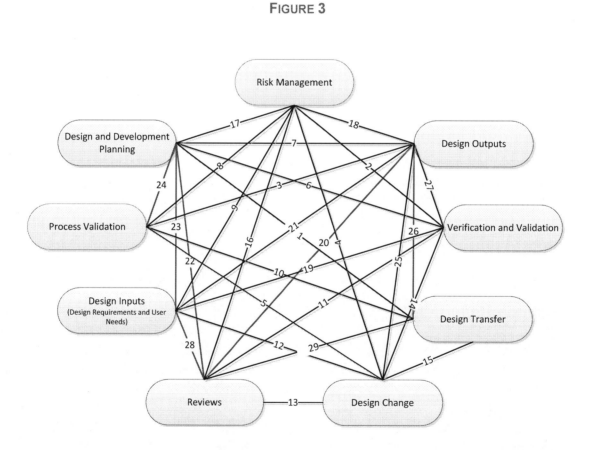

Medical Device Regulation Consulting and Training – www.Procenius.com

The numbers referenced in this matrix (Table 1) are defined in Table 2 to explain how these design control elements interface with each other.

TABLE 1

	Risk Mgt.	Design Output	V&V	Design Transfer	Design Change	Reviews	Design Inputs	Process Val.	Design & Dev. Plans
Risk Mgt.		18	2	--	4	16	9	8	17
Design Output			27	26	25	20	21	3	7
V&V				--	14	11	19	--	6
Design Transfer					15	29	--	10	1
Design Change						13	12	5	--
Reviews							28	--	22
Design Inputs								--	23
Process Validation									24
Design and Development Plans									

Table 2 provides the functional interfaces between each design control element and a detail description of how these design control elements interact.

Medical Device Regulation Consulting and Training – www.Procenius.com

TABLE 2

Relationship ID#	Design Control Activity Interface	Description of Design Control Activity Interface, Relationship and Traceability
1	Design Transfer	The design and development plan should specify timing and responsibility of design transfer activities such as design transfer reviews, completion of process validation, completion of production inspection specifications, DHR forms, and manufacturing procedures, etc. The design and development plan should also specify timing of design transfer phases (as applicable). It is best practice to reference the design transfer checklist document # in the design and development plan as design transfer is occurring and as the design and development plan is updated.
	Design & Development Plan	
2	Risk Management	The risk assessment is typically used to refine acceptance criteria in verification and validation protocols and to influence verification/validation methods. Even though the design input requirements will drive the acceptance criteria, the risk assessment will influence such things as the required confidence level and method of verification or validation. For lower risk design features or performance requirements, lower confidence levels may be acceptable. It may also be acceptable to perform verification by inspection or by analysis for lower risk features, where this may not be the case for higher risk features which would typically drive verification by testing.
	Verification and Validation	In some instances when a risk assessment is performed on a manual process or assesses variability of a user during human factors studies, it may be appropriate to use the results of verification or validation to lower the original probability of occurrence of harm. This may be justified in some instances if the original identified probability of occurrence of harm is based on team member subjective input and not on objective data. If the verification or validation was performed by hundreds or thousands of manual users which repeat the same operation, risk assessment reviewers may be inclined to use this data to justify reducing the probability of occurrence. If this approach is justified, the verification/validation report should be referenced as a risk control method (even though technically it is not a control).

3	Design Output	The <u>design outputs</u> from the design process (i.e. drawings) which define the device are used to guide <u>process validation</u> acceptance criteria. The <u>design outputs</u> will specify critical features and inspection criteria which will be translated into manufacturing product acceptance criteria. The manufacturing acceptance criteria will be used to drive acceptance criteria in the <u>process validation</u> (Process Performance Qualification and Product Performance Qualification).
	Process Validation	
4	Risk Management	Every time a <u>design change</u> is proposed, a <u>risk assessment</u> should be performed (or an existing risk assessment should be reviewed) to determine if the <u>design change</u> will impact/alter the current risk levels.
	Design Change	
5	Design Change	Every time a <u>design change</u> is proposed, the impact to the design outputs should be assessed to determine if the change will invalidate the <u>process validation</u> associated with those design outputs. (e.g. did a critical feature or acceptance criteria on the design output change which would require re-validation of the process which makes the device)
	Process Validation	
6	Verification & Validation	The <u>design and development plan</u> should specify timing and responsibility of <u>verification and validation</u> activities such as protocol development, execution and report generation. It is best practice to reference the <u>verification and validation</u> protocol and reports document #'s in the design and development plan when V & V is completed and when the <u>design and development plan</u> is updated.
	Design and Dev. Plan	

7	Design Output	The <u>design and development plan</u> should specify timing and responsibility of <u>design output</u> activities such as software code, component drawings, electrical schematics, manufacturing procedures, inspection requirements, etc. It is best practice to reference the <u>design output document #'s</u> (usually high level) in <u>the design and development plan as design outputs</u> are being created and when the <u>design and development plan</u> is updated.
	Design and Dev. Plan	
8	Risk Management	A <u>design risk assessment</u> will identify device hazards which may lead to patient harm. These hazards will be used as inputs into the process risk assessment for a device manufacturing process. (The hazards in the process risk assessment should contain a reference back to where they were initially identified in the design risk assessment.) The process risk assessment will evaluate what process steps may lead to these hazards occurring. Those process steps which have a high probability of causing these hazards (higher risk) should be given additional <u>process development and validation scrutiny</u>. As an example, if a manufacturing process generates a device feature which is critical to the safety of the device, that process step should have higher process capability requirements ($1.33\ C_{pk}$ vs. $2.00\ C_{pk}$) than other features which are not as high risk.
	Process Validation	
9	Risk Management	Typically design <u>risk assessments</u> and <u>design inputs</u> should be developed simultaneously. The initial version of <u>the risk assessment</u> will identify hazards and associated risks which may need to be mitigated. An ideal method of mitigating risk is to generate a <u>design input</u> requirement which will lead to generating an output that is intended to mitigate the risk (via design control). It is best practice to reference these requirements and the verification reports (evidence of verifying that the outputs meet the design inputs) in the "risk control" field of the <u>risk assessment</u>. This documentation practice provides objective evidence that the design control feature was implemented and verified. The residual risk evaluation should be performed with consideration of the completed verification which may in turn lead to a lower residual risk. For those identified risks which lead to creating design inputs, it is also best practice to reference the line item # (or ID#) from the risk assessment in the design input requirement line item to provide the source of the design input requirement (source = risk assessment).
	Design Inputs	

Medical Device Regulation Consulting and Training – www.Procenius.com

10	Design Transfer	Process validation for device manufacturing processes should be a required design transfer activity. Process validation should be specified as a requirement on the design transfer checklist. The process validation report(s) should be referenced in the design transfer checklist to provide objective evidence that process validation was completed. This also provides easy traceability during internal or external inspections.
	Process Validation	
11	Verification and Validation	Verification and validation protocols and reports should be reviewed prior to approval. Informal individual reviews are acceptable, a formal design review is not required.
	Reviews	
12	Design Change	Revisions to design input documents require changes to be approved through a formal change control process.
	Design Inputs	When making design changes (i.e. to design outputs), an impact assessment should be performed to determine if the design inputs (or associated verifications and validations) are affected by the change.
13	Design Change	Design changes should be reviewed prior to implementing the design change. Reviews can be individual or formal team design reviews (meetings).
	Reviews	

14	Verification and Validation	When making <u>design changes</u> (changes to design inputs or outputs), a verification and validation assessment should be performed to determine if the <u>design change</u> affects the validity of a previously performed verification or validation. If the validity of the verification or validation is in question, additional verification or validation may be required.
	Design Change	
15	Design Transfer	When making <u>design changes</u> (changes to design inputs or outputs), an impact assessment should be performed to determine if the design change affects the <u>production specifications</u> that were created during <u>design transfer</u>.
	Design Change	
16	Risk Management	<u>Risk assessments</u> and <u>risk management reports</u> should be <u>reviewed</u> prior to approval.
	Reviews	
17	Risk Management	The <u>design and development plan</u> should specify timing and responsibility of <u>risk management</u> activities/deliverables such as a risk analysis, risk management plan and report. It is best practice to reference the <u>risk management plan and report</u> document # in the <u>design and development plan</u>.
	Design and Development Plan	

Medical Device Regulation Consulting and Training – www.Procenius.com

18	Risk Management	During the risk analysis process, design outputs are reviewed to identify hazards that may be associated with the output.
	Design Output	As a result of the initial risk analysis and evaluation, risk mitigation may be required. Design controls to mitigate risk are implemented by modifying or creating design outputs.
19	Verification and Validation	Verification and Validation protocols should contain acceptance criteria which should be derived from the design inputs. The protocol should also include a trace matrix to tie the verification or validation test case to the input that is being verified/validated.
	Design Inputs	
20	Design Outputs	Design outputs should be reviewed prior to approval and release. Individual review of outputs are acceptable, formal design reviews are not required.
	Reviews	
21	Design Outputs	Design inputs guide the development of the design outputs during the design process.
	Design Inputs	Design verification is performed to show that design outputs meet design inputs. A traceability matrix is used to tie design outputs back to design inputs. See traceability section in verification chapter for more details.

22	Reviews	
	Design and Development Plan	The design and development plan should specify when design reviews will be held, who is responsible for leading the reviews and what type of reviews will be held. It is best practice to reference the design review meeting minute's document # in the design and development plan as design reviews are executed.
23	Design Inputs	
	Design and Development Plan	The design and development plan should specify what type of inputs will be developed, when the inputs should be completed, and who will be responsible for developing the inputs.
24	Process Validation	
	Design and Development Plan	The design and development plan should specify when process validation will be held and who is responsible for leading process validation activities (i.e. protocol development).
25	Design Output	A change control process is required for all design changes (changes to design inputs or design outputs).
	Design Change	As part of the change control process, an impact assessment should be performed to determine what outputs are affected by the change. It is best practice to include the change control reference number in the revision record of the output to tie the output revision to the change control record.

Medical Device Regulation Consulting and Training – www.Procenius.com

26	Design Output	During the design transfer process, production specifications (design outputs) will be developed to support the production process.
	Design Transfer	Also, design outputs which document the device design (i.e. device drawings) will be used to develop the production specifications during design transfer (also design outputs).
27	Design Output	Design verification is performed to show that design outputs meet design inputs.
	Verification and Validation	Verification/Validation protocols should reference the design output document(s) # that are being used during verification or validation.
28	Reviews	Design inputs should be reviewed in a formal design review(s). If a design input requirement is developed or modified in a review, the document # of the meeting minutes from the review should be referenced in the design input requirement as the source of that requirement (traceability).
	Design Inputs	
29	Design Transfer	It is best practice to hold a formal design transfer review to ensure that all design transfer activities and deliverables have been completed.
	Reviews	

Medical Device Regulation Consulting and Training – www.Procenius.com

2.0 Medical Device Classifications (I,II,III)

2.1. Introduction

It is essential that a medical device manufacturer understand how their device will be classified prior to dedicating significant resources to the development of the device. The amount of resources (time and money) required to develop each level of device classification can vary greatly depending on the class, type of device and intended use. Frequently manufacturers will often make strategic business decisions as to whether or not the device should be developed based solely on the device classification. A majority of medical device manufacturers only develop class two devices and will not pursue class three device concepts due to the intensive resources required to develop and submit these devices for FDA Premarket Approval (PMA).

The remainder of this chapter is FDA's explanation of medical device classifications and associated submission types. Direct references from the FDA website are noted.

2.2. Explanation of Class I, II, III Medical Devices

Reference: (FDA Medical Device Classes Define, 2014)

The Medical Device Amendments of 1976 to the Federal Food, Drug and Cosmetic Act established three regulatory classes for medical devices. The three classes are based on the degree of control necessary to assure the various types of devices are safe and effective.

Class I – These devices present minimal potential for harm to the user and are often simpler in design than Class II or Class III devices. Examples include enema kits and elastic bandages. 47% of medical devices fall under this category and 95% of these are exempt from the regulatory process.

Class II – Most medical devices are considered Class II devices. Examples of Class II devices include powered wheelchairs and some pregnancy test kits. 43% of medical devices fall under this category.

Class III – These devices usually sustain or support life, are implanted or present potential unreasonable risk of illness or injury. Examples of Class III devices include implantable pacemakers and breast implants. 10% of medical devices fall under this category.

Exempt – If a device falls into a generic category of exempted Class I devices, a premarket notification application and FDA clearance is not required before marketing the device in the U.S. However, the manufacturer is required to register their establishment and list their generic product with FDA. Examples of exempt devices are manual stethoscopes, mercury thermometers and bedpans.

Section 510(k) of the Food, Drug and Cosmetic Act requires those device manufacturers who must register to notify FDA their intent to market a medical device. This is known as Premarket Notification (PMN) or 510(k). Under 510(k), before a manufacturer can market a medical device in the United States, they must demonstrate to FDA's satisfaction that it is substantially equivalent (as safe and effective) to a device already on the market. If FDA rules the device is "substantially equivalent," the manufacturer can market the device. If the device you are researching has been in commercial distribution before 1976 or is substantially equivalent to a device already on the market, you should search FDA's 510(k) releasable database.

A primary safeguard in the way FDA regulates medical devices is the requirement that manufacturers must submit to FDA a Premarket Approval (PMA) application if they wish to market any new products that contain new materials or differ in design from products already on the market. A PMA submission must provide valid scientific evidence collected from human clinical trials showing the device is safe and effective for its intended use. If the device you are researching is life sustaining or presents a potential, unreasonable risk of illness or injury, you should search FDA's Premarket Approval (PMA) releasable database.

Investigational Device Exemption (IDE) - An IDE allows the investigational device to be used in a clinical study to collect safety and effectiveness data required to support a Premarket Approval (PMA) application and in some rare situations a Premarket Notification (510(k)) submission. Only a small percentage of 510(k)s require clinical data to support a marketing clearance by the Food and Drug Administration (FDA). An IDE limits the distribution of an investigational device only to the sites identified in the IDE application. In addition to FDA requirements, clinical studies of devices are also monitored by Institutional Review Boards (IRB) located at hospitals or other facilities where the clinical studies are conducted. An IRB is composed of medical experts and lay persons.

The purpose of an IRB's review is to assure ethical principles are in place for patient selection criteria, and that adequate informed consent information exists to identify the risks to patients. The IRB acts as FDA's surrogate to oversee the protection of human subjects who participate in the clinical studies. The initial risk determination of a clinical study and/or device is made by an IRB in most cases. The IRB determines if a device/clinical study is significant risk or non-significant risk. The FDA can overrule any risk determination made by an IRB. If the IRB determines that a device/clinical study is significant risk the applicant must submit an IDE application to the FDA. The FDA must approve the application prior to the applicant enrolling patients in the clinical study. If the IRB determines that the clinical study/device is non-significant risk the applicant can enroll patients without submitting an IDE application to the FDA. The clinical study will be monitored by the IRB under the abbreviated requirements of the IDE regulations in 21 CFR 812.2(b).

FDA will not disclose the existence of an IDE because the information is considered confidential.

2.3. How to Classify Medical Devices

Reference: (FDA Devcie Classification, 2014)

The Food and Drug Administration (FDA) has established classifications for approximately 1,700 different generic types of devices and grouped them into 16 medical specialties referred to as panels. Each of these generic types of devices is assigned to one of three regulatory classes based on the level of control necessary to assure the safety and effectiveness of the device. The three classes and the requirements which apply to them are:

Device Class and Regulatory Controls

1. Class I General Controls

   * With Exemptions

   * Without Exemptions

2. Class II General Controls and Special Controls

   * With Exemptions

   * Without Exemptions

3. Class III General Controls and Premarket Approval

The class to which your device is assigned determines, among other things, the type of premarketing submission/application required for FDA clearance to market. If your device is classified as Class I or II, and if it is not exempt, a 510k will be required for marketing. All devices classified as exempt are subject to the limitations on exemptions. Limitations of device exemptions are covered under 21 CFR xxx.9, where xxx refers to Parts 862-892. For Class III devices, a premarket approval application (PMA) will be required unless your device is a pre-amendments device (on the market prior to the passage of the medical device amendments in 1976, or substantially equivalent to such a device) and PMA's have not been called for. In that case, a 510k will be the route to market.

Device classification depends on the *intended use* of the device and also upon *indications for use*. For example, a scalpel's intended use is to cut tissue. A subset of intended use arises when a more specialized indication is added in the device's labeling such as, "for making incisions in the cornea". Indications for use can be found in the device's labeling, but may also be conveyed orally during sale of the product. A discussion of the meaning of intended use is contained in The 510(k) Program: Evaluating Substantial Equivalence in Premarket Notification [510(k)].

In addition, classification is risk based, that is, the risk the device poses to the patient and/or the user is a major factor in the class it is assigned. Class I includes devices with the lowest risk and Class III includes those with the greatest risk.

Medical Device Regulation Consulting and Training – www.Procenius.com

As indicated above, all classes of devices are subject to General Controls. General Controls are the baseline requirements of the Food, Drug and Cosmetic (FD&C) Act that apply to all medical devices, Class I, II, and III.

2.4. <u>How to Determine Classification</u>

Reference: (FDA Devcie Classification, 2014)

To find the classification of your device, as well as whether any exemptions may exist, you need to find the regulation number that is the classification regulation for your device. There are two methods for accomplishing this: go directly to the classification database and search for a part of the device name, or, if you know the device panel (medical specialty) to which your device belongs, go directly to the listing for that panel and identify your device and the corresponding regulation. You may make a choice now, or continue to read the background information below. If you continue to read, you will have another chance to go to these destinations.

If you already know the appropriate panel you can go directly to the CFR and find the classification for your device by reading through the list of classified devices. If you're not sure, you can use the keyword directory in the PRODUCT CODE CLASSIFICATION DATABASE. In most cases this database will identify the classification regulation in the CFR. You can also check the classification regulations below for information on various products and how they are regulated by CDRH.

Each classification panel in the CFR begins with a list of devices classified in that panel. Each classified device has a 7-digit number associated with it, e.g., 21 CFR 880.2920 - Clinical Mercury Thermometer. Once you find your device in the panel's beginning list, go to the section indicated: in this example, 21 CFR 880.2920 . It describes the device and says it is Class II. Similarly, in the Classification Database under "thermometer", you'll see several entries for various types of thermometers. The three letter product code, FLK in the database for Clinical Mercury Thermometer, is also the classification number which is used on the Medical Device Listing form.

Once you have identified the correct classification regulation go to: What are the Classification Panels below and click on the correct classification regulation or go to the CFR Search page. Some Class I devices are exempt from the premarket notification and/or parts of the good manufacturing practices regulations. Approximately 572 or 74% of the Class I devices are exempt from the premarket notification process. These exemptions are listed in the classification regulations of 21 CFR and also has been collected together in the Medical Device Exemptions document.

2.5. Is the Product a Medical Device?

2.5.1. Medical Device Definition

Reference: (FDA Device Determination, 2014)

Medical devices range from simple tongue depressors and bedpans to complex programmable pacemakers with micro-chip technology and laser surgical devices. In addition, medical devices include in vitro diagnostic products, such as general purpose lab equipment, reagents and test kits, which may include monoclonal antibody technology. Certain electronic radiation emitting products with medical application and claims meet the definition of medical device. Examples include diagnostic ultrasound products, x-ray machines and medical lasers. If a product is labeled, promoted or used in a manner that meets the following definition in section 201(h) of the Federal Food Drug & Cosmetic (FD&C) Act it will be regulated by the Food and Drug Administration (FDA) as a medical device and is subject to premarketing and post marketing regulatory controls. A device is:

"an instrument, apparatus, implement, machine, contrivance, implant, in vitro reagent, or other similar or related article, including a component part, or accessory which is:

o   recognized in the official National Formulary, or the United States Pharmacopoeia, or any supplement to them,

o   intended for use in the diagnosis of disease or other conditions, or in the cure, mitigation, treatment, or prevention of disease, in man or other animals, or

o   intended to affect the structure or any function of the body of man or other animals, and which does not achieve its primary intended purposes through chemical action within or on the body of man or other animals and which is not dependent upon being metabolized for the achievement of any of its primary intended purposes."

This definition provides a clear distinction between a medical device and other FDA regulated products such as drugs. If the primary intended use of the product is achieved through chemical action or by being metabolized by the body, the product is usually a drug. Human drugs are regulated by FDA's Center for Drug Evaluation and Research (CDER). Biological products which include blood and blood products, and blood banking equipment are regulated by FDA's Center for Biologics Evaluation and Research (CBER). FDA's Center for Veterinary Medicine (CVM) regulates products used with animals. If your product is not a medical device but regulated by another Center in the FDA, each component of the FDA has an office to assist with questions about the products they regulate. In cases where it is not clear whether a product is a medical device there are procedures in place to use DICE Staff Directory to assist you in making a determination.

2.5.2. <u>Class I/II Exemption</u>

Most Class I devices and a few Class II devices are exempt from the premarket notification [510(k)] requirements subject to the limitations on exemptions. However, these devices are not exempt from other general controls. All medical devices must be manufactured under a quality assurance program, be suitable for the intended use, be adequately packaged and properly labeled, and have establishment registration and device listing forms on file with the FDA.

A few Class I devices are additionally exempt from the GMP requirements with the exception of complaint files and general record keeping requirements.

Class I/II Devices Exempt from 510(k) and class I Devices Exempt from GMPs

Devices exempt from 510(k) are:

- preamendment devices not significantly changed or modified; or

- Class I/II devices specifically exempted by regulation.

For purposes of 510(k) decision-making, the term "preamendment device" refers to devices legally marketed in the U.S. by a firm before May 28, 1976 and which have not been:

- significantly changed or modified since then; and

- for which a regulation requiring a PMA application has not been published by FDA.

Devices meeting this description are referred to as "grandfathered" and do not require a 510(k).

The Food, Drug and Cosmetic Act under section 513(d)(2)(A) authorizes FDA to exempt certain generic types of Class I devices from the premarket notification [510(k)] requirement. FDA has exempted over 800 generic types of Class I devices and 60 class II devices from the premarket notification requirement. The 510(k) exemption is with certain limitations, which are so noted in ".9" of each chapter (See FDA Device Classification, 2014). It is important to confirm the exempt status and any limitations that apply with 21 CFR Parts 862-892 or the PRODUCT CODE CLASSIFICATION DATABASE or subsequent FR announcements on class I exemptions and class II exemptions.

If a manufacturer's device falls into a generic category of exempted Class I devices as defined in 21 CFR Parts 862-892, a premarket notification application and FDA clearance is not required before marketing the device in the U.S.

3.0 Design and Development Planning

3.1. Overview

After a preliminary review of the design control regulation it may not be obvious to device developers why planning is important to the FDA. After all, the FDA's purpose is to protect public health, right? Why would they care about how product development is planned? The FDA does not have a significant vested interest in having products launch on time; so why do they care about planning?

Their first priority is to "allow no harm" by establishing regulations and inspecting medical device manufacturers which will encourage safe development and manufacturing. Their second priority is not to be a barrier for devices that may be beneficial to those that are in need of new technology or procedures. So even though the FDA is not necessarily interested in the timely launch of a product, they do understand that effective planning is essential for the development of a safe and effective device.

Essentially the design and developing plan helps manufacturers "think ahead" before just jumping into product development. There are already significant unknown surprises and challenges that are inherent in the development process, planning will help minimize these foreseeable challenges.

Planning allows project managers to identify activities, deliverables, personnel and resources required to develop a device. Management will typically use the plan to allocate personnel and resources to support development. In the absence of a plan, teams may jump into development unprepared, understaffed and underfunded. As a result, milestones will be missed, completion of project deliverables will be rushed, risks will be taken and an ineffective and unsafe device may be developed.

3.2. Design and Development Plan Quick Reference Summary

TABLE 3

Purpose	Design and development planning is needed to ensure that the design process is appropriately controlled and that device quality objectives are met. (FDA D.C. Guidance, 2015)
Regulation	21 CFR 820.30 (b) (FDA): Each manufacturer shall establish and maintain plans that describe or reference the design and development activities and define responsibility for implementation. The plans shall identify and describe the interfaces with different groups or activities that provide, or result in, input

Medical Device Regulation Consulting and Training – www.Procenius.com

	to the design and development process. The plans shall be reviewed, updated, and approved as design and development evolves. (FDA QS Regulation, 2015)
Standards	ISO 13485 (7.3.1) (ISO 13485, 2007)
Guidance	21 CFR 820.30 (b) (FDA) — FDA Design Control Guidance for Medical Device Manufacturers (FDA D.C. Guidance, 2015)
	ISO 13485 (7.3.1) — Medical Devices – Quality Management Systems – Guidance on the Application of ISO 13485:2003 (ISO 14969, 2004)
Timing of Design and Development Planning Relative to the Research and Development Cycle	**Figure 4** The two humps in Figure 4 depict the relationship and the relative amount of research and development activities performed during the design and development cycle. The shaded area is the typical time when initial development planning occurs and when the design and development plan is generated, reviewed and approved.
Deliverables	1. Design and Development Plan (DDP) will typically contain the following (FDA D.C. Guidance, 2015): • Description of the goals and objectives of the design and development program; (i.e. what is to be developed) • Delineation of organizational responsibilities with respect to assuring quality during the design and development phase; to include interface with any contractors; • Identification of the major tasks to be undertaken, deliverables for each task, and individual or organizational responsibilities (staff and

	resources) for completing each task; • Scheduling of major tasks to meet overall program time constraints; • Identification of major reviews and decision points; • Selection of reviewers, the composition of review teams, and procedures to be followed by reviewers; • Controls for design documentation; • Notification activities. 2. Sub-Plans may be required to provide a sufficient level of detail planning for complex designs (e.g. – regulatory, mechanical, electrical, software, labeling, and validation master plan). Sub-Plans may be included as part of the general DDP or may be only referenced and independently reviewed and approved.
The Plan Should Establish	• The major tasks required to develop the product • The time involved for each major task • The resources and personnel required • The allocation of responsibilities for completing each major task • The prerequisite information necessary to start each major task and the interrelationship between tasks • The form of each task output or deliverable • Constraints, such as applicable codes, standards, and regulations • Tasks for all significant design activities, including verification and validation tasks, should be included in the design and development plan. For example, if clinical trials are anticipated, there may be tasks associated with appropriate regulatory requirements. • For complex projects, rough estimates may be provided initially, with the details left for the responsible organizations to develop. As development proceeds, the plan should evolve to incorporate more up to date information. (FDA D.C. Guidance, 2015)
Review	The type and method of review is dependent upon the complexity of the device and size of the organization. In typical organizations an effective review includes an individual review of the design and development plan

	(DDP) and a formal design review. A final draft of the DDP should be reviewed by required approvers and design review attendees. The reviewers should thoroughly review the content of the DDP prior to the formal design review. During the review, the reviewers should be prepared to challenge and discuss issues, errors or concerns that they have identified in the DDP. The sign of an effective review process is often indicated by multiple revisions of the draft document. The process of getting input from the reviewers and coming to a consensus as to what should and can be realistically accomplished to meet all stakeholder requirements is the essence of the purpose of the review process. Reviewers attending formal design reviews should include qualified individuals in all functional areas that may have critical feedback to the design being reviewed. **Typical Reviewers**: Cross Functional Team Quality Assurance Regulatory Affairs R&D / Engineering Marketing Operations Independent Reviewer(s) Project Management Other Stake Holders
Approval	Approvers of the DDP typically include a cross functional team and executive management (or mid-level management for larger organizations). The team should have the expertise to provide input about the feasibility of completing cross functional requirements (i.e. technical, regulatory, marketing, quality,). Management's approval indicates that they agree with the development plan including target dates, deliverables and requested resources. Approvals should be documented manually or electronically with signature and date. Electronic approvals should be in compliance with 21 CFR part 11.

	Typical Approvers: Cross Functional Team Quality Assurance Regulatory Affairs R&D / Engineering Marketing Operations Project Management Other Stake Holders
Revisions	The DDP is a living document and should be updated and revised as the design evolves. The DDP should be revised to be relative and current with the execution of development activities. The initial revision typically contains high level and nonspecific development plans whereas subsequent revisions will contain increasingly more specific detailed plans. The DDP may be revised as necessary throughout the design process and will typically follow the same review and approval process which was required for the initial version.
Best Practices	• Use matrices to communicate the interaction or correlation of information • Have documents in draft status for design review prior to approval • Reviewers should be given sufficient time to review documents prior to design reviews and approval • The FDA Design Control Guidance Document (FDA D.C. Guidance, 2015) suggests that the DDP should include high level milestones and deliverable dates. It is typically acceptable to have a target range for deliverable due dates. Specific target dates are not required but if used, frequent updates to the DDP are often required due to variability in product development timing. A detailed project schedule can be managed and approved separately which is typically less burdensome to keep updated and approved.

Templates	Visit *Procenius.com* to download design and development plan templates.

3.3. Regulation (21 CFR 820.30 (b)) - Design and Development Planning

Each manufacturer shall establish and maintain plans that describe or reference the design and development activities and define responsibility for implementation. The plans shall identify and describe the interfaces with different groups or activities that provide, or result in, input to the design and development process. The plans shall be reviewed, updated, and approved as design and development evolves. (FDA QS Regulation, 2015)

3.4. Design Control Guidance Document (21 CFR 820.30 (b))

Design and development planning is needed to ensure that the design process is appropriately controlled and that device quality objectives are met. The plans must be consistent with the remainder of the design control requirements. The following elements would typically be addressed in the design and development plan or plans:

- Description of the goals and objectives of the design and development program; i.e., what is to be developed

- Delineation of organizational responsibilities with respect to assuring quality during the design and development phase to include interface with any contractors Identification of the major tasks to be undertaken, deliverables for each task, and individual or organizational responsibilities (staff and resources) for completing each task

- Scheduling of major tasks to meet overall program time constraints

- Identification of major reviews and decision points

- Selection of reviewers, the composition of review teams and procedures to be followed by reviewers

- Controls for design documentation

- Notification activities

Planning enables management to exercise greater control over the design and development process by clearly communicating policies, procedures and goals to members of the design and development team. Planning also provides a basis for measuring conformance to quality system objectives.

Design activities should be specified at the level of detail necessary for carrying out the design process. The extent of design and development planning is dependent on the size of the developing organization and the size and complexity of the product to be developed. Some manufacturers may have documented policies and procedures which apply to all design and development activities. For each specific development program, such manufacturers may also prepare a plan which spells out the project-dependent elements in detail and incorporates the general policies and procedures by reference. Other manufacturers may develop a comprehensive design and development plan which is specifically tailored to each individual project.

In summary, the form and organization of the planning documents are less important than their content. The following paragraphs discuss the key elements of design and development planning.

3.4.1. Organizational Responsibilities

The management responsibility section of the quality system requirements requires management to establish a quality policy and implement an organizational structure to ensure quality. These are typically documented in a quality manual or similarly named document. In some cases, however, the design and development plan rather than the quality manual is the best vehicle for describing organizational responsibilities relative to design and development activities. The importance of defining responsibilities with clarity and without ambiguity should be recognized. When input to the design is from a variety of sources, their interrelationships and interfaces (as well as the pertinent responsibilities and authorities) should be defined, documented, coordinated and controlled. This might be the case, for example, if a multidisciplinary product development team is assembled for a specific project, or if the team includes suppliers, contract manufacturers, users, outside consultants or independent auditors.

3.4.2. Task Breakdown

The plan establishes, to the extent possible:

- The major tasks required to develop the product
- The time involved for each major task
- The resources and personnel required
- The allocation of responsibilities for completing each major task
- The prerequisite information necessary to start each major task and the interrelationship between tasks
- The form of each task output or deliverable
- Constraints, such as applicable codes, standards, and regulations

Tasks for all significant design activities, including verification and validation tasks, should be included in the design and development plan. For example, if clinical trials are anticipated, there may be tasks associated with appropriate regulatory requirements.

For complex projects, rough estimates may be provided initially, with the details left for the responsible organizations to develop. As development proceeds, the plan should evolve to incorporate more and better information.

The relationships between tasks should be presented in such a way that they are easily understood. It should be clear which tasks depend on others, and which tasks need to be performed concurrently. Planning should reflect the degree of perceived development risk; for example, tasks involving new technology or processes should be spelled out in greater detail, and perhaps be subjected to more reviews and checks, than tasks which are perceived as routine or straightforward.

The design and development plan may include a schedule showing starting and completion dates for each major task, project milestone or key decision points. The method chosen and the detail will vary depending on the complexity of the project and the level of risk associated with the device. For small projects, the plan may consist of only a simple flow diagram or computer spreadsheet. For larger projects, there are a number of project management tools that are used to develop plans. Three of the most commonly used are the Program Evaluation and Review Technique (PERT), the Critical Path Method (CPM), and the Gantt chart. Software is available in many forms for these methods. When selecting these tools, be careful to choose one that best fits the needs of the project. Some of the software programs are far more complex than may be necessary.

Unless a manufacturer has experience with the same type of device, the plan will initially be limited in scope and detail. As work proceeds, the plan is refined. Lack of experience in planning often leads to optimistic schedules, but slippage may also occur for reasons beyond the control of planners. Some examples include personnel turnover, materiel shortage or unexpected problems with a design element or process. Sometimes the schedule can be compressed by using additional resources, such as diverting staff or equipment from another project, hiring a contractor or leasing equipment.

It is important that the schedule be updated to reflect current knowledge. At all times, the plan should be specified at a level of detail enabling management to make informed decisions and provide confidence in meeting overall schedule and performance objectives. This is important because scheduling pressures have historically been a contributing factor in many design defects which caused injury. To the extent that good planning can prevent schedule pressures, the potential for design errors is reduced.

However, no amount of planning can eliminate all development risk. There is inherent conflict between the desire to maximize performance and the need to meet business objectives, including development deadlines. In some corporate cultures, impending deadlines create enormous pressure to cut corners. Planning helps to combat this dilemma by ensuring management awareness of pressure points. With awareness, decisions are more likely to be made with appropriate oversight and consideration of all relevant factors. Thus, when concessions to the clock must be made, they can be justified and supported. (FDA D.C. Guidance, 2015)

3.5. <u>Timing of Design and Development Activities and Deliverables</u>

The FDA does not specify at what point in the development process when design and development planning should begin or end but the following graphical models give some clarity as to when initial planning will occur relative to research and development activities.

The two humps in FIGURE 5 depict the relationship and the relative amount of research and development activities performed during the design and development cycle. The shaded area is the typical time when initial development planning occurs and when the design and development plan is generated, reviewed and approved.

Figure 5

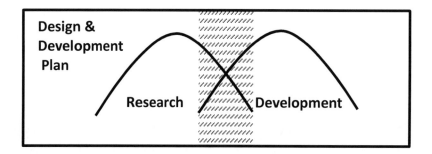

3.6. <u>Interpretation, Application, & Discussion (21 CFR 820.30 (b))</u>

*When the FDA says... **"shall establish and maintain plans"**....* they are indicating that the plan needs to be documented, implemented and revised as product development progresses. Updates to the plan may be scheduled to coincide with planned phases and/or on an as needed basis. Some projects that are straight forward with low risk may only require the plan to be updated at specified intervals according to the project plan or standard operating procedures. On the other hand, in scenarios where there are technical challenges and high project risks, the plan may be updated many times to accommodate delays that are typically experienced in these situations.

Medical Device Regulation Consulting and Training – www.Procenius.com

Quality Systems Regulation Preamble States:

Comment 71

"This section has been revised to state that ``plans shall be reviewed, updated, and approved as design and development evolves,'' indicating that changes to the design plan are expected. A design plan typically includes at least proposed quality practices, assessment methodology, recordkeeping and documentation requirements, and resources, as well as a sequence of events related to a particular design or design category. These may be modified and refined as the design evolves. However, the design process can become a lengthy and costly process if the design activity is not properly defined and planned. The more specifically the activities are defined up front, the less need there will be for changes as the design evolves." (FDA Preamble, 2015)

The FDA also says,**.... *"plans that describe or reference the design and development activities"...*** The regulation gives the flexibility of "describing" or making "reference" to the "design and development activities". The FDA uses this wording to give manufacturers flexibility during development of the plans and therefore can be written for a wide range of device design complexity. For relatively simple medical devices (such as surgical gloves), the design and development plan (DDP) may fully describe in great detail all that is required to plan the development of the device. On the other hand, complex devices such as MRI machines may require a DDP that references many other sub-plans that are approved separately from the overall governing DDP. In this case sub-plans may be needed to address the development of typical aspects of the device such as software, hardware and electrical systems. Each of these areas is highly technical and complex and may need their own sub-plan to adequately define the development activities and assignments. In addition to sub-plans that reference technical aspects of the design, other typical sub-plans may include a regulatory plan, validation master plan, labeling plan, risk management plan, quality plan, detailed project schedule, etc.

The word **"activities"** in this regulation means just about anything that is performed by an individual or team in the process of developing the device. The **"activities"** (which often result in deliverables) that are required to complete development of the device should be included in the DDP. The FDA specifically states that the plan should ***"define responsibility for implementation"*** of these activities or deliverables. In simple product development projects with small teams it is ideal to assign individuals that will actually be performing the activities. In complex projects where activities are completed by teams, it is more common to see the names of the project leads or department heads that are assigned to those activities. Some companies choose to put the department names or functional groups that are assigned to the activity, but more often than not it is preferred to assign a name to the activity. When names are assigned, people take notice. It is more likely that if one person is assigned a task, they will take ownership of ensuring the activity gets completed on time. In cases when whole departments are assigned, the possibility exists that no one will take responsibility and deliverables won't get completed on schedule.

Medical Device Regulation Consulting and Training – www.Procenius.com

Quality Systems Regulation Preamble States:

Comment 69

"In making this change, FDA notes that Sec. 820.20(b)(1) requires manufacturers to establish the appropriate responsibility for activities affecting quality, and emphasizes that the assignment of specific responsibility is important to the success of the design control program and to achieving compliance with the regulation. Also, the design and development activities should be assigned to qualified personnel equipped with adequate resources as required under Sec. 820.20(b)(2)." (FDA Preamble, 2015)

When the FDA states, ***"The plans shall identify and describe the interfaces with different groups or activities that provide, or result in, input to the design and development process***, what they are really trying to say is that they want the manufacturers to thoroughly think about and plan what resources are required, how they are going to interact with each other and how are those interactions are going to effectively produce the desired result.

In practice, one of the best ways to present these interactions is in some type of matrix[BP1] which correlates deliverables (or activities) vs. resources, start dates, finish dates, targeted design phase, document number of deliverables (for traceability), etc.

Quality Systems Regulation Preamble States:

Comment 70

"Many organization functions, both inside and outside the design group, may contribute to the design process. For example, interfaces with marketing, purchasing, regulatory affairs, manufacturing, service groups, or information systems may be necessary during the design development phase. To function effectively, the design plan must establish the roles of these groups in the design process and describe the information that should be received and transmitted." (FDA Preamble, 2015)

#1 Best Practice – Use matrices to communicate the interaction or correlation of information.

Using matrices is often an effective method for communicating development plans to management, the development team and the FDA. During a typical inspection the FDA may review thousands of pages of documents, therefore any tools that will increase the efficiency of communicating this massive amount of information to reviewers should be implemented if possible. (see the example at the end of this chapter)

Medical Device Regulation Consulting and Training – www.Procenius.com

As the old saying goes, "the devil is in the details." Effective planning will allow engineers, project managers and executive management to fully understand the scope and extent of the work required to complete device development and will give management the information needed to allocate adequate resources to the project and to set realistic timelines.

Those that have worked in the medical device industry and with the FDA have come to realize that the FDA is **BIG** on planning, **VERY** big on planning, and rightly so. As a general rule, the FDA wants to see this pattern:

1. Plan the activities
2. Perform the planned activities
3. Report what activities were actually performed and the results of the planned activities

The first step of this pattern is the planning step which also includes documents like verification and validation protocols (step two and three are implementation and reporting which will be discussed in later chapters).

When the FDA states, "**The plans shall be reviewed, updated, and approved as design and development evolves,**" they are trying to convey that the plan should be thoroughly understood, revised as needed, and formally approved throughout the development process.

Quality Systems Regulation Preamble States:

Comment 69

"Therefore, the approval is consistent with ISO 9001:1994 and would not be unduly burdensome since the FDA does not dictate how or by whom the plan must be approved. The regulation gives the manufacturer the necessary flexibility to have the same person(s) who is responsible for the review also be responsible for the approval of the plan if appropriate." (FDA Preamble, 2015)

It is best practice to have a draft version[BP2] of the design and development plan (DDP) which should typically be reviewed individually and in design reviews. Prior to approval of the DDP, the approvers should be given sufficient time to read and understand the DDP content and intent of the plan. After reviewers have had the opportunity to read the DDP, it is best practice[BP3] to review the DDP during a design review which will give all attendees the opportunity to address (or challenge) any concerns or issues that may arise. As a result of the review, decisions will be made and actions will be assigned that may require updates to the DDP. This may include changing unrealistic target dates, deliverable assignments or updates with new requirement deliverables.

#2 Best Practice – Have documents in draft status for design review prior to approval.

To increase the efficiency of the review and approval process, "near final" drafts of documents (prior to design review) should be reviewed by the design review attendees. After the results of the design review are documented, the drafts of the documents can be easily updated and then approved to reflect the outcome of the design review. (see the design review chapter for more detail)

#3 Best Practice – Reviewers should be given sufficient time to review documents prior to design reviews and approval.

Reviewers should be given sufficient time to review all documents prior to approving and holding a design review. If insufficient time is provided, reviewers may be inadequately prepared for design review discussion and/or individual review prior to document approval. (see design review chapter for more detail)

It is important to understand that the DDP should be used as a *living* document. Just as product development can never be perfectly planned from the beginning, neither can the DDP be completely and accurately written to predict the future. As required changes in the development process occur, the plan should be updated periodically. The FDA is very aware that product development is often unpredictable and that plans often change. As a matter of fact, the FDA expects to see multiple revisions of the DDP and may be suspicious if it was never revised. The decision to update the DDP should be based heavily on when significant changes to the development of the product are required. The DDP should be updated as discussions of deviating from the current approved plans become finalized.

Typically the initial version of the DDP may only include the initial plans that are known at that point in time and therefore the plan will have relatively minimal content. As product development progresses the plan should be updated as additional information becomes available. As an example, the initial revision of the DDP may include deliverable dates that are specified by quarters of the year (3 month time period). As the target dates get closer and more confidence and understanding of the deliverable requirements are understood, the deliverable date will most likely be able to be refined within a month, week or even a specific day.

Approval of the DDP (as well as other documents) is typically performed by a handwritten signature and date or by an electronic signature (see 21 CFR part 11), either of which is an acceptable document approval method. If hand written signatures are used for approval it is best practice to provide the printed name next to the signature line to allow easy association of names with signatures if required during an FDA inspection or internal audit. Either type of approval method is acceptable as long as 21 CFR part 11 is followed for electronic signatures on a validated software system. These approval methods are applicable for all design and development documents that are subject to FDA inspection.

The development activities and resource assignments indicated in the DDP typically affect many departments and therefore require a greater number of approval signatures than other development documents (e.g. risk assessments, design inputs, verification protocols). In small to medium size companies, approvals will typically include executive level management members such as VP of Quality, VP of Engineering, VP of Marketing and VP of Regulatory Affairs. In larger corporations, lower to mid-level management will typically approve the DDP. The intent of having executive management approve the DDP is twofold: 1) To receive management's approval of the team's plan to develop the product 2) To receive approval of resources (e.g. people, money, equipment) that the project manager has requested. Other department heads and stake holders should also be considered as approvers and/or to provide input to the DDP as appropriate for the organization. The FDA does not directly specify that the stake holders are required to approve the DDP but they do indicate under 21 CFR 820.20 (sub-part B, Management Responsibility) that management should be involved and aware of activities pertaining to the quality system. Figure 6 below indicates typical stakeholders that will have significant input to the DDP.

FIGURE 6

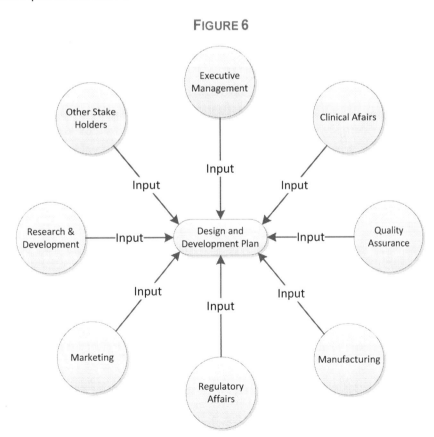

Medical Device Regulation Consulting and Training – www.Procenius.com

It should be noted that the previous paragraph stated "the team's plan" should be approved by management. This is a key concept that needs to be accepted and understood by management for product development teams to be successful. In smaller companies, executive management has a tendency to directly manage and influence development plans. As companies grow, this becomes impractical, inefficient and unwise. Management's role should not include extending significant influence in directing detailed development plans. Management has the best intentions, but they are often too far removed from the technical hurdles and detail work that is required to effectively develop the DDP. The team is in the trenches every day, and they are therefore realistic with their target dates and are greatly in tune with technical challenges and risks that are just around the corner.

Ideally an executive sponsor will develop a project charter in conjunction with the project manager to establish high level requirements that will initially be approved by executive management. The project manager will present these requirements to the team who will in turn develop a DDP with realistic target dates and resource plans. During the review of the DDP, management will typically either cut requested resources or reduce development time from the proposed plan. If resources and/or time are cut from the plan, it is up to the team (primarily the project manager) to communicate the impact to the target launch data as a result of the resources being denied. This situation epitomizes one of the reasons the FDA requires a DDP. At this point in the review and approval process of the DDP, a cross functional team and executive management have to come to a consensus as to what should and can be realistically accomplished to meet all stakeholder requirements. If a review of the DDP is thoroughly performed, the final version of the DDP may go through multiple revisions before all stakeholders are satisfied. On the other hand if the DDP always flies through the approval process on the first draft and stakeholders are not invested in the plan, the DDP is a plan on paper only and becomes ineffective and a waste of time. This typically happens when management is only concerned about "checking the regulatory box" to meet regulatory requirements but is not interested in using the DDP as an effective planning tool.

Even though getting the DDP through the approval process may seem as difficult as getting an act of congress passed, in the end, the team and management can have confidence that the plan has been thoroughly reviewed and vetted[BP4]. This type of rigorous review gives the proposed design greater potential for being a successful product, not to mention being compliant to the regulations.

#4 Best Practice – The DDP should be thoroughly reviewed and vetted.

If approvers of the DDP are not fully invested in the plan, the development of the product will suffer and the safety and effectiveness of the device may be compromised. Management should establish a culture in the organization which prioritizes the development of effective design and development plans. This will greatly benefit the success of the product and compliance to regulatory requirements. (see the design review chapter for more detail)

3.6.1. Quality Systems Manual: Design and Development Planning

DESIGN AND DEVELOPMENT PLANNING

Excerpt from the "Quality Systems Manual: A Small Entity Compliance Guide"
(Withdrawn from FDA website 12 December 2013)
(FDA QS Manual, 2013)

Developing a new device and introducing it into production are very complex tasks. For many new devices and associated manufacturing processes that use software, these tasks are further complicated because of the importance of software, and the possibility of subtle software errors. Without thorough planning, program control, and design reviews, these tasks are virtually impossible to accomplish without errors or leaving important aspects undone. The planning exercise and execution of the plans are complex because of the many areas and activities that should be covered. Some of the key activities are:

- determining and meeting the user/patients requirements;
- meeting regulations and standards;
- developing specifications for the device;
- developing, selecting and evaluating components and suppliers;
- developing and approving labels and user instructions;
- developing packaging;
- developing specifications for manufacturing processes;
- verifying safety and performance of prototype and final devices;
- verifying compatibility with the environment and other devices;
- developing manufacturing facilities and utilities;
- developing and validating manufacturing processes;

- training employees;
- documenting the details of the device design and processes; and,
- if applicable, developing a service program.

To support thorough planning, the QS regulation requires each manufacturer to establish and maintain plans that describe or reference the design and development activities and define responsibility for implementation.

The plans should be consistent with the remainder of the design controls. For example, the design controls section of the quality system requires a design history file (DHF) [820.30(j)] that contains or references the records necessary to demonstrate that the design was developed in accordance with the:

1. approved design plan, and
2. regulatory requirements.

Thus, the design control plans should agree with, and require meeting, the quality system design control requirements. One of the first elements in each design plan should be how you plan to meet each of the design control requirements for the specific design you plan to develop; that is, the design plans should support all of the required design control activities. Such plans may reference the quality system procedures for design controls in order to reduce the amount of writing and to assure agreement.

Interface

Design And Development Planning section 820.30(b) states:

"The plans shall identify and describe the interfaces with different groups or activities that provide, or result in, input to the design and development process..."

If a specific design requires support by contractors such as developing molds, performing a special verification test, clinical trials, etc., then such activities should be included or referenced in the plan and proactively implemented in order to meet the interface and general quality system requirements. Of course, the interface and general requirements also apply to needed interaction with manufacturing, marketing, quality assurance, servicing or other internal functions.

Proactive interface is a important aspect of concurrent engineering. Concurrent engineering is the process of concurrently, to the maximum feasible extent, developing the product and the manufacturing processes. This valuable technique for reducing problems, cost reduction and time saving cannot work without proactive interface between all involved parties throughout all stages of the development and initial production program.

Structure of Plans

Each design control plan should be broad and complete rather than detailed and complete. The plan should include all major activities and assignments such as responsibility for developing and verifying the power supplies rather than detailing responsibility for selecting the power cords, fuse holders and transformers. Broad plans are:

- easier to follow;
- contain less errors;
- have better agreement with the actual activities; and
- will require less updating than detailed plans.

Over the years, several manufacturers have failed to follow this advice and opted for writing detailed design control procedures. They reported being unable to finish writing the over-detailed procedures and were unable to implement them.

Regardless of the effort in developing plans, they usually need updating as the development activities dictate. Thus, the QS regulation requires in 820.30(a) that the plans shall be reviewed, updated, and approved as the design and development evolves. The details of updating are left to the manufacturer; however, the design review meetings are a good time and place to consider, discuss and review changes that may need to be made in the design development plan.

3.7. Case Study – Design and Development Planning (MRI To Go Inc.)

Thorough planning is the first step in setting realistic expectations for management. As any experienced project manager (PM) knows, the sooner management experiences a reality check during product development; the easier course corrections can be made. Unfortunately early effective planning does not always occur and unrealistic expectations are made by which time there is enormous pressure to meet timeline expectations.

The following is a theoretical case study of ineffective planning which results in non-compliance and potential risk to the patient.

The marketing team of a medical device manufacturer that designs and manufactures MRI machines (MRI To Go Inc. or MRI T.G.) identifies a market need for a product that can easily be transported from room to room by a maximum of two hospital employees. The executive management team of MRI T.G. sees this as a potentially very profitable product. From their initial assessment there does not seem to be significant technical challenges or risks. Essentially they think, "how difficult could it be? Just put some wheels on our current product and that should be it, right?" (or something like that)

They also fail to foresee the significant resources needed to support the product development activities. After reviewing the results from the preliminary business case and technical feasibility assessment, management asks marketing to run a market assessment of the market opportunity and penetration. The analysis comes back positive and therefore management communicates next year's revenue and profit projections to the corporate office based on expected revenue from the new product (*MRI OnWheels*).

Management creates and approves the project charter with little input from the product development team. Aggressive target dates and requirements are set based on high level planning, marketing analysis, and technical risk assessments. The PM realizes that the target dates are aggressive and feels like he should get the project going right away. He decides that in order to meet the aggressive time line there is no time for feasibility studies so he immediately starts assigning resources to requirements and deliverables that are contained on the project charter. Within the first few months of the project the PM realizes that he has not initiated a design and development plan (DDP). At this point in the project he does not see the point of writing the plan because assignments have already been made and work has already begun. A few weeks later during a project audit the quality assurance representative reminds him that a DDP must be completed and approved to be compliant with internal procedures and with FDA regulation. With reluctance, the PM throws together a shell of a DDP and gets it pushed through the approval cycle to "check the regulatory box" to ensure the development activities will be found to be compliant during the next inspection.

As product development progresses, the PM begins to feel resistance from his team about completing their assigned deliverables and tasks. It turns out that their functional managers (direct supervisors) have not given the project high priority and they will therefore not be able to adequately support the project deliverables and activities. In addition to this hurdle, the team is confused about what deliverables are required and when they are due. Many of the team members are conscientious and want to hit the target launch date and therefore take on more work than they are assigned (or take on work that they think they are assigned). As a result of this confusion, deliverables are not completed on time, and major milestone dates are missed. Even with the current hurdles, the PM marches on to try and make up for lost time.

As time goes by, engineers on the team tell the PM that that there are huge technical challenges with the basic product concept. During the initial management assessment of the product concept they did not think about the risks involved in using MRI machines in standard hospital rooms that have unsecured metal objects that may contribute to significant hazards during a MRI procedure. They also did not realize that typical power requirements of an MRI machine are greater than those available in a standard hospital room.

The PM is feeling pressure to try and salvage the project that is having so many problems without giving management a complete picture of the situation; therefore he avoids providing details of the development progress and marches on. Meanwhile management has heard a rumor that there is trouble with the progress of the product but the PM has not yet communicated those problems. They have confidence in their PM so they will wait until the next product review meeting to find out more about the rumors. During the product review meeting, management asks very pointed questions about the development of the product (MRI *OnWheels*). At this point the PM realizes that there is no way that the product can be launched on time and finally tells management about the issues that the project is facing. Management is surprised and immediately goes into "save the day mode". They start trying to come up with quick fixes and "work arounds" that are either unpractical or borderline unethical. The last thing they will consider is to move the target launch date. After all, they have made revenue commitments to the corporate office which they are not about to default on.

They eventually start putting pressure on the development team to go back and "re-assess" the design, risk assessment and other design decisions to see if there is some way to quickly overcome these hurdles. After the team "re-assesses" these decisions they somehow come up with different conclusions than they originally decided. Documentation is revised and rationales are written to explain the design changes. In this case the development team elevated their risk tolerance due to pressure from management to meet the product launch date.

3.8. Case Study Analysis

Unfortunately the scenario previously explained happens all too often. The root cause of these situations is typically due to poor planning. The problem was initiated when management committed to a launch date prior to adequately understanding the resources, technical risk and time required to launch the product. If management had allowed the PM to adequately plan and assess the resources needed to meet project deliverables they would have had a realistic picture of what it would take to complete development of the device prior to committing resources. A design and development plan also would have prevented confusion of project assignments between team members and would have minimized the potential for late deliverables.

A design and development plan is both a planning tool and a communication tool between management and the development team. Instead of management having to hear about project issues through the rumor mill, periodic design reviews and updates to the DDP would have effectively communicated problems with the product development as the project progressed.

Under initial review of this case study it may be tempting to point fingers at the PM as the main culprit in this scenario, but in this case the blame should also be shared with management. Yes it is true that the PM delayed the creation and approval of the DDP, but his decision to delay was based on pressure from management's aggressive timelines. The PM was in survival mode to do everything and anything to meet the deadline. In addition, management did not convey the importance of regulatory compliance within the company so the PM also did not think it was critically important.

Medical Device Regulation Consulting and Training – www.Procenius.com

3.9. Case Study Lessons Learned

It is unfortunate that this scenario occurs in many organizations but the good news is that things can change. The following are lessons learned that should be implemented to improve the organization's effectiveness in design and development planning:

- Management should convey a culture of compliance. This can only happen if management puts compliance as a first priority in word, action, and procedure. The product should be developed "the right way" as a first priority and then on time as a second priority.

- Adequate planning time should be given to the product development team so they can provide realistic timeline and resource requirements prior to management committing to revenue promises (or other similar business projections).

- Management should not put undue pressure on the development teams to go back and "re-assess" design decisions (a.k.a taking short cuts or risks). The establishment of the development team with independent reviewers acts as a "checks and balances" system which minimizes the biased influenced from some stakeholders to influence decisions based on pressure to meet financial goals. This undue influence is often against an organizations procedure and borders on unethical business practices.

- The project manager is responsible to push back to management if unrealistic timelines are set which may compromise the safety and effectiveness of the product. Short cuts in developing design and development documents should not be used to just "check the regulatory box". The effective use of a Design and Development plan is a useful tool that increases the likelihood of developing a safe and effective product and should be used in compliance with FDA regulation.

3.10. Design and Development Plan Matrix (Template)

Table 4 is an example of a design and development plan matrix which is an effective tool for planning design control deliverables. Development phases, deliverable owners, planned start/finished dates are all tied together in this plan.

A = Document should be approved in applicable phase

R = Review is required in applicable phase

TABLE 4

	Phase I	Phase II	Phase III	Phase IV	Owner	Deliverables	Planned Start	Planned Finish	Comments, Plans, Rationale
Design Development Plan	A	A	A	A					
Subsidiary Plans									
Electrical Plan	A	A							
Mechanical Plan	A	A							
Software Plan	A	A							
Regulatory Plan	A	A							
Labelling Plan	A	A							
Project Schedule (Detailed)	A	A	A	A					
Phase Reviews									
Phase I (Planning & Requirements)	R								
Phase II (Design & Verification)		R							
Phase III (Validation & Design Transfer)			R						
Phase IV (Launch)				R					

Medical Device Regulation Consulting and Training – www.Procenius.com

	Phase I	Phase II	Phase III	Phase IV	Owner	Deliverables	Planned Start	Planned Finish	Comments, Plans, Rationale
Design Reviews									
Sub-System/Component Design Review(s)		R							
Product Level Design Review I		R							
Product Level Design Review II		R							
Design Transfer Design Review		R							
Validation Design Review			R						
Labeling Review		R							
Design Input									
Design Input Requirements (DIR)	A	A							

Risk Management									
Risk Assessment (Design)	A	A	A						
Design Verification									
Design Verification protocol(s)		A							

Design Verification report(s)		A							
Trace Matrix		A							
Design Outputs									
Design Documentation		A							
Device Master Record		A	A	A					

Design Validation										
Validation Master Plan	A	A								
Validation Master Report		A	A							
Design Validation Protocol(s)			A							
Design Validation Report(s)				A						
Design Transfer										
Design Transfer Protocol		A								
Design Transfer Report		A	A							
Traceability										
Essential Design Output List		A	A							
Design History File										
DHF	A	A	A	A						

3.11. Templates

Visit *Procenius.com* to download design and development plan templates.

4.0 Design Input

4.1. Overview

Design inputs is the general term used in the regulation which refers to requirements and user needs that should be used to drive the preliminary concept design through final detailed design. Design inputs are what the users want, what is required by regulation or what is needed for a device to be safe and effective. Design inputs do not specify the details of how a device is designed but rather act as boundaries that must be maintained while filling in the gaps of the design details.

To further illustrate the concept of design inputs, the analogy of designing and building a house can be used. A future home owner wants a house designed such that it can be kept at a constant 71 +/- 0.25 F° all year round. For this user need to be achieved there are certain lower level requirements that must be specified by the architect and sub-contractors to ultimately meet the 71 +/- 0.25 F° higher level requirement (user need). For example,

- The heating and cooling contractor must specify the correct size furnace, air conditioner, and duct work to allow the adequate air flow to each part of the house. Other considerations would be the number and location of air vents in each room and sources of heat generation such as the refrigerator, lights, windows and oven.

- The correct insulation rating for the wall, ceiling and floor insulation must be specified in order to minimize heat transfer through the house walls and ceilings.

- The electrical contractor has to specify the power requirements into the home to operate the furnace and air conditioner (as well as other power requirements to operate appliances and lights in the house). This includes specifying the correct wire gauge sizes, correct relay ratings, and breaker box components.

- A thermostat must be specified that has the correct resolution and accuracy to hold the temperature at the 71 degree requirement.

- The house has to meet local building codes which also become inputs to the design of the house.

The *take away* from this example is that there are many sources and levels of inputs that will guide the design of a medical device. This example also illustrates how many lower level technical requirements can be generated from relatively few user needs (in this case one user need 71 +/- 0.25 F°) .

The most important thing to keep in mind while developing design requirements is to ensure that requirements are identified which will lead to a safe and effective device. Requirements should not be burdensome, but on the contrary, they should be a valuable tool used to bring clarity to the design process. The initial development of design requirements may seem burdensome and a waste of time, but the time and resources invested up front in the design process to develop robust requirements will more than pay for itself in later development phases or after product launch by preventing costly rework or re-design due to inadequate design requirements. The FDA preamble states the following concerning this topic:

Quality Systems Regulation Preamble:

> **Comment 82**
>
> *"All the requirements are essential to assuring the safety and effectiveness of devices. FDA does not believe that these requirements place undue burden on designers or require additional documentation with no value added. These basic requirements are necessary to assure the proper device performance, and, therefore, the production of safe and effective devices, and are acknowledged and accepted as such throughout the world."* (FDA Preamble, 2015)

4.2. Design Input Quick Reference Summary

TABLE 5

Purpose	Design input is the starting point for product design. The requirements which form the design input establish a basis for performing subsequent design tasks and validating the design. (FDA D.C. Guidance, 2015)
Definition	Design input means the physical and performance requirements of a device that are used as a basis for device design. (FDA QSR , 2014)
Regulation	21 CFR 820.30 (c): Each manufacturer shall establish and maintain procedures to ensure that the design requirements relating to a device are appropriate and address the intended use of the device, including the needs

	of the user and patient. The procedures shall include a mechanism for addressing incomplete, ambiguous, or conflicting requirements. The design input requirements shall be documented and shall be reviewed and approved by a designated individual(s). The approval, including the date and signature of the individual(s) approving the requirements, shall be documented. (FDA QS Regulation, 2015)
Standard(s)	ISO 13485 (7.3.2) (ISO 13485, 2007)
Guidance	21 CFR 820.30 (c) (FDA) — FDA Design Control Guidance for Medical Device Manufacturers (FDA D.C. Guidance, 2015) ISO 13485 (7.3.2) — Medical Devices – Quality Management Systems – Guidance on the Application of ISO 13485:2003 (ISO 14969, 2004)
Timing of Design Inputs Relative to the Research and Development Cycle	Figure 7 The two humps in Figure 7 depict the relationship and the relative amount of research and development activities performed during the design and development cycle. The shaded area is the typical time when inputs are generated, reviewed, approved and implemented.

Deliverables	1. **User Needs** User needs are quantifiable requirements that are identified as being needed for the safe and effective use of the device by the user or patient. The user needs are typically high level performance, functional and interface requirements for which the user/patient has the most interest or concern. 2. **Design Input Requirements (DIR)** This is a document that contains system level and sub-system level design requirements. (e.g. software, mechanical, electrical, performance, biocompatibility, sterilization, reliability, labeling, regulatory). For complex devices, sub-system level requirements may be documented and approved in a separate requirements document.
Types of Design Input Requirements	1. **Functional Requirements** Functional requirements specify what the device does, focusing on the operational capabilities of the device and processing of inputs and the resultant outputs. 2. **Performance Requirements** Performance requirements specify how much or how well the device must perform, addressing issues such as speed, strength, response times, accuracy, limits of operation, etc. This includes a quantitative characterization of the use environment; including, for example, temperature, humidity, shock, vibration, and electromagnetic compatibility. Requirements concerning device reliability and safety also fit into this category. 3. **Interface Requirements** Interface requirements specify characteristics of the device which are critical to compatibility with external systems; specifically, those characteristics which are mandated by external systems and outside the control of the developers. One interface which is important in every case is the user and/or patient interface. (FDA D.C. Guidance, 2015)

Medical Device Regulation Consulting and Training – www.Procenius.com

Examples of Design Input Requirements	<ul><li>Performance requirements (including normal use, storage, handling, and maintenance)</li><li>Human factors/usability requirements</li><li>Safety and reliability requirements</li><li>Toxicity and biocompatibility requirements</li><li>Electromagnetic compatibility requirements</li><li>Limits/tolerances</li><li>Implemented controls from output of risk assessment</li><li>Failures in the field</li><li>Performance of similar/competitive designs</li><li>Labeling requirements</li><li>Training requirements</li><li>Regulations or standards</li><li>Sterility requirements</li><li>Field service requirements</li><li>Packaging requirements</li><li>User and patient needs</li></ul>
Characteristics of Effective Design Input Requirements	<ul><li>Measureable and able to be quantifiably verified and validated</li><li>Contain strong command statements such as "shall"</li><li>Concise and unambiguous (typical requirements are no more than one sentence)</li><li>Specify the design intent but not how the device should be designed</li></ul>

	• Consider regulatory requirements, standards, performance, functional, user interface, and output from risk analysis • Non-conflicting with other requirements • Comprehensive – FDA expects detail requirements that should be defined at high and low level subsystems. • Traceable – It is best practice to document the source of the requirement in the DIR to allow future (and current) product development teams to understand the driver of the requirement. In some cases it may shed light on determining applicability of the requirement for future design revisions. • Feasibility - It is typically best practice to perform feasibility testing to determine if the requirement can be achieved prior to performing formal verification and validation. • Address Functionality, Performance and User/Patient Interface • Organize Requirements for Efficiency – It is typically best practice to organize requirements in a design input document by function (Mechanical, Software, Electrical, System) or by type (Functional, Performance, Interface)
Process of Developing Design Input Requirements	**1. Determine the Use Case** Use cases are narrative descriptions of how developers anticipate users will use a device. Use cases will also help developers understand user needs and is typically performed by a marketing team and/or clinical specialists. **2. Translate Use Case into User Needs** This step is often considered one of the most difficult steps in developing design requirements. The subjective-narrative use case needs to be translated into quantifiable user needs. This step is typically performed by a cross functional team such as marketing and engineering.

Medical Device Regulation Consulting and Training – www.Procenius.com

3. **Translate User Needs into Design Requirements**
This step in the process involves the challenge of accurately translating user needs into lower level design requirements that will allow developers to design a device that will meet the needs of the user. This step is typically performed by technical team members such as engineers and scientists.

4. **Implement Regulatory Requirements and Standards**
Regulatory requirements and/or commonly accepted industry standards should be integrated into the design requirements to ensure the device is compliant to applicable standards and regulations.

5. **Implement Controls from Risk Assessment into Design Requirements**
As a result from performing a design risk analysis, design controls (risk controls) will be identified to mitigate unacceptable risks which should be translated into design requirements.

6. **Review Design Input Requirements (DIR)**
Prior to approval, the design requirements should be reviewed individually and ideally in a design review where questions, concerns and issues can be addressed.

7. **Approve Design Input Requirements**
The DIR should be formally approved by a qualified cross functional team that has the expertise required to thoroughly understand the device design and all of the requirements.

8. **Design Feasibility Testing**
After initial approval of the design requirements (or earlier in some cases), it is best practice to build a prototype to provide feedback to the development team about the feasibility of the design being able to meet the initial requirements. As a result of design feasibility testing, the DIR should be able to be updated and revised with feasible design requirement values. This practice increases the probability of passing verification and validation the first time.

Medical Device Regulation Consulting and Training – www.Procenius.com

	9. Design Input Requirement Revisions After design feasibility is performed and as development progresses the DIR should be updated, revised and approved to replace subjective requirements or "TBD's" with objective and specific verifiable design requirements prior to performing verification and validation activities.
Review	The type and method of review is dependent upon on the complexity of the device and size of the organization. In typical organizations an effective review includes an individual review and a formal design review. A final draft of the DIR should be reviewed by required approvers and design review attendees. The reviewers should thoroughly review the content of the DIR prior to the formal design review. During the review, the reviewers should be prepared to challenge and discuss issues, inadequacies, errors, or concerns that they have identified in the DIR. The sign of an effective review process is often indicated by multiple revisions of the draft document. The process of getting cross functional team input and coming to a consensus as to what should and can be realistically accomplished to meet all user needs and design requirements is the purpose of reviewing design inputs. Reviewers attending formal design reviews should include qualified individuals in all functional areas that may have critical contribution to the design inputs being reviewed. **Typical Reviewers** Cross Functional Team Quality Assurance Regulatory Affairs R&D / Engineering Marketing Project Management

Medical Device Regulation Consulting and Training – www.Procenius.com

	Other Stake Holders Independent Reviewer
Approval	The DIR is typically approved by a cross functional development team. The team should have the expertise to provide input about the feasibility of the device and its ability to meet the specified requirements. (i.e. technical, regulatory, marketing, quality). Management may also be included as approvers for design inputs. Approvals should be documented manually with signature and date or electronically to be in compliance with 21 CFR part 11. **Typical Approvers:** <u>Cross Functional Team</u> Quality Assurance Regulatory Affairs R&D / Engineering Marketing Project Management Other Stake Holders
Revisions	The DIR is a living document and should be updated and revised as the design evolves. The DIR should be revised as additional requirements are identified and as more specific and objective values are determined. Design inputs may be revised as necessary throughout the design process and will typically follow the same review and approval process which was required for the initial version. Revisions to design inputs require compliance to design change regulation *21CFR 820.30 (I)*.

Medical Device Regulation Consulting and Training – www.Procenius.com

Best Practices	• Invest the necessary resources early in the development cycle to ensure appropriate and accurate design inputs are established. • Perform human factors testing for all instances where human interface with the device may lead to unacceptable risk due to human error. • User needs and design requirements should include a range of acceptable values. • Design input documents should include (or reference) specific design requirements from regulations and standards. • Correctly written requirements will only specify the design intent, not how the device should be designed. • Design safety controls, which are outputs from a risk analysis, should be interpreted and captured in the design requirements. • Design requirements should be developed from user needs, regulations / standards and risk mitigation controls. • Build and test a prototype to adequately evaluate the design and provide feasible requirement values.
Templates	Visit **Procenius.com** to download design input requirement templates.

4.3. Regulation (21 CFR 820.30 (c)) - Design Input

Each manufacturer shall establish and maintain procedures to ensure that the design requirements relating to a device are appropriate and address the intended use of the device, including the needs of the user and patient. The procedures shall include a mechanism for addressing incomplete, ambiguous, or conflicting requirements. The design input requirements shall be documented and shall be reviewed and approved by a designated individual(s). The approval, including the date and signature of the individual(s) approving the requirements, shall be documented. (FDA QS Regulation, 2015)

4.4. Definition 21 CFR 820.3(f) – Design Input

Design input means the physical and performance requirements of a device that are used as a basis for device design. (FDA QSR , 2014)

4.5. Design Control Guidance Document (21 CFR 820.30 (c))

Design input is the starting point for product design. The requirements which form the design input establish a basis for performing subsequent design tasks and validating the design. Therefore, development of a solid foundation of requirements is the single most important design control activity.

Many medical device manufacturers have experience with the adverse effects that incomplete requirements can have on the design process. A frequent complaint of developers is that "there's never time to do it right, but there's always time to do it over." If essential requirements are not identified until validation, expensive redesign and rework may be necessary before a design can be released to production.

By comparison, the experience of manufacturers that have designed devices using clear-cut, comprehensive sets of requirements is that rework and redesign are significantly reduced and product quality is improved. They know that the development of requirements for a medical device of even moderate complexity is a formidable, time-consuming task. They accept the investment in time and resources required to develop the requirements because they know the advantages to be gained in the long run.

Unfortunately, there are a number of common misconceptions regarding the meaning and practical application of the quality system requirements for design input. Many seem to arise from interpreting the requirements as a literal prescription, rather than a set of principles to be followed. In this guidance document, the focus is on explaining the principles and providing examples of how they may be applied in typical situations.

4.5.1. Concept Documents Versus Design Inputs

In some cases, the marketing staff, who maintain close contact with customers and users, determine a need for a new product, or enhancements to an existing product. Alternatively, the idea for a new product may evolve out of a research or clinical activity. In any case, the result is a concept document specifying some of the desired characteristics of the new product.

Some members of the medical device community view these marketing memoranda, or the equivalent, as the design input. However, that is not the intent of the quality system requirements. Such concept documents are rarely comprehensive, and should not be expected to be so. Rather, the intent of the quality system requirements is that the product conceptual description be elaborated, expanded, and transformed into a complete set of design input requirements which are written to an engineering level of detail.

This is an important concept. The use of qualitative terms in a concept document is both appropriate and practical. This is often not the case for a document to be used as a basis for design. Even the simplest of terms can have enormous design implications. For example, the term "must be portable" in a concept document raises questions in the minds of product developers about issues such as size and weight limitations, resistance to shock and vibration, the need for protection from moisture and corrosion, the capability of operating over a wide temperature range, and many others. Thus, a concept document may be the starting point for development, but it is not the design input requirement. This is a key principle-the design input requirements are the result of the first stage of the design control process.

4.5.2. Research and Development

Some manufacturers have difficulty in determining where research ends and development begins. Research activities may be undertaken in an effort to determine new business opportunities or basic characteristics for a new product. It may be reasonable to develop a rapid prototype to explore the feasibility of an idea or design approach, for example, prior to developing design input requirements. But manufacturers should avoid falling into the trap of equating the prototype design with a finished product design. Prototypes at this stage lack safety features and ancillary functions necessary for a finished product, and are developed under conditions which preclude adequate consideration of product variability due to manufacturing.

4.5.3. Responsibility for Design Input Development

Regardless of who developed the initial product concept, product developers play a key role in developing the design input requirements. When presented with a set of important characteristics, it is the product developers who understand the auxiliary issues that must be addressed, as well as the level of detail necessary to design a product. Therefore, a second key principle is that the product developer(s) ultimately bear responsibility for translating user and/or patient needs into a set of requirements which can be validated prior to implementation. While this is primarily an engineering function, the support or full participation of production and service personnel, key suppliers, etc., may be required to assure that the design input requirements are complete.

Care must be exercised in applying this principle. Effective development of design input requirements encompasses input from both the product developer as well as those representing the needs of the user, such as marketing. Terminology can be a problem. In some cases, the product conceptual description may be expressed in medical terms. Medical terminology is appropriate in requirements when the developers and reviewers are familiar with the language, but it is often preferable to translate the concepts into engineering terms at the requirements stage to minimize miscommunication with the development staff.

Another problem is incorrect assumptions. Product developers make incorrect assumptions about user needs, and marketing personnel make incorrect assumptions about the needs of the product designers. Incorrect assumptions can have serious consequences that may not be detected until late in the development process. Therefore, both product developers and those representing the user must take responsibility for critically examining proposed requirements, exploring stated and implied assumptions, and uncovering problems.

Some examples should clarify this point. A basic principle is that design input requirements should specify what the design is intended to do while carefully avoiding specific design solutions at this stage. For example, a concept document might dictate that the product be housed in a machined aluminum case. It would be prudent for product developers to explore why this type of housing was specified. Perhaps there is a valid reason-superior electrical shielding, mechanical strength, or reduced time to market as compared to a cast housing. Or perhaps machined aluminum was specified because a competitor's product is made that way, or simply because the user didn't think plastic would be strong enough.

Not all incorrect assumptions are made by users. Incorrect assumptions made by product developers may be equally damaging. Failure to understand the abuse to which a portable instrument would be subjected might result in the selection of housing materials inadequate for the intended use of the product.

There are occasions when it may be appropriate to specify part of the design solution in the design input requirements. For example, a manufacturer may want to share components or manufacturing processes across a family of products in order to realize economies of scale, or simply to help establish a corporate identity. In the case of a product upgrade, there may be clear consensus regarding the features to be retained. However, it is important to realize that every such design constraint reduces implementation flexibility and should therefore be documented and identified as a possible conflicting requirement for subsequent resolution.

4.5.4. Scope and Level of Detail

Design input requirements must be comprehensive. This may be quite difficult for manufacturers who are implementing a system of design controls for the first time. Fortunately, the process gets easier with practice. It may be helpful to realize that design input requirements fall into three categories. Virtually every product will have requirements of all three types.

- Functional requirements specify what the device does, focusing on the operational capabilities of the device and processing of inputs and the resultant outputs.

- Performance requirements specify how much or how well the device must perform, addressing issues such as speed, strength, response times, accuracy, limits of operation, etc. This includes a quantitative characterization of the use environment, including, for example, temperature, humidity, shock, vibration, and electromagnetic compatibility. Requirements concerning device reliability and safety also fit into this category.

- Interface requirements specify characteristics of the device which are critical to compatibility with external systems; specifically, those characteristics which are mandated by external systems and outside the control of the developers. One interface which is important in every case is the user and/or patient interface.

What is the scope of the design input requirements development process and how much detail must be provided? The scope is dependent upon the complexity of a device and the risk associated with its use. For most medical devices, numerous requirements encompassing functions, performance, safety, and regulatory concerns are implied by the application. These implied requirements should be explicitly stated, in engineering terms, in the design input requirements.

Determining the appropriate level of detail requires experience. However, some general guidance is possible. The marketing literature contains product specifications, but these are superficial. The operator and service manuals may contain more detailed specifications and performance limits, but these also fall short of being comprehensive. Some insight as to what is necessary is provided by examining the requirements for a very common external interface. For the power requirements for AC-powered equipment, it is not sufficient to simply say that a unit shall be AC-powered. It is better to say that the unit shall be operable from AC power in North America, Europe, and Japan, but that is still insufficient detail to implement or validate the design. If one considers the situation just in North America, where the line voltage is typically 120 volts, many systems are specified to operate over the range of 108 to 132 volts. However, to account for the possibility of brownout, critical devices may be specified to operate from 95 to 132 volts or even wider ranges. Based on the intended use of the device, the manufacturer must choose appropriate performance limits.

There are many cases when it is impractical to establish every functional and performance characteristic at the design input stage. But in most cases, the form of the requirement can be determined, and the requirement can be stated with a to-be-determined (TBD) numerical value or a range of possible values. This makes it possible for reviewers to assess whether the requirements completely characterize the intended use of the device, judge the impact of omissions, and track incomplete requirements to ensure resolution.

For complex designs, it is not uncommon for the design input stage to consume as much as thirty percent of the total project time. Unfortunately, some managers and developers have been trained to measure design progress in terms of hardware built, or lines of software code written. They fail to realize that building a solid foundation saves time during the implementation. Part of the solution is to structure the requirements documents and reviews such that tangible measures of progress are provided.

Medical Device Regulation Consulting and Training – www.Procenius.com

At the other extreme, many medical devices have very simple requirements. For example, many new devices are simply replacement parts for a product, or are kits of commodity items. Typically, only the packaging and labeling distinguishes these products from existing products. In such cases, there is no need to recreate the detailed design input requirements of the item. It is acceptable to simply cite the predecessor product documentation, add any new product information, and establish the unique packaging and labeling requirements.

4.5.5. <u>Assessing Design Input Requirements for Adequacy</u>

Eventually, the design input must be reviewed for adequacy. After review and approval, the design input becomes a controlled document. All future changes will be subject to the change control procedures, as discussed in [the Design Change chapter].

Any assessment of design input requirements boils down to a matter of judgment. As discussed in [the Design Review chapter], it is important for the review team to be multidisciplinary and to have the appropriate authority. A number of criteria may be employed by the review team.

- Design input requirements should be unambiguous. That is, each requirement should be able to be verified by an objective method of analysis, inspection, or testing. For example, it is insufficient to state that a catheter must be able to withstand repeated flexing. A better requirement would state that the catheter should be formed into a 50 mm diameter coil and straightened out for a total of fifty times with no evidence of cracking or deformity. A qualified reviewer could then make a judgment whether this specified test method is representative of the conditions of use.

- Quantitative limits should be expressed with a measurement tolerance. For example, a diameter of 3.5 mm is an incomplete specification. If the diameter is specified as 3.500±0.005 mm, designers have a basis for determining how accurate the manufacturing processes have to be to produce compliant parts, and reviewers have a basis for determining whether the parts will be suitable for the intended use.

- The set of design input requirements for a product should be self-consistent. It is not unusual for requirements to conflict with one another or with a referenced industry standard due to a simple oversight. Such conflicts should be resolved early in the development process.

- The environment in which the product is intended to be used should be properly characterized. For example, manufacturers frequently make the mistake of specifying "laboratory" conditions for devices which are intended for use in the home. Yet, even within a single country, relative humidity in a home may range from 20 percent to 100 percent (condensing) due to climactic and seasonal variations. Household temperatures in many climates routinely exceed 40 °C during the hot season. Altitudes may exceed 3,000 m, and the resultant low atmospheric pressure may adversely affect some kinds of medical equipment. If environmental conditions are fully specified, a qualified reviewer can make a determination of whether the specified conditions are representative of the intended use.

- When industry standards are cited, the citations should be reviewed for completeness and relevance. For example, one medical device manufacturer claimed compliance with an industry standard covering mechanical shock and vibration. However, when the referenced standard was examined by a reviewer, it was found to prescribe only the method of testing, omitting any mention of pass/fail criteria. It was incumbent on the manufacturer in this case to specify appropriate performance limits for the device being tested, as well as the test method.

4.5.6. Evolution of the Design Input Requirements

Large development projects often are implemented in stages. When this occurs, the design input requirements at each stage should be developed and reviewed following the principles set forth in this section. Fortunately, the initial set of requirements, covering the overall product, is by far the most difficult to develop. As the design proceeds, the output from the early stages forms the basis for the subsequent stages, and the information available to designers is inherently more extensive and detailed.

It is almost inevitable that verification activities will uncover discrepancies which result in changes to the design input requirements. There are two points to be made about this. One is that the change control process for design input requirements must be carefully managed. Often, a design change to correct one problem may create a new problem which must be addressed. Throughout the development process, it is important that any changes are documented and communicated to developers so that the total impact of the change can be determined. The change control process is crucial to device quality.

The second point is that extensive rework of the design input requirements suggests that the design input requirements may not be elaborated to a suitable level of detail, or insufficient resources are being devoted to defining and reviewing the requirements. Managers can use this insight to improve the design control process. From a design control perspective, the number of requirements changes made is less important than the thoroughness of the change control process. (FDA D.C. Guidance, 2015)

4.6. Timing of Design Input Activities and Deliverables

The FDA does not specify at what point in the design and development process when inputs should be defined and approved but the following graphical models give some clarity as to when design inputs typically begin and end relative to research and development activities.

The two humps in Figure 8 depict the relationship and the relative amount of research and development activities performed during the design and development cycle. The shaded area is the typical time when inputs are generated, reviewed, approved and implemented.

Medical Device Regulation Consulting and Training – www.Procenius.com

Figure 8

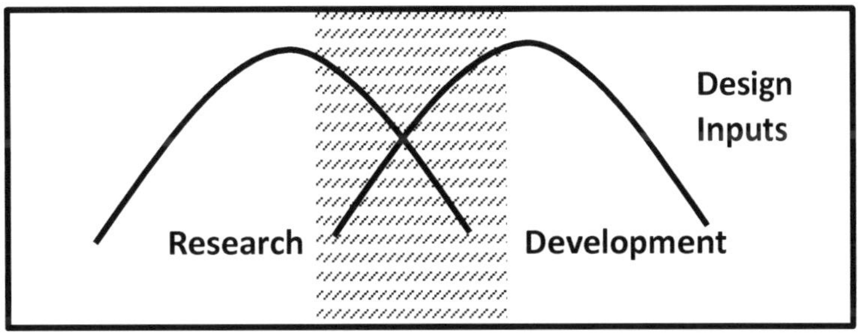

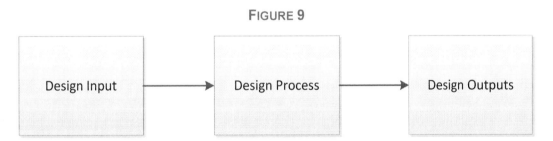

4.7. Design Input and Output Fundamentals

Before moving on to the detailed interpretation of the design inputs regulation, it is important to establish a fundamental understanding of design inputs. In the simplest terms, design inputs are the most basic information that developers use to initiate and finalize a design.

Figure 9 shows a simple and idealistic process flow of how design inputs feed into the design process.

FIGURE 9

Design Input	→	Design Process	→	Design Outputs

The following examples are provided in Table 6 to more fully understand how design inputs feed into the design process and then how design outputs are generated from that process.

4.7.1. How Design Inputs Result in Design Outputs Through the Design Process

TABLE 6

Design Inputs (Requirements)	Design Process	Design Output
The MRI machine's electrical system shall operate at 120V at less than 16 amps.	Components such as motors, actuators and LEDs rated for 120V that will meet functional requirements will be specified but will not exceed a total of 16 amps during operation. The design process will include design iterations, informal bench testing, feasibility studies and prototyping.	Once a viable design has been identified, the components and configuration of the design will be documented. A bill of materials (list of all components) and an electrical schematic (defines the configuration and layout of the components and wiring) are the design outputs.
The overall size of the MRI machine shall be less than 9' 6" (long) X 4' 8" (wide) X 6' 6" (high)	A 3D design envelope that will be no greater than 9' 6" (long) X 4' 8" (wide) X 6' 6" (high) will be defined in a CAD system. The sub-systems and components will be designed and specified to operate within the required maximum design envelope.	The design envelope will be defined in a 3D CAD system and will be electronically stored as a 3D model. The details of the design will be stored as a 2D drawing and bill of materials. The CAD files, drawings and bill of materials are the design outputs.

Medical Device Regulation Consulting and Training – www.Procenius.com

The dialysis catheter shall have a flow rate of 400 ml per minute at 10psi.	An iterative flow analysis to determine the minimum internal cross sectional area required to meet the flow requirement will be performed. Other requirements will also have to be considered that will drive material type, the external diameter and profile of the catheter extrusion.	The final cross sectional geometry and material will be defined in a 3D CAD system and will be electronically stored as a 3D model. The detail of the design will be stored as a 2D drawing and bill of materials. The CAD files, drawings and bill of materials are the design outputs.
The x-ray machine's software system shall display features to operate fluoroscopy, still images and deep tissue images from the main interface screen.	The software developers will develop code for the main interface page of the software such that all required image types are available from the main interface screen.	The software code will define the image display information that will meet the image requirement. The software code is therefore the output of the software design effort. Any documentation that supports the software code will also be part of the design output.

Table 6 is intended to show how design requirements form the initial framework of the design by putting in place boundaries and constraints that guide developers down the path to the optimal design that will meet user needs. Design requirements are not meant to specify every aspect of the design, but are needed to keep the design on the intended path. There is a critical balance between the design being over constrained and under constrained that should be optimized prior to initiating the design process. If the design is over constrained then the requirements specify too many design details which may lead to a design that is not technically feasible, impossible to manufacture or very costly. If the design is under constrained then there are not enough requirements to adequately enable designers to meet user needs.

As mentioned in the design control guidance, "… development of a solid foundation of requirements is the single most important design control activity". [BP1] (FDA D.C. Guidance, 2015) Just as a building constructed on an unstable foundation will eventually crumble and fall, so too will a design that is based on incomplete, ambiguous, or conflicting design requirements.

> **#1 Best Practice – Development of solid design requirements is the single most important design control activity.**
>
> Invest the necessary resources early in the development cycle to ensure appropriate and accurate design inputs are established.

4.8. Interpretation & Application (21 CFR 820.30 (c))

*The regulation states**, "Each manufacturer shall establish and maintain procedures to ensure that the design requirements relating to a device are appropriate and address the intended use of the device, including the needs of the user and patient"** ...*

To "*establish*" means to define, document (in writing or electronically), and implement. (FDA QSR , 2014)

The FDA is saying that the device manufacturer/developer must have a documented procedure(s) that defines the "what, who, how, why and when" of how design inputs are created and applied. The FDA wants to ensure that a standard design input requirement (DIR) procedure has been created, vetted, reviewed and approved.

The procedure must be "maintained" (or in other words revised and updated) as required to be current with the actual practices being used to develop the design input requirements in the organization. Typically this procedure is maintained by the department that is responsible for new product development such as development engineering or R&D.

The regulation also states that the procedure shall "**ensure that the design requirements relating to a device are appropriate...**". The word "*appropriate*" as mentioned here may sound like a wide open interpretation but the FDA is trying to convey that the manufacturer's procedure must provide a consistent method of developing design inputs that are applicable for the intended use of the device. The procedure must also guide the generation of workable, accurate, and effective requirements for design teams to use during product development.

The regulation also states that the procedure shall ensure that the design input requirements "**address the intended use of the device...**". This phrase in the regulation should prompt developers to take actions which are necessary to fully understand and define how the device will be used. In theory the intended use is straight forward and easily addressed. The medical device intended use is essentially how the medical device manufacturer expects (or intends) a user and/or patient to use the device (see IMPORTANT CONCEPTS* below). Designers will use the intended use as the basis for developing design inputs therefore it is crucial that the intended use is established <u>prior</u> to creating design inputs.

> **IMPORTANT CONCEPTS***
>
> **Intended Use vs. Indications for Use**
>
> There is often confusion in the medical device industry between intended use and indications for use. The best definitions which distinguish between the two terms is found in 21 CFR 814.20(b)(3)(i),
>
> **Intended Use** - means the general purpose of the device or its function, and encompasses the indications for use.
>
> **Indications for Use**… describes the disease or condition the device will diagnose, treat, prevent, cure or mitigate, including a description of the patient population for which the device is intended.

Even though the medical device manufacturer will formally specify how the device should be used in device labeling, the manufacturer should also consider variations of how the users may use the device under typical situations. Manufacturers are not expected to anticipate and mitigate risks for extreme off label use of the device but they should consider and design the device in anticipation of expected use conditions even though they may not be intended.

As an example of interpreting intended use into requirements, our *MRI OnWheels* case study from the previous chapter discussed a portable MRI machine that could be transported and used in various rooms in a hospital environment. At first review this intended use would drive requirements like:

- *No more than X lbs of horizontal force will be required by the user to transport the machine.*
- *The machine must be able to function with X voltage and Y power.*
- *The machine must be able to be transported across standard doorway thresholds less than or equal to Z inches.*
- *The MRI shall be compliant to ISO XXX.XX to prevent electromagnetic interference with other surrounding equipment.*

In a perfect world these design requirements seem reasonable and expected. Unfortunately there are other anticipated scenarios that the device will experience that should be considered. Less than obvious design inputs will typically come from sales or service representatives in the field that see firsthand day in and day out how similar machines are actually used. As an example, they may see devices similar to the *MRI OnWheels* that are used as "battering rams" to

Medical Device Regulation Consulting and Training – www.Procenius.com

open swinging hospital doors as they travel to the emergency room. They may also see clinicians try to pull the machine across the floor by pulling the power cord. Obviously the intended use of this device would not have led developers to anticipate these extreme conditions, but the FDA will expect manufacturers to do their due diligence to thoroughly understand and gather all design requirements that can practically and reasonably be identified to ensure the safety and effectiveness of the device. Under these expected conditions, it is possible that the safety and effectiveness of the device would be compromised and therefore it is the responsibility of developers to add design requirements that will lead to design features that will mitigate these anticipated risks. In this example design requirements might be:

- *The machine shall function safely and effectively as intended after receiving X number of frontal impacts with a force of Y lbs.*

- *The machine shall function safely and effectively as intended after X lbs. of tension applied to the power cord Y number of times.*

The initial development of these types of inputs may be far, few and in between but as experience with the product (or similar products) increases, the DIR will become more detailed, refined and improved which will eventually result in a highly effective design.

4.8.1. <u>Design Input Sources (User Needs, Risk Controls, Regulations)</u>

Design inputs typically come from three sources: Marketing Inputs, Regulatory Bodies & Standards Organizations, and Risk Assessments. Figure 10 shows these three sources of inputs and how they translate into design requirements.

Medical Device Regulation Consulting and Training – www.Procenius.com

FIGURE 10

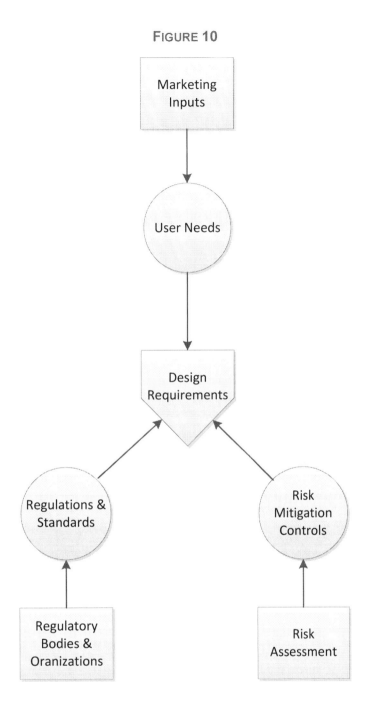

4.8.2. Design Inputs Derived from User Needs

Interpretation of *"...**Needs of the user and patient**..."* as defined in 21 CFR 820.30 (c) tends to be applied in many ways across the medical device industry. The first thing to understand is that user and patient needs are not typically identified directly from feedback from a sales representative or product manager (marketing rep.). Yes, it is true that these roles will be part of the development team that will develop the DIR and yes it is also true that these roles will help the team identify the "voice of the customer" but more often than not these inputs are very subjective and "soft" marketing descriptors such as, the device must be "easy to use", "light" and "reliable". These may seem totally reasonable to the user and they know what these terms mean, but unfortunately these terms are subjective and are unable to be effectively validated. Some may say, "but these are what the users want, how can you say that they are not the user needs?". It is true that these are the needs that the users have identified but they are not the "user needs" that should be documented in formal design inputs that will be used to validate the device.

The user needs that will be validated should be defined in such a manner that is measureable and objective (in most cases) to minimize subjectivity and ambiguity during development and validation. There are various ways to represent the relationship between user needs and design requirements. Figure 11 is a typical way to visualization how marketing inputs flow down to user needs, to design requirements, and eventually down to sub-system requirements.

Medical Device Regulation Consulting and Training – www.Procenius.com

FIGURE 11

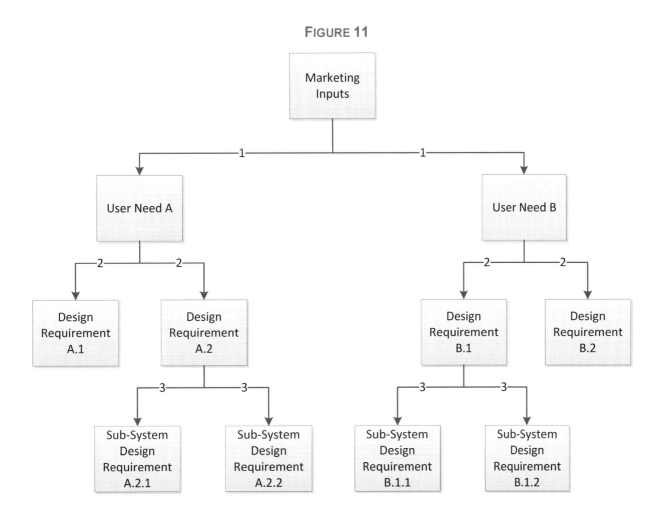

Medical Device Regulation Consulting and Training – www.Procenius.com

Table 7 is an example of how a marketing input is translated into design requirements and how the design requirements and user needs are verified/validated. The numbers listed in Table 7 are defined in Table 8.

———————————————————————————————→

TABLE 7

Marketing Input/Use Case	Interpreted User Need	Design Requirement	How Verified	How Validated
1	2	5	11	17
		6	12	
	3	7	13	18
		8	14	
	4	9	15	19
		10	16	

Medical Device Regulation Consulting and Training – www.Procenius.com

TABLE 8

1	The user wants to be able to use the MRI machine in an emergency room environment.
2	The device shall be able to be plugged into and powered by a standard U.S. 120V @ 15 amp electrical outlet in an emergency room.
3	The device shall be able to be transported as in an emergency room suite with aisle and door ways that are 10'(long) X 5' (wide) X 6' 8" (high).
4	The device shall not cause other medical devices in the emergency room to malfunction from the intended use and operation. (e.g. EMI, power, mechanically)
5	The software system shall operate at 120 V @ less than 0.3 amps
6	The electrical system shall operate at 120V @ less than 16 amps
7	The overall size of the device shall be less than 9' 5" (long) X 4' 8" (wide) X 6' 6" (high)
8	The device shall function as intended and without damage after being rolled over a .250 high threshold with a full radius tangential to the ground.
9	The device shall be compliant to EMC directive IEC 60601-1-2.
10	The device shall not incur power draw spikes greater than 10 amps during normal operation, start up or shut down.

11	Approved protocol used in R&D test environment to verify that the software operates on120V @ less than .3 amps.
12	Approved protocol used in R&D test environment to verify that the software operates on120V @ less than 16 amps.
13	Approved protocol used in R&D test environment to verify (measure overall size of machine) that the overall size of the device is less than 9' 5" (long) X 4' 8" (wide) X 6' 6" (high)
14	Approved protocol used in R&D test environment to verify rolling over a .250" threshold 800 times (determined from reliability requirement). Test method to check basic functionality is performed.
15	Approved protocol used in R&D test environment to verify that there is acceptable EMI (electrical magnetic interface) levels from the machine according to the standard.
16	Approved protocol used in R&D test environment to verify that the max current draw spike was less than 10 amps.
17	A clinician will follow an approved validation protocol, while in a hospital emergency room, that instructs him to plug in the device, turn on the device and perform basic device functions. This validates that the device is functional using the available power source.
18	A clinician will follow an approved validation protocol while in a hospital emergency room that instructs him to maneuver the device through a door way, over a threshold, and through an aisle way that is 10'(long) X 3' (wide) X 6' 8"ft (high).

Medical Device Regulation Consulting and Training – www.Procenius.com

19	A clinician will follow an approved validation protocol, while in a hospital emergency room, that instructs him to operate the device and other specified devices in the area. The other devices will be monitored to ensure that no interference or malfunctions of other devices occur.

Table 7 shows how one marketing input can lead to three user needs and six design requirements. From this one marketing input, there is the potential for significantly more user needs which can propagate into numerous design requirements. It would not be uncommon for a system of this magnitude to have hundreds if not over a thousand design requirements.

Collecting marketing inputs (top tier of Figure 11 and first column of Table 7) is relatively easy compared with defining user needs. Marketing inputs are typically collected from market research such as surveys or interviews. Translating market inputs into user needs (link 1, Figure 11) is often the most difficult step in this process because a substantial amount of user interface is often required to accurately translate qualitative marketing input into quantitative (objective) user needs which requires significant resources (time and money). Resource constraints aside, link 1 in Figure 11 also requires the skill set of an experienced marketing, clinical specialist and engineering team that is able to develop an accurate method for translating marketing inputs into user needs. These methods may be performed by surveys or user testing using prototypes that can quantifiably capture the needs of the user.

Due to limited availability of prototypes, product managers may be tempted to have users use a single prototype (or use a single data point approach) during marketing research to quantify a specific value for the feature in question. As an example, the product manager for *MRI OnWheels* will perform market research in an attempt to determine if the force required to transport the MRI prototype is acceptable to the user. Unfortunately the results from the market research will only identify a single data point that is acceptable to the user.

Ideally[BP2] market research will be performed to determine a range of force values that is acceptable to users of the *MRI OnWheels.* Instead of having one prototype, multiple prototypes with variable transporting forces would help quantify an acceptable range for the design requirement. If multiple prototypes are not practical it may be possible to modify the force of one prototype to simulate different force values. Determining a range of acceptable values will provide flexibility to the engineering team during the design phase and will increase the probability of the device passing validation.

> **#2 Best Practice – User needs and design requirements should Include a range of acceptable values.**
>
> Determining a range of acceptable values will provide flexibility to the engineering team during the design phase and will increase the probability of the device passing validation.

If the translation of marketing input to the user need is not fully understood, is misinterpreted, or is not adequately researched (link 1, Figure 11), the risk of failing design validation dramatically increases.

Translation from user needs to design requirements (link 2, Figure 11) and then from design requirements to sub-system design requirements (link 3, Figure 11) is relatively easy. These levels can be performed with internal resources using established procedures or engineering/scientific techniques.

Figure 11 depicts a multilevel design requirement scenario that is typical in average to highly complex devices. Highly complex devices may require even more levels of requirements in contrast with very simple devices that may only require a one tier design requirement structure.

4.8.3. Importance of Human Factors: (User Needs and Design Validation)

The FDA emphasizes that design inputs and user needs should be identified and refined by "conduct[ing] appropriate human factors studies" as stated in comment 72 of the quality systems regulation preamble. Even though this is not required in the design control regulation it is industry best practice[BP3] to perform human factors testing for all instances where human interface with the device may lead to unacceptable risk due to human error.

> **#3 Best Practice – Perform human factors testing for all instances where human interface with the device may lead to unacceptable risk due to human error.**

Medical Device Regulation Consulting and Training – www.Procenius.com

Quality Systems Regulation Preamble:

Comment 72

"FDA emphasizes, however, that the section requires the manufacturer to ensure that the design input requirements are appropriate so the device will perform to meet its intended use and the needs of the user. In doing this, the manufacturer must define the performance characteristics, safety and reliability requirements, environmental requirements and limitations, physical characteristics, applicable standards and regulatory requirements, and labeling and packaging requirements, among other things, and refine the design requirements as verification and validation results are established. For example, when designing a device, the manufacturer should conduct appropriate <u>human factors studies</u>, analyses, and tests from the early stages of the design process until that point in development at which the interfaces with the medical professional and the patient are fixed. The human interface includes both the hardware and software characteristics that affect device use, and good design is crucial to logical, straight forward, and safe device operation. The <u>human factors</u> methods used (for instance, task/function analyses, user studies, prototype tests, mock-up reviews, etc.) should ensure that the characteristics of the user population and operating environment are considered. In addition, the compatibility of system components should be assessed."
(FDA Preamble, 2015)

In recent years the FDA has issued Human Factors draft guidance in an effort to help device manufactures develop better practices when trying to understand user needs and design risks associated with device and user interface scenarios. The guidance outlines best practices for implementing human factors testing in both a development and validation environment.

Human factors testing goes above and beyond traditional marketing research and concept testing. Human factors/usability testing evaluates user performance using the product in an environment that is similar to how the device will be used in a clinical setting. These are typically one-on-one testing sessions using strict scientific and experimental methods. In contrast marketing research and concept testing is relatively informal, not scientific in nature and is typically not in an actual or simulated use environment.

Human factors testing not only helps developers identify user needs early in the development cycle, it also hones in the design and mitigates risk as development progresses to ensure the device is safe and effective and will actually meet user needs.

To effectively explain the purpose of human factors testing, the following excerpt has been taken from, "FDA Human Factors Requirements Change the Landscape of Medical Device Development", by David Hirning and Virginia Lang (Hirning, 2013).

"Human Factors Engineering is based on research, scientific/experimental method, statistics, human physiology and cognitive information processing. It is the combination of engineering, human physiology, behavioral performance and cognitive science. Human

Factors Engineering is a scientific discipline that studies how humans interact with devices, products and/or systems. It approaches design with the user as the focal point. Human Factors Engineering ensures that devices, products and systems are safe, effective and usable by their intended users.

The FDA requires** device manufacturers to create a use-based risk analysis for their products. By creating this risk analysis, medical device manufacturers do a thorough examination of their product(s) from the point of view of the user. The risk analysis then becomes the basis of the human factors/usability testing. One important aspect of the risk analysis is the proposed mitigations for high-risk/high-frequency tasks. Instructions for use, training and product patient inserts are no longer considered appropriate mitigations. Instead, appropriate mitigations must be related to the design of the device. So, how do you know that these design mitigations are accurate? That is where human factors/usability testing comes into the picture.

[Using Human Factors to Mitigate Design Risks]

… Human Factors have methods to evaluate those mitigations early in the product development cycle. The FDA calls these formative testing/methods. These tests are evaluative in purpose. Getting your product in front of users will quickly tell you if your design mitigations are accurate. In addition, it will give you the opportunity to make changes to your product very early in your product development cycle. As you know, identifying product problems early in the cycle will enable lower cost changes than if you waited until just before launch. What goes into a formative test?

Formative testing uses a prototype of the device and puts it into the hands of users. Formative testing sits at the center of the development cycle to align the actual model of human interaction with the ultimate design of the device or system.

[Formative Testing to Identify Design Input and User Needs during Development]

…Finding out you have some serious design problems with your device early in the development cycle will cost less to fix than if you find out at the end of the product development cycle. You might actually want to do two or three rounds of formative human factors/usability testing. Then when you get to the summative testing, you are assured that you have mitigated all of the risks through design changes.

[Summative Testing to Validate Design]

What is a summative human factors/usability test? The summative test is the final test, which renders a pass/fail judgment on a device, product or system. This test validates that the device, product or system is safe, effective and usable by the all intended user groups. It differs from the formative test in that now you have to use a device that represents exactly the device that is going to be launched to the market."

Medical Device Regulation Consulting and Training – www.Procenius.com

**FDA regulation does not currently require user base risk analysis as indicated in the referenced article but it is typically expected as industry practice and is indicated in human factors draft guidance.

Formative Testing

Formative testing is explained by the FDA in the following excerpt from the Human Factors Draft Guidance (FDA Human Factors, 2011):

> "Formative evaluations are conducted to inform product development in progress. These evaluations derive information from user interaction with devices under conditions of varying degrees of formality and may include various simulated-use testing approaches. Formative studies that involve use of the device by representative end users are useful for identifying problems that were not identified or sufficiently understood using analytical methods, early in the design process when they can be addressed more easily and less expensively."

Summative Testing (Human Factors Design Validation)

Summative testing is explained by the FDA in terms of design validation in the following excerpt from the Human Factors Draft Guidance (FDA Human Factors, 2011):

> "The human factors validation test demonstrates that the intended users of a medical device can safely and effectively perform critical tasks for the intended uses in the expected use environments. It is particularly important during validation testing to use a production version of the device, representative device users, actual use or simulated use in an environment of appropriate realism, and to address all aspects of intended use. Validation is often carried out under conditions of simulated use, but, if necessary, further evaluation can be undertaken under conditions of actual use in a clinical study..."

Integration of Formative and Summative Testing into Product Development

Figure 12 illustrates the integration of formative and summative testing into a typical product development cycle.

Medical Device Regulation Consulting and Training – www.Procenius.com

FIGURE 12

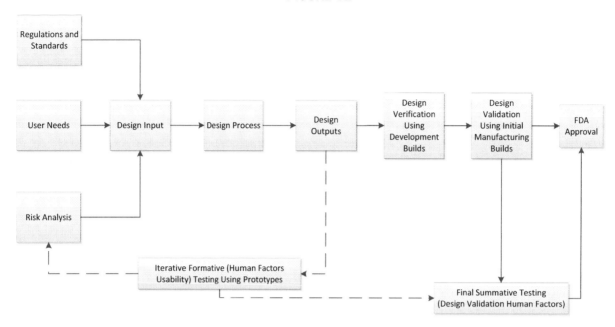

In addition to the FDA draft guidance on the subject of Human Factors (FDA Human Factors, 2011), the FDA does officially recognize device specific and general standards by national and international standards bodies as listed in Table 9.

(FDA HUMAN FACTORS, 2011)

TABLE 9

Standard	Title	Main Purpose
AAMI/ANSI HE75:2009	*Human Factors Engineering – Design of Medical Devices*	Comprehensive reference that includes general principles, usability testing, design elements, integrated solutions
ISO/IEC 62366:2007	*Medical devices – Application of usability engineering to medical devices*	HFE/UE process applied to all medical devices, with emphasis on risk management

ANSI/AAMI/ISO 14971:2007	*Medical Devices – Application of risk management to medical devices*	Risk management process for medical devices
IEC 60601-1-8:2006	*Medical electrical equipment — Part 1-8: General requirements for basic safety and essential performance — Collateral Standard: General requirements, tests and guidance for alarm systems in medical electrical equipment and medical electrical systems*	HFE/UE process applied to alarm systems for medical electrical equipment and systems

Medical Device Regulation Consulting and Training – www.Procenius.com

4.8.4. Design Inputs Derived from Regulations and Standards

Although many design requirements are derived from user needs, regulations and industry standards may also be a significant source of design requirements. As an example, the FDA specifies medical device labeling requirements in 21 CFR 801. There are also numerous ISO standards that are often required by European notified bodies or competent authorities for medical device approval or industry accepted standards such as IEC 60601-1-2. These standards should be referenced or contained in the DIR.

If references to standards or regulations are used in design input documents, the references should be specific[BP4] to applicable sections or requirement ID's as applicable. General high level references to regulations should not be referenced. High level references such as: "The device shall meet all requirements of 21 CFR 801" leads to potential problems. Problems often arise during verification and validation because it is typically discovered at that point that some of the requirements in the referenced standard or regulation are not applicable to the device. A revision to the design input document is now required and/or deviations have to be documented in the verification and validation reports that will need to explain why the requirements were not applicable and therefore do not have to be verified or validated. This type of "cleanup work" never looks good in an FDA inspection. It is always better to perform the due diligence of documenting the requirements accurately prior to beginning any major design work. It is also an indication to the FDA that sufficient time was not invested into development of the design requirements.

#4 Best Practice – Design input documents should include (or reference) specific design requirements from regulations and standards.

Design input documents should include specific references to applicable regulation and/or standards. High level regulations/standard requirements may lead to non-compliance issues or insufficient verification or validation activities.

4.8.5. Design Inputs Derived from Risk Analysis Controls

Design requirements are also derived from risk mitigation controls which are developed from the risk [BP5] analysis process. This will typically occur as the development team is analyzing risks associated with the device design through evaluation of anticipated risk scenarios and feedback from formative human factors testing.

It is best [BP5] practice to implement the risk mitigation controls into design requirements to ensure the control is not inadvertently lost from the device design. The requirement that is generated

Medical Device Regulation Consulting and Training – www.Procenius.com

from the risk control does not need to specify how the design should function but as with all requirements it should communicate the intent of the risk control but should also leave developers flexibility of how they want to meet user needs.

As an example, during the risk analysis of the *MRI OnWheels,* the development team determines that there is an unacceptable risk in the design which allows the machine to be transported (e.g. inadvertently rolls) during operation. This event may cause the power cord to become unplugged which in turn leads to loss of power during a MRI scan. The development team assigns the engineering team to implement a design feature that prevents the machine from being transported during operation. The engineering team develops a simple yet effective solution. They put standard brakes on the wheels that will automatically engage when the machine is operated. Testing is performed with acceptable performance results on the new brake design. The development team evaluates the mitigation to the design which lowers the risk level to an acceptable level. The risk assessment is revised and the design modification is implemented into the system design but before closing out the risk line item in the risk assessment, the team should highly consider creating a new requirement that will ensure that this risk is permanently addressed in future design revisions. If not, the risk control to prevent transportation during operation may be lost or overlooked in future design revisions.

Over the years, the design will most likely change in response to user requests or internal business needs. As an example, this may happen when a few users complain about the brakes limiting the maneuvering capability of the machine during a scan. So, the sustaining engineering team evaluates the impact of removing the brakes from the design. They thoroughly review the risk assessment and design inputs to assess what the impact of removing the brakes may have on the safety and effectiveness of the design. During the review of the risk assessment, the team would ideally make the connection that the brakes were implemented into the design to mitigate the "transport during operation" hazard. Unfortunately because the risk is not directly tied to the design of the brakes, this connection may not be made.

The best way to ensure safety controls are not lost from the design intent is to implement the control into the requirements[BP5]. In this case the requirement may simply say something like, "The system shall not be able to be transported while operating a scan". This is a clear requirement that should be very apparent to reviewers while making a determination of whether or not the design change should be implemented. To ensure the risk is tied to the design requirement, the risk ID# from the risk assessment document should be traced directly to the design input requirement in the DIR and vice versa. This technique will allow forward and backwards traceability between the DIR and the risk assessment.

If requirements are correctly written, they will only specify the design intent, not how the device should be designed. In our previous example, a requirement should never specify that "brakes" should be required. The power of correctly written requirements conveys the design intent but will also allow designers flexibility to consider numerous design solutions to meet the requirement[BP6].

Medical Device Regulation Consulting and Training – www.Procenius.com

#5 Best Practice – Design safety controls which are outputs from a risk analysis should be interpreted and captured in the design requirements.

To ensure the intent of the design safety controls are not lost during product revisions, the design requirements should be revised to include a requirement that captures the intent of the safety control but does not specify the exact design that was implemented. A reference in both the risk assessment and design requirements should be made to link the risk mitigation and design requirement together so future design teams understand the source and resolution of the risk mitigation.

#6 Best Practice – Correctly written requirements will only specify the design intent, not how the device should be designed.

If requirements are correctly written, they will only specify the design intent, not how the device should be designed. The power of correctly written requirements conveys the design intent but will also allow designers flexibility to consider numerous design solutions to meet the requirement.

#7 Best Practice – Design requirements should be developed from user needs, regulations / standards and risk mitigation controls.

Effective design requirements are typically derived from a variety of sources including but not limited to regulations, industry standards, risk assessments and user needs.

4.8.6. Addressing Incomplete, Ambiguous, or Conflicting Requirements

The regulation states, *"The procedures shall include a mechanism for addressing incomplete, ambiguous, or conflicting requirements."* During the initial process of documenting the design input requirements, developing the design, or performing verification, it is fairly typical that design requirements are often found to be incomplete, ambiguous or conflicting. It is also often expected that the initial revision of design inputs may not include quantifiable requirements that are able to be objectively verified but as the design progresses design requirements should become more specific and quantified.

Inexperienced teams that are developing new and unique products often have a difficult time creating objective, complete, and non-conflicting requirements. It is often difficult for teams to foresee the insufficiencies in the design inputs until they have actually been tested. The best design input requirements are often a result from lessons learned from similar products that have previously been developed. Unfortunately the best lessons learned happen during verification and validation (v&v) testing at which point incomplete, ambiguous or conflicting requirements become painfully obvious. When this is the case, teams will be spending their time trying to salvage the v&v and revising the requirements as needed in hopes that the revised requirements will lead to a more successful v&v the second time around. During v&v these issues can cause major problems for the team, but the team should take advantage of this opportunity by documenting what they have learned to bolster the next revision of the design requirements.

The FDA realizes that the creation of insufficient requirements is frequently a significant deficiency in the medical device industry therefore they have specified that "...*The procedures shall include a mechanism for addressing incomplete, ambiguous, or conflicting requirements"*. Manufacturers have flexibility of what "mechanism" or method they use to address these insufficiencies, but typically the preferred method is to take advantage of the design review forum. Design reviews are an ideal setting for resolving incomplete, ambiguous or conflicting design requirements. Experienced cross functional teams in attendance at design reviews should have the expertise to resolve the most challenging design requirement issues.

The design input requirements shall be documented and shall be reviewed and approved by a designated individual(s).

This line in the regulation requires that design requirements are documented. Traditionally this means the requirements are captured on paper or electronically.

"...**shall be reviewed...**" Ideally review of the design input requirements will mean a cross functional team of experts will thoroughly evaluate and understand the content and intent of the requirements. Each expert should not only understand their area of expertise but should also understand the interface of other requirements from other functional areas. They should also thoroughly understand how the requirements will affect the safety and effectiveness of the device. This level of understanding requires that the reviewers know the intended use of the device including patient population, indications for use, risks associated with the device and other factors which are highly impacted by the design input requirements.

Review of the design input requirements (DIR) should be taken seriously. The accuracy and completeness of the DIR is essential to the success of the device. If reviewers fail to invest the needed time to perform a thorough review of the DIR they are not only jeopardizing the commercial success of the device, but they are also putting users at risk. As with any review of medical device development documents (i.e. DIR, DDP, Risk Assessment) reviewers have an ethical responsibility to invest the time required to ensure that the design input requirements are robust, thorough, and accurate.

A draft version of design input requirements (DIR) are typically reviewed individually and in formal design reviews. Prior to approval of the DIR, the approvers should be given sufficient time to read and understand the DIR content and intent of the requirements. After reviewers have had the opportunity to read the DIR, it is best practice to review the DIR during a design review which will give all of the attendees the opportunity to address (or challenge) any concerns or issues that may arise. As a result of the review, decisions will be made and actions will be assigned that may require updates to the DIR.

"The approval, including the date and signature of the individual(s) approving the requirements, shall be documented."

Due to the fact that design requirements have such a significant impact on the success of a design, more approval signatures will typically be required relative to other type of development documents. In small to medium size companies approvals may include upper level management members such as the VP of Quality, VP of Engineering, VP of Marketing, and VP of Regulatory Affairs. In larger corporations, lower to mid-level management may approve the DIR. Other department heads and stake holders should also be considered as approvers and/or to provide input to the DIR as appropriate for the organization. The FDA does not directly specify the stake holders required to approve design inputs but they do indicate under 21 CFR 820.20 (sub-part B, Management Responsibility) that management should be involved and aware of activities pertaining to the quality system which makes it seem reasonable that management should review and approve design input requirements when feasible.

4.9. Characteristics of Well Defined User Needs and Design Requirements

- Measureable and able to be quantifiably verified and validated

- Contain strong command statements such as "shall"

- Concise and unambiguous (Typical requirements are no more than one sentence)

- Specify the design intent but not how the device should be designed

- Consider regulatory requirements, industry standards, performance, functional, user interface, and outputs from risk analysis

- Non-conflicting with other requirements

- Comprehensive – FDA expects detail requirements that should be defined at high and low level subsystems.

- Traceable – It is best practice to document the source of the requirement in the DIR to allow future (and current) product development teams to understand the driver behind the requirement. In some cases it may shed light on determining applicability of the requirement for future design revisions.

- Feasibility - It is typically best practice to perform feasibility testing to determine if the requirement can be achieved prior to performing formal verification and validation.

- Address Functionality, Performance and User/Patient Interface

- Organize Requirements for Efficiency – It is typically best practice to organize requirements in a design input document by function (Mechanical, Software, Electrical, System) or by type (Functional, Performance, Interface)

4.10. <u>Step by Step Process of Creating Design Input Requirements</u>

1. Determine the Use Case

The first step in developing requirements is to identify the user needs. One of the best ways of doing this is by developing use cases. Use cases are narrative descriptions of how developers anticipate users will use a device. Developers should elicit the input from users, marketing, and sales representatives. In our *MRI OnWheels* example, a use case would sound something like this:

> *A clinician will use the mobile MRI machine in the emergency room environment. One clinician will be performing the MRI scan. The clinician will be capturing images of multiple anatomy types such as blood vessels, bone and core chest cavity organs. The clinician will need to copy, send and/or transfer the image to external locations. A maximum of two clinicians will be available to transport the machine to multiple floors in a hospital environment.*

This is a brief excerpt of a use case that may typically be paragraphs if not pages in length. The intent of this exercise is to get a full detail description of how users need, want and intend to use the machine. Even though this is a short description of how the machine will be used, it has the potential to affect many functional aspects of the machine and will lead to potentially hundreds of requirements.

Refer to Table 7 in this chapter for an example of how the use case (or marketing inputs) are translated into user needs and design input requirements.

2. Translate Use Case into User Needs

With the expertise of a cross functional team which may include a clinical expert (i.e. physician, nurse), product manager (marketing), engineer (all types), human factor representative and QA representative, the use cases should be evaluated and translated into user needs as previously specified. This is often a time consuming step that is very iterative due to the nature of researching and understanding the details of how the use case can be quantified into objective user needs.

Refer to Table 7 in this chapter for an example of how the use case (or marketing inputs) are translated into user needs and design input requirements.

3. Translate User Needs into Design Requirements by a Technical Team

This step in the process is typically performed by technical team members such as engineers with input from product managers (marketing). It is not uncommon for the team to be focused or specialized in technical areas such as software development, electrical engineering or mechanical engineering. Their job is to accurately translate user needs into lower level design requirements that will allow developers to design a device that will meet the needs of the user. The same process can and should be repeated for lower sub-level requirements if needed to adequately define the design requirements.

4. Implement Regulatory Requirements and Standards

Identification of applicable regulatory requirements and standards should be relatively straightforward. In most cases device manufacturers deal with similar type products which have commonly accepted regulatory requirements and industry standards that will be common for similar devices. Over time device manufacturers may develop a standards and regulatory list that is typical for their industry and may be modified to accommodate applicable regulations and standards for specific industries, technologies or countries.

5. Implement Controls from Risk Assessment

As a result from performing a design risk analysis, design controls will be identified to mitigate unacceptable risks. As previously discussed, design controls should be captured as requirements in the design input requirements document to ensure that the reason and intent of the design control is not lost over time.

6. Review Design Input Requirements

Prior to approval, the design requirements should be reviewed individually and ideally in a formal design review where questions, concerns and issues can be addressed. Both reviews should include resolving conflicting requirements, ambiguity and lack of clarity that may exist in early drafts or versions of the design input requirements. Reviewers should also ensure that requirements are written objectively such that they may be easily and consistently verified.

7. Approve Initial Design Input Requirements

After feedback from the review process is implemented into the design input requirements (DIR), the document should be formally approved by a qualified cross functional team that has the expertise required to thoroughly understand the device design and requirements. This will be the initial design input requirements document that may only have broad, subjective requirements or TBD place holders which will be refined and updated into a comprehensive set of objective requirements as the device is developed.

8. Design Feasibility Testing (Human Factors / Formative Testing)

After initial approval of the design requirements, it is best practice to build a prototype [BP8] (or earlier in some cases) to provide feedback to the development team about the feasibility of the design meeting the initial requirements. At this point in development many product concepts are killed because feasibility tests demonstrate that the design concept cannot meet the requirements and user needs. Those concepts that meet initial design requirements or are close to meeting requirements will often be pursued. Additional product development may prove that some improvements to the design will enable the requirements and user needs to be met. Other times additional marketing research may conclude that there may be alternative intended uses with different user needs that the design concept may more easily meet. Under no circumstances should user needs be changed to match the capability of the device unless there is a real and reasonable intended use that has been identified that the current capability of the design can meet. Other than this scenario, there is typically not a good reason to change an intended use or user needs. Changing user needs or intended uses based solely on the intent of passing validation is not only unethical but it is also bad business. Eventually these types of practices will result in a product that the user finds to be ineffective and will reject it for a competitor's product.

As a result of design feasibility testing, the DIR should be updated and revised to include feasible design requirement values that are based on an iterative design process which allows for potentially multiple design approaches to meet the user needs. As an inherent result of the iterative design process, adequate feedback is integrated back into the requirements as the design changes and will greatly increase the probability of passing verification and validation the first time.

9. Design Input Requirement Revisions

Due to many unknown factors during early stages of device development, preliminary revisions of the DIR may not include details and specific objective requirements. It is not uncommon that "To Be Determined" (TBD) will be a place holder for specific values in design requirements and user needs. After design feasibility is performed and as development progresses the DIR should be updated, revised and approved to replace subjective requirements or "TBD" with objective and specific verifiable design requirements prior to performing verification and validation activities.

#8 Best Practice – Build and test a prototype(s) to adequately evaluate the design and provide feasible requirement values.

After initial approval of the design requirements, it is best practice to build a prototype(s) (or earlier in some cases) to provide feedback to the development team about the feasibility of the design meeting the initial requirements. As a result of design feasibility testing, the DIR should be updated and revised to include feasible design requirement values that are based on an iterative design process which allows for potentially multiple design approaches to meet the user needs. As an inherent result of the iterative design process, adequate feedback is integrated back into the requirements as the design changes and will greatly increase the probability of passing verification and validation the first time.

4.10.1. Quality Systems Manual: Design Input

DESIGN INPUT

Excerpt from the "Quality Systems Manual: A Small Entity Compliance Guide"
(Withdrawn from FDA website 12 December 2013)
(FDA QS Manual, 2013)

Design input means the physical and performance requirements of a device that are used as a basis for device design [820.3(f)].

Section 820.30(c) Design Input, requires that each manufacturer shall establish and maintain procedures to make certain that the design requirements relating to a device are appropriate

---

Medical Device Regulation Consulting and Training – www.Procenius.com

and address the intended use of the device, including the needs of the user and patient. Also, a design requirement in 820.130 requires that each manufacturer shall make certain that device packaging and shipping containers are designed and constructed to protect the device from alteration or damage during the customary conditions of processing, storage, handling, and distribution. The intent of 820.130 is to add the broad conditions that are considered for a package design. Packaging design activities should be done according to design controls. Likewise, the design of the content and physical parameters of labeling are covered by design controls. Manufacturers that are exempt from design controls shall labeling and packaging specifications in the DMR (820.181) and are encouraged to use the QS design controls as guidance.

The input procedures shall address incomplete, ambiguous, or conflicting requirements. The design input requirements shall be documented and shall be reviewed and approved by a designated individual(s). The approval, including the date and signature of the individual(s) approving the requirements, shall be documented.

Under a design control system, manufacturers should identify device requirements during the design input phase or beginning of the design activity. Design input includes determining customer needs, expectations and requirements plus determining regulatory, standards, and other appropriate requirements. These various requirements are documented by the manufacturer in a set of device requirements. A set of design input requirements, when converted to engineering terminology, finalized and accepted as part of the device master record is called a device or product specification.

The design input phase usually is a continuum because intensive and formal input requirements activities usually occur near the beginning of the feasibility phase and continue to the early physical design activities. After the initial design input phase there are also intensive and formal activities to reduce the input requirements to engineering-type input specifications -- usually called a product or device specification.

At the opposite end of the design program, the last event is initial production which may be pilot production or the beginning of routine production. Whether a manufacturer starts with pilot or routine production depends on the nature of the new device and associated production. Pilot devices may be distributed after design validation of initial units is completed if they meet all of the device master record and other GMP requirements. Some manufacturers, however, use the pilot models in training programs for technical writers, production and service personnel, etc. Pilot models are also commonly used in early marketing displays.

After the concept of the new device design is established, the following basic design input questions should have been answered:

1. What is the real need for the new device?

2. Where will the new device be used?
3. Who will use the new device?
4. How will the new device be used?
5. With what devices will the new device be used?
6. How long will the new device be used? and
7. Other questions related to the specific device to be developed.

Designing a device and verifying that it meets customer requirements are expensive and time consuming activities. Therefore, to control these activities and increase the probability of achieving desired safety and performance characteristics, device, software, and process requirements and specifications should be thoroughly reviewed and approved before physical design and development begins. As the design evolves, the hardware, software, packaging, labeling, etc., shall be verified [820.30(f)] and reviewed [820.30(e)] versus their latest specifications to verify that design input requirements have been met.

Input Checklists

Device requirements should identify all of the desired performance, physical, safety and compatibility characteristics of the proposed device and, ultimately, the finished device. Design input also includes requirements for labeling, packaging, manufacturing, installation, maintenance and servicing. The final device specifications should cover ALL of the device characteristics. The device specifications may incorporate other specifications by reference such as reference to the manufacturer's list of specifications for a type of device, to specific paragraphs in standards, or to all of a standard, etc. with respect to a referenced specification. It should be very clear exactly what is going to be met. A failure to properly address characteristics or factors such as immunity from transients in the power source, thermal stress, electromagnetic compatibility (EMC), packaging protection, shipping stability, proper maintenance, etc., can have disastrous consequences.

It is possible to diligently develop device requirements and still forget one or more elements in the final specification. Hopefully, no key factors will be left out. To reduce the probability of a requirement or characteristic being left out, a specification checklist(s) may be used during the design input phase. A checklist should be developed that is broad based but also germane to the product line of the manufacturer. If used, a checklist should be part of a standard operating procedure such as a Design Input Specification Procedure.

The input requirements should cover any standards that the manufacturer plans for the device to meet. In the United States, information about essentially all national and international standards may be obtained from the American National Standards Association (ANSI), 11 West 42nd Street, New York, New York, 10036, phone 212-642-4900. ANSI is a private organization, which monitors most of the standards activity in the United States and foreign activity in which U.S. citizens "officially" participate. Thus, ANSI can supply addresses and other information about all well-established standards writing groups. Also, ANSI has for sale many different types of standards including quality system standards. For example, the International Electrotech Commission has a draft design review standard, "Guide on Formal Design Review" (plus a supplement), which should be helpful to product assurance/design control personnel.

The QS regulation requires that the input procedures shall address incomplete, ambiguous, or conflicting requirements. Thus, every reasonable effort should made to collect all of the requirements from which the designers can generate detailed design specifications that are clear, correct and complete.

At the end of the major aspects of the design input stage, the design input requirements shall be documented and shall be reviewed and approved by a designated individual(s). The approval, including the date and signature of the individual(s) approving the requirements, shall be documented.

A documented device specification or set of specifications derived from the input requirements should exist at the beginning of the physical design project. The device and other related specifications should be kept current as the design of the device, packaging, labeling and manufacturing processes evolve during the development program. As the physical design evolves, the specifications usually become more specific and more detailed.

The device specification will undergo changes and reviews as the device design evolves. However, one goal of market research and initial design reviews is to establish complete device requirements and specifications that will minimize subsequent changes.

Old versions of the input requirements and later the input specifications, are put in the design history file (DHF) or indexed in the computer as part of the DHF to help show that the design plan was followed.

4.11. Case Study – Developing Design Requirements (MRI To Go Inc.)

A product manager is attending a medical device show to get feedback on a newly launched fixed room MRI machine. During the show he has a discussion with a clinician that works 3rd shift (11pm-7am) in the emergency room of a hospital. During their discussion the clinician expresses his frustration that he often has a patient that has experienced major trauma to vital organs and requires immediate assessment of the damage. Unfortunately the hospital is understaffed on 3rd shift and typically does not have resources to perform needed MRI scans in the middle of the night. Typically patients are required to wait until the first shift staff arrives before a scan can be performed.

Qualified personnel to perform the MRI scan are available in the emergency room (ER) but they do not have the time to take the patient up to the 18th floor to perform the scan using the fixed room MRI machine. The clinician is frustrated because this valuable resource that is in high demand is unable to be used because of the unavailability of the system in the ER.

The product manager takes note of the clinician's frustration and sees it as an opportunity to meet an unmet customer need. The product manager takes this problem back to his marketing team for evaluation. After further discussion the team decides that this unmet need is worth pursuing. They get approval to perform initial market research to determine if this issue is a widespread problem.

The initial market research confirms that this problem is very common among most hospitals. Evidence from initial market research justifies a significant increase in budget for a second round of market research in an effort to understand the size of the market opportunity. The second round of market research shows an even greater demand for a product that will solve this problem.

Marketing research efforts have identified the following items as marketing inputs to the new concept design.

- The user wants to be able to use the MRI machine in the ER.
- The user wants to be able to easily roll the machine with no more than two people required to push it from room to room.
- The user interface must be easy to use.
- The user wants to be able to easily distinguish between organs that have a wide range of density (i.e. bone vs. skin).
- The user wants to know when the scan is complete while working on a patient in another room.
- The MRI machine must be small enough to fit in standard hospital rooms with other standard hospital equipment.

After reviewing the marketing inputs the business development and marketing team are ecstatic. The team gets together and comes up with some device concepts of what the new device might look like. They present their concepts to executive management who quickly approves the pursuit of the new concepts.

The product managers then present their ideas to the engineering team to get input on the device concept. This is a critical point in the development of the device that could make or break the success of the product. The engineering team has at least three development strategies that will result in three possible scenarios.

Strategy 1. Initiate the full design and development of the device immediately only using the marketing inputs.

Medical Device Regulation Consulting and Training – www.Procenius.com

Strategy 2. Initiate the process of developing the initial version of user needs and design requirements using the marketing inputs and then pursue the full design and development of the device.

Strategy 3. Initiate the process of developing the initial version of user needs and design requirements using the marketing inputs. Then develop a prototype to determine proof of concept and feasibility. Next, update the design requirements with measureable and objective requirements derived from feasibility testing prior to beginning full design and development of the device.

Results from following Strategy 1

The eager engineering team leader (ETL) realizes that product development is already behind schedule and wants to do everything he can to get back on schedule so he pursues full development using marketing inputs to guide the design effort. The ETL quickly realizes that to initiate the design many assumptions have to be made. For instance, one of the marketing inputs says, *"The user wants to be able to easily roll the machine with no more than two people required to push it from room to room."* In an effort to understand what "easy" means to "two people", the ETL gets his team together to try to come up with reasonable assumptions about the acceptable inertial and frictional resistance that would be acceptable to the user.

The team consists mostly of men that are an average height of 5' 10" and weigh 200+ lbs. Unfortunately the typical profile of users will be women that are 5' 6" and weigh an average of 135 lbs. This is just one of many assumptions the team makes from the marketing inputs that leads to the device being designed on an unsure foundation of requirements. The consequence of this initial and inaccurate assumption causes the overall allowable weight requirement of the system to be too high, it also leads to the incorrect wheels to be specified and the incorrect center of gravity to be calculated. As more time and money are invested into the design, it becomes more difficult to make a course correction to fix the problem. Unfortunately this misstep may not be found until validation is performed by which time it is too late. It is also unfortunate that this situation may also tempt manufacturers to rationalize why there was error in the validation and will either change the requirements or validate under a new method that will most likely allow the device to pass the validation (unethical).

Lessons Learned from Strategy 1

- Never commit full or partial design and development resources to a project based only on marketing inputs if they have not been derived into objective and measurable user needs and design requirements.

- Short cuts taken early in the develop cycle often lead to major issues during later phases of development

- Assumptions are ok during initial concept and prototype testing, but major assumptions should be confirmed prior to dedicating major time and resources to significant design and development activities.

Results from following Strategy 2

Just as in scenario 1, the eager engineering team leader (ETL) realizes that product development is already behind schedule and wants to do everything he can to get back on track. Fortunately, this time he realizes that marketing inputs must be translated into defined user needs before initiating the design. Now his team has a high level, quantitative user need for the marketing input: *"The user wants to be able to easily roll the machine with no more than two people required to push it from room to room."* With the help of marketing research and the product manager, the following user need was derived: "A clinician shall only be required to apply a maximum horizontal force of 40 lbs. to transport the system."

The ETL is ecstatic about having defined requirements for the system. He no longer feels that he has to make unknown assumptions to design the device. He immediately takes this new requirement to his team leads and they quickly discuss how they will distribute the weight budget in the system.

After the design has been finalized, design validation is initiated. As part of the validation, two clinicians attempt to role the system down the hall of a hospital. They immediately discover that the system will not budge! They really lean into it without any success. The engineering team is immediately called up to investigate the problem. They determine the root cause of the problem is due to three errors made during development.

1. Miscommunication between design teams resulted in each module (3 modules in the system) requiring a maximum of 40 lbs. of horizontal force instead of the total required force being split between modules.

2. Inconsistent assumptions about wheel design and its friction coefficient resulted in increased friction forces that added to the actual horizontal force.

3. Inconsistent application of the moment arm where the force would be applied relative to the center of gravity resulted in a higher than expected horizontal resistance force.

    Unfortunately lower level requirements were never identified therefore lower level verification testing was never required.

Medical Device Regulation Consulting and Training – www.Procenius.com

Lessons Learned from Strategy 2

- Always develop system level and low level sub-system design requirements to ensure all design requirements are adequately understood and documented.

- Low level design requirements reduce the risk of making incorrect design assumptions such as the friction coefficient of the wheel design as discussed in this case scenario.

- Assumptions are ok during initial concept and prototype testing, but major assumptions should be confirmed prior to dedicating major time and resources to significant design and development activities.

Results from following Strategy 3

Just as in scenario 1, the eager engineering team leader (ETL) realizes that product development is already behind schedule and wants to do everything he can to get back on schedule but this time he realizes taking short cuts will only cause major problems and delays. The ETL estimates the time required to translate marketing inputs into user needs, system requirements and sub-system level requirements. He realizes that the time required to perform this exercise will not support the project schedule but he also realizes that not doing it will delay the project even more due to unforeseen design problems caused by incomplete design inputs. He convinces management that putting the time required into developing comprehensive requirements will significantly increase the probability of developing a safe and effective product.

Therefore the marketing inputs were translated into user needs and feasibility testing was performed which provided input for development of the detail design requirements. A solid foundation of multiple level design requirements were created and full development was initiated. As development of the device progressed, minimal assumptions were made and major project risks were avoided. As a result of these good design and development practices the product met user needs, was determined to be safe and effective and was therefore a successful product.

Lesson Learned from Strategy 3

- To ensure the device is developed in accordance with user needs and is also developed to be safe and effective, first priority should be given to the development of a solid foundation of user needs and design inputs requirements no matter what management or commercial pressures exist.

4.12. Templates

Visit *Procenius.com* to download design input templates.

Medical Device Regulation Consulting and Training – www.Procenius.com

5.0 Design Output

5.1. <u>Overview</u>

Design outputs are the results from the design process. Just as the design inputs are used to guide the device design, the outputs fill in the details of the design and allow the device to be manufactured, inspected, verified and validated. Examples of design outputs include drawings, schematics, software code and 3D models.

Just as in the design inputs chapter, the analogy of designing and building a house will be used to further illustrate the concept of design outputs. In this example, an architect will draft house plans which will specify detail dimensions, building materials, HVAC specifications and other general design details. These drawings may be reviewed and approved by a senior architect, civil engineer, HVAC specialist, the city building inspector and the future home owner. After approval, these plans will be used by the general contractor to build the home to meet all stakeholder requirements.

The *take away* from this example is that there are many aspects of the detailed design that must be documented and adequately approved by appropriate stakeholders to ensure the design is safe, effective, meets user requirements and can be correctly built.

The FDA preamble states the following concerning design outputs:

Quality Systems Regulation Preamble:

Comment 76

"Design output are the design specifications which should meet design input requirements, as confirmed during design verification and validation and ensured during design review. The output includes the device, its labeling and packaging, associated specifications and drawings, and production and quality assurance specifications and procedures. These documents are the basis for the DMR. The total finished design output consists of the device, its labeling and packaging, and the DMR." (FDA Preamble, 2015)

Medical Device Regulation Consulting and Training – www.Procenius.com

5.2. Design Output Quick Reference Summary

TABLE 10

Purpose	Design outputs allow adequate assessment of conformance to design input requirements and identify the characteristics of the design that are crucial to the safe and proper functioning of the device.
Definition	Design output means the results of a design effort at each design phase and at the end of the total design effort. The finished design output is the basis for the device master record. The total finished design output consists of the device, its packaging and labeling, and the device master record. (FDA D.C. Guidance, 2015)
Regulation	21 CFR 820.30 (d): Each manufacturer shall establish and maintain procedures for defining and documenting design output in terms that allow an adequate evaluation of conformance to design input requirements. Design output procedures shall contain or make reference to acceptance criteria and shall ensure that those design outputs that are essential for the proper functioning of the device are identified. Design output shall be documented, reviewed, and approved before release. The approval, including the date and signature of the individual(s) approving the output, shall be documented. (FDA QS Regulation, 2015)
Standard(s)	ISO 13485 (7.3.3) (ISO 13485, 2007)

Guidance	21 CFR 820.30 (d) (FDA)	FDA Design Control Guidance for Medical Device Manufacturers (FDA D.C. Guidance, 2015)

	ISO 13485 (7.3.3)	Medical Devices – Quality Management Systems – Guidance on the Application of ISO 13485:2003 (ISO 14969, 2004)
Timing of Design Outputs Relative to the Research and Development Cycle	FIGURE 13 Design Outputs Research Development The two humps in Figure 13 depict the relationship and the relative amount of research and development activities performed during the design and development cycle. The shaded area is the typical time when outputs are generated, reviewed, approved and implemented in the life cycle.	
Types of Design Outputs	<ul><li>Risk Assessment (Output of Risk Analysis)</li><li>Design Documentation (or electronic files, software)</li><li>Drawings (components, assemblies, raw material, etc.)</li><li>Verification Reports (Output of Verification Activities)</li><li>Validation Master Report</li><li>Manufacturing Process Documentation</li><li>Acceptance criteria and quality assurance procedures</li><li>Manufacturing Process Validation Report(s)</li><li>Installation and Servicing Instructions</li><li>Labeling</li><li>Device Master Record (Compilation of Design Outputs)</li></ul>	

Effective Design Output Characteristics	• Acceptance criteria is clearly defined • Design outputs essential for the proper functioning of the device are identified
Review	The type and method of review is dependent upon on the complexity of the device and size of the organization. In typical organizations an effective review includes an individual review and a formal comprehensive design review. Because design outputs can range from very simple component drawings to highly complex software system code, the type and level of required reviews will vary greatly. For simple components, the review may only require the designer, an independent technical expert and a quality assurance representative. There may be numerous components that fall into this category and it is reasonable for reviews to be performed at an individual level. These lower component outputs may feed into a larger sub-system that will be reviewed during a formal comprehensive design review. This is typically a good forum for reviewers to raise concerns about the outputs that they discovered during their independent review. Reviewers attending formal design reviews should include qualified individuals in all functional areas that may have critical feedback about the outputs being reviewed. **Typical Reviewers:** *Individual only* **Individual & formal comprehensive design review* **Components[†]** Small Cross Functional Team Quality Assurance*[†] Designer (person who created the output)*[†] Independent Technical Expert*[†]

	System or Sub-System Level Outputs
	
	    <u>Large Cross Functional Team</u>
	
	    Quality Assurance**
	
	    Regulatory Affairs**
	
	    Technical Expert (i.e. R&D / Engineering)**
	
	    Project Management**
	
	    Marketing**
	
	    Clinical Affairs**
	
	    Other Stake Holders**
	
	[†] *According to design control guidance* (FDA D.C. Guidance, 2015), *design reviews;* "Each design document which constitutes the formal output, or deliverable, of a design task is normally subject to evaluation activities, sometimes referred to as informal peer review, supervisory review, or technical assessment. These activities, while they may be called reviews, are often better described as verification activities, because they are not intended to be comprehensive, definitive, and multidisciplinary in their scope."
	
	Therefore review of outputs that fall under this scope <u>are not required</u> to be reviewed according to formal design review requirements 21CFR 820.30 (E) but may be informally and individually reviewed.

Approval	Just as reviewers may vary greatly depending on the complexity of the design output, so too will the required approvals. The same rationale for choosing reviewers based on design output complexity as previously mentioned should be applied when identifying approval roles. Approvals should be documented manually with signature and date (hand written or electronically to be in compliance with 21 CFR part 11).

Medical Device Regulation Consulting and Training – www.Procenius.com

	Typical Approvers
	
	    <u>Components</u>
	
	    Quality Assurance*
	
	    Designer (person who created the output)*
	
	    Independent Technical Expert*
	
	    <u>System or Sub-System Outputs</u>
	
	    Quality Assurance**
	
	    Regulatory Affairs**
	
	    Technical Expert (i.e. R&D / Engineering)**
	
	    Project Management**
	
	    Marketing**
	
	    Clinical Affairs**
	
	    Other Stake Holders**

Revisions	Design outputs may be revised as necessary throughout the design process and will typically follow the same review and approval process which was required for the initial version. Revision to design outputs require compliance to design change regulation *21CFR 820.30 (I)*.
Best Practice	• Develop an Essential Design Output List • Hold design reviews for multiple discipline design components or systems
Templates	Visit ***Procenius.com*** to download design output templates.

Medical Device Regulation Consulting and Training – www.Procenius.com

5.3. Regulation (21 CFR 820.30 (d)) - Design Output

Each manufacturer shall establish and maintain procedures for defining and documenting design output in terms that allow an adequate evaluation of conformance to design input requirements.

Design output procedures shall contain or make reference to acceptance criteria and shall ensure that those design outputs that are essential for the proper functioning of the device are identified.

Design output shall be documented, reviewed, and approved before release.

The approval, including the date and signature of the individual(s) approving the output, shall be documented. (FDA QS Regulation, 2015)

5.4. Definition 21 CFR 820.3(g) – Design Output

Design output means the results of a design effort at each design phase and at the end of the total design effort. The finished design output is the basis for the device master record. The total finished design output consists of the device, its packaging and labeling, and the device master record. (FDA QSR , 2014)

5.5. Design Control Guidance Document (21 CFR 820.30 (d))

The quality system requirements for design output can be separated into two elements: Design output should be expressed in terms that allow adequate assessment of conformance to design input requirements and should identify the characteristics of the design that are crucial to the safety and proper functioning of the device. This raises two fundamental issues for developers:

What constitutes design output?

Are the form and content of the design output suitable?

The first issue is important because the typical development project produces voluminous records, some of which may not be categorized as design output. On the other hand, design output must be reasonably comprehensive to be effective. As a general rule, an item is design output if it is a work product, or deliverable item, of a design task listed in the design and development plan, and the item defines, describes, or elaborates an element of the design implementation. Examples include block diagrams, flow charts, software, high-level code, and system or subsystem design specifications. The design output in one stage is often part of the design input in subsequent stages.

Design output includes production specifications as well as descriptive materials which define and characterize the design.

Medical Device Regulation Consulting and Training – www.Procenius.com

5.5.1. Production Specifications

Production specifications include drawings and documents used to procure components, fabricate, test, inspect, install, maintain, and service the device, such as the following:

- assembly drawings

- component and material specifications

- production and process specifications

- software machine code (e.g., diskette or master EPROM)

- work instructions

- quality assurance specifications and procedures

- installation and servicing procedures

- packaging and labeling specifications, including methods and processes used

In addition, as discussed in Section H (Design Transfer), production specifications may take on other forms. For example, some manufacturers produce assembly instructions on videotapes rather than written instructions. Similarly, a program diskette, used by a computer-aided milling machine to fabricate a part, would be considered a production specification. The videotape and the software on the program diskette are part of the device master record.

5.5.2. Other Descriptive Material

Other design output items might be produced which are necessary to establish conformance to design input requirements, but are not used in its production. For example, for each part which is fabricated by computer-aided machine, there should be an assembly drawing which specifies the dimensions and characteristics of the part. It is a part of the design output because it establishes the basis for the machine tool program used to fabricate the part. Other examples of design output include the following:

- the results of risk analysis

- software source code

- results of verification activities

- biocompatibility test results

- bioburden test results

5.5.3. Form and Content

Manufacturers must take steps to assure that the design output characterizes all important aspects of the design and is expressed in terms which allow adequate verification and validation. Two basic mechanisms are available to manufacturers to accomplish these objectives.

First, the manufacturer proactively can specify the form and content of design output at the planning stage. For some types of design output, form and content may be codified in a consensus standard which can be referenced. In other cases, a manufacturer could specify the desired characteristics, or even simply specify that the form and content of an existing document be followed.

Second, form and content can be reviewed retroactively as a part of the design verification process. For example, the verification of design output could include assessing whether specified documentation standards have been adhered to.

As these examples illustrate, conformance with the quality system requirements concerning design output generally requires no "extra" effort on the part of the manufacturer, but simply the application of some common sense procedures during the planning, execution, and review of design tasks. (FDA D.C. Guidance, 2015)

5.6. Timing of Design Output Activities and Deliverables

The FDA does not specify at what point in the design and development process when outputs should be defined and approved but the following graphical model gives some clarity as to when design outputs typically begin relative to research and development activities.

The two humps in the Figure 14 depict the relationship and the relative amount of research and development activities performed during the design and development cycle. The shaded area is the typical time when outputs are generated, reviewed, approved and implemented in the life cycle.

FIGURE 14

Medical Device Regulation Consulting and Training – www.Procenius.com

5.7. Interpretation & Application (21 CFR 820.30 (d))

In the most basic terms, design outputs are the result of the design effort. The design control guidance gives the following definition,

> *"As a general rule, an item is design output if it is a work product, or deliverable item, of a design task listed in the design and development plan, and the item defines, describes, or elaborates an element of the design implementation."* (FDA D.C. Guidance, 2015)

Figure 15 shows a somewhat simple process flow of how design outputs are a result of design inputs and the design process.

FIGURE 15

To more fully understand how design outputs are a result of the design process, the following examples are provided in Table 11.

5.7.1. Examples of How Design Outputs are the Result of the Design Process

TABLE 11

Design Inputs (requirements)	Design Process	Design Output
The MRI machine's electrical system shall operate at 120V at less than 16 amps	Components such as motors, actuators and LEDs rated for 120V that will meet functional requirements will be specified but will not exceed a total of 16 amps during operation. The design process will include design iterations,	Once a viable design has been identified, the components and configuration of the design will be documented. A bill of materials (list of all components) and an electrical schematic (defines

	informal bench testing, research and prototyping.	the configuration and layout of the components and wiring) are the design outputs.
The overall size of the MRI machine shall be less than 9.5'(long) X 4' 8" (wide) X 6' 6" (high)	A 3D design envelope that will be no greater than 9.5'(long) X 4' 8" (wide) X 6' 6"(high) will be defined in a CAD system. The sub-systems and components will be designed and specified to operate within the required maximum design envelope.	The design envelope will be defined in a 3D CAD system and will be electronically stored as a 3D model. The detail of the design will be stored as a 2D drawing and bill of materials. The CAD files, drawings and bill of materials are the design outputs.
The dialysis catheter shall have a flow rate of 400 ml per minute at 10psi.	An iterative flow analysis to determine the minimum internal cross sectional area required to meet the flow requirement will be performed. Other requirements will also have to be considered that will drive material type, the external diameter and profile of the catheter extrusion.	The final cross sectional geometry and material will be defined in a 3D CAD system and will be electronically stored as a 3D model. The detail of the design will be stored as a 2D drawing and bill of materials. The CAD files, drawings and bill of materials are the design outputs.
The x-ray machine's software system shall display options to operate fluoroscopy, still image and deep tissue images from the main interface screen.	The software developers will develop the code for the main interface page of the software such that all required image types are available from the main page.	The software code will define the image display information that will meet the image requirement. The software code is the output of the software design effort. Any documentation that supports the software code will also be part of the design output.

Medical Device Regulation Consulting and Training – www.Procenius.com

5.7.2. Characteristics of an Effective and Compliant Design Output Procedure

When the FDA states **"Each manufacturer shall establish and maintain procedures for defining and documenting design output..."** (FDA QS Regulation, 2015) they are saying...

To "*establish*" means to define, document (in writing or electronically), and implement. (FDA QSR , 2014)

They are also saying that the manufacturer that is designing the product must have a documented procedure(s) that defines the "what, who, how, why and when" of how design outputs are created (documented) and applied. The FDA wants to ensure that a standard design output procedure has been created, vetted, reviewed and approved. The procedure must be "maintained" (in other words revised and updated) as required to be current with the intended and approved design output activities. Typically this procedure is assigned to the department that is responsible for product development such as (Development Teams or Engineering).

The regulation also states that the procedure shall define and document "...**design output in terms that allow an adequate evaluation of conformance to design input requirements...**". (FDA QS Regulation, 2015)

"Adequate evaluation of conformance to design inputs" means that the design outputs are effectively defined such that there is no ambiguity or difficulty using them to verify the device design to the design input requirements.

The Quality Systems Regulation Preamble states:

Comment 77

"*...the design output must be documented and expressed in terms that can be verified against the design input requirements.*" (FDA Preamble, 2015)

The Quality Systems Regulation Preamble states:

Comment 82

"*Design output, requires that the output be documented in a fashion that will allow for verification and validation.*" (FDA Preamble, 2015)

The MRI machine's overall size requirement in Table 11 can be used as an example of adequately defined design outputs. In this case the design output would be a mechanical drawing that would define the overall dimensions of the design including the tolerance range. Just as the design input requirements are objective and measureable, so should the design outputs. In this case the design output defines the overall dimensions of the machine as 9' X 2' X 6' (+/- 2 in.). A simple evaluation of this design output to the design input requirement (9.5' X 4' 8" X 6' 6") clearly shows that the design will meet this requirement.

Medical Device Regulation Consulting and Training – www.Procenius.com

In an alternative scenario where the drawing may not have the overall dimensions of the MRI machine fully defined or without tolerances, it would be significantly more difficult to determine if the device design will actually meet the design input requirement. This scenario may become a challenge during verification and validation because the design being verified (or validated) is not fully defined. In this case if the dimensions are not defined then how can the design be verified to the design input requirements?

The next line of the regulations states, "**Design output procedures shall contain or make reference to acceptance criteria...**". (FDA QS Regulation, 2015) This means that design output procedures should require design outputs to have acceptance criteria. It is rare that the design output procedure would contain specific acceptance criteria for specific design outputs (i.e. drawings) but it is typical that a design output procedure would specify the type of acceptance criteria that is permitted and the business requirements for how that acceptance criteria is documented.

In the previous example of the MRI machine the acceptance criteria would be the overall size of the machine (as designed) which would also include the dimension tolerances. Having clearly defined, quantifiable and objective acceptance criteria will effectively allow device manufacturers the ability to accept or reject the device during "in process" inspections or during "receiving inspections" based upon the specified acceptance criteria.

Ambiguous acceptance criteria leads to "ambiguous" product quality. If the definition of quality is: "the extent to which a product conforms to its acceptance criteria", then it is reasonable to assume that clear, measureable and objective acceptance criteria must be defined to make that assessment.

The next line of the regulations states, "... **make reference to acceptance criteria and shall ensure that those design outputs that are essential for the proper functioning of the device are identified**". (FDA QS Regulation, 2015)

In this statement the FDA wants to ensure that the design is thoroughly reviewed and analyzed for those design outputs that define essential specifications that must be met for the device to function properly. This type of review and analysis most naturally occurs during the risk analysis and design input development activities. The risk analysis will determine what components or functions of the device are essential for ensuring the device is safe and effective. In addition, design outputs which are directly driven by design input requirements will be key indicators that the outputs are essential for the proper functioning of the device.

To ensure that essential design outputs are appropriately identified, it is typically best practice[BP1] to develop an "Essential Design Output List" (EDOL). This list will typically include the outputs from the trace matrix (see verification chapter) that are being verified, outputs that are associated with high risk functions and outputs that are essential for the device to function effectively. The EDOL will become invaluable during an FDA inspection when agency inspectors ask for developers to produce the device's essential design outputs. It is also a very effective tool when

Medical Device Regulation Consulting and Training – www.Procenius.com

developing the verification and validation strategy. The EDOL and risk assessment should be used as the basis for justifying the verification and validation strategy that will be documented in the validation master plan.

A typical EDOL will include, as a minimum, the following sections:

- Purpose
- Scope
- Table of Outputs with description and unique identifier / document number
- Rationale for each output as to why it is essential (ideal but optional if it is impractical for large number of outputs)
- Review and approval by applicable team members (i.e. Quality Assurance, R&D etc.)

#1 Best Practice – Develop an *Essential Design Output List* (EDOL)

It is best practice to develop an "Essential Design Output List". This list will typically include the outputs from the trace matrix that are being verified and outputs that are associated with high risk functions of the device that are essential to its proper functioning.

5.7.3. Trace Matrix

As mentioned in the design output best practice, a design trace matrix is a verification tool to link the design input requirements to the output being verified with the report documenting the results of the verification or validation. This topic is discussed in greater detail in the design verification chapter.

TABLE 12

ID	Design Input Requirement	Output (being verified)	Results (verification/validation)
1.0	The overall size of the MRI machine shall be less than 9.5' (long) X 4' 8" (wide) X 6' 6" (high)	System Level Drawing (Drawing Number)	Results from verification (Report Number)

Medical Device Regulation Consulting and Training – www.Procenius.com

2.0	The MRI machine's electrical system shall operate at 120V at less than 16 amps	System Level Electrical Schematic (Drawing Number)	Results from verification (Report Number)

The outputs identified in the trace matrix are by no means the only essential design outputs but they are arguably some of the most essential. This approach is merely a rule of thumb that will easily identify most, if not all, of the essential design outputs. As previously mentioned, the remaining essential design outputs will most likely be identified through the risk analysis process.

5.7.4. What Type of Design Outputs Should be Reviewed in a Design Review?

The next line in the regulation states, "**Design output shall be documented, reviewed, and approved before release.**" (FDA QS Regulation, 2015) This line in the regulation requires that design outputs are documented. Traditionally this means the outputs are captured on paper or electronically in a document control system.

The regulation also states that outputs shall be"...**reviewed...**". (FDA QS Regulation, 2015) The term "review" is open to interpretation and does not necessarily refer to a formal design review in this context. According to the FDA, a "formal design review" as specified in 21 CFR 820.30 (e), is "comprehensive, definitive and multidisciplinary in scope" (FDA D.C. Guidance, 2015). The "review" requirement in this part of the regulation does not refer to a formal design review but is intended to ensure that the output is appropriately "evaluated" such that the design outputs will meet design requirements and design intent. The level of reviews for outputs should be specified by the device manufacturer in the design output procedure which should be in proportion to the complexity and scope of the content being reviewed. Reviews of simple device components may only be "informal peer reviews, supervisory reviews or technical assessments" as defined by the FDA [or evaluation activities]. (FDA D.C. Guidance, 2015)

In practice, all design outputs should be reviewed [evaluated] prior to being approved but not all levels of design outputs need to be interrogated during a formal design review. For inexperienced device manufacturers it can be challenging when trying to determine the appropriate level (i.e. – component, sub-system, system, etc) at which design outputs should be formally reviewed. As a general rule, it is best practice[BP2] to hold a formal design review for component, sub-system, system level or device level designs if the design output directly impacts multiple cross functional team member's interests (i.e. engineering, marketing, quality, regulatory, clinical affairs, R&D). The key term the FDA uses is "multidisciplinary in scope" which indicates that those design outputs that impact multiple disciplines should be formally reviewed. Complex designs (i.e. MRI, x-ray, CT machines) typically require design reviews which usually cover sub-systems all the way up to device level designs. Formal review of component level design outputs is often not practical for complex devices and are only typically reviewed during design reviews for simple devices with few components (i.e. catheters, syringes, etc). In some cases even lower level or simple components in complex systems may be reviewed in a formal design review if the component impacts a cross functional team. As an example, an EMI (electrical magnetic interference) shied is typically a simple sheet metal component, but its design characteristics can impact the mechanical, electrical and software performance of the device if not properly designed. For this reason a formal design review of this component may be required to ensure representatives from each functional area (mechanical, electrical and software) are represented in the review.

#2 Best Practice – Hold design reviews for multiple discipline design components or systems

It is best practice to hold a formal design review for component, sub-system, system level or device level designs if the design output directly impacts multiple cross functional team member's interests (i.e. engineering, marketing, quality, regulatory, clinical affairs, R&D).

A draft version of design outputs are typically reviewed individually and in design reviews. Prior to approval of the outputs, the approvers should be given sufficient time to thoroughly understand the details of the design outputs. After reviewers have had the opportunity to individually review the outputs, it is best practice to allow reviewers the opportunity to address (or challenge) any concerns or issues that they may have concerning design outputs during a formal design review. As a result of the review, decisions will be made and actions will be assigned that may require updates to the outputs.

5.7.5. What Does Approval and Release of Design Outputs Mean?

…[design output shall be] …approved before release. ….The approval, including the date and signature of the individual(s) approving the output, shall be documented. (FDA QS Regulation, 2015)

Approvals should be documented manually with signature/date or electronically to be in compliance with 21 CFR part 11.

…**before release…;** "release" means the output is officially approved and is allowed to be used as an official document to build, manufacture or inspect the device for development or for production activities. A released document should be version controlled and changes to released documents should be controlled through a change control process.

The Quality Systems Regulation Preamble states:

Comment 77

"Design output can be ``released" or transferred to the next design phase at various stages in the design process, as defined in the design and development plan. The design output is reviewed and approved before release or transfer to the next design phase or production. The design output requirements are intended to apply to all such stages of the design process." (FDA Preamble, 2015)

In other words, design outputs should be reviewed (or evaluated), approved and version controlled for each stage of development (i.e. - concept, feasibility, verification and validation phases).

5.8. Types of Design Outputs

Figure 16 gives a graphical representation of the design and development of a medical device from initial planning through verification and design transfer. Typical design outputs used during development are indicated by letters **A-G** in Figure 16.

A – Risk Assessment (Output of Risk Analysis) – Risk analysis activities are an iterative process between the design requirements and the design process. As a result from these activities, a risk assessment is created, reviewed and approved.

B – Design Documentation (or electronic files, software) – Design documentation is a result of the developers creating a design that meets design input requirements, otherwise known as the "design process". Design documentation typically includes mechanical drawings, electrical schematics, flowcharts etc. Traditionally engineering drawings / schematics were in a 2D paper format. In recent decades drawings have been stored as electronic CAD files that would also fall under this category.

C – Verification Reports (Output of Verification Activities) – These reports include the results (data, pass/fail, etc.) and methods used to perform each individual verification activity. Validation reports (not shown in this figure) are also outputs.

D – Validation Master Report – This is typically a report that is a summary of the results from all verification activities that is derived from the verification and validation reports. In other words it is the report which compliments the validation master plan (VMP).

E – Manufacturing Process Requirements – This document is somewhat unique because it is considered an output of the design process but an input to the manufacturing development process. However, using the FDA's definition of design output being a "work product or deliverable", this document will be considered a design output.

Medical Device Regulation Consulting and Training – www.Procenius.com

F – Manufacturing Process Documentation – These are various types of procedures that define the manufacturing process and records of activities including but not limited to: work instructions, inspection methods, equipment/process procedures & training records.

G –Manufacturing Process Validation Report(s) – These reports include the results (data, pass/fail etc.) and methods used to perform process validation. These reports provide evidence that the process successfully passed the process validation acceptance criteria (or failed as the case may be).

H –Purchasing (not included in Figure 16) – Documents which specify details about purchase components, raw materials, assemblies, software, and labeling are design outputs. Outputs used for purchasing may also be used to specify component performance specifications.

I –Installation and Servicing (not included in Figure 16) – Other types of outputs include documentation that is used by the user or service field representatives to install and or service the device.

J –Labeling (not included in Figure 16) – Labeling that is used to communicate with the user critical device information such as intended use, warnings, instructions for use, performance specifications and storage requirements are also design outputs.

FIGURE 16

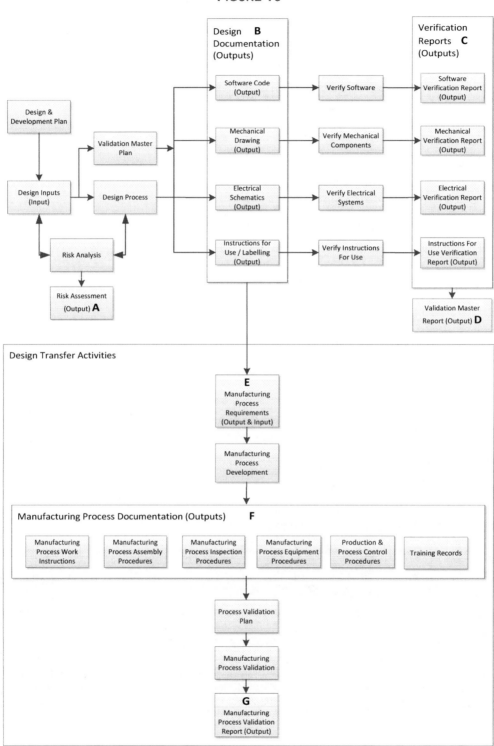

5.9. The Device Master Record (The Recipe) vs. Outputs

Even though the "device master record" (DMR) is formally addressed in 21 CFR 820.181, (not in the design control regulation 21 CFR 820.30) to fully understand design outputs it is essential to understand the concept of the device master record.

The Quality Systems Regulation Preamble states:

Comment 76

..."The output includes the device, its labeling and packaging, associated specifications and drawings, and production and quality assurance specifications and procedures. These documents are the basis for the device master record (DMR). The total finished design output consists of the device, its labeling and packaging, and the DMR." (FDA Preamble, 2015)

Comment 90...

..."The DMR contains the documentation necessary to produce a device. The final design output from the design phase, which is maintained or referenced in the DHF, will form the basis or starting point for the DMR. Thus, those outputs must be referred to or placed in the DMR. The total finished device design output includes device specifications and drawings, as well as all instructions and procedures for production, installation, maintenance, and servicing." (FDA Preamble, 2015)

The easiest way to understand the DMR is to think of it as a "recipe" for the device. As an analogy, a recipe for a birthday cake typically describes the required ingredients and how it should be cooked. The DMR is very much the same, it will typically specify the raw materials, component / assembly drawings, labeling, manufacturing instructions, process instructions, inspection instructions, etc. In simple terms, the DMR can be thought of as the documents (or electronic files) that define what materials, components, software, and labelling that are needed to make the device and the instructions for how the device is manufactured, processed, packaged and inspected. The DMR should not include development documents such as the DDP, DIR, risk assessments, verification or validation protocols/reports, memos, meeting minutes, etc.

A final DMR should be approved as part of a design transfer deliverable when the design is approved for commercialization and production. When released to production, the DMR becomes a living "recipe" that will drive the development and sustaining of the manufacturing process. Over time the design may change which will drive a change to the DMR. The DMR should be revised as design changes occur.

Figure 17 gives a graphical representation of design outputs as they relate to the design and development process and how a subset of the outputs make up the DMR as indicated.

FIGURE 17

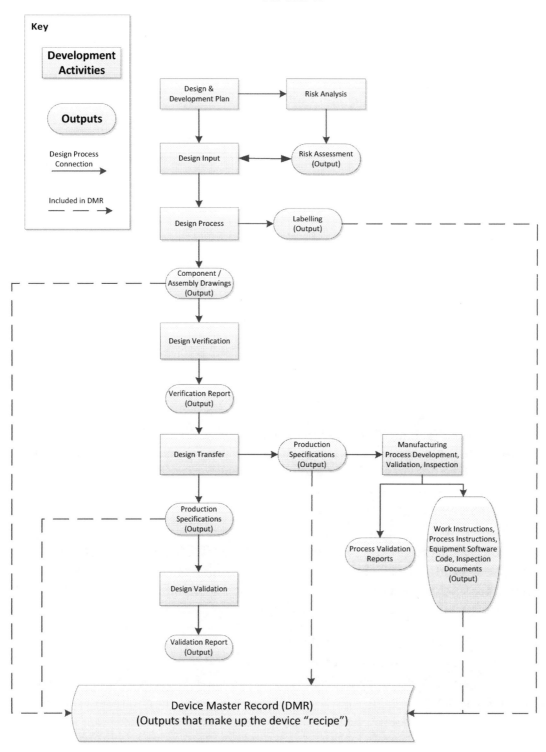

Medical Device Regulation Consulting and Training – www.Procenius.com

5.10. Quality Systems Manual: Design Output

DESIGN OUTPUTS

Excerpt from the "Quality Systems Manual: A Small Entity Compliance Guide"
(Withdrawn from FDA website 12 December 2013)
(FDA QS Manual, 2013)

Design output per 820.3(g) means the results of a design effort at each design phase and at the end of the total design effort. The finished design output is the basis for the device master record. The total finished design output consists of the device, its packaging and labeling, and the device master record. Device master record (DMR) means a compilation of records containing the procedures and specifications for a finished device.

The design output at each phase are documents and physical design elements that are either complete or are used to move the design effort into the next phase. For example, the first design output will usually be the design requirements document. From the requirements and their engineering knowledge, the designers will derive the preliminary design specifications. Then the physical design begins. For example, the designers may begin the selection of known routine components that are part of the design and begin documenting their purchasing and acceptance requirements documented to meet 820.50 Purchasing Controls, (b) Purchasing Data which requires that each manufacturer shall establish and maintain data that clearly describe or reference the specified requirements, including quality requirements, for purchased or otherwise received product and services.

Other components will be selected as the design evolves. The design output for some special or new components, or components in unusual applications, will include verification protocols, purchasing and acceptance requirements.

Many of the design output documents are documents that directly form part of the DMR. The remaining DMR documents are created by quality assurance, production engineering, process engineering, technical writing, installation and servicing, etc., using design output data and information. For example, the finished device final-test methods and some installation and/or servicing test methods and data forms may be derived from the design verification protocol(s). When all of these design and documentation activities are completed, the DMR is complete. When the DMR is complete and initial production units, including packaging, meets all specifications, the total finished design output exists.

To generate the design output per the QS regulation in 820.30(d), three activities are required. Each of these is listed and discussed below.

---

1. Each manufacturer shall establish and maintain procedures for defining and documenting design output in terms that allow an adequate evaluation of conformance to design input requirements.

2. Design output procedures shall contain or make reference to acceptance criteria and ensure that those design outputs that are essential for the proper functioning of the device are identified.

3. Design output shall be documented, reviewed, and approved before release. The approval, including the date and signature of the individual(s) approving the output, shall be documented.

Documenting Design Output (1)

Documenting design output in terms that allow an adequate evaluation of conformance to design input requirements is a significant requirement and design activity. A common technique for achieving this conformance is listed below.

• Convert the general input requirements to specific design engineering specifications and give each item a line/paragraph number.

• Develop the design to meet all of the parameters and characteristics in the design engineering specification.

• Generate a verification requirement document(s) and test method(s) for the design and give each requirement/parameter/characteristic the same line/paragraph number that it has in the design engineering specification.

• Generate a verification data form that lists each requirement/parameter/characteristic and give each requirement/parameter/characteristic the same line/paragraph number that it has in the design engineering specification.

Each of these documents has a different drawing number but the line/paragraph numbers are the same. The first of these documents may be used as the beginning format for the next one. Therefore, it is almost impossible to leave out an element. Thereafter, when the verification is performed and documented, conformance or lack of conformance from input to output is known.

Acceptance Criteria (2)

The verification documents and data contain more information than is typically needed for production evaluation and acceptance of components, in-process items and finished devices.

Medical Device Regulation Consulting and Training – www.Procenius.com

Therefore, it is easy to copy and modify verification documents to meet the quality system requirement that: design output procedures shall contain or make reference to acceptance criteria and ensure that those design outputs that are essential for the proper functioning of the device are identified. In fact, this technique of deriving test procedures from the verification protocols also yields the test method(s) and data form(s) needed to meet the DMR requirements for QA procedures and acceptance criteria in 820.181(c).

Design Output Approval (3)

The third and final output requirement is that: design output shall be documented, reviewed, and approved before release. The approval, including the date and signature of the individual(s) approving the output, shall be documented. This means that:

• Manufacturers may choose to have a group review certain documents and have individuals review other documents.

• Output documents that are directly part of the DMR are reviewed, dated and signed by the author which is current practice; and reviewed, dated and approved by individual(s) designated by the manufacturer. As appropriate, these reviews should cover technical issues as well as adequacy for use in production, purchasing, servicing, etc. DMR documents that are generated and approved under 820.30 automatically meet the approval requirements of 820.40, Document Controls and do not have to be re-approved under 820.40.

• Design output reports, data and any other document that will be used to create documents in the DMR are reviewed, dated and signed by the author which is current practice; and reviewed, dated and approved by individual(s) designated by the manufacturer.

Design output also includes the physical design which, of course, is not intended to be signed, and dated. The approval for the physical design is the validation that is done on initial production units.

5.11. Templates

Visit **Procenius.com** to download design output templates.

Medical Device Regulation Consulting and Training – www.Procenius.com

6.0 Design Reviews

6.1. Overview

The purpose of conducting design reviews during the design phase is to ensure the design satisfies the design input requirements for the intended use of the device and the needs of the user. Design reviews can be powerful design activities which have the potential to significantly improve the safety, effectiveness and eventual success of the device. Correctly executed design reviews go above and beyond a simple presentation of the design. Effective design reviews will typically involve a cross functional team which challenges the design and seeks to optimize the design by attempting to meet all stakeholder requirements. The power of design reviews comes from open debates (constructive discussions) between cross functional stakeholders in an effort to have their needs met. During these discussions (or debates) suggestions are made, problems are found and actions are assigned.

6.2. Quick Reference Summary

TABLE 13

Purpose	• To provide a systematic assessment of design results, including the device design and the associated designs for production and support processes; • To provide feedback to designers on existing or emerging problems; • To assess project progress • To provide confirmation that the project is ready to move on to the next stage of development. (FDA D.C. Guidance, 2015)

Medical Device Regulation Consulting and Training – www.Procenius.com

Definition	A design review is a documented, comprehensive, systematic examination of a design to evaluate the adequacy of the design requirements, to evaluate the capability of the design to meet these requirements and to identify problems. (FDA D.C. Guidance, 2015)
Regulation	21 CFR 820.30 (e): Each manufacturer shall establish and maintain procedures to ensure that formal documented reviews of the design results are planned and conducted at appropriate stages of the device's design development. The procedures shall ensure that participants at each design review include representatives of all functions concerned with the design stage being reviewed and an individual(s) who does not have direct responsibility for the design stage being reviewed, as well as any specialists needed. The results of a design review, including identification of the design, the date, and the individual(s) performing the review, shall be documented in the design history file (the DHF). (FDA QS Regulation, 2015)
Standard(s)	ISO 13485 (7.3.4) (ISO 13485, 2007)

Guidance	21 CFR 820.30 (e) (FDA)	FDA Design Control Guidance for Medical Device Manufacturers (FDA D.C. Guidance, 2015)
	ISO 13485 (7.3.4)	Medical Devices – Quality Management Systems – Guidance on the Application of ISO 13485:2003 (ISO 14969, 2004)

Timing of Design Reviews Relative to the Research and Development Cycle	FIGURE 18 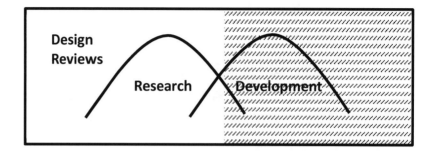 The two humps in Figure 18 depict the relationship and the relative amount of research and development activities performed during the design and development cycle. The shaded area is the typical time when design reviews are executed.
Deliverable	**Design Review Meeting Minutes** The FDA does not specify how reviews should be documented but best practice is to use meeting minutes to record actions and to summarize the discussion. Meeting minutes should include the following: • Name of the product being reviewed ("identification of the design") • Date of review ("the date") • Name of the specific output (system, sub-system, or component) being reviewed as applicable ("identification of the design") • Design review attendees (specify who is required and who is optional with title and role) ("individuals performing the review") • Summary and key points of the discussion • Critical decisions made • Action items including what, by when, and by who • The approved meeting minutes with closed actions should be included or referenced in the Design History File

Medical Device Regulation Consulting and Training – www.Procenius.com

Types of Design Reviews	The following types of reviews are common but the possibilities are by no means limited to this list. The type and scope of reviews should be held to meet the needs of the medical device manufacturer. **Phase Reviews** Phase reviews are used to review results from phase activities and to close out major design phases. These reviews act as the *gate* that must be approved prior to moving to the next design phase. **Concept Phase Reviews** Concept reviews are held at the end of the concept phase to review the results of concept testing and to determine if development activities should continue in the next phase of development (feasibility). **Feasibility Phase Reviews** Feasibility reviews are held at the end of the feasibility phase to review the results of feasibility testing and to determine if development activities should continue in the next phase of development (verification). **Verification Phase Reviews** Verification reviews are held at the end of the verification phase to review the results of verification testing and to determine if development activities should continue in the next phase of development (validation).

Types of Design Reviews	**Validation Phase Reviews** Validation reviews are held at the end of the validation phase to review the results of validation testing and to determine if development activities should continue in the next phase of development (launch). **Launch Phase Reviews** Launch reviews are held at the end of the launch phase to ensure all commercial/business requirements have been met and to determine if the device is ready for commercialization. **Technical Design Reviews** Technical design reviews are used to assess the technical aspects of the device. **System Level Reviews** System reviews are used to review the technical aspects of complex devices. These type of reviews assess the high level interaction and function between multidisciplinary technical aspects of the device such as software, mechanical and electrical. **Sub System Reviews** Sub-System reviews are lower level reviews and are typically very technical. These will review the function of the design based on lower level design requirements.

Characteristics of an Effective Design Review	• Attendees are qualified with necessary expertise to adequately evaluate the design • Attendees should include multidisciplinary independent reviewers • The atmosphere during the review is non-threatening to reviewers and open constructive criticism is welcome; Synergy and teamwork should exist during reviews to allow the full potential of the cross functional team's expertise to be effectively utilized • Concerns, actions and questions are addressed in the review or documented for later resolution; Concerns, actions and questions are tracked until they are resolved and closed • Focused on finding problems, not resolving them • The reviewers should be given sufficient time to read the review documents prior to the review so they have adequate time to thoroughly understand the design • Scheduled with enough time to cover all required topics • Provides a systematic assessment of design results, including the device design and the associated designs for production and support processes; • Provides feedback to designers on existing or emerging problems; • Assess project progress and/or provide confirmation that the project is ready to move on to the next stage of development
Best Practices	• Design reviews should be documented using meeting minutes • Narrow Scope and Frequent Design Reviews • Use a phase gate development strategy and phase reviews • Design review strategies should be customized to meet the needs of the organization

Templates	Visit *Procenius.com* to download design review meeting minute templates.

6.3. Regulation (21 CFR 820.30 (e)) - Design Review

Each manufacturer shall establish and maintain procedures to ensure that formal documented reviews of the design results are planned and conducted at appropriate stages of the device's design development.

The procedures shall ensure that participants at each design review include representatives of all functions concerned with the design stage being reviewed and an individual(s) who does not have direct responsibility for the design stage being reviewed, as well as any specialists needed.

The results of a design review, including identification of the design, the date, and the individual(s) performing the review, shall be documented in the design history file (the DHF). (FDA D.C. Guidance, 2015)

6.4. Definition 21 CFR 820.3 (h) – Design Review

(h) *Design review* means a documented, comprehensive, systematic examination of a design to evaluate the adequacy of the design requirements, to evaluate the capability of the design to meet these requirements, and to identify problems. (FDA QSR , 2014)

6.5. Design Control Guidance Document (for 21 CFR 820.30 (e))

In general, formal design reviews are intended to:

- provide a systematic assessment of design results, including the device design and the associated designs for production and support processes;

- provide feedback to designers on existing or emerging problems;

- assess project progress; and/or

- provide confirmation that the project is ready to move on to the next stage of development.

Many types of reviews occur during the course of developing a product. Reviews may have both an internal and external focus. The internal focus is on the feasibility of the design and the produceability of the design with respect to manufacturing and support capabilities. The external focus is on the user requirements; that is, the device design is viewed from the perspective of the user.

The nature of reviews changes as the design progresses. During the initial stages, issues related to design input requirements will predominate. Next, the main function of the reviews may be to evaluate or confirm the choice of solutions being offered by the design team. Then, issues such as the choice of materials and the methods of manufacture become more important. During the final stages, issues related to the verification, validation, and production may predominate.

The term "review" is commonly used by manufacturers to describe a variety of design assessment activities. Most, but not all, of these activities meet the definition of formal design reviews. The following exceptions may help to clarify the distinguishing characteristics of design reviews.

- Each design document which constitutes the formal output, or deliverable, of a design task is normally subject to evaluation activities, sometimes referred to as informal peer review, supervisory review, or technical assessment. These activities, while they may be called reviews, are often better described as verification activities, because they are not intended to be comprehensive, definitive, and multidisciplinary in their scope. Rather, their purpose is to confirm that design output meets design input. Verification activities affect and add to the design output, and are themselves subject to subsequent design review.

- Developers may conduct routine or ad hoc meetings to discuss an issue, coordinate activities, or assess development progress. Decisions from such meetings may not require formal documentation; however, if a significant issue is resolved, this should be documented. If the outcome results in change to an approved design document, then applicable change control procedures should be followed, as discussed in Section I (Design Changes).

Control of the design review process is achieved by developing and implementing a formal design review program consistent with quality system requirements. The following issues should be addressed and documented in the design and development plan(s).

6.5.1. Number and Type of Reviews

It is a well-accepted fact that the cost to correct design errors increases as the design nears completion, and the flexibility to implement an optimal solution decreases. When an error is discovered at the end of the development cycle, difficult decisions have to be made regarding an acceptable corrective action. When that corrective action is implemented in haste, the result is often an unintended consequence leading to a new problem. Thus, formal design reviews should be planned to detect problems early. A corollary is that planners should presume that problems will be detected, and allocate a reasonable amount of time to implement corrective actions. Typically, formal reviews are conducted at the end of each phase and at important milestones in the design process.

As discussed in Section C (Design Input), it is beneficial in almost every case to conduct a formal review of the design input requirements early in the development process. The number of reviews depends upon the complexity of the device.

- For a simple design, or a minor upgrade to an existing product, it might be appropriate to conduct a single review at the conclusion of the design process.

- For a product involving multiple subsystems, an early design task is to allocate the design input requirements among the various subsystems. For example, in a microprocessor-based system, designers must decide which functions will be performed by hardware and which by software. In another case, tolerance buildup from several components may combine to create a clearance problem. System designers must establish tolerance specifications for each component to meet the overall dimensional specification. In cases like these, a formal design review is a prudent step to ensure that all such system-level requirements have been allocated satisfactorily prior to engaging in detailed design of each subsystem.

- For complex systems, additional reviews are often built into the development plan. For example, engineering sketches may be developed for prototyping purposes prior to development of production drawings. Evaluation of the prototype would typically culminate in a formal design review. Similarly, software development commonly includes a high-level design phase, during which requirements are elaborated to a greater level of detail and algorithms are developed to implement key functions. A formal design review would typically be conducted to review this work prior to beginning detailed coding.

There are a number of approaches to conducting formal design reviews at the end of the design process. In some organizations, engineering essentially completes the design, tests an engineering prototype, and conducts a formal design review prior to turning the design over to manufacturing. In such cases, an additional review will be needed after the design has been validated using production devices.

In some instances, components having long lead times may enter production prior to completion of the overall device design. The primary motivation for early production is to reduce time to market. The manufacturer runs the business risk that the design review at the end of the design process will uncover a defect that must be corrected in production devices before any devices are distributed.

All of these approaches to scheduling formal design reviews are valid. What is important is that the manufacturer establish a reasonable rationale for the number and type of reviews, based on sound judgment.

6.5.2. Selection of Reviewers

In determining who should participate in a formal design review, planners should consider the qualifications of reviewers, the types of expertise required to make an adequate assessment, and the independence of the reviewers. Each of these concerns is discussed briefly in the following paragraphs.

6.5.3. Qualifications

Formal design reviews should be conducted by person(s) having technical competence and experience at least comparable to the developers. For a small manufacturer, this may require that an outside consultant be retained to participate in the evaluation of the design.

A manufacturer will often employ one or more specialists to conduct certain types of specialized assessments which are beyond the capabilities of the designers. For example, a mechanical engineer may be retained to perform a structural analysis of a design, and perhaps conduct vibration testing to verify its performance under stress. Such specialists may be assigned to participate in the formal design review. Alternatively, they may be assigned to make an independent assessment and submit observations and recommendations to the reviewers. Either approach is valid.

6.5.4. Types of Expertise Required

Many medical device designs involve a number of technologies, such as electronics, mechanics, software, materials science, or pneumatics. In addition, a variety of clinical and manufacturing issues may influence the design. Manufacturers should carefully consider which interests should be represented at formal design reviews. Subtle distinctions in reviewer perspective may have dramatic impact on device quality. For example, the marketing department of a small manufacturer shared a new design with several surgeons on their advisory board. The surgeons all thought the design was terrific. Subsequently, the manufacturer invited two experienced operating room nurses to participate in the final design review. During the course of the review, it became apparent that while surgeons may be the customers, nurses are the primary users of the device, and no one up to that point had consulted with any nurses. The nurses at the design review didn't like some of the features of the design. After some further market survey, the manufacturer decided to make changes to the design to accommodate these concerns. It was unfortunate (and expensive) in this case that the user requirements were not considered until late in the development cycle, but the design review was ultimately very successful.

6.5.5. Independence

The formal design review should include at least one individual who does not have direct responsibility for the design stage under review. In a small company, complete independence is very difficult to obtain. Within the context of formal design reviews, the practical solution is simply to ensure a fresh perspective, based on the principle that those who are too close to the design may overlook design errors. Thus, reviewers will often be from the same organization as the developers, but they should not have been significantly involved in the activities under review. As discussed in the following section, the formal design review procedures play a large role in assuring independent and objective reviews.

6.5.6. Resolution of Concerns

The reviewers consider concerns raised during the evaluation portion of the formal design review and decide on an appropriate disposition for each one. There is wide variation in the way companies implement decision-making processes. In some cases, the reviewers play an advisory role to the engineering manager or other company official, who directs the formal design review and ultimately selects a course of action. In other cases, the reviewers are given limited or broad authority to make decisions and commit resources to resolve problems. The approach used should be documented.

In the real world, reviews often leave unresolved issues. Therefore, review procedures should include a process for resolving differences, and provide reviewers with enough leeway to make practical decisions while protecting the integrity of the process.

6.5.7. Implementation of Corrective Actions

Not all identified concerns result in corrective actions. The reviewers may decide that the issue is erroneous or immaterial. In most cases, however, resolution involves a design change, a requirements change, or a combination of the two. If the solution is evident, the reviewers may specify the appropriate corrective action; otherwise, an action item will be assigned to study the problem further. In any case, action items and corrective actions are normally tracked under the manufacturer's change control procedures.

6.5.8. Relationship of Design Reviews to Verification and Validation

In practice, design review, verification, and validation overlap one another, and the relationship among them may be confusing. As a general rule, the sequence is: verification, review, validation, review.

Medical Device Regulation Consulting and Training – www.Procenius.com

In most cases, verification activities are completed prior to the design review, and the verification results are submitted to the reviewers along with the other design output to be reviewed. Alternatively, some verification activities may be treated as components of the design review, particularly if the verification activity is complex and requires multidisciplinary review.

Similarly, validation typically involves a variety of activities, including a determination that the appropriate verifications and reviews have been completed. Thus, at the conclusion of the validation effort, a review is usually warranted to assure that the validation is complete and adequate. (FDA D.C. Guidance, 2015)

6.6. Timing of Design Reviews

The FDA does not specify at what point in the design and development process when design reviews should be held but the following graphical models give some clarity as to when design reviews typically begin relative to research and development activities.

The two humps in Figure 19 depict the relationship and the relative amount of research and development activities performed during the design and development cycle. The shaded area is the typical time when design reviews are executed.

One interesting aspect of this figure is how it depicts design reviews occurring after development has ended. The reason for this is to illustrate that design reviews should continue beyond production release. When a significant change is made to a design post production release, a design review should be held and documented just as in development to ensure the design is adequately reviewed.

FIGURE 19

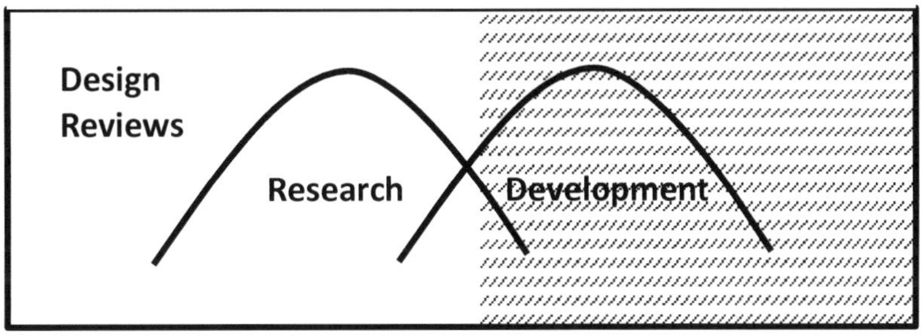

Medical Device Regulation Consulting and Training – www.Procenius.com

6.7. Interpretation & Application (21 CFR 820.30 (e))

When the FDA states in the regulation that **"Each manufacturer shall establish and maintain procedures to ensure that formal documented reviews of the design results are planned and conducted... at appropriate stages of the device's design development."** (FDA D.C. Guidance, 2015) ...they are saying:

To "establish" means to define, document (in writing or electronically), and implement. They are also saying that the manufacturer that is designing the product must have a documented procedure(s) which defines the "what, who, how, why and when" of how formal design reviews are recorded, planned and executed.

The Quality Systems Regulation Preamble states:

> **Comment 79**
>
> *"FDA agrees with the first comment and has rewritten the requirement to make clear that design reviews must be conducted at appropriate stages of design development, which must be defined in the established design and development plan. The number of design reviews will depend on the plan and the complexity of the device."* (FDA Preamble, 2015)

Like other aspects of design control, FDA likes to see design reviews planned. Typically a design review procedure will specify general requirements for design or phase reviews at defined phase gates in the development process. It is also typical that design and phase reviews are planned in the design and development plan which indicates completion of critical milestones during development.

When the FDA says"**...formal documented reviews...",** they are trying to convey that the intent of these reviews are to provide a structured and systematic method of vetting the design. These reviews are not just another development status meeting or a problem solving meeting used to review technical problems, but instead are meetings that are held to review the design and are typically comprehensive, definitive, and multidisciplinary in scope to find problems and approve designs. To promote these practices, the design review procedure should specify the process and deliverables (i.e. meeting minutes) for ensuring a structured and systematic method of reviewing designs for consistent and effective design review implementation.

6.7.1. How to Document Design Reviews

"...The results of a design review, including identification of the design, the date, and the individual(s) performing the review, shall be documented in the design history file (the DHF)..." (FDA D.C. Guidance, 2015)

Medical Device Regulation Consulting and Training – www.Procenius.com

The Quality Systems Regulation Preamble states:

Comment 79

"FDA also amended the requirements so that the results of a design review include identification of the design, the date, and the individual(s) performing the review. Thus, multiple reviews can occur and the manufacturer must document what is being reviewed, when, and by whom." (FDA Preamble, 2015)

The FDA does not specify how reviews should be documented but best practice is to use meeting minutes[BP1] to record action items, document critical decisions and to document a summary of the discussion. Meeting minutes should include the following:

- Name of product being reviewed ("identification of the design")*
- Date of review ("the date")*
- Name of the specific output (system, sub-system, or component) being reviewed as applicable ("identification of the design")*
- Design review attendees (specify who is required and who is optional with title and role) ("individuals performing the review")*
- Summary and key points of the discussion
- Critical decisions made
- Action items including what, by when and by who
- The approved meeting minutes with closed actions should be included or referenced in the Design History File*

Items labeled with a "*" are indicated as required in the regulation. (FDA D.C. Guidance, 2015)

#1 Best Practice – Design reviews should be documented using meeting minutes

The FDA does not specify how reviews should be documented but best practice is to use meeting minutes to record action items, document major decisions and to document a summary of the discussion.

6.7.2. Meeting Minutes Documentation Process

1. The person assigned to documenting meeting minutes will ensure meeting minutes are accurately recorded and formatted.

2. At this point the development team will review and address the meeting minutes and actions to determine what actions are feasible and applicable for the product scope. After this assessment, actions will either be immediately implemented, planned for future implementation with a specific due date or eliminated.

3. The results from the assessment will be recorded in the meeting minutes and will be approved by the required reviewers/roles which will typically be specified in a design review standard operating procedure (SOP) or a document approval SOP.

4. The actions should be implemented as specified in the approved meeting minutes.

5. The status of the actions should be tracked to ensure that all actions are completed by the due date.

6. Once all actions are completed (or closed), a summary of the completed actions and/or references to the document which provides evidence of completion (or action item being addressed) should be referenced in a closed action items record.

7. The record of the closed action items should be approved by the original approvers or key stakeholders.

Typically when the FDA refers to the "result" of an activity, more often than not the "results" are design outputs or the results from design verifications and validations. So when they say, "...**formal documented reviews of the design results...**" (FDA QS Regulation, 2015), they are implying that design outputs and verification/validation results should be reviewed during design reviews. This does not mean that all levels of design outputs should be reviewed during a formal design review. For practicality sake, high level design outputs are reviewed in formal design reviews and low level design outputs are reviewed as technical evaluations prior to approval.

When they say, "**ensure...reviews...are planned and conducted at appropriate stages of the device's design development...**" (FDA QS Regulation, 2015) they are expecting that the type and scope of reviews should be specified when planning development activities. The design and development plan is expected to contain the design review plan including the type and timing of reviews. The timing of reviews can be planned to coincide with planned design phases or to coincide with the completion of specific milestones, systems, modules or components.

"**The procedures shall ensure that participants at each design review include representatives of all functions concerned with the design stage being reviewed...**" (FDA QS Regulation, 2015) This line of the regulation specifies that cross functional team members, management and other stakeholders should be in attendance as applicable to the items being reviewed.

The Quality Systems Regulation Preamble states:

Comment 78

"Design review includes the review of design verification data to determine whether the design outputs meet functional and operational requirements, the design is compatible with components and other accessories, the safety requirements are achieved, the reliability and maintenance requirements are met, the labeling and other regulatory requirements are met, and the manufacturing, installation, and servicing requirements are compatible with the design specifications. Design reviews should be conducted at major decision points during the design phase." (FDA Preamble, 2015)

For reviews that are only intended to evaluate small components or subsystems of the design, it is typical to only have a few engineers (or product experts), an independent reviewer and a quality assurance representative. For larger technical system reviews it is typical to have more cross functional team members such as engineers (multidiscipline), quality assurance, regulatory, marketing, manufacturing/operations, human factors, and technical service (service systems in the field). These cross functional team members should have the necessary experience, expertise and qualifications to adequately evaluate the safety and effectiveness of the system being reviewed. The intent of having a cross functional team is to ensure a thorough review is performed by multidiscipline stakeholders that will have different perspectives and agendas. If all functional areas are not represented, the perspective of the review team will be bias and/or limited. Each functional team member has a unique perspective based on their expertise and background that can effectively optimize the design to ensure a consensus is reached and all stakeholders' needs are satisfied.

At times these cross functional teams may become at odds with each other because of conflicting interests but these disagreements and challenges are what makes the cross functional review so effective. During a review, an effective team will optimize the design in such a way that will satisfy each team member's interests. This is not to say that everyone will get everything they want, or anything they want for that matter. Tradeoffs and compromises will have to be made but at the end of the day a safe and effective design that meets the business's needs should be the result. If this cannot be achieved teams may need to "go back to the drawing board".

For reviews that are larger in scope that provide design phase status updates (often called phase reviews), cross functional team members, as well as upper management, are typical reviewers. It is typical that management may actually attend the reviews or just may approve of the decisions made through approval of formal meeting minutes from the review.

6.7.3. Independent Reviewers

"The procedures shall ensure that participants at each design review include...... an individual(s) who does not have direct responsibility for the design stage being reviewed..." (FDA D.C. Guidance, 2015)

The Quality Systems Regulation Preamble states:

Comment 79

" FDA never intended to mandate that an individual without design responsibility conduct the design reviews and, to clarify its position, has rewritten the requirement. The requirement now states that the procedures shall ensure that each design review includes an individual(s) who does not have direct responsibility for the design stage being reviewed. This requirement will provide an ``objective view'' from someone not working directly on that particular part of the design project, to ensure that the requirements are met. In making this change, FDA also notes that it was not FDA's intention to prohibit those directly responsible for the design from participating in the design review." (FDA Preamble, 2015)

There are at least two reasons why an independent reviewer(s) is required:

1. To Avoid Errors - The design control guidance states, *"Within the context of formal design reviews, the practical solution is simply to ensure a fresh perspective, based on the principle that those who are too close to the design may overlook design error"* (FDA D.C. Guidance, 2015). This is a common problem in the design world. Designers develop designs with a strategy and perspective that makes sense to them. Unfortunately their perspective may not consider all anticipated scenarios which may result in a poor design. An independent reviewer will provide a fresh look and possibly a different perspective that may significantly improve the effectiveness of the design and find camouflaged errors.

2. To Avoid Groupthink - Group think is described as: *"A phenomenon developed in groups and marked by the consensus of opinion without critical reasoning or evaluation of consequences or alternatives. Groupthink evolves around a common desire to not upset the balance of a group of people by creating conflict, with creativity and individuality considered potentially harmful traits that should be avoided.*

   Groupthink in a business setting can cause employees and their bosses to overlook potential problems in the pursuit of consensus thinking. Because individual critical thinking is deemphasized or frowned upon, employees may self-censor themselves and not bring up alternatives or risks for fear of upsetting the status quo." (Investopedia LLC, 2015)

The occurrence of group think can be detrimental on product development teams. "Group Think" exists if the team becomes more worried about "going along with the group" than what is best for the safety and effectiveness of the device. Independent reviewers can break the "group think" cycle and can influence the team to think objectively and ask probing questions that were not previously explored.

During product development, the initial formation of a cross functional team will typically bring sufficient diversity to the group that may inherently avoid the groupthink phenomenon, but as development progresses the risk of groupthink increases. During initial stages of development team members have their own ideas of what the product should do and how it should work. These different perspectives will be challenged within the team until a resolution and/or compromise is eventually made. Some of these decisions may have minor impact on the safety and effectiveness of the design. Over time, more and more of these decisions build upon each other to the point that the design is far below the "bar" that most of the group initially expected. This may happen for a variety of reasons. The dynamics of the group may include a few dominant personalities which will influence decisions over more passive members. Any resistance that the passive members may introduce may be subdued by the dominant team members. Over time the team will tend to fall in line with the "path of least resistance" and will rationalize their decisions based on logic, when in reality they were based on a sub-conscience desire to conform to the team's momentum.

Dominant team members are often thought to be those that are forceful in their tone and demeanor and have a tendency to intimidate or manipulate the team. Though this may sometimes be the case, more often than not, dominant team members are those that use their position (executive management) to persuade the team to come in line with their agenda. Team members may feel that their job is at risk if they don't conform to an executive's perspective.

Other types of dominant team members may include articulate intellectuals that have the ability to logically rationalize just about anything. These team members are the ones that can pretty much convince the team during a meeting that the sky is green and the grass is blue. In the meeting it all makes since and the team has no problem with the idea. The intellectual team member has the ability to manipulate and persuade the team to meet his agenda using clever debating skills and proposed logic, yet the arguments are often unfounded.

As the product target launch date gets closer, the team may be under pressure to meet their deadlines. This type of high pressure environment encourages groupthink because the team's individual perspectives and agendas become less important and is over taken by the schedule pressures. Now the team's interests are aligned around the launch date and groupthink starts to make the sky look green and the grass look blue.

To avoid groupthink the team's interests, knowledge and experience should be diverse such as on a cross functional team. As a final check, an independent reviewer(s) should review the design. Independent reviewers should have the expertise and background to adequately

Medical Device Regulation Consulting and Training – www.Procenius.com

evaluate the design but should not be directly influenced by managers that are applying schedule pressure.

6.7.4. Type of Independent Reviewers and Requirements

Ideally an independent reviewer from each functional area (engineering, marketing, regulatory, quality, etc.) should attend the review to adequately evaluate the multidisciplinary aspects of the design. In smaller companies this may not be feasible. In many cases small medical device manufacturers will have a member of their quality department be their independent reviewer. Members of the quality department should be by definition *independent* and will typically be under less pressure to compromise the safety and effectiveness of the design.

Independent Reviewer Requirements
- Independent reviewers must be adequately qualified to understand the design and provide critical feedback
- Independent reviewers should not have been involved in development of the current aspect of the design being reviewed but are allowed to have been involved in aspects of the design which have been previously developed (or will be developed).

6.7.5. Specialist Reviewers

"The procedures shall ensure that participants at each design review include...... as well as any specialists needed." (FDA QS Regulation, 2015)

This simply means that if the design being reviewed cannot be effectively understood or explained (as applicable) by typical reviewers or presenters, specialists should be called upon to assistant in explaining the design or interpreting/reviewing the effectiveness and safety of the design. In very small companies which may only have one engineer (as an example), an external consultant may be called upon to be an independent and a specialist.

6.7.6. Design Reviews = Course Correction

Design reviews are ideal forums for making course corrections. Frequently developers are so involved in launching the product they do not take time to step back and take a look at their progress and the direction the design is heading. Design reviews are an ideal time to have the development team and independent reviewers take a thorough overview of the design and look at how the design is developing and if it is meeting its requirements and intended use. If things are starting to veer off track, design reviews should catch such deviations and will allow the team to make course corrections before significant resources have been dedicated to any given path.

Medical Device Regulation Consulting and Training – www.Procenius.com

The FDA realizes that if effective and frequent design reviews are not performed, developers may end up with a product right before target launch that does not meet user needs, is unsafe or ineffective. By this time manufacturers have committed significant time and resources and have also committed projected revenue to investors based on the new product forecasts. Unfortunately, instead of canceling development or going back to the drawing board, manufacturers either try the "band aid approach" by trying to fix the problem with minimal time and resources or they turn a blind eye to the problem and come up with some rationale of why it is acceptable. Either tactic is unacceptable and unethical.

Instead of trying to make one huge course correction at the end of development, small and frequent course corrections are significantly more effective and can potentially reduce patient and project risk. It is best practice[BP2] to err on the side of having too many design reviews with a narrow scope than to have too infrequent and too large scope reviews. Frequent and narrow scope reviews will increase the potential of catching design flaws that lead to an ineffective or unsafe design.

#2 Best Practice – Narrow Scope and Frequent Design Reviews

It is best practice to err on the side of having too many design reviews with a narrow scope than to have too infrequent and too large scope reviews. Frequent and narrow scope reviews will increase the potential of catching design flaws that lead to an ineffective or unsafe design.

6.7.7. Types of Design Reviews

Since most manufactures focus on developing a family of common products it is often most efficient to define the type and scope of reviews in a design review standard operating procedure (SOP). The following are examples of types of design reviews that may be used during product development. The FDA does not specify the scope or types of reviews which are required during development but the following list includes typical reviews that are used in complex medical devices that may involve multidisciplinary systems like mechanical, electrical and software. For simpler designs, only one type of design review or a sub-set of these review types may suffice.

Phase Reviews (formal design reviews) – Phase reviews are used to close out design phases. These reviews act as the *gate* that must be approved prior to moving to the next design phase. These reviews are typically a high level review of deliverables such as design requirements, the validation master plan, validation master report (summary of verification and validation reports) and the design transfer report. Depending on the size of the manufacturer, management may attend the review or at least approve the phase review meeting minutes which indicates that they approve further development of the product. In addition to management attendees, cross functional team members that have roles in marketing, engineering, quality, regulatory and manufacturing are also typical phase review attendees.

Phase reviews may include a review of the following topics:

- Product Safety

- Human Factors

- Product Effectiveness

- Manufacturability

- Marketability

- Confirmation that product is ready to move to the next stage of development

- Review of design control activities and deliverables (i.e. high level inputs, verification, validation, risk assessment)

- Early recognition of patient risk associated with the design

- Clinical acceptance

- Ensuring the design satisfies the design input requirements for intended use and user needs

- Ensuring compliance to all regulatory requirements

- Ensuring the design is consistent with the regulatory path and strategy

- Ensuring all design and development activities are compliant with all internal SOP's

System Design Reviews (formal design reviews) – System reviews are used to review the technical aspects of a complex device. These types of reviews assess the high level interaction and function between multidisciplinary aspects of the device such as software, mechanical and electrical. In other words this review is to make sure that everything is working together correctly. Traditionally separate functional groups will design and test their respective function of the design at a sub-system level. The systems review will

Medical Device Regulation Consulting and Training – www.Procenius.com

ensure that these separate design and development activities have been effectively integrated. For complex devices the development team may include a "systems team" that is responsible for ensuring the design integration from all departments and will be responsible for leading the system level design review.

System reviews may include a review of the following topics:

- Product Safety

- Product Effectiveness

- Manufacturability

- Ensuring the design satisfies the design input requirements for intended use and user needs

- Review of design control activities and deliverables (i.e. low level inputs, verification, validation)

- Compliance to all regulatory requirements

- Technical and functional integration between multi-functional systems

- Risk Assessment

- Human Factors

Sub-System Design Reviews (formal design reviews) – Sub-System reviews are lower level reviews that focus on smaller sub-system designs and are typically very technical. These are more than just a peer review or "one over one" technical review. These will evaluate the function of the design based on lower level design requirements.

Sub-system reviews may include a review of the following topics:

- Product Safety

- Product Effectiveness

- Manufacturability

- Ensuring the design satisfies the design input requirements for intended use and user needs

- Compliance to all regulatory requirements

- Functionality

- Risk Assessment

Medical Device Regulation Consulting and Training – www.Procenius.com

<u>Component Reviews (technical assessment or evaluation)</u> – The scope of component reviews are typically on the component level. These are informal evaluation activities that are not considered formal design reviews by the FDA. The scope usually only involves one technical discipline and is usually a peer evaluation, supervisory review or technical assessment. Typically this would be a one on one review of a drawing / schematic or a document being routed for review and approval. Because the FDA considers these activities to be evaluation or assessment activities, 21 CFR 820.30 (e) regulation requirements <u>do not</u> apply (i.e. independent reviewer, documentation, planning, etc.)

Component reviews may include a review of the following topics:

- Effectiveness

- Functionality

- Manufacturability

- Safety

<u>Other Reviews (formal design reviews)</u> – In addition to phase, system and sub-system reviews there may be other type of formal reviews that the project requires that are focused on different aspects of the design and development but are based on the same principles as previously discussed such as:

- Labeling - Review of device labeling

- Design Transfer - Identification and review of all design transfer activities to ensure that all design specifications were correctly translated into production specifications.

- Design Validation - Review of validation plans and/or results

- Design Verification - Review of verification plans and/or results

A key principle to remember is that the number and type of reviews should be based on the manufacturer's needs which is often a function of the complexity of the device, organizational structure, and the size of the company. For startup medical device manufacturers of simple devices, only a few design reviews may be required. For complex devices in large organizations, there may be 10-30 design reviews (or more).

Medical Device Regulation Consulting and Training – www.Procenius.com

6.7.8. Characteristics of an Effective Design Review

- Attendees are qualified with necessary expertise to adequately evaluate the design; Reviews should be conducted by person(s) having technical competence and experience at least comparable to the developers

- Attendees should include multidisciplinary independent reviewers

- The atmosphere during the review is non-threatening to reviewers and open constructive criticism is welcome; Synergy and teamwork should exist during reviews to allow the full potential of the cross functional team's expertise to be effectively utilized

- Concerns, actions and questions are addressed in the review or documented for later resolution; Concerns, actions and questions are tracked until they are resolved and closed

- Focused on finding problems, not resolving them

- The reviewers should be given sufficient time to read the review documents prior to the review so they have adequate time to thoroughly understand the design

- Scheduled with enough time to cover all required topics

- Provides a systematic assessment of design results, including the device design and the associated designs for production and support processes;

- Provides feedback to designers on existing or emerging problems;

- Assess project progress and/or provide confirmation that the project is ready to move on to the next stage of development

6.7.9. Phase Gate Product Development Strategy and Phase Reviews

Many medical device manufacturers use a phase gate[BP3] development strategy and associated phase reviews to ensure that certain deliverables of the design are completed prior to initiating and completing dependent deliverables. A prime example of this is the initial development of the design and development plan, design requirements, risk assessment, and validation master plan (see validation chapter). These early deliverables set the stage for downstream activities such as creating the design, verification and validation. If any of the early deliverables are not completed prior to completing the downstream activities, there is significant risk that the design will not pass verification and validation.

The Quality Systems Regulation Preamble states:

Comment 79

"FDA agrees with the first comment and has rewritten the requirement to make clear that design reviews must be conducted at appropriate stages of design development, which must be defined in the established design and development plan. The number of design reviews will depend on the plan and the complexity of the device." (FDA Preamble, 2015)

Examples of phase gate reviews are illustrated in Figure 20 through Figure 25 (end of chapter). In these examples the phase gate reviews are: Planning/Requirements, Design/Verify/Transfer, Validation and Launch. These are only examples of different type of phase reviews. Each device manufacturer should develop their own design phase gate process and procedures to meet the unique needs of their business environment.

#3 Best Practice – Use a phase gate development strategy and phase reviews

It is best practice to use a phase gate development strategy and associated phase reviews to ensure that certain deliverables of the design are completed prior to initiating and completing dependent deliverables. Phase gate reviews are popular in the medical device industry because the formal review structure increases the probability of compliance to design control regulation.

Medical Device Regulation Consulting and Training – www.Procenius.com

6.8. Quality Systems Manual: Design Reviews

DESIGN REVIEWS

Excerpt from the "Quality Systems Manual: A Small Entity Compliance Guide"
(Withdrawn from FDA website 12 December 2013)
(FDA QS Manual, 2013)

Design review [820.30(e)] is one of the key design control elements in a quality system. The objectives of design review are stated in the definition of design review in 820.3(h) as follows:

Design review means a documented, comprehensive, systematic examination of a design to evaluate the adequacy of the design requirements, to evaluate the capability of the design to meet these requirements, and to identify problems.

To meet the systematic design review requirement, device design and design reviews should progress through defined and planned phases starting with the design input phase and continuing through validation of initial production units or lots. Subsequent activities are usually design changes.

To meet the design review comprehensive requirement, assessments should include a formal review of the main device and subsystems, including accessories, components, software; labeling, and packaging; production and resource needs; and installation and service, if needed. The scope includes performance, physical safety, compatibility with other devices, overall device system requirements, human factors, and environmental compatibility.

Even though users or medical practitioners will be aware of direct medical requirements, they may not be fully aware of physical safety, compatibility, system, human factors, and environmental requirements. Thus, the reviews of the design input and the design should extend beyond merely satisfying user-stated requirements in order to assure that safety and effectiveness goals are met.

As the development program progresses, the reviews should cover producibility and production documentation such as assembly drawings, manufacturing instructions, test specifications, test procedures, etc.

The extent and frequency of design reviews depends on the complexity and significance of the device being evaluated.

When the design program is a redesign of an existing device, a special effort should be made to assure that data obtained from previous failures, complaints, and service records are made available and reviewed by those responsible for design, design input and design review.

Combination Devices

Marketing submissions to FDA for drug delivery, drug coated, etc., devices are required to have appropriate data that supports combination claims. The verification of combination devices requires interaction between device, drug or other manufacturers. Records of this interaction, such as design review meeting minutes, are required in order to meet the interface requirements of 820.30(b), Design and Development Planning. The labeling and particularly the cross-labeling of combination devices should be carefully analyzed during verification and validation activities, and design review meetings.

Preparation For Reviews

The designated moderator or other designated employee should announce the formal review meetings with appropriate lead time and include an agenda.

Persons who are making presentations should prepare and distribute information to help clarify review issues and help expedite the review. However, the intent of the quality system is not that presentations be so formal and elaborate that designers are spending excessive time on presentations rather than on designing a safe and effective device.

Persons who plan to attend a review meeting should come prepared to discuss the key issues on the agenda and issues related to the current design phase. Design review meetings are a great educational forum. However, design review meetings should not be used as a primary tool to educate or bring new employees or unprepared employees up-to-speed. To do so detracts from the intent of the meeting and detracts from the intent of the GMP requirements. Obviously, design review is also an excellent educational tool. However, new, or new-to-the-project employees should be primarily oriented by other means that do not detract from the primary function of design review meetings.

Why Design Reviews

Design reviews are conducted for design definition, selection and adequacy; communication; and resolution of problems and issues. For example, the design review of the design input requirements and subsequent design input specifications for the device, labeling, packaging and accessories is performed to help select the best and/or needed characteristics and requirements, usually from among many available and sometimes conflicting inputs.

The design review of the initial requirements allows input from all parties. Various people may participate and "buy in" or "become part of the program." As the design input and review activities progress, any conflicts are resolved and the preliminary specifications for the device,

Medical Device Regulation Consulting and Training – www.Procenius.com

accessories, labeling, and packaging are established. Herein, the device, accessories, labeling and packaging is called the device system. Because of the establishment of these input requirements and subsequent specifications, plus interface and communication during the reviews, all personnel are directed toward the goal of developing the "exact" same device system.

As the development progresses and the design and production processes evolve, design reviews reduce errors, help avoid problems, help find existing problems, help propose solutions, increase producibility and reduce production transfer problems. The relentless inquiry during design reviews will expose needed design input requirements and/or design corrections that otherwise may have been overlooked.

Throughout the design program and particularly toward the end of the development cycle, design reviews help assure that the final design of the device system meets the current design requirements and specifications.

Types Of Design Review Meetings

Design review meetings may be grouped into two levels such as:

- total or major program review meetings, and
- sub-program or team review meetings.

Some of the review meetings need to be total or major program review meetings because this is the only type of review meeting that will satisfy all of the GMP review requirements, particularly the interface requirement for interaction between or among different organizational groups. However, sub-program, team and contractor review meetings are design review meetings, are subject to quality system design controls, and should be conducted in a manner that meets the GMP requirements. Sub-program or team meetings are encouraged as these can be very effective and efficient in reviewing and resolving sub-program issues.

The records of total program and team meetings are part of the device design history file. The team review records or a summary of team records and the current design documentation are to be available, as appropriate, at total program review meetings.

Design review meetings are called under two scenarios:

- first are the meetings that are preplanned and called at least on a per design phase;

- second are ad hoc meetings that are covered in the broad plans and are called to review or resolve a specific problem or issue.

The preplanned design review meetings and ad hoc meetings are part of the planning and interaction that are required in 820.30(b), Design and Development Planning. That is, the manufacturer should expect, plan for, and encourage appropriate ad hoc meetings as well as the major design review meetings. Reasonable notes and copies of significant engineering documents discussed during total device system, ad hoc, contractor, and other review meetings are part of the device design history file.

Design Review Requirements

The objectives of design review are stated in the definition noted above. How these objectives are to be achieved are presented in the design review requirements. The main design review requirements are in 820.30(e) of the QS regulation as follows:

Each manufacturer shall establish and maintain procedures to ensure that formal documented reviews of the design results are planned and conducted at appropriate stages of the device's design development. The procedures shall ensure that participants at each design review include representatives of all functions concerned with the design stage being reviewed and an individual(s) who does not have direct responsibility for the design stage being reviewed, as well as any specialists needed. The results of a design review, including identification of the design, the date, and the individual(s) performing the review, shall be documented in the design history file.

There are four requirements related to design reviews:

1. The meetings should be formal. That is, key attendees are designated and the meetings are conducted at least once per stage/phase, are planned, are announced or are periodic, have an appropriate agenda, notes are recorded, etc., according to the manufacturer procedure for design reviews.

The design review procedure should be broad and complete in that it contains information about all of the requirements. However, the procedure should not be so detailed that it cannot be followed. Over the years, several manufacturers have failed to follow this advice, tried to write detailed design QA procedures, and have reported that they were unable to finish writing the over-detailed procedures and were unable to implement them.

2. To meet the definition of design review in 820.3(h), the review should include persons who are intimately knowledgeable about the technical characteristics of the design such as performance, safety, compatibility, etc. In many manufacturers this can only be done by those persons responsible for the design. However, reviews are to be objective, unbiased examinations by appropriately trained personnel which should include an individual(s) not responsible for the design. The moderator of the review meeting may be one of the persons not responsible for the design.

Medical Device Regulation Consulting and Training – www.Procenius.com

To meet interface and other review requirements, the review meetings should, as appropriate, include representatives of R&D, Engineering, Technical Support Services, Production Engineering, Manufacturing, Quality Assurance, Marketing, Installation and Servicing,

Purchasing and contractors. Design review should, as applicable and at the appropriate phase, include those responsible for coordinating or managing preclinical and clinical studies.

3. Pre- and post-review meeting significant responsibilities and assignments should be documented [820.30(b)]. These assignments are not unusual -- they are simply ordinary work required to develop a new product or modify an existing product. The progress and/or results of such assignments would typically be reported at the next review meeting. Documentation is not required for detailed day-to-day development activities that are part of the designer's routine job.

4. The design review meeting results are made a part of the device design history file. The results should include minutes and should include notes, or annotated draft drawings and annotated draft procedures that played a significant role during the design review. Such documents help show that plans were followed, verification/validation was reviewed, and, to some extent, how the design evolved.

The QS regulation does not require that every document mentioned, referenced or used during a design review be placed in the design history file.

The device design review meeting minutes should include information such as:

- moderator and attendees,
- date and design phase/stage,
- plans and/or agenda,
- problems and/or issues to identify and solve,
- minutes and reports, and
- follow-up report(s) of solutions and/or the next review covers the solutions and remaining issues.

Manufacturers may use a form to capture some of this information for minutes such the device, date, moderator, attendees, major phase, problems, assignments, etc. The device design review minutes are a key and required part of the design history file. The minutes also help consolidate development information and the current minutes are also a brief record of some of the immediate development tasks to be done.

End Of Initial Design

The design control requirements, particularly design validation, give clear insight into when the initial design effort is completed. The end of the total design effort has not been reached until it is known that the initial production devices, when transferred to production and produced per the device master record, meet all of the current design specifications. This fact can only be determined by performing design validation on one or more samples of the finished production units as required by 820.30(g). Initial production and subsequent validation are well defined stages; and, therefore, design review(s) shall be performed as required by 820.30(e), Design Review.

Thus the design validation of initial production should be followed by a "final" design review to meet the design review requirement. If the validation of the final design and subsequent design review(s) reveal design problems, then design changes are required to correct these problems.

Design changes require another design verification and, where appropriate, validation and review of all parts or the affected parts of the device system.

6.9. Case Study – Planning and Implementing Design Reviews (MRI To Go Inc.)

The project manager (PM) for MRI *OnWheels* has been tasked with planning and implementing design reviews for his project. He knows that the design of the system is complex and involves development activities from various functional groups. His goal is to find the right balance between the right type, scope and frequency of design reviews that will be sufficiently adequate to review the design but will not over burden resources. The project manager has decided to structure the project in four phases as outlined in Figure 20 through Figure 22: 1) planning & requirements, 2) design, verify & transfer, 3) validation and 4) launch.

(Project implementation strategies are not specified by the FDA but some form of a phase-gate development strategy seems to naturally align with design control regulatory requirements in contrast to other strategies. Implementing effective development strategies under design controls requirements will be addressed in more detail in a later chapter.)

The project manager's initial objective is to ensure that the team can determine the technical, clinical and commercial feasibility of the device's intended use prior to committing extensive resources to full product development. Therefore after concept testing is completed, feasibility testing is performed prior to initiating phase I.

After feasibility has been passed, phase I is initiated. The development plan is approved, risk assessment is completed, design requirements are identified and the validation master plan is finalized. Prior to closing phase I a phase review is held to ensure the results from all phase I activities are sufficiently completed prior to moving on to phase II.

Medical Device Regulation Consulting and Training – www.Procenius.com

Phase II includes design, testing and verification of each defined sub-system (mechanical, electrical and software). Design reviews are held to review the details of the design which is iterated as required from feedback from the review. After successful completion of the product design, verification testing is initiated which is then followed by another design review to evaluate the results of the verification testing. After the individual sub-system reviews are completed, system level verification is performed which is followed by a system level design review to ensure the sub-systems have been sufficiently integrated. Finally a phase review is held to close out phase II. Design transfer activities and design changes are executed in parallel with phase II activities.

> *(For less complex devices that do not have multiple sub-systems or have less complex designs, one phase review to cover all aspects of the design may sufficient to adequately evaluate the design. Implementation[BP4] of a design review strategy should consider what is most efficient for the organization but should also ensure compliance to FDA regulations. The strategy should take into consideration design review type, scope and frequency. Design review strategies should be customized for the organization and should not be strictly duplicated from other organizations without a full evaluation of the strategy's strengths and weaknesses.)*

Following the close of Phase II, validation activities begin in phase III, design transfer activities are completed and the risk assessment is closed out. After the completion of these activities, a phase III design review is held which closes out validation and design transfer. The review will evaluate the results from validation and design transfer to ensure that all activities in this phase are completed in such a manner that meet product requirements, internal procedures and FDA regulation. All design control activities are closed at the completion of phase III. Finally, regulatory submissions are executed and business deliverables are completed prior to closing phase IV.

#4 Best Practice – Design review flow strategies should be customized to meet the needs of the organization

Implementation of a design review flow strategy should consider what is most efficient for the organization but should also ensure compliance to FDA regulations. The strategy should take into consideration design review type, scope and frequency. Design review strategies should be customized for the organization and should not be strictly duplicated from other organizations without a full evaluation of the strategy's strengths and weaknesses.

Medical Device Regulation Consulting and Training – www.Procenius.com

Complex Design Review Flow Strategy Example (Phase I)

FIGURE 20

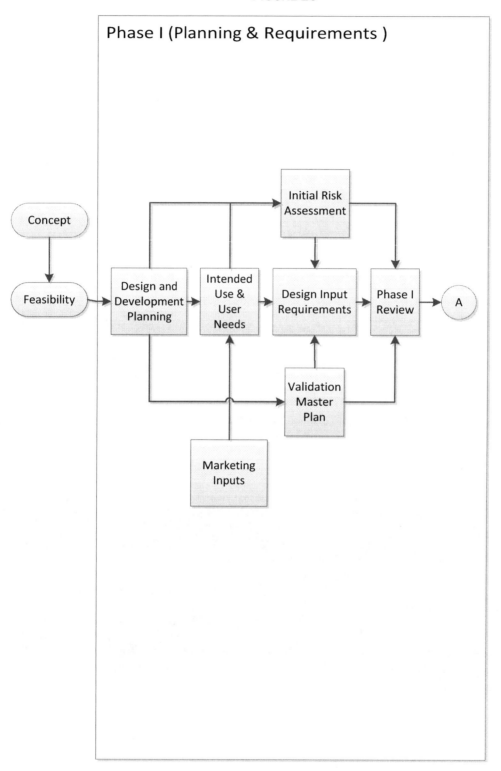

Medical Device Regulation Consulting and Training – www.Procenius.com

Complex Design Review Flow Strategy Example (Phase II)

FIGURE 21

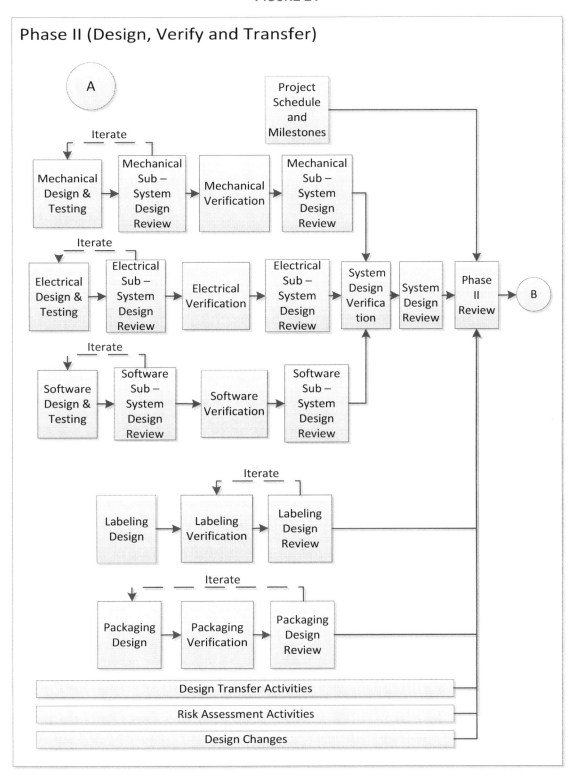

Medical Device Regulation Consulting and Training – www.Procenius.com

Complex Design Review Flow Strategy Example (Phase III & IV)

FIGURE 22

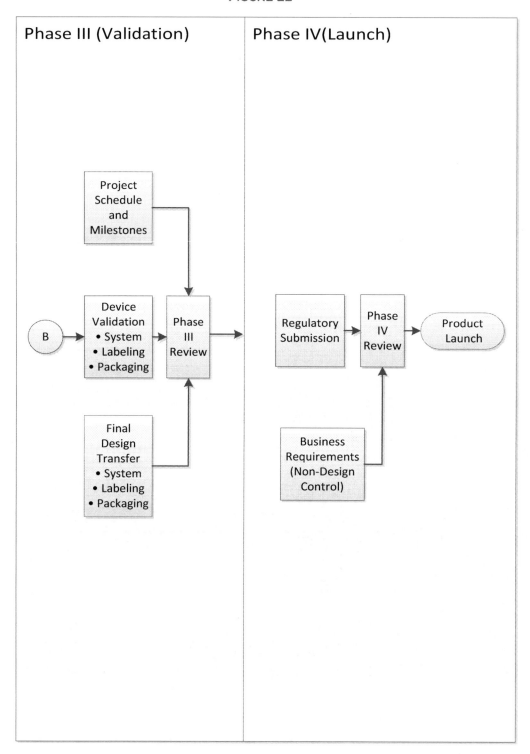

Medical Device Regulation Consulting and Training – www.Procenius.com

For less complex designs, a simpler design review flow strategy can be used as depicted in Figure 23 through Figure 25 which minimizes the number of required reviews. The key point to remember is that the design review flow strategy should be customized to effectively work with the complexity level of the design.

Simple Design Review Flow Strategy Example (Phase I)

FIGURE 23

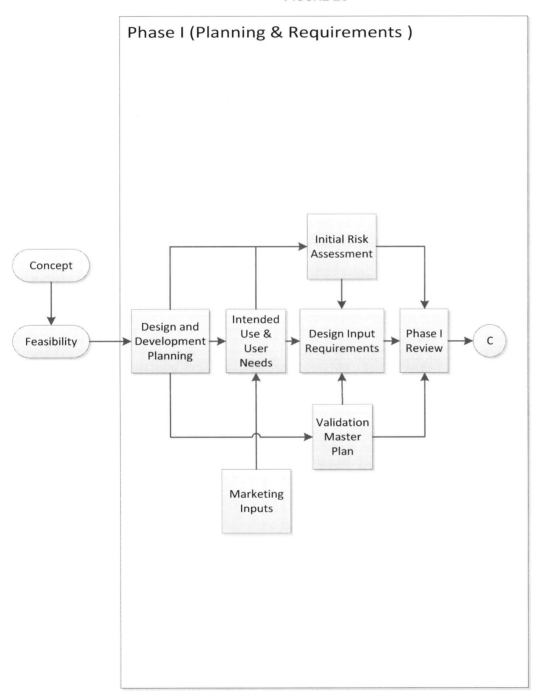

Medical Device Regulation Consulting and Training – www.Procenius.com

Simple Design Review Flow Strategy Example (Phase II)

FIGURE 24

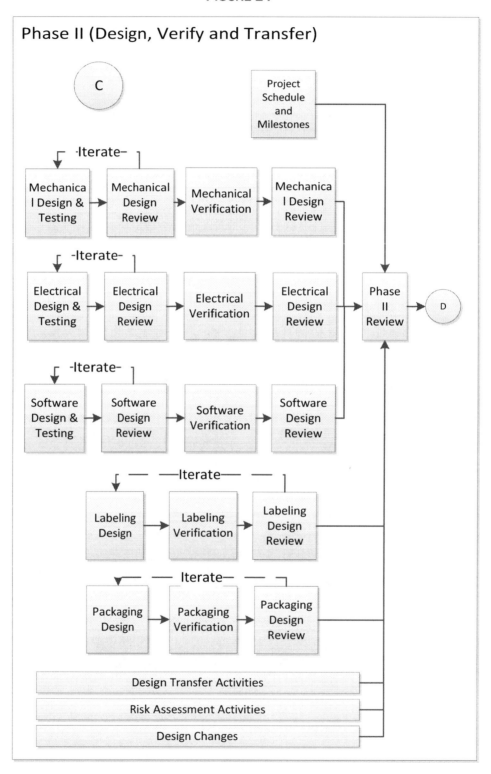

Simple Design Review Flow Strategy Example (Phase III & IV)

FIGURE 25

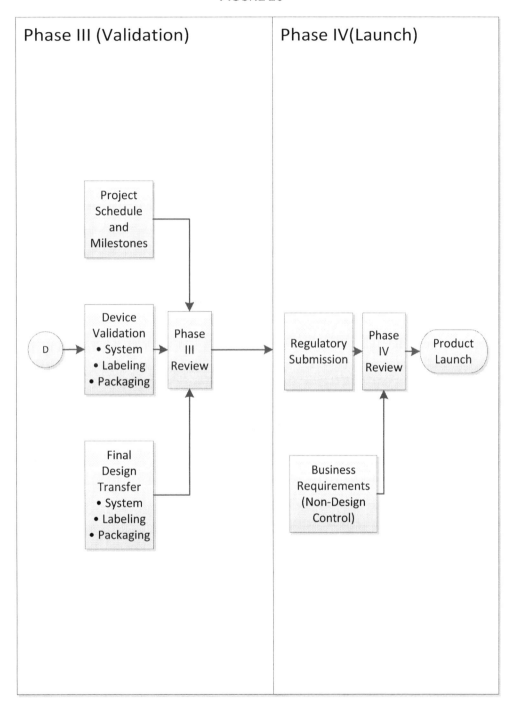

6.10. Templates

Visit *Procenius.com* to download design review meeting minute templates.

7.0 Design Verification

(Principles common to both design verification and validation are indicated by (*V&V*))

7.1. Overview

Design verification is simply a practice during medical product development which ensures that a device is being designed to meet its design requirements. A medical device design engineer has all of the best intentions to design the device to perform and function to meet these design requirements but for one reason or another these intentions may fall short and unfortunately the intended design functionality and performance can be lost. To ensure the device performs as intended, design verification will confirm that the design meets design input requirements during the design processes and not just at the end of development.

It is often said that design verification ensures that the "device was designed right", and design validation ensures that the "right device was designed". Or in other words, design verification ensures that the design meets the engineering requirements and design validation ensures that the device actual does what the user needs it to do in a safe and effective way.

7.2. Principles and Models Common to Both Design Verification and Validation

There are typically a significant number of common principles and models used to implement and explain design verification and validation. Most of these common principles and models will be presented in this chapter. In an effort to reduce duplicating material in the Design Validation chapter, those sections indicated with (*V&V*) in this chapter will indicate those principles and techniques which are applicable to both design verification and validation.

7.3. Quick Reference Summary

TABLE 14

Purpose	Design verification confirms that the design is effectively being designed to meet design input requirements during development.

Medical Device Regulation Consulting and Training – www.Procenius.com

Definition	Verification means confirmation by examination and provision of objective evidence that specified requirements have been fulfilled. (FDA QSR , 2014)
Regulation	21 CFR 820.30 (f): Each manufacturer shall establish and maintain procedures for verifying the device design. Design verification shall confirm that the design output meets the design input requirements. The results of the design verification, including identification of the design, method(s), the date, and the individual(s) performing the verification, shall be documented in the Design History File. (FDA QS Regulation, 2015)
Standard(s)	ISO 13485 (7.3.5) (ISO 13485, 2007)
Guidance	21 CFR 820.30 (f) (FDA) — FDA Design Control Guidance for Medical Device Manufacturers (FDA D.C. Guidance, 2015)
	ISO 13485 (7.3.5) — Medical Devices – Quality Management Systems – Guidance on the Application of ISO 13485:2003 (ISO 14969, 2004)

Timing of Design Verification Relative to the Research and Development Cycle	FIGURE 26 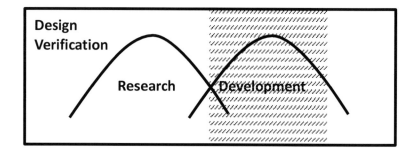 The two humps in Figure 26 depict the relationship and the relative amount of research and development activities during the design and development cycle. The shaded area is the typical time when design verification is executed.
Verification Methods	• **Verification by Inspection (VBI)** - This method typically requires creating an approved verification protocol which defines how the verifier will inspect approved outputs, such as design specifications or drawings, to ensure they meet design requirements. This type of verification may be as simple as reviewing a component drawing to ensure the drawing specifies the material type required by the design input requirements. • **Verification by Analysis (VBA)** - VBA's are typically performed on simple components or design features which can be effectively analyzed by industry accepted methods or standards such as engineering stress or heat transfer formulas. Complex designs or design features which involve multi-physics analysis should be verified by testing. Even in today's world of advanced software analysis tools, there are underlying assumptions made by imperfect humans which may compromise the accuracy of the result. Analysis tools are ideal for upfront analysis of preliminary designs to land the design in the "ballpark" but should not be relied upon for verifying designs requirements which have multi-physics interaction such as reliability, vibration, or fatigue.

	• **Verification by Testing (VBT)** - Verification by testing is typically performed when other less resource intensive methods are inadequate to verify that the design meets the design input requirements. Even though this method is considered by most engineers to be the safest verification method to ensure product performance, it should not always be immediately considered as the default method. Extensive VBT can be very time and resource intensive. VBT is typically ideal for verifying multi-physics interaction such as reliability, vibration, or fatigue that cannot be verified by inspection or by analysis. • **Rationale (not performing verification)** - A rationale can be written to justify why verification is not required for some design inputs. More often than not these rationales are based on similarities between the new design and a previously verified design. Rationales should be based on data or facts, not opinions.
Types of Verification Tests (examples only, not all inclusive)	• Comparative tests with proven design • Simulated use in the laboratory • Animal model tests • Biocompatibility tests • Material and device compatibility tests, • Functional tests after sterilization • Reliability tests • Performance tests • Tests of compatibility with other devices • Environmental emission and susceptibility tests

Medical Device Regulation Consulting and Training – www.Procenius.com

Design Verification vs. Design Validation	The best way to think about design verification is as a method of confirming that developers are staying on track during the design process. In other words, do the specifications (outputs) being developed meet the design input requirements?

When the design process was initiated, developers started with initial design requirements that guided them through the preliminary design phase. At the completion of each subsequent phase of development or at the completion of a significant module of the design, developers should confirm (or verify) that what they have designed during each phase meets the original and subsequent requirements. Verification may be performed on small components, sub-system modules, or the full scale medical device depending on the design requirements identified.

Design verification focuses on "Did we design the device right (correctly)?" or in other words, does the design meet or satisfy all of the design requirements so the device will perform as designed (or as intended)? Design validation focuses on, "Did we design the right device?" or in other words, does the device do what the user needs it to do safely and effectively? Does it meet their needs?

Design verification focuses on verifying the design as the design is progressing and validation is performed on the final medical device.

So for design verification always think "verification confirms that the device is on track as development is occurring". For design validation think, "validation confirms that the final device meets the user's needs after development is completed".

"Whereas verification is a detailed examination of aspects of a design at various stages in the development, design validation is a cumulative summation of all efforts to assure the design will conform with users need and intended use(s), given expected variations in components, materials, manufacturing processes, and the use environment." (FDA D.C. Guidance, 2015) |

		Design Verification	Design Validation
Comparison of Design Verification vs. Design Validation Requirements/Activities	May be performed on prototypes, early designs modules, sub-systems or components	X	
	Confirms that the design output meets the design input requirements as the device is being developed	X	
	Should be performed throughout product development on interim and final design outputs	X	
	May be performed in a lab or bench top setting (actual conditions not required)	X	
	Performed under defined operating conditions on initial production units, lots or batches or their equivalents		X
	Ensure device conforms to defined user needs and intended uses		X
	Shall include testing of production units under actual or simulated use conditions		X
	Shall include software validation		X
	Shall include risk analysis where appropriate		X
	The results of the design (validation/verification), method(s), the date, and the individual(s) performing the (validation/verification) shall be documented in the DHF	X	X

Medical Device Regulation Consulting and Training – www.Procenius.com

Process of Planning and Executing Design Verification	1. Approve Design Input Requirements 2. Create and Approve a Validation Master Plan (VMP) (Optional) 3. Create and Approve Verification Protocols 4. Train Personnel Executing Verification 5. Prepare Equipment (if needed for verification) 6. Prepare the Design Output / Medical Device 7. Execute Verification 8. Create Verification Report 9. Verification Results Should Be Reviewed 10. Approve Verification Report 11. Create Validation Master Report (VMR)(optional)
Design Review	21 CFR 820.30 (E) states (FDA D.C. Guidance, 2015): *"As a general rule, the [design review and verification] sequence is: verification, review, validation, review."* So typically design verification is executed and the results of verification are reviewed. The type and method of review is dependent upon on the complexity of the device and size of the organization. In typical organizations, an effective review will include the results from the design verification documented in individual reports or a summary of verification results listed in a validation master plan. Reviewers attending formal design reviews should include qualified individuals in all functional areas that may have critical input to the verification results being reviewed.

Medical Device Regulation Consulting and Training – www.Procenius.com

Design Review	**Typical Reviewers** For early prototype or lower level verifications a limited number of reviewers may only be required* but for review of final system level reviews additional team members are more appropriate. <u>Cross Functional Reviewers</u> Quality Assurance* R&D / Engineering* Marketing Human Factors Regulatory Affairs Project Management Independent Reviewer* Other Stake Holders
Deliverable(s)	• Protocol • Report • Supporting Data • Training Documentation • Protocol Deviations (if applicable)
Approval **(Protocols and Reports)**	Approval of design verification protocol and report (and validation master plan/report) typically includes cross functional team members. The team should have the technical expertise to provide input as to how the verification should be executed and how to interpret the results. Approvals should be documented manually with signature and date or electronically to be in compliance with 21 CFR part 11.

	Typical Protocol or Report Approvers For early prototype or lower level verifications, a limited number of approvers may only be required* for verification protocol/report approval but for review of final system level protocol/report approvals, additional team members could be more appropriate. <u>Cross Functional Approvers</u> Quality Assurance* R&D / Engineering* Marketing Human Factors Regulatory Affairs Project Management Other Stake Holders
Revisions	Design verification protocols should be revised and updated as the design progresses to reflect the design output or design input changes which could occur in each new design iteration. Design verification reports (and validation master report) will not typically be revised unless the report is used as an ongoing compilation of multiple verifications such as in a validation master report. In the case where a verification fails and is later performed again, the same report should be revised to reflect the latest results of the same verification.

Medical Device Regulation Consulting and Training – www.Procenius.com

Best Practices	• The verification method chosen should ultimately be based on patient/user risk. • It is best practice that rationales should be based on data or facts, not opinions. • It is best practice to leverage previously verified designs whenever possible to minimize unnecessary development work. • Use a pre-approved verification protocol and a post approved report (results). • It is best practice to increase the level of verification documentation as the design progresses.
Templates	Visit *Procenius.com* to download design verification protocol/report templates.

7.4. Regulation (21 CFR 820.30 (f)) - Design Verification

Each manufacturer shall establish and maintain procedures for verifying the device design. Design verification shall confirm that the design output meets the design input requirements. The results of the design verification, including identification of the design, method(s), the date, and the individual(s) performing the verification, shall be documented in the Design History File. (FDA QS Regulation, 2015)

7.5. Definition 21 CFR 820.3 (Z.2.aa) – [Design] Verification

[Design] Verification means confirmation by examination and provision of objective evidence that specified requirements have been fulfilled. (FDA QSR , 2014)

7.6. Design Control Guidance Document (for 21 CFR 820.30 (f))

Verification and validation are associated concepts with very important differences. Various organizations have different definitions for these terms. Medical device manufacturers are encouraged to use the terminology of the quality system requirements in their internal procedures.

To illustrate the concepts, consider a building design analogy. In a typical scenario, the senior architect establishes the design input requirements and sketches the general appearance and construction of the building, but associates or contractors typically elaborate the details of the various mechanical systems. Verification is the process of checking at each stage whether the output conforms to requirements for that stage. For example: does the air conditioning system deliver the specified cooling capacity to each room? Is the roof rated to withstand so many newtons per square meter of wind loading? Is a fire alarm located within 50 meters of each location in the building?

At the same time, the architect has to keep in mind the broader question of whether the results are consistent with the ultimate user requirements. Does the air conditioning system keep the occupants comfortable throughout the building? Will the roof withstand weather extremes expected at the building site? Can the fire alarm be heard throughout the building? Those broader concerns are the essence of validation.

In the initial stages of design, verification is a key quality assurance technique. As the design effort progresses, verification activities become progressively more comprehensive. For example, heat or cooling delivery can be calculated and verified by the air conditioning designer, but the resultant air temperature can only be estimated. Occupant comfort is a function not only of delivered air temperature, but also humidity, heat radiation to or from nearby thermal masses, heat gain or loss through adjacent windows, etc. During the latter design phases, the interaction of these complex factors may be considered during verification of the design.

Validation follows successful verification, and ensures that each requirement for a particular use is fulfilled. Validation of user needs is possible only after the building is built. The air conditioning and fire alarm performance may be validated by testing and inspection, while the strength of the roof will probably be validated by some sort of analysis linked to building codes which are accepted as meeting the needs of the user-subject to possible confirmation during a subsequent severe storm.

7.6.1. Types of Verification Activities

Verification activities are conducted at all stages and levels of device design. The basis of verification is a three-pronged approach involving tests, inspections, and analyses. Any approach which establishes conformance with a design input requirement is an acceptable means of

Medical Device Regulation Consulting and Training – www.Procenius.com

verifying the design with respect to that requirement. In many cases, a variety of approaches are possible.

Complex designs require more and different types of verification activities. The nature of verification activities varies according to the type of design output. The intent of this guidance document is not to suggest or recommend verification techniques which should be performed by device manufacturers. Rather, the manufacturer should select and apply appropriate verification techniques based on the generally accepted practices for the technologies employed in their products. Many of these practices are an integral part of the development process, and are routinely performed by developers. The objective of design controls is to ensure adequate oversight by making verification activities explicit and measuring the thoroughness of their execution. Following are a few examples of verification methods and activities.

- Worst case analysis of an assembly to verify that components are derated properly and not subject to overstress during handling and use.

- Thermal analysis of an assembly to assure that internal or surface temperatures do not exceed specified limits.

- Fault tree analysis of a process or design.

- Failure modes and effects analysis.

- Package integrity tests.

- Biocompatibility testing of materials.

- Bioburden testing of products to be sterilized.

- Comparison of a design to a previous product having an established history of successful use.

For some technologies, verification methods may be highly standardized. In other cases, the manufacturer may choose from a variety of applicable methods. In a few cases, the manufacturer must be creative in devising ways to verify a particular aspect of a design.

Some manufacturers erroneously equate production testing with verification. Whereas verification testing establishes conformance of design output with design input, the aim of production testing is to determine whether the unit under test has been correctly manufactured. In other words, production testing is designed to efficiently screen out manufacturing process errors and perhaps also to detect infant mortality failures. Typically, a small subset of functional and performance tests accomplish this objective with a high degree of accuracy. Therefore, production testing is rarely, if ever, comprehensive enough to verify the design. For example, a leakage test may be used during production to ensure that a hermetically-sealed enclosure was properly assembled. However, the leakage test may not be sensitive enough to detect long-term diffusion of gas through the packaging material. Permeability of the packaging material is an intrinsic property of the material rather than an assembly issue, and would likely be verified using a more specialized test than is used during production.

7.6.2. Documentation of Verification Activities

Some verification methods result in a document by their nature. For example, a failure modes and effects analysis produces a table listing each system component, its postulated failure modes, and the effect of such failures on system operation.

Another self-documenting verification method is the traceability matrix. This method is particularly useful when the design input and output are both documents; it also has great utility in software development. In the most common form of the traceability matrix, the input requirements are enumerated in a table, and references are provided to each section in the output documents (or software modules) which address or satisfy each input requirement. The matrix can also be constructed "backwards," listing each feature in the design output and tracing which input requirement bears on that feature. This reverse approach is especially useful for detecting hidden assumptions. Hidden assumptions are dangerous because they often lead to overdesign, adding unnecessary cost and complexity to the design. In other cases, hidden assumptions turn out to be undocumented design input requirements which, once exposed, can be properly tracked and verified.

However, many verification activities are simply some sort of structured assessment of the design output relative to the design input. When this is the case, manufacturers may document completion of verification activities by linking these activities with the signoff procedures for documents. This may be accomplished by establishing a procedure whereby each design output document must be verified and signed by designated persons. The presence of the reviewers' signatures on the document signifies that the design output has been verified in accordance with the signoff procedure. (FDA D.C. Guidance, 2015)

7.7. Timing of Design Verification Activities and Deliverables

The FDA does not specify at what point in the design and development process when design verification should begin but the following graphical models give some clarity as to when design verification typically begins and ends relative to research and development activities.

The two humps in Figure 27 depict the relationship and the relative amount of research and development activities during the design and development cycle. The shaded area is the typical time when design verification is planned and executed.

Medical Device Regulation Consulting and Training – www.Procenius.com

FIGURE 27

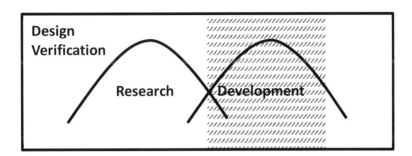

7.8. Interpretation & Application (21 CFR 820.30 (f))

When the FDA states in the regulation that **"Each manufacturer shall establish and maintain procedures for verifying the design."**, they are saying that the manufacturer of the design must have a documented procedure(s) that defines the "what, who, how, why and when" for the verification process. The FDA wants to ensure that a standard design verification procedure has been created, vetted, reviewed and approved.

The procedure must be "maintained" (in other words revised and updated) as required to be current with the intended and approved design verification activities. Typically this procedure is assigned to the department that is responsible for product development such as (Development Teams or Engineering).

"Design verification shall confirm that the design output meets the design input requirements." This sentence from the regulation is saying that development teams need to verify, check, prove, substantiate, etc. that the outputs (see below) conforms to the design requirement's design intent. Design intent is achieved by the outputs satisfying the requirements through verification activities such as testing, analysis or inspection.

This sentence of the design verification regulation can be admittedly difficult to fully understand for most people (and difficult to explain abstractly for that matter). To offer a better explanation, a review of design output examples, method of verification and examples of verifications are explained below.

As a review, these are some examples of design outputs that may be verified:

- assembly drawings

- component and material specifications

- production and process specifications

- software machine code (e.g., diskette or master EPROM)

- work instructions

- quality assurance specifications and procedures

- installation and servicing procedures

- packaging and labeling specifications, including methods and processes used

- the results of risk analysis

- software source code

- results of verification activities

- biocompatibility test results

- bioburden test results

7.8.1. Verification Methods

Development teams have essentially three ways to confirm or verify that these outputs will "meet" the design input requirements: Testing, Analysis and/or Inspection. The verification method chosen should ultimately be based on patient/user risk[BP1]. The high level strategy and plan of how design verification (and design validation) will be performed should be specified in a validation master plan which will be addressed later in this chapter.

#1 Best Practice – The verification method chosen should ultimately be based on patient/user risk.

At times, the optimal verification method is not obvious. When not obvious or if the decision is somewhat subjective, a risk analysis should be performed to weigh the risk vs. benefit of the verification methods being considered. (i.e. – verify by test or analysis of a multi-physics thermal analysis; not always straight forward)

FDA Design Control Guidance states:

> "The basis of verification is a three-pronged approach involving tests, inspections, and analyses." (FDA D.C. Guidance, 2015)

Medical Device Regulation Consulting and Training – www.Procenius.com

7.8.1.1. Verification by Inspection (VBI)

Verification by inspection is typically by far the least resource intensive verification method. This method typically requires creating an approved verification protocol (discussed later in this chapter) which defines how the verifier will inspect approved outputs, such as design specifications or drawings, to ensure they meet design requirements. This type of verification may be as simple as reviewing a component drawing to ensure the drawing specifies the material type required by the design input requirements. See Table 15 for more examples.

7.8.1.2. Verification by Analysis (VBA)

Verification by analysis is typically executed by technical professionals such as engineers or scientists. Just as with VBI, an approved protocol is required which will define the method for how the analysis will be performed. VBA's are typically performed on simple components or design features which can be effectively analyzed by industry accepted methods or standards such as engineering stress or heat transfer formulas. Complex designs or design features which involve multi-physics analysis should be verified by testing. Even in today's world of advanced software analysis tools, there are underlying assumptions made by imperfect humans which may compromise the accuracy of the result. Analysis tools are ideal for straight forward analysis of preliminary designs to land the design in the "ballpark" but should not be relied upon for verifying designs requirements which have multi-physics interaction such as reliability, vibration, or fatigue. See Table 15 for examples.

7.8.1.3. Verification by Testing (VBT)

VBT typically involves using an approved protocol to execute a test case to verify the design requirements. Verification by testing is typically performed when other less resource intensive methods are inadequate to verify that the design meets the design input requirements. Even though this method is considered by most engineers to be the safest verification method to ensure product performance, it should not always be immediately considered as the default method. Extensive VBT can be very time and resource intensive. VBT is typically ideal for verifying multi-physics interaction such as reliability, vibration, or fatigue that cannot be verified by inspection or by analysis.

7.8.1.4. Rationale (Not Performing Verification)

The fourth way that is sometimes acceptable to the FDA is to write a rationale as to why verification is not required. More often than not these rationales are based on similarities between the new design and a previously verified design. It is best practice that rationales[BP2] should be based on data or facts, not opinions. The next section addresses this in more detail.

> **#2 Best Practice – It is best practice that rationales should be based on data or facts, not opinions.**
>
> Rationales based on opinion or even "expert experience" will not typically provide sufficient objective evidence to justify not performing verification.

7.8.2. Referencing Data from Equivalent Designs to Reduce Verification Effort

The Quality Systems Regulation Preamble states:

Comment 84

"…FDA agrees in part with the comment. The revised language of Sec. 820.30(f) will permit the use of data from prior experimentation when applicable. When using data from previous experimentation, manufacturers must ensure that it is adequate for the current application." (FDA Preamble, 2015)

The FDA does not intend to overburden device manufacturers. They understand that data from previously executed verifications on equivalent design features (e.g. components or sub-assemblies) can be leveraged to minimize re-verification of outputs that would be non-value added activities. Although allowed, it is critical to remember that even minor design changes from the previously verified design could very easily and significantly impact the validity of the verification results. Any design change should be seriously evaluated before leveraging data from previously verified outputs, hence the need for a robust design change process as defined in the Design Change chapter. With these guidelines in mind, it is best practice to leverage[BP3] previously verified designs whenever possible to minimize unnecessary development work.

> **#3 Best Practice – It is best practice to leverage previously verified designs whenever possible to minimize unnecessary development work.**
>
> Re-verification of outputs with equivalent (or very similar) design features relative to the new design is a non-value added activity.

Medical Device Regulation Consulting and Training – www.Procenius.com

7.8.3. Types of Verification Testing

Types of Verification Tests (examples only, not all inclusive)

- Comparative tests with proven design
- Simulated use in the laboratory
- Animal model tests
- Biocompatibility tests
- Material and device compatibility tests
- Functional tests after sterilization
- Reliability tests
- Performance tests
- Tests of compatibility with other devices and
- Environmental emission and susceptibility tests

7.8.4. Examples of Verification Methods

Ultimately the best way to understand design verification is by example or application. Table 15 gives examples of how the design progresses from design inputs all the way through design verification.

The numbers listed in TABLE 15 are defined in TABLE 16 below.

TABLE 15

Design Input Requirements	Design Process	Design Output	Verification Method	Design Verification Examples
1	11	17	23	33
2	12	18	24	34
3	13	19	25	35
4	14	20	26	36
5	15	21	27	37
6			28	38
7			29	39
8	16	22	30	40
9			31	41
10			32	42

Medical Device Regulation Consulting and Training – www.Procenius.com

TABLE 16

1	The MRI machine's electrical system shall operate at 120V at less than 16 amps.
2	The overall size of the MRI machine shall be less than 9.5'(long) X 4' 8" (wide) X 6' 6"ft (high)
3	The dialysis catheter shall have a flow rate of 400 ml per minute at 10psi.
4	The x-ray machine's software system shall display options to operate fluoroscopy, still image and deep tissue images from the main interface screen.
5	The x-ray machines articulating arm shall function as intended through 10,000 cycles at 360 degree rotations.
6	A surgical scalpel shall support a bending load greater than 20 lbs. force.
7	A surgical scalpel shall support an axial load (resistance to buckling) greater than 10 lbs. force.
8	A surgical scalpel shall be made from materials that can conform to ASTM E2314 (cleanliness standards)
9	A surgical scalpel shall be made from materials that are biocompatible as determined by ISO-10993.
10	A surgical scalpel shall weigh more than 0.5 ounces but no more than 4 ounces.
11	Components such as motors, actuators and LEDs rated for 120V that will meet functional requirements will be specified but will not exceed a total of 16 amps during operation. The design process will include design iterations, informal bench testing, research and prototyping.
12	A 3D design envelope that will be no greater than 9.5' (long) X 4' 8" (wide) X 6' 6"ft (high) will be defined in a CAD system. The sub-systems and components will be designed and specified to operate within the required maximum design envelope.
13	An iterative flow analysis to determine the minimum internal cross sectional area required to meet the flow requirement will be performed. Other requirements will also have to be considered that will drive material type, the external diameter and profile of the catheter extrusion.

14	The software developers will develop the code for the main interface page of the software such that all required image types are available from the main page.
15	Components and materials that are rated for high reliability (high cycles) applications to meet the design requirement will be identified and integrated as part of the design.
16	Multiple design iterations are evaluated with various combinations of materials, features, components, and geometries. All compounding requirements are considered during design: weight, strength (axial and bending loads), biocompatibility and cleaning. A 0.25 in. diameter cylindrical shaft design using 440C stainless steel has been determined to be the optimal design.
17	Once a viable design has been identified, the components and configuration of the design will be documented. A bill of materials (list of all components) and an electrical schematic are the design outputs. (defines the configuration and layout of the components and wiring)
18	The design envelope will be defined in a 3D CAD system and will be electronically stored as a 3D model. The detail of the design will be stored as a 2D drawing and bill of materials. The CAD files, drawings and bill of materials are the design outputs.
19	The final cross sectional geometry and material will be defined in a 3D CAD system and will be electronically stored as a 3D model. The detail of the design will be stored as a 2D drawing and bill of materials. The CAD files, drawings and bill of materials are the design outputs.
20	The software code will define the image display information that will meet the image requirement. The software code is therefore the output of the software design effort. Any documentation that supports the software code will also be part of the design output.
21	The design of the articulating arm using the high cycle components and materials will be documented in a 3D CAD system or on drawings.
22	The design of the scalpel and material will be documented in a 3D CAD system or on drawings.
23	Test
24	Analysis

25	Test
26	Inspection
27	Test
28	Analysis
29	Analysis
30	Inspection
31	Inspection
32	Analysis
33	The system is tested by measuring the power draw by the system during operation. Verification passes if the power draw is less than 16 amps @ 120V.
34	For simplicity, verification can be performed by analysis. The drawings or 3D model can be used to evaluate if the design will meet this requirement. (This could also be performed by testing (measuring) the actual system.)
35	Even though modern fluid dynamic analysis software is very advanced, there is sufficient variability in fluid viscosity, extrusion friction forces and variability in extrusion geometry to warrant testing the catheter. The catheter is flow tested to ensure the catheter can meet the 400 ml flow requirement at 10psi.
36	Verification is executed by confirming that the main interface screen displays options for operating fluoroscopy, still images and deep tissue images.
37	Verification should be performed by testing. Most moderate, to complex designs with reliability requirements should be tested. Interaction between unique materials, components, and the intended design application make it very difficult if not impossible to accurately predict the end of the design's functional life due to wear, creep, corrosion or fatigue.
38	Verification by analysis can be easily justified because the geometry of a standard cylindrical shaped scalpel can be easily and accurately analyzed using a thoroughly proven moment formula for loads causing stress from bending.

Medical Device Regulation Consulting and Training – www.Procenius.com

39	Verification by analysis can be easily justified because the geometry of a standard cylindrical shaped scalpel can be easily and accurately analyzed using a thoroughly proven buckling formula for axial loads.
40	Verification by inspection can be easily justified because 440C stainless steel is a common material that has been previously proven to meet ASTM E2314 cleanliness standards. References linking the design to previous verifications or published studies should be documented in the verification report.
41	Verification by inspection can be easily justified because 440C stainless steel is a common material that has been previously proven to meet ISO 10993 biocompatibility standards. References linking the design to previous verifications or published studies should be documented in the verification report.
42	Verification by analysis can be easily justified because the geometry of a standard cylindrical shaped scalpel can be easily and accurately analyzed using a simple density to weight derivation or by using validated CAD software to verify the weight.

7.8.5. Verification Results Shall Be Documented In the Design History File

*When the FDA says…"***The results of the design verification, including identification of the design, method(s), the date, and the individual(s) performing the verification, shall be documented in the Design History File.***"*, they are saying that details of the verification needs to be recorded and approved in a document which is included in the design history file. As the FDA is known for saying, "If it isn't documented, it didn't happen". It is best practice[BP4] and industry standard (and is expected by the FDA) to use a pre-approved verification protocol and a post approved report (results) as diagramed in Figure 28. Pre-approval of the protocol before executing verification ensures that questionable results are not considered after the verification was performed. The FDA realizes that developers are more likely to be less bias and will make decisions more objectively about acceptance criteria if determined, documented and approved **prior** to performing and seeing the results of the verification.

FIGURE 28

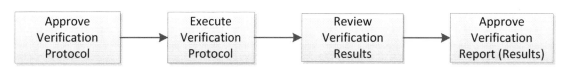

#4 Best Practice – Use a pre-approved verification protocol and a post approved report (results).

FDA expects a pre-approved protocol (including acceptance criteria) **before** verification is executed. A post approval report of the results is also expected which provides objective evidence of the verification pass/fail status. "If it isn't documented, it didn't happen"

7.8.6. Traditional Validation and Verification Model (V&V Model) (*V&V*)

Figure 29 is the traditional V&V model which depicts the abstract relationship between User Needs – Design Validation – Medical Device and Design Input Requirements – Design Verification – Design Outputs.

FIGURE 29

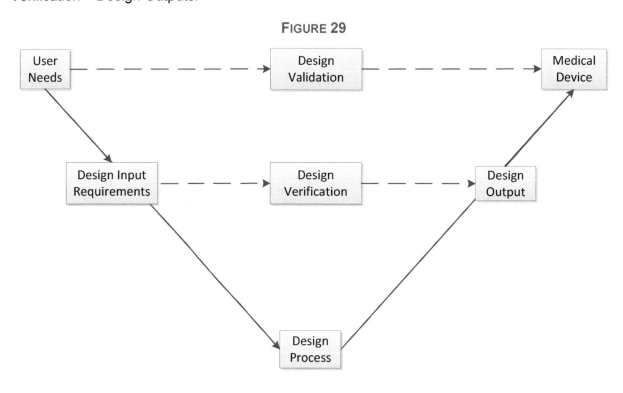

7.8.7. Complex Medical Device Verification w/ Sub-System Verification (*V&V*)

Figure 30 is a variation of the traditional V&V model for complex medical devices which depict the relationship between system level requirements and verification with sub-system requirements and verification.

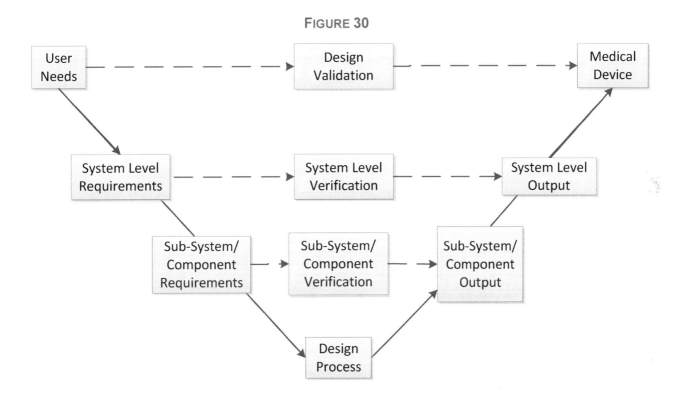

FIGURE 30

Medical Device Regulation Consulting and Training – www.Procenius.com

7.8.8. Complex Medical Device Verif. w/ Concurrent Sub-System Verif. (*V&V*)

To understand this model,   Figure 31 breaks out the sub-system verification V-model (SVM) as shown below. The SVM will be used in Figure 26 to show concurrent sub-system verifications.

FIGURE 31

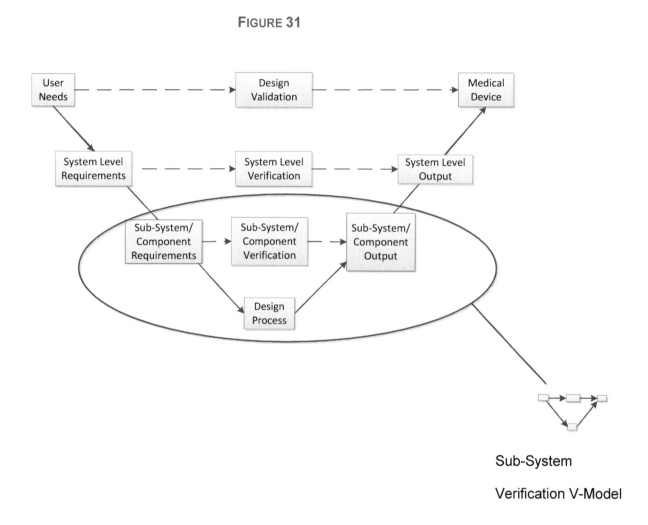

Sub-System

Verification V-Model

Figure 32 is a flattened version of the traditional V&V model for complex medical devices which depicts concurrent verification activities between system level and sub-system level verifications.

This model shows how user needs are translated into system requirements then into sub-system requirements. The sub-system requirements are then verified independently and often concurrently. The letters which run vertically A to C represent different sub-systems or

Medical Device Regulation Consulting and Training – www.Procenius.com

components such as the electrical, software, and mechanical systems. Numbers 1 to 3...
represent the number of sub-system design verification iterations for each sub-system that may
need to be performed to determine a safe and effective design. Early iterations (design versions)
may start as prototypes that are progressively iterated until the final design is solidified. As
design iterations are performed, the design will be refined until it will meet all design input
requirements.

Eventually the sub-system designs and verifications will be finalized in preparation for system
level design verification. The system level design used for system level design verification will
integrate all of the final sub-system designs and will be representative of the final design
configuration prior to design validation.

FIGURE 32

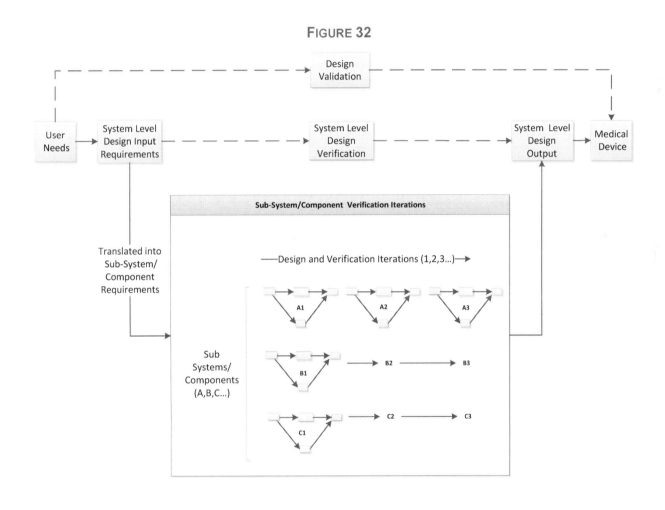

Medical Device Regulation Consulting and Training – www.Procenius.com

7.9. Design Verification vs. Design Validation (*V&V*)

At times there can be significant confusion between design verification and validation. The best way to think about design verification is as a method of confirming that developers are staying on track during the design process. In other words, the design specifications (outputs) should be checked during the development process to ensure that the design input requirements are being met.

At completion of each phase of development or at the completion of a significant module of the design, developers should perform verification activities. Verification may be performed on labeling, small components, sub-system modules, or the full scale medical device depending on the design requirements identified.

FDA Design Control Guidance states:

> *"Verification is the process of checking at each stage whether the output conforms to requirements for that stage."*

> *"Verification activities are conducted at all stages and levels of device design."*

> *"During the latter design phases, the interaction of these complex factors [sub-systems or components] may be considered during verification of the design."* (FDA D.C. Guidance, 2015)

Design verification focuses on "Did we design the device right (correctly)?" or in other words, does the design meet or satisfy all of the design requirements so the device will perform as designed (or as intended)? Design validation focuses on, "Did we design the right device?" or in other words, does the device do what the user needs it to do safely and effectively? Does it meet their needs?

Since the design process is a progressive process, developers may perform verification on the same component, module or sub-system multiple times until the design is finalized. Initial verifications may be performed on early prototypes to confirm that the design is progressing correctly. As the design progresses, the outputs should become closer and closer to the final configuration in preparation for final verification and validation. If early verifications are performed on devices which are not representative of the final design, they should be re-verified to ensure the latest design still meets the design input requirements (i.e. final verification). Figure 33 depicts the iterative design verification and design process.

FIGURE 33

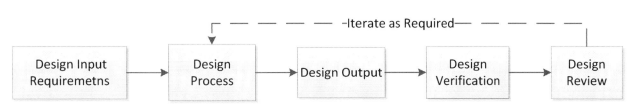

Once the design outputs are finalized and the results of all verifications are accepted in applicable design reviews, the documented device design used for verification should be translated into production specifications during design transfer and should be used to manufacture the device in its final configuration. The final configuration of the medical device, which may be manufactured during initial production lots, should be used for design validation. Prototypes or non-production versions of the device should not be used for design validation. Figure 34 shows how the final approved design outputs are used to configure the medical device used for design validation.

FIGURE 34

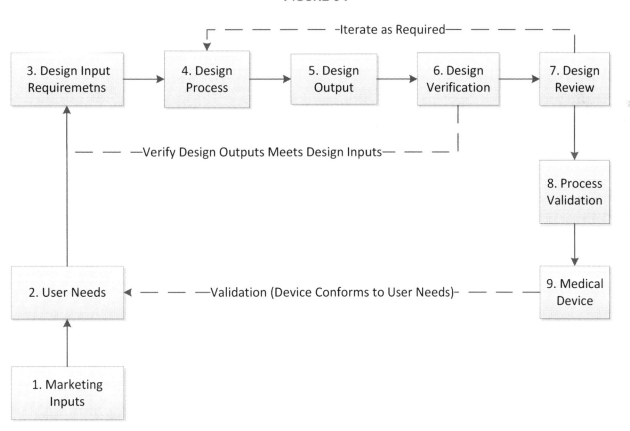

Design verification focuses on verifying the design as the design is progressing and validation focuses on validating the final medical device. So for design verification always think "verification confirms that the device is on track as development is occurring". For design validation think, "validation confirms that the final device meets the user's needs after development is completed".

Even though design verification occurs throughout development on prototypes and early development devices, the FDA also indicates that a "final verification" is required on the actual production device under actual or simulated conditions.

The Quality Systems Regulation Preamble states:

Comment 80

"Final design validation, however, cannot be done on prototypes because the actual devices produced and distributed are seldom the same as the research and development prototypes. The final verification and validation, therefore, must include the testing of actual production devices under actual or simulated use conditions." (FDA Preamble, 2015)

So this concept of "final verification" seems like it would be over burdensome to require device manufacturers to perform verification on "production devices". On the other hand, it makes logical sense that the final device configuration (or final design output) should be verified just as any previous design output that was verified to design input requirements. It is common industry practice to use a final design configuration that is expected to be equivalent to the final production device, but not actual production devices. Since the design validation regulation allows validation to be performed on an "equivalent" design configuration it is safe to assume production equivalent devices can be used for "final verification" also.

It's also interesting to note that the FDA considers verifications to be under the *umbrella* of design validation as stated in the guidance.

FDA Design Control Guidance states:

"Whereas verification is a detailed examination of aspects of a design at various stages in the development, <u>design validation is a cumulative summation of all efforts to assure the design will conform with users need and intended use(s)</u>, given expected variations in components, materials, manufacturing processes, and the use environment." (FDA D.C. Guidance, 2015)

In practice, this concept of "final design verification" can be confusing. Essentially what the FDA is saying is that the results of a verification is only valid to support the overall final device validation effort if performed on a production equivalent device. In situations where the overall device configuration has changed but some components haven't, the verification results from those unchanged components may be valid as long as those components were verified independently. Or in other words, verification results may be used in support of the validation effort for device configurations or components that have not changed.

Example

From the *MRI OnWheels* example, if the reliability requirements of a mechanical articulating arm is being verified, the testing may be performed on a benchtop where the articulating arm has been isolated from the rest of the MRI machine. Even though the rest of the device may have changed, as long as the components of the articulating arm have not change, the reliability data for the verification may be used to support the final verification requirements.

The Quality Systems Regulation Preamble also supports this principle:

Comment 81

"…Certain aspects of design validation can be accomplished during the design verification, but design verification is not a substitute for design validation…" (FDA Preamble, 2015)

Since design input requirements are derived from user needs and are verified on the final device configuration, it is only logical that the "final verification" falls under the "*cumulative summation of all efforts to assure the design conforms with users need and intended use(s)*". After all, meeting the design input requirements is part of predicting that the final device will conform with user needs and intended use during validation.

This is an advanced design control concept which is best explained by Figure 35. In this figure each column represents a design stage with different iterations of the design. As the design progresses, it is shown how results of each design review provides input to the next design stage. In addition it shows how each design phase requires a new verification to ensure the latest configuration of the design is adequately verified. The final verification (in this case iteration IV) is verified using the final device configuration prior to entering design validation.

All verifications from early prototypes to the final device configuration are illustrated by the *Design Verification* call out in Figure 35. But interestingly enough, since the final verification is considered part of design validation, it is also indicated in the *Design Validation* call out.

FIGURE 35

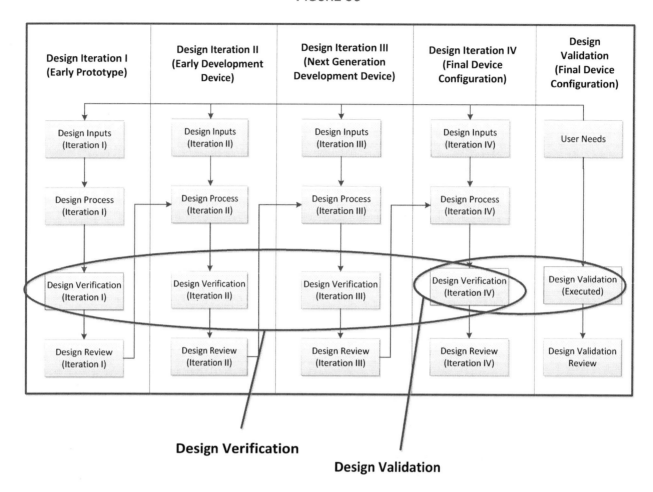

Design Verification

Design Validation

As previously explained, for practicality sake, those design features that remain the same from iteration to iteration do not require re-verification, only those features which have changed need to be re-verified (or features that may have been affected by other design changes). The need to re-verify a design feature of the next design iteration should be evaluated in a design change control which should evaluate the impact and risk associated with the change. The impact and risk analysis should provide sufficient information to decide whether or not the design feature should be re-verified or re-validated.

To easily compare the regulatory requirements between design verification and validation, the following table provides a quick reference summary.

Comparison of Design Verification vs. Design Validation Requirements/Activities (*V&V*)

TABLE 17

Regulatory Requirements	Design Verification	Design Validation
May be performed on prototypes, early designs modules, sub-systems or components (initial verification)	X	
Confirms that the design output meets the design input requirements as the device is being developed	X	
Should be performed throughout product development using interim and final design outputs	X	
May be performed in a lab or bench top setting (actual conditions not required)	X	
Performed under defined operating conditions on initial production units, lots or batches or their equivalents		X
Ensure device conforms to defined user needs and intended uses		X
Shall include testing of production units under actual or simulated use conditions		X
Shall include software validation		X
Shall include risk analysis where appropriate		X
The results of the design (validation/verification), method(s), the date, and the individual(s) performing the (validation/verification) shall be documented in the DHF	X	X

Medical Device Regulation Consulting and Training – www.Procenius.com

7.10. Process for Planning and Executing Design Verification and Validation (V&V*)

1. **Approve Design Input Requirements (Design Validation: User Needs for Validation)**
   The design input requirements which are being verified must be approved prior to approving the design verification protocol and executing the verification. The verification protocol should reference (and be traceable to) the approved design requirements document as the source of the requirements that are being verified.

2. **Create and Approve a Validation Master Plan (VMP)**
   A validation master plan (VMP) is called many things and means many things to different medical device manufacturers. The source of this inconsistent terminology and definition is inherently due to no formal definition provided by the FDA. As a matter of fact, the FDA does not require a validation master plan although validation planning is recommended for complex devices and is often expected during inspections.

   FDA Design Control Guidance states:

   > *VALIDATION PLANNING. Planning for validation should begin early in the design process. The performance characteristics that are to be assessed should be identified, and validation methods and acceptance criteria should be established. For complex designs, a schedule of validation activities and organizational or individual responsibilities will facilitate maintaining control over the process. The validation plan should be reviewed for appropriateness, completeness, and to ensure that user needs and intended uses are addressed. (FDA D.C. Guidance, 2015)*

   A validation master plan in this context is essentially the high level plan for how a development team plans to verify design input requirements and validate user needs for a device. Therefore the design input document is the main input to the VMP. Decisions in this plan will determine the following:
   - What aspects of the design needs to be verified or validated (i.e. requirements and outputs)
   - How will verification and validation be performed (sub-systems, modules, phases)
   - What type of verification will be performed (inspection, test, analysis, rationale)
   - What resources will be assigned to perform the verification and validation
   - When will verification and validation be performed

3. **Create and Approve Verification/Validation Protocols**
   Verification protocols should be planned, drafted, reviewed and approved. Since the VMP drives the creation of the verification and validation protocols, the VMP should be approved prior to approving verification and validations protocols.

Medical Device Regulation Consulting and Training – www.Procenius.com

4. **Train Personnel Executing Verification/Validation**

   The people which have been designated to execute the verification should be trained to fully understand the details of the protocol requirements and methods. Training should be documented and should include: name of personnel trained, date, trainer and content of training.

5. **Prepare Equipment**

   Standard equipment used to perform the verification/validation should be identified in the protocol (if known at the time) or in the final report including make, model and serial number. Equipment should be calibrated and a gage R&R (repeatability and reproducibility) should be performed as necessary.

6. **Prepare the Design Output / Medical Device**

   The design output or medical device being verified or validated should be procured and identified by lot, make, model or serial number as applicable to ensure its configuration is traceable. The outputs and design inputs should be "frozen" and version controlled during verification. This is to ensure the version of the design inputs and outputs being verified are accurately identified in the verification report.

7. **Execute Verification/Validation**

   The verification/validation protocol should be executed as specified in the protocol.

8. **Create Verification/Validation Report**

   Objective evidence should be collected as a result of executing the verification/validation. Data should be captured and recorded as part of the verification report. The report should also include a clear conclusion statement which indicates if the results completely passed, failed or partially passed.

   If any aspect of the verification/validation protocol is not followed, a deviation report detailing the extent of the deviation should be documented. The results and impact of the deviation should be evaluated using a risk analysis to determine the validity of the results of the verification/validation. A full rationale/explanation should be included in the verification/validation report explaining the validity (or invalidity) of the results. The deviation should be approved by the same approvers of the verification/validation protocol and report.

9. **Verification/Validation Results Should Be Reviewed**

   The verification/validation results should be reviewed in a formal design review.

FDA Design Control Guidance states:

> *"RELATIONSHIP OF DESIGN REVIEW TO VERIFICATION AND VALIDATION.*
> *In practice, design review, verification, and validation overlap one another, and the relationship among them may be confusing. As a general rule, the sequence is: verification, review, validation, review.*
>
> *In most cases, verification activities are completed prior to the design review, and the verification results are submitted to the reviewers along with the other design output to be reviewed. Alternatively, some verification activities may be treated as components of the design review, particularly if the verification activity is complex and requires multidisciplinary review."* (FDA D.C. Guidance, 2015)

10. Approve Verification/Validation Report

The results and conclusion of the report should be approved by the same approvers which approved the verification protocol.

11. Create Validation Master Report (VMR)

The validation master report is to compliment the validation master plan. The VMR is a summary of all of the high level results (i.e. pass/fail) for each verification or validation performed. Just as the VMP is not required by the FDA, neither is the VMR but it is a very convenient document for inspectors to understand the overall results of verification and validation without having to dig through the individual details of each validation or verification report.

7.11. Verification by Trace Matrix (*V&V*)

FDA Design Control Guidance states:

> *"Another self-documenting verification method is the traceability matrix. This method is particularly useful when the design input and output are both documents; it also has great utility in software development. In the most common form of the traceability matrix, the input requirements are enumerated in a table, and references are provided to each section in the output documents (or software modules) which address or satisfy each input requirement."* (FDA D.C. Guidance, 2015)

The trace matrix is comprised of several columns that trace the evolution of the user needs through the design translation, into design requirements, verification and validation reports, and finally output documents. The trace matrix is a living document throughout development of the device. Many columns of the trace matrix should be completed as development progresses. The trace matrix should be reviewed in design reviews during development and finalized prior to final device approval.

Table 12 (from Design Output chapter) is an example of a trace matrix showing traceability from design outputs back to design input requirements. A trace matrix is a great tool to ensure outputs are created during development and adequately verified/validated prior to device launch. It is also a valuable tool for internal and external inspectors which enables them to easily tie outputs to inputs.

The example in Table 18 is a trace matrix in its most basic form which ties requirements, to outputs, to verification. This example also only has two rows where in practice a trace matrix may have hundreds of requirements depending on device complexity. The FDA does not require a trace matrix but will often expect one while performing an inspection.

Basic Trace Matrix Example (*V&V*)

TABLE 18

ID	Design Input Requirement	Output (being verified)	Results of Design Verification
1.0	The overall size of the MRI machine shall be less than 9.5'(long) X 4' 8" (wide) X 6' 6" (high) (Reference the DIR document number and requirement ID#)	System Level Drawing (Drawing Number)	Results from verification (Report Number)
2.0	The MRI machine's electrical system shall operate at 120V at less than 16 amps (Reference the DIR document number and requirement ID#)	System Level Electrical Schematic (Drawing Number)	Results from verification (Report Number)

More thorough trace matrices will include additional columns such as:

- User Needs
- Source of User Need or Design Requirement (Marketing Inputs, Risk Assessment, Standard/Regulation)
- Process Validation (Process Qualification and Product Performance Qualification)

Table 19 is an example of an advanced trace matrix which ties the source of user needs all the way through process validation.

Source of User Need: This column is used to document the source from where the user need was identified. These references typically come from marketing or publication research. The marketing research report number or publication reference should be referenced in this column.

User Need: This column is used to document the user needs. The actual user need can be documented in this column or a reference can be made to the user need document number. (See design inputs chapter for more details about user needs)

Risk Assessment (Driver): As a risk analysis is performed, risks will be identified which require implementation of controls into the design which will mitigate the risk. As described in the design input chapter, risk controls can be translated into the design as design input requirements. Typically the ID# and risk assessment document number which was the sources of the control is referenced in this column. ("Driver" indicates that the risk assessment drives the design input requirement)

Example: A risk assessment identifies a risk of exposure to x-ray radiation. The risk is high enough to require a mitigation control. A design requirement is derived from this mitigation control which specifies a maximum dose of radiation allowed per image taken.

Design Input Requirements (DIR): The design input requirements are translated from user needs, risk assessment controls (driver) or regulations/standards. Design input requirements should be objective and measureable to enable effective design verification. Typically the ID# and DIR document number which was the sources of the control is referenced in this column.

Outputs: The outputs document consists of the components, assembly or device which was verified or validated. Typically a drawing number for the output is referenced in this column.

Risk Assessment (Driven): The driven risk assessment column is used to document how a pre-existing requirement will satisfy a risk control in order to mitigate risk. The risk assessment ID# and risk assessment document should be referenced in this column. ("Driven" indicates that an output generated to satisfy a DIR requirement will satisfy a control to mitigate risk)

Medical Device Regulation Consulting and Training – www.Procenius.com

Results of Verification: This column is used to document the verification report number that was used to verify a design output to a design input requirement.

Results of Validation: This column is used to document the validation report that was used to validate the medical device to the user need.

Process Requirements: This column is used to document the process requirements which will be used to develop the manufacturing process and inspection criteria.

Process Outputs: This column is used to document the process outputs such as the manufacturing and inspection procedures.

Results of Process Validation: This column is used to document the process validation report(s) that is associated with the output that is being manufactured.

This level of traceability is not required by FDA but will lend itself to more thorough and robust development practices and will make FDA inspections go smoother. An effectively designed trace matrix can help a FDA inspector understand how design elements are tied together and will more likely give the inspector greater confidence in the device manufacturer's ability to follow design control regulation.

Advanced Trace Matrix (*V&V*)

TABLE 19

ID	Source of User Need	User Need/Risk Assessment (driver)/ Standard	Design Input Requirement	Output (being verified)	Results of Design Verification	Results of Design Validation
1	Marketing research (Report #)	The MRI machine shall be able to be transported through a 3' (wide) by 6' 8" (high) door (Reference User Need document number and requirement ID#)	The overall size of the MRI machine shall be less than 9.5'(long) X 4' 8" (wide) X 6' 6" (high) (Reference the DIR document number and requirement ID#)	System Level Drawing (Drawing #)	Results from verification (Report #)	Design Validation Report Document Number and ID#
2	Marketing research (Report #)	The MRI machine shall be powered using a U.S. standard 120V wall outlet. (Reference User Need document number)	The MRI machine's electrical system shall operate at 120V at less than 16 amps (Reference the DIR document number)	System Level Electrical Schematic (Drawing #)	Results from verification (Report #)	Design Validation Report Document Number and ID#

Medical Device Regulation Consulting and Training – www.Procenius.com

The trace matrix is continued below in Table 20. Reference ID#'s in rows 1 & 2 from Table 19.

TABLE 20

ID	Risk Assessment (controls)	Process Requirements	Process Outputs	Results of Process Validation
1	Risk Assessment Document/Report Number and ID#	Process Requirements document driven from critical design outputs	Process documentation to produce the device in manufacturing.	Product Performance Qualification and Process Qualification (Report #)
2	Risk Assessment Document/Report Number and ID#	Process Requirements document driven from critical design outputs	Process documentation to produce the device in manufacturing.	Product Performance Qualification and Process Qualification (Report #)

7.12. Verification Protocol and Report Best Practices and Requirements

Just as the design progresses during development, so should the formality of verification documentation. It is best practice[BP5] to increase the level of verification documentation as the design progresses. Verification of early design prototypes can simply be documented in a lab notebook with minimal information but by the time final verification is performed it is typical to have a formal and detailed protocol and report. This progressive verification documentation approach should be specified in a design verification standard operating procedure. As indicated by "*" in the next section, these elements are the absolute minimum requirements for design verification at all phases of the design as specified by *21 CFR 820.30(f)*.

> **#5 Best Practice – It is best practice to increase the level of verification documentation as the design progresses.**
>
> Allowing for progressive verification documentation in design verification SOP's allows needed flexibility during early development while still being compliant to *21 CFR 820.30(f)*.

Final verification protocols should be approved and should include the following:

Required by 21 CFR 820.30(f) as noted; other items are best practice but not required.

- *Identification of the design
  - Name, part numbers, components and design outputs being verified

- *Verification method
  - Step by step procedure defining how the verification should be executed
  - Specifying by analysis, test or inspection

- Purpose and scope

- Reference to design requirements being verified
  - It is common to have a "mini" trace matrix within the protocol to trace the requirement from the design input requirement document to the protocol's test I.D.

- Required expertise or training of the person executing the verification protocol

- Objective acceptance criteria
  - Acceptance criteria should be quantitative that can be objectively measured. Tolerances, standard deviations etc. should be provided for expected variable data

- Sample size and sample size rationale (e.g. statistical justification)
  - Should be based on statistical confidence levels in most cases

- Each test case shall be uniquely/sequentially numbered, to allow for traceability to design input requirements.

Medical Device Regulation Consulting and Training – www.Procenius.com

Verification report should be approved and should contain the following:

Required by 21 CFR 820.30(f) as noted

- *Identification of the design
- *Verification method (protocol can be referenced)
- *Results (e.g. data) from executing the design verification protocol
- *Conclusion from the results; including Pass/Fail according to acceptance criteria
- Documentation of traceability of design (test process) used during verification; Including material lot information or component serial number traceability as applicable
- *Date verification was performed
- *Record of person who executed the verification
- Record of (or reference to) person trained to verification protocol
- Record of deviations (or reference to) should be included in the report

*The verification report should be referenced by (or contained in) the design history file (DHF). (See Design History File chapter for more details)

7.13. Quality Systems Manual: Design Verification and Validation

DESIGN VERIFICATION AND VALIDATION

Excerpt from the "Quality Systems Manual: A Small Entity Compliance Guide"
(Withdrawn from FDA website 12 December 2013)
(FDA QS Manual, 2013)

Each manufacturer shall establish and maintain procedures for verifying the device design. Design verification [820.30(f)] shall confirm that the design output meets the design input requirements. The results of the design verification, including identification of the design, method(s), the date, and the individual(s) performing the verification, shall be documented in the DHF.

Validation [820.30(g)] means confirmation by examination and provision of objective evidence that the particular requirements for a specific intended use can be consistently fulfilled.

Process validation means establishing by objective evidence that a process consistently produces a result or product meeting its predetermined specifications.

Design validation means establishing by objective evidence that device specifications conform with user needs and intended use(s).

Verification means confirmation by examination and provision of objective evidence that specified requirements have been fulfilled.

Each manufacturer shall establish and maintain procedures for validating the device design. Design validation shall be performed under defined operating conditions on initial production units, lots, or batches, or their equivalents. Design validation shall ensure that devices conform to defined user needs and intended uses and shall include testing of production units under actual or simulated use conditions. Design validation shall include software validation and risk analysis, where appropriate. The results of the design validation, including identification of the design, method(s), the date, and the individual(s) performing the validation, shall be documented in the DHF.

Design verification is always done versus specifications. Therefore, to control the specifications and increase the probability of achieving desired safety and performance characteristics, device, software, labeling, packaging and any other specifications should be complete and thoroughly reviewed before development commences. As the hardware and software designs evolve, they should be evaluated versus their current specifications.

Verification and validation should be done with test equipment calibrated and controlled according to quality system requirements. Otherwise, there is limited confidence in the data.

Verification and validation should also be done according to a written protocol(s). The protocol(s) should include defined conditions for the testing. The protocol(s) should be approved before being used. Test protocol(s) are not perfect for a design, particularly a new design. Therefore, the designers and other verification personnel carefully annotate any ongoing changes to a protocol. Likewise, the verification personnel should record technical comments about any deviations or other events that occurred during the testing. The slightest problem should not be ignored. During design reviews, the comments, notes and deviations may be as important as test data from the formal protocol(s).

Design Evaluation versus Specifications

The original design of devices and any subsequent changes should be verified by appropriate and formal laboratory, animal, and in vitro testing. Risk analysis should be conducted to identify possible hazards associated with the design. Failure Mode Effects Analysis and Fault Tree Analysis are examples of risk analysis techniques.

Appropriate laboratory and animal testing followed by analysis of the results should be

Medical Device Regulation Consulting and Training – www.Procenius.com

carefully performed before clinical testing or commercial distribution of the devices. The manufacturer should be assured that the design is safe and effective to the extent that can be determined by various scientific tests and analysis before clinical testing on humans or use by humans. For example, the electrical, thermal, mechanical, chemical, radiation, etc., safety of devices usually can be determined by laboratory tests.

Clinical testing is not needed for many substantially equivalent devices (See 21 CFR Part 807 Subpart E - Premarket Notification Procedure). Where it is needed, such as for complex substantially equivalent devices or new devices, clinical testing on humans should meet the applicable requirements in the Investigational Device Exemption (IDE) regulations (21 CFR Parts 812 and 813).

The general IDE regulation (21 CFR Part 812) exempts a manufacturer during the "premarketing phase" from the following provisions of the FD&C Act:

- Misbranding,
- Registration of the Establishment,
- Premarket Notification [510(k)],
- FDA Performance Standards,
- Premarket Approval,
- Production sections ONLY of the Good Manufacturing Practices,
- Color Additives,
- Banned Devices, and
- Restricted Devices.

Don't be misled by this list of exemptions -- being exempted from these provisions does not mean that a manufacturer may develop a new device under uncontrolled conditions and then test it on humans. Devices being clinically tested are not exempt from section 501(c) of the FD&C Act, which states that a device is adulterated if it does not meet a manufacturer's quality claims. Devices being manufactured for use in clinical studies under an IDE are exempt ONLY from the production section of the QS regulation. They are not exempt from design controls listed in 820.30. In addition, the IDE regulation has labeling requirements in 812.5 and quality assurance requirements in
812.20(b)(3) that shall be met. Further, manufacturers should remember that human subjects are also protected through the courts via product liability laws and actions. In summation, protection of manufacturer interests, human test subjects, practitioners, and patients requires that all medical devices be developed, evaluated, and manufactured under a total quality system.

Laboratory testing to force a failure takes considerable time and the "culprit" may not fail during the testing. Another evaluation technique is Failure Mode and Effects Analysis (FMEA) in which failures are assumed to occur. FMEA is useful for evaluating reliability, safety, and general quality where, for example, the evaluator assumes that:

- each component fails,
- each subsystem or subassembly fails,
- the operator makes errors, and
- the power source is interrupted and immediately restarted.

The probability of each failure actually occurring and, if it does, the resulting effect are analyzed. Then, where needed and feasible, hazards and faulty performance are designed out of the device or reduced; or compensated or prevented/reduced by interlocks, warning signs, explicit instructions, alarms, etc. Risks, of course, cannot always be removed from medical devices, but they should be known and controlled to the extent feasible with existing technology.

Failure Mode and Effects Analysis (FMEA) is a very powerful and cost-effective technique. Note that it takes very little time to assume that a component or subsystem is going to fail versus the time required to test to failure. The idea is not to promote one method above the other because a reasonable amount of both actual testing and failure mode and effects analysis should be done before a device is clinically tested and/or placed into production.

Besides using FMEA there are also other human factor and validation process techniques that can be used in developing an overall risk analysis. These techniques include: timelines, workload analysis, failure analysis, alternative calculations, testing including animal testing, auditing the design output, design reviews, demonstrations, and comparing a new design to a proven design etc. The users should be considered components when developing a fault tree and failure mode effects analysis.

All evaluation results should be reviewed by product development personnel who compare the tests and FMEA results with specifications, including safety and performance standards, to make certain that the desired level of intrinsic quality has been designed into the device. Also, the appropriate design of manufacturing processes, including validation where appropriate, is needed to assure that production can achieve the level of quality designed into the device.

Software Validation

Software is evaluated and reviewed versus the software specifications during the ongoing development of the device design. When a "final" prototype(s) is available, the software and hardware are validated to make certain manufacturer specifications for the device and process are met. Some aspects of hardware evaluation were discussed above. Aspects specific to software are covered below.

Before testing the software in actual use, the detailed code should be visually reviewed versus flow charts and specifications. All cases, especially decision points and error/limit handling, should be reviewed and the results documented.

Medical Device Regulation Consulting and Training – www.Procenius.com

In all cases, algorithms should be checked for accuracy. Recalls have occurred because algorithms were incorrectly copied from a source and, in other cases, because the source algorithm was incorrect. During the development phase, complex algorithms may need to be checked by using a test subroutine program written in a high-order language, if the operational program is written in a low-level language.

The validation program is planned and executed such that all relevant elements of the software and hardware are exercised and evaluated. The testing of software usually involves the use of an emulator and should include testing of the software in the finished device.

The testing includes normal operation of the complete device; and this phase of the validation program may be completed first to make certain that the device meets the fundamental performance, safety and labeling specifications. Concurrently or afterward, the combined system of hardware and software should be challenged with abnormal inputs and conditions. As appropriate, these inputs and conditions include such items as:

- operator errors;
- induced failure of sensors and cables or other interconnects;
- induced failure of output equipment;
- exposure to static electricity;
- power loss and restart;
- simultaneous inputs or interrupts; and,
- as appropriate, deliberate application of none, low, high, positive, negative, and extremely high input values.

The results of the software and combined device system validation are included in the design reviews.

Labeling Verification

During verification, the complete device is exercised such that all labeling, displays, and outputs are generated, reviewed, and the results documented. During the verification, all displayed prompts and instructions are checked versus the manufacturer's and FDA's labeling requirements and versus the operator manual.

Printed labeling and screen displays should be checked to see if they are directed to the user and not to the system designers, which is a common fault found in labeling. Displayed text should be short and to the point. Because displays are brief, keywords should be carefully selected to match system characteristics, yet transfer the maximum information to the user. The text of references to controls or other parts of the system should match the labeling on the device. Data, identifications, or other key information displayed should be current, complete, unambiguous, and accurate.

During verification, all prompts and instructions should be followed exactly by the device test or other operators and such action should result in correct operation of the device. Prompts and instructions should appropriately match the instructions in the operator's manual. The evaluation should include verification that any screen or other displays meet the requirements of, and have been approved per, the manufacturer's policy/procedure for design of labeling.

Patient and procedure data on printouts should be correct; therefore, printouts should undergo a verification similar to that performed for the screen or other displays. In addition, the printouts should be evaluated with respect to their "cold" information transfer characteristics. Will the printouts be quickly and clearly understood a few weeks later when the reader is not reading the displays, operating the device, or looking at the patient? All printouts should also meet the manufacturer's design control policy/procedure requirements for labeling. Likewise, patient data or other key information transmitted to a remote location should be correct; therefore, it should be checked for accuracy, completeness, and identification. Annotated copies of verified labeling, printouts, etc. and associated notes and any checklists should be placed in the design history file.

The overall device specifications usually have requirements that cover user/operator error prevention and control. Along with operator training, such errors are controlled by:

- adequate instruction manuals,
- adequate device labels,
- display of adequate prompts and correct instructions,
- status (history) reports,
- exclusion of certain erroneous inputs or actions, and
- adequate human factors design.

Also, for some devices, it may be important to control the order in which data can be entered by the operator. In emergency situations or because of distractions, it may be important to present the operator with a brief history or status report of recent actions. During the verification, the listed items should be evaluated versus the specifications, and checked for completeness and appropriate- ness. A checklist or matrix may be used to aid in the review of labeling.

Medical Device Regulation Consulting and Training – www.Procenius.com

7.14. Case Study – The Importance of Design Verification (MRI To Go Inc.)

A project manager (PM) for MRI TO GO INC. has just been given the approval to initiate the *MRI OnWheels* project. The PM quickly determines that the schedule is very aggressive. Initial planning indicates there is a significant amount of work required by his team to deliver the product on time. As the project manager tries to work different scenarios to launch on time, he notices that there are significant resources and time planned by engineering to complete design verification. He schedules a meeting with the engineering project lead (EPL) in hopes to somehow reduce some of the planned verification deliverables or activities.

The meeting with the engineering project lead does not go as planned. Initially the EPL does not budge on reducing the verification scope or deliverables. Eventually the PM and EPL narrow their options down to the following:

> **Option 1.** Keep the schedule "as is" and assume the likely scenario that the product launch will be delayed.
>
> **Option 2.** Eliminate a minimal subset of verification activities that will allow the project to get back on schedule.
>
> **Option 3.** Evaluate the planned verification activities using a risk based approach to determine if the scope of lower risk device features can be minimized.

Option 1

In this scenario the EPL gets his way and the verifications are executed as planned. As predicted by the PM the product launched six months late and the business unit misses its revenue goals for the year. In addition to the loss revenue, a competitor launches a product in direct competition to the *MRI OnWheels* and is first to market which enables them to secure major industry accounts.

Lessons Learned from Option 1

Any time an internal functional department has too much decision making power (e.g. quality, regulatory, engineering, marketing etc.), businesses will eventually have serious problems. In this case engineering was a strong influence which swayed the project manager and management not to reduce verification scope which led to a delayed launch. If this pattern is continually repeated, MRI TO GO INC. will be out of business.

Option 2

In this scenario the PM gets his way and the project progresses smoothly up until design validation is initiated. As the team takes the device into validation, they begin to realize that their product is severely inadequate. Most of the validations eventually fail and the product launch is now behind schedule by 3 months. The engineering team is tasked with investigating the cause of the validation failures.

After performing a thorough investigation, the engineering team determines that there are some fundamental design flaws that cannot easily be fixed. The news is reported to management for further review.

As management evaluates the predicament they come up with three options:

1. To avoid major design rework which could take up to a year, the product scope could be reduced which would reduce some competitive product features. This would allow for the product to launch sooner but the company would probably lose market share.

2. The company could spend the time to perform a full rework to correct all of the problems but again, they would probably lose market share.

3. They could try to perform a quick fix on some of the minor problems and "change validation strategies" so they will be more likely to pass validation the second time around.

Management decisions 1 & 2 are legitimate business decisions for which there is no right or wrong answer. Decision 3 on the other hand may be considered unethical to most people, including the FDA. "Changing validation strategy" is another word for revising requirements or approving validation strategies that they know will pass.

Lessons Learned from Option 2

- Because the decision was made to reduce the scope of verification during development, many of the critical design features were not adequately challenged to ensure all of the design input requirements were met. As a result, the final validation failed.
- Taking short cuts during verification will lead to problems in final validation.
- It takes time to do the right thing but it takes twice as long to fix problems from doing the wrong thing.
- Failing validation will often lead to a delayed launch which in turn leads to scenarios where manufacturers are pressured to make unethical decisions such as decision 3. This gets to the heart of why the FDA requires design controls. The theory is that the more effective and efficient companies are at developing designs, the more likely they will produce safe and effective products and at the same time meet their business goals. The FDA realizes that if a company continues to fall short of its business goals due to an inadequate development process, the more likely they will give in to the temptation to make unethical decisions.

Option 3

In this scenario, a balanced approach is taken which balances risk with business needs. It turns out that engineering had not taken the time to optimize the verification plan to meet the business needs. After a risk assessment was performed and additional planning was completed, it was determined that since the new product leveraged much of previously verified designs, rationales could be written to waive the need for many of the originally planned verifications.

As a result of this balanced approach, final validation passed without major issue and the product was launched within 2 weeks of the planned launch date.

Lessons Learned from Option 3

- The idea presented in scenario 3 took a little more time to develop and execute but in the end the company's business goals were achieved, a safe and effective product was validated and the company remained in compliance to FDA regulations.
- A balanced cross functional team/management decision typically results in the best decision.

7.15. Templates

Visit *Procenius.com* to download design verification protocol/report templates.

8.0 Design Validation

(Principles common to both design verification and validation are indicated by (*V&V*))

8.1. Overview

Design validation is the final comprehensive check to ensure the medical device has been designed and manufactured correctly to meet the needs of the user in a safe and effective way. Early in the design process marketing and engineers got together to translate marketing research and user needs into design requirements. The engineers used these requirements to design the device in an effort to make a device that meets the user's needs. Design validation is to confirm that the engineers got it right.

These questions will be answered through design validation.

- Were the user needs translated correctly into design requirements?
- Is the final manufactured device safe and effective?
- Does the device do what user needs it to do?

(Repeated from Design Verification chapter) It is often said that design verification ensures that the "device was designed right", and design validation ensures that the "right design was designed". Or in other words, design verification ensures that the design meets the engineering requirements and design validation ensures that the device actual does what the user needs it to do in a safe and effective way.

8.2. Principles and Models Common to Both Design Verification and Validation

There are typically a significant number of common principles and models used to implement and explain design verification and validation. Many of these common principles and models have already been presented in the Design Verification chapter. In an effort to reduce duplicating material in this chapter, those sections indicated with **(*V&V*)** in the Design Verification chapter will indicate those principles and techniques which are applicable to both design verification and validation.

Medical Device Regulation Consulting and Training – www.Procenius.com

8.3. Quick Reference Summary

TABLE 21

Purpose	Design validation is a cumulative summation of all efforts to assure that the design will conform with user needs and intended use(s), given expected variations in components, materials, manufacturing processes, and the use environment. (FDA D.C. Guidance, 2015)
Definition	Validation means confirmation by examination and provision of objective evidence that the particular requirements for a specific intended use can be consistently fulfilled. (FDA QSR , 2014) 1. Process Validation means establishing by objective evidence that a process consistently produces a result or product meeting its predetermined specifications. 2. Design Validation means establishing by objective evidence that device specifications conform with user needs and intended use(s).
Regulation	21 CFR 820.30 (g): Each manufacturer shall establish and maintain procedures for validating the device design. Design validation shall be performed under defined operating conditions on initial production units, lots, or batches, or their equivalents. Design validation shall ensure that devices conform to defined user needs and intended uses and shall include testing of production units under actual or simulated use conditions. Design validation shall include software validation and risk analysis, where appropriate. The results of the design validation, including identification

	of the design, method(s), the date, and the individual(s) performing the validation, shall be documented in the Design History File. (FDA D.C. Guidance, 2015)
Standard(s)	ISO 13485 (7.3.6) (ISO 13485, 2007)

Guidance	21 CFR 820.30 (f) (FDA)	FDA Design Control Guidance for Medical Device Manufacturers (FDA D.C. Guidance, 2015)
	ISO 13485 (7.3.6)	Medical Devices – Quality Management Systems – Guidance on the Application of ISO 13485:2003 (ISO 14969, 2004)

Timing of Design Validation Relative to Research and Development Cycle	FIGURE 36 The two humps in Figure 36 depict the relationship and the relative amount of research and development activities during the design and development cycle. The shaded area is the typical time when design validation is executed.

| | Design Verification vs. Design Validation | Design verification focuses on "Did we design the device right (correctly)?" or in other words, does the design meet or satisfy all of the design requirements so the device will perform as designed (or as intended)? Design validation focuses on, "Did we design the right device?" or in other words, does the device do what the user needs it to do safely and effectively? Does it meet their needs?

Design verification focuses on verifying the outputs as the design is progressing and validation is performed on the final medical device. So for design verification always think "verification confirms that the device is on track as development is occurring". For design validation think, "validation confirms that the final device meets the user's needs after development is completed".

"Whereas verification is a detailed examination of aspects of a design at various stages in the development, design validation is a cumulative summation of all efforts to assure the design will conform with users need and intended use(s), given expected variations in components, materials, manufacturing processes, and the use environment." (FDA D.C. Guidance, 2015) |

Design Verification vs. Design Validation

Design verification focuses on "Did we design the device right (correctly)?" or in other words, does the design meet or satisfy all of the design requirements so the device will perform as designed (or as intended)? Design validation focuses on, "Did we design the right device?" or in other words, does the device do what the user needs it to do safely and effectively? Does it meet their needs?

Design verification focuses on verifying the outputs as the design is progressing and validation is performed on the final medical device. So for design verification always think "verification confirms that the device is on track as development is occurring". For design validation think, "validation confirms that the final device meets the user's needs after development is completed".

"Whereas verification is a detailed examination of aspects of a design at various stages in the development, design validation is a cumulative summation of all efforts to assure the design will conform with users need and intended use(s), given expected variations in components, materials, manufacturing processes, and the use environment." (FDA D.C. Guidance, 2015)

Comparison of Design Verification vs. Design Validation Requirements/Activities

	Design Verification	Design Validation
May be performed on prototypes, early designs modules, sub-systems or components (initial verification)	X	
Confirms that the design output meets the design input requirements as the device is being developed.	X	
Is typically performed throughout product development on interim and final design outputs.	X	
May be performed in a lab or bench top setting (actual	X	

	conditions not required).		
	Performed under defined operating conditions on initial production units, lots or batches or their equivalents.		X
	Ensure device conforms to defined user needs and intended uses.		X
	Shall include testing of production units under actual or simulated use conditions.		X
	Shall include software validation.		X
	Shall include risk analysis where appropriate.		X
	The results of the design (validation/verification), method(s), the date, and the individual(s) performing the (validation/verification) shall be documented in the DHF.	X	X
Process of Planning and Executing Design Validation	1. Approve User Needs 2. Create and Approve a Validation Master Plan (VMP) (Optional) 3. Create and Approve Validation Protocols 4. Train Personnel Executing Validation 5. Prepare the Design Output / Medical Device 6. Execute Validation 7. Create Validation Report 8. Validation Results Should Be Reviewed 9. Approve Validation Report 10. Create Validation Master Report (VMR)(optional)		

	21 CFR 820.30 (E) states (FDA D.C. Guidance, 2015): *"As a general rule, the [design review and validation] sequence is: verification, review, validation, review."* So typically design validation is executed and the results of validation are reviewed. The type and method of review is dependent upon on the complexity of the device and size of the organization. In typical organizations, an effective review will include the results from the design validation documented in individual reports or a summary of validation results listed in a validation master plan. Reviewers attending formal design reviews should include qualified individuals in all functional areas that may have critical input to the validation results being reviewed.
Design Review	**Typical Reviewers** <u>Cross Functional Reviewers</u> Quality Assurance* R&D / Engineering* Marketing Human Factors Regulatory Affairs Project Management Clinical Specialist (physician, nurse, clinician, etc.) Independent Reviewer* Other Stake Holders

Medical Device Regulation Consulting and Training – www.Procenius.com

Deliverable(s)	<ul><li>Protocol</li><li>Report</li><li>Supporting Data</li><li>Training Documentation</li><li>Protocol Deviations (if applicable)</li></ul>
Approval **(Protocols and Reports)**	Approval of design validation protocol and report (and validation master plan/report) typically includes cross functional team members. The team should have the clinical expertise to provide input as to how the validation should be executed in a clinical setting and how to interpret the results. Approvals should be documented manually with signature and date or electronically to be in compliance with 21 CFR part 11. **Typical Protocol or Report Approvers** Cross Functional Approvers Quality Assurance* R&D / Engineering* Marketing Human Factors Regulatory Affairs Clinical Specialist (physician, nurse, clinician, etc.) Other Stake Holders
Revisions	Design validation protocols should be revised and updated as needed to adapt to changes in design validation strategy. Design validation reports (and validation master report) will not

Medical Device Regulation Consulting and Training – www.Procenius.com

	typically be revised unless the report is used as an ongoing compilation of multiple validations such as in a validation master report. In some cases if validations fail, the same report should be revised to reflect the latest results of the same validation.
Best Practices	• Use a pre-approved validation protocol and a post approved report (results) • Validation and Verification Method Decisions Require Risk vs. Benefit Analysis
Templates	Visit *Procenius.com* to download validation protocol/report templates.

8.4. Regulation (21 CFR 820.30 (g)) - Design Validation

Each manufacturer shall establish and maintain procedures for validating the device design. Design validation shall be performed under defined operating conditions on initial production units, lots, or batches, or their equivalents. Design validation shall ensure that devices conform to defined user needs and intended uses and shall include testing of production units under actual or simulated use conditions. Design validation shall include software validation and risk analysis, where appropriate. The results of the design validation, including identification of the design, method(s), the date, and the individual(s) performing the validation, shall be documented in the Design History File. (FDA D.C. Guidance, 2015)

8.5. Definitions 21 CFR 820.3 (y&z) – [Design] Validation

(y) *Specification* means any requirement with which a product, process, service, or other activity must conform.

(z) *Validation* means confirmation by examination and provision of objective evidence that the particular requirements for a specific intended use can be consistently fulfilled.

1. *Process Validation* means establishing by objective evidence that a process consistently produces a result or product meeting its predetermined specifications.

2. *Design Validation* means establishing by objective evidence that device specifications conform with user needs and intended use(s).

(FDA D.C. Guidance, 2015)

8.6. Design Control Guidance Document (for 21 CFR 820.30 (g))

Whereas verification is a detailed examination of aspects of a design at various stages in the development, design validation is a cumulative summation of all efforts to assure that the design will conform with user needs and intended use(s), given expected variations in components, materials, manufacturing processes, and the use environment.

8.6.1. Validation Planning

Planning for validation should begin early in the design process. The performance characteristics that are to be assessed should be identified, and validation methods and acceptance criteria should be established. For complex designs, a schedule of validation activities and organizational or individual responsibilities will facilitate maintaining control over the process. The validation plan should be reviewed for appropriateness, completeness, and to ensure that user needs and intended uses are addressed.

8.6.2. Validation Review

Validation may expose deficiencies in the original assumptions concerning user needs and intended uses. A formal review process should be used to resolve any such deficiencies. As with verification, the perception of a deficiency might be judged insignificant or erroneous, or a corrective action may be required.

Medical Device Regulation Consulting and Training – www.Procenius.com

8.6.3. Validation Methods

Many medical devices do not require clinical trials. However, all devices require clinical evaluation and should be tested in the actual or simulated use environment as a part of validation. This testing should involve devices which are manufactured using the same methods and procedures expected to be used for ongoing production. While testing is always a part of validation, additional validation methods are often used in conjunction with testing, including analysis and inspection methods, compilation of relevant scientific literature, provision of historical evidence that similar designs and/or materials are clinically safe, and full clinical investigations or clinical trials.

Some manufacturers have historically used their best assembly workers or skilled lab technicians to fabricate test articles, but this practice can obscure problems in the manufacturing process. It may be beneficial to ask the best workers to evaluate and critique the manufacturing process by trying it out, but pilot production should simulate as closely as possible the actual manufacturing conditions.

Validation should also address product packaging and labeling. These components of the design may have significant human factors implications, and may affect product performance in unexpected ways. For example, packaging materials have been known to cause electrostatic discharge (ESD) failures in electronic devices. If the unit under test is delivered to the test site in the test engineer's briefcase, the packaging problem may not become evident until after release to market.

Validation should include simulation of the expected environmental conditions, such as temperature, humidity, shock and vibration, corrosive atmospheres, etc. For some classes of device, the environmental stresses encountered during shipment and installation far exceed those encountered during actual use, and should be addressed during validation.

Particular care should be taken to distinguish among customers, users, and patients to ensure that validation addresses the needs of all relevant parties. For a consumer device, the customer, user, and patient may all be the same person. At the other extreme, the person who buys the device may be different from the person who routinely uses it on patients in a clinical setting. Hospital administrators, biomedical engineers, health insurance underwriters, physicians, nurses, medical technicians, and patients have distinct and sometimes competing needs with respect to a device design.

8.6.4. Validation Documentation

Validation is a compilation of the results of all validation activities. For a complex design, the detailed results may be contained in a variety of separate documents and summarized in a validation report. Supporting information should be explicitly referenced in the validation report and either included as an appendix or available in the design history file.

Medical Device Regulation Consulting and Training – www.Procenius.com

8.7. Timing of Design Validation Activities and Deliverables

The FDA specifies that design validation should follow successful design verification. The following graphical models give some clarity as to when design validation typically begins and ends relative to research and development activities.

The two humps in Figure 38 depict the relationship and the relative amount of research and development activities during the design and development cycle. The shaded area is the typical time when design validation is planned and executed.

FIGURE 38

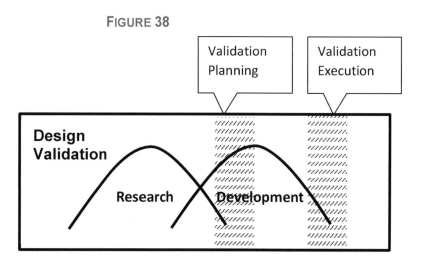

8.8. Interpretation & Application (21 CFR 820.30 (g))

When the FDA states *"Each manufacturer shall establish and maintain procedures for validating the device design.",* they are saying that the manufacturer of the design must have a documented procedure(s) that defines the "what, who, how, why and when" of how validation is performed. The FDA wants to ensure that a standard design validation procedure has been created, vetted, reviewed and approved. The procedure must be "maintained" (in other words revised and updated) as required to be current with the intended and approved design validation activities. Typically this procedure is assigned to the department that is responsible for product development such as (Development Teams or Engineering).

8.8.1. Validation Should be Performed Under Defined Operating Conditions

"Design validation shall be performed under defined operating conditions…". This sentence is saying that the device being used for design validation should be manufactured under defined operating conditions (controlled) and the actual design validation activity should be executed under defined operating conditions (i.e. using an approved protocol) which typically specifies:

- Environment
- Qualifications of people performing the validation
- Method
- Identification of the device being validated
- Sample size and sample size rationale
- Acceptance criteria

8.8.2. Validation - Perform on Initial Production Units, Lots or Batches

"...on initial production units, lots, or batches, or their equivalents". The intent of this sentence is to require design validation to be performed on products which were produced on production equipment by production workers in the production environment by a defined, approved and validated process or procedure. The FDA wants to make sure final acceptance of the product is executed on the final version of the device design and from the final validated manufacturing process. The FDA is well aware of all of the potential risks involved during design transfer between R&D and a production environment. There are endless possibilities of things that can go wrong when the design is taken out of the experienced hands of the developers to the high volume production world. The underlined phrase from the guidance below indicates that design validation includes consideration for "...variations in components, materials, manufacturing processes..." (FDA D.C. Guidance, 2015). Using initial production units, lots or batches supports this statement. This statement also indicates that design validation should be performed on devices produced from a validated process.

The Quality Systems Regulation Preamble states:

Comment 80

"FDA understands that it is not always practical to conduct clinical studies on finished production units and, therefore, the use of prototypes in clinical studies is acceptable. When prototype devices are used on humans they must be verified as safe to the maximum extent feasible. Final design validation, however, cannot be done on prototypes because the actual devices produced and distributed are seldom the same as the research and development prototypes. The final verification and validation, therefore, must include the testing of actual production devices under actual or simulated use conditions." (FDA Preamble, 2015)

This sentence of the regulation [*"...on initial production units, lots, or batches, or their equivalents"...*] is really straight forward except the FDA throws in *"...or their equivalents."* This phrase does allow manufacturers some flexibility during validation but in some cases manufacturers have probably leveraged this phrase well beyond what the FDA originally intended.

The Quality Systems Regulation Preamble states:

Comment 81

"When equivalent devices are used in the final design validation, the manufacturer must document in detail how the device was manufactured and how the manufacturing is similar to and possibly different from initial production. Where there are differences, the manufacturer must justify why design validation results are valid for the production units, lots, or batches. Manufacturers should not use prototypes developed in the laboratory or machine shop as test units to meet these requirements. Prototypes may differ from the finished production devices. During research and development, conditions for building prototypes are typically better controlled and personnel more knowledgeable about what needs to be done and how to do it than are regular production personnel. When going from laboratory to scale-up production, standards, methods, and procedures may not be properly transferred, or additional manufacturing processes may be added. Often, changes not reflected in the prototype are made in the device to facilitate the manufacturing process, and these may adversely affect device functioning and user interface characteristics. Proper testing of devices that are produced using the same methods and procedures as those to be used in routine production will prevent the distribution and subsequent recall of many unacceptable medical devices." (FDA Preamble, 2015)

"Equivalents" are typically devices used for validation that were not manufactured from the validated production process but from a process (or method) which is "equivalent" to the production process. Manufacturers should provide the documented rationale that describes how the equivalent devices were found to be production equivalent, e.g., assembly procedures and test protocols, etc., along with results and/or letter to the design history file outlining the rationale for equivalence. Particular care must be taken to document rationales when personnel other than routine production personnel are utilized to build devices that will be used for validation.

Where manufacturers get into trouble is when they perform design validation with devices before the production manufacturing process has been validated or even established. The intent behind this strategy is to allow the development team the option to validate the design in parallel or before the process validation (which typically takes significant time) is performed to shorten development time and launch the product sooner. While in theory this strategy would be in compliance, in practice it is usually not.

The biggest problem with this approach is that there is often a significant difference between the process (or methods) used to produce the validation devices (pre-process validation/design transfer) and the process that will be used in production. If this happens, development teams will then attempt to prove equivalency by comparing critical features or functionality between the two devices through analysis or testing. Unfortunately this approach has increased risk because development teams cannot always possibly foresee all of the potential differences between devices manufactured by two different production methods. At this point revalidation of the design using devices from a validated process is the next prudent step.

It is situations like this, after manufacturers have invested significant resources into design validation that they may be tempted to unjustly rationalize that revalidation is not required. Under most circumstances this would not be in compliance with FDA regulations and considered unethical.

8.8.3. Design Validation: Conformance to User Needs and Intended Uses

"Design validation shall ensure that devices conform to defined user needs and intended uses*...", this sentence in the regulation confirms that developers "designed the right" device. "Conforming to defined user needs and intended uses" means, "does the device do what the user needs it to do safely and effectively? Does it meet their needs?" These questions are answered by the results of design validation.

IMPORTANT CONCEPTS*

Intended Use vs. Indications for Use

There is often confusion in the medical device industry between intended use and indications for use. The best definitions which distinguish between the two terms is found in 21 CFR 814.20(b)(3)(i),

Intended Use - means the general purpose of the device or its function, and encompasses the indications for use.

Indications for Use... describes the disease or condition the device will diagnose, treat, prevent, cure or mitigate, including a description of the patient population for which the device is intended.

8.8.4. Traditional Validation and Verification Model (V&V Model) (*V&V*)

Those new to design controls may find it difficult to understand how validation relates to verification, design inputs, outputs, etc. Figure 39 shows a traditional V&V model which depicts the abstract relationship between User Needs – Design Validation – Medical Device and Design Input Requirements – Design Verification – Design Outputs.

FIGURE 39

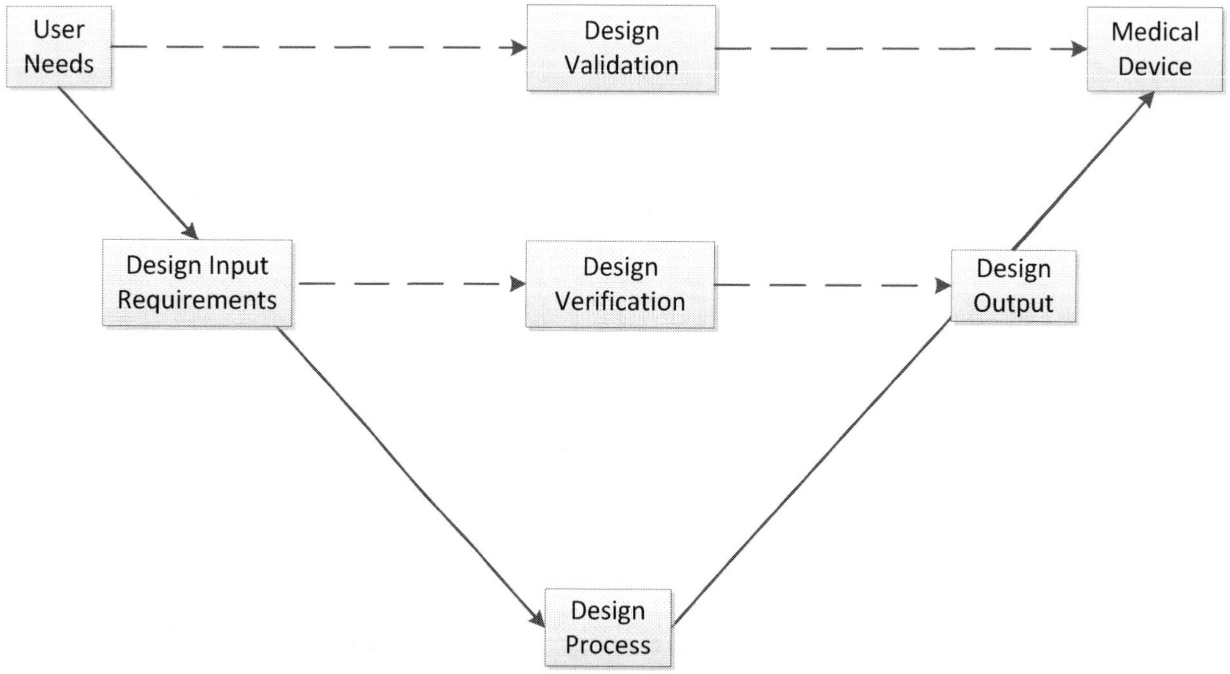

Medical Device Regulation Consulting and Training – www.Procenius.com

8.8.5. Complex V&V Model with Sub-System Verification (*V&V*)

Figure 40 is a variation of the traditional V&V model from complex medical devices which depicts the relationship between system level requirements and verification with sub-system requirements and verification.

FIGURE 40

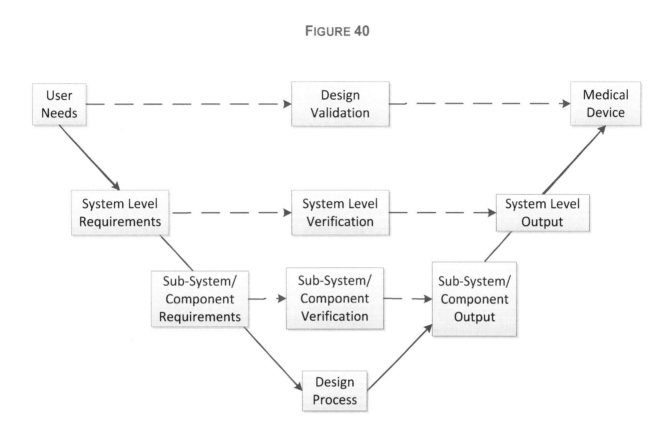

8.8.6. Validation of Production Units Under Actual or Simulated Use Conditions

"...and shall include testing of production units under actual or simulated use conditions." Again, the FDA emphasizes that design validation should be performed using "production units". They also make it clear that validation should be performed as it actually will be used in its intended environment by its intended users. Clinical trials are typically the ultimate method used for validating device safety and effectiveness of class III devices for which a PMA (Premarket Approval) is required. Class II devices, which are determined to be substantially equivalent, often do not require clinical trials and may only require reference to design verification or validation study results.

Medical Device Regulation Consulting and Training – www.Procenius.com

Quality Systems Regulation Preamble states:

Comment 81

"In addition, finished devices must be tested for performance under actual conditions of use or simulated use conditions in the actual or simulated environment in which the device is expected to be used. The simulated use testing provision no longer requires that the testing be performed on the first three production runs. However, samples must be taken from units, lots, or batches that were produced using the same specifications, production and quality system methods, procedures, and equipment that will be used for routine production. FDA considers this a critical element of the design validation. The requirement to conduct simulated use testing of finished devices is found in the original CGMP in Sec. 820.160, as part of finished device inspection. This requirement has been moved to Sec. 820.30(g) because FDA believes that simulated use testing at this point is more effective in ensuring that only safe and effective devices are produced. Manufacturers must also conduct such tests when they make changes in the device design or the manufacturing process that could affect safety or effectiveness as required in the original CGMP in Sec. 820.100(a)(2). The extent of testing conducted should be governed by the risk(s) the device will present if it fails. FDA considers these activities essential for ensuring that the manufacturing process does not adversely affect the device.

Design validation may also be necessary in earlier stages, prior to product completion, and multiple validations may need to be performed if there are different intended uses. Proper design validation cannot occur without following all the requirements set forth in the design control section of the regulation." (FDA Preamble, 2015)

In some instances "simulated use conditions" are acceptable when a reasonable and logical rationale can be supported with objective evidence that a simulated use condition is an acceptable substitute for the actual conditions. As justification for using simulated use conditions, a risk vs. benefit analysis should be performed to show that the relative risk of the simulated condition is low. As always, the justification should be documented in the design history file.

8.8.7. Design Validation Shall Include Software Validation

"Design validation shall include software validation……., where appropriate."
Manufacturers should take note that the FDA specifies that software validation should be included as part of design controls in this section which is a rarely specific section of the

Medical Device Regulation Consulting and Training – www.Procenius.com

regulation which should not be taken lightly. FDA has great concern over software validation and has high expectations for its implementation.

The Quality Systems Regulation Preamble states:

Comment 83

"Software must be validated when it is a part of the finished device. FDA believes that this control is always needed, given the unique nature of software, to assure that software will perform as intended and will not impede safe operation by the user. Risk analysis must be conducted for the majority of devices subject to design controls and is considered to be an essential requirement for medical devices under this regulation, as well as under ISO/CD 13485 and EN 46001. FDA has replaced the phrase ``where applicable" with ``where appropriate" for consistency with the rest of the regulation." (FDA Preamble, 2015)

Even though software validation is only briefly mentioned in this section of the regulation and the preamble, there is extensive discussion and guidance around software verification discussed in FDA guidance, *"General Principles of Software Validation; Final Guidance for Industry and FDA Staff"* (FDA SW Validation, 2012). This guidance explains in great detail the FDA's expectations and suggested software validation methodologies. This guidance is very much aligned with the design control guidance with respect to design reviews, verification and validation etc. but also addresses concepts and issues which are inherently unique in software development and validation. The scope of this guidance includes not only device software but also medical device manufacturing and quality systems software used by medical device manufacturers.

The "….**where appropriate"** should be interpreted as if your device contains or uses software. It is not suggesting that software validation is not required in some circumstances. Some level of software validation is always required dependent upon risk.

8.8.8. Design Validation Shall Include Risk Analysis

"Design validation shall include... risk analysis, where appropriate." Final risk analysis should be performed during the validation phase to ensure the risk controls put in place actually work to mitigate risks and do not cause any adverse effects from implementing the risk controls

In reality and in application, the FDA expects risk analysis to be a very integral part of medical device development. There are a few places the FDA addresses risk analysis for medical device development which are found in: 21 CFR 820.30 (G), Design Control Guidance and the Quality System Regulation Preamble.

FDA Design Control Guidance states (FDA D.C. Guidance, 2015)**:**

> **"RISK MANAGEMENT AND DESIGN CONTROLS.** Risk management is the systematic application of management policies, procedures, and practices to the tasks of identifying, analyzing, controlling, and monitoring risk. It is intended to be a framework within which experience, insight, and judgment are applied to successfully manage risk. It is included in this guidance because of its effect on the design process.
>
> Risk management begins with the development of the design input requirements. As the design evolves, new risks may become evident. To systematically identify and, when necessary, reduce these risks, the risk management process is integrated into the design process. In this way, unacceptable risks can be identified and managed earlier in the design process when changes are easier to make and less costly."

The Quality Systems Regulation Preamble states:

Comment 83

"Risk analysis must be conducted for the majority of devices subject to design controls and is considered to be an essential requirement for medical devices under this regulation, as well as under ISO/CD 13485 and EN 46001. ….FDA believes that sufficient domestic and international guidelines are available to provide assistance to manufacturers for the validation of software and risk analysis." (FDA Preamble, 2015)

"…When conducting a risk analysis, manufacturers are expected to identify possible hazards associated with the design in both normal and fault conditions. The risks associated with the hazards, including those resulting from user error, should then be calculated in both normal and fault conditions. If any risk is judged unacceptable, it should be reduced to acceptable levels by the appropriate means, for example, by redesign or warnings. An important part of risk analysis is ensuring that changes made to eliminate or minimize hazards do not introduce new hazards. Tools for conducting such analyses include Failure Mode Effect Analysis and Fault Tree Analysis, among others." (FDA Preamble, 2015)

As referenced in comment 83 of the QSR Preamble, international guidelines and standards are widely accepted in the medical device industry such as ISO 14971 (Risk Management System for Medical Devices). Compliance to this standard is typically acceptable and is frankly expected by most FDA inspectors.

Again as mentioned before, the *"....***where appropriate"** should be interpreted as where risk analysis should be applied in the development process. It is not suggesting that risk analysis is not required under some circumstances. Some level of risk analysis is always required.

As previously explained, a final risk analysis should be performed as part of design validation. (see the Risk Analysis chapter for more commentary on the FDA's expectations for risk analysis and interpretation of ISO 14971)

8.8.9.   Design Validation Shall Be Documented in the Design History File

*When the FDA says…"***The results of the design validation including identification of the design, method(s), the date, and the individual(s) performing the verification, shall be documented in the Design History File."***,* they are saying that details of the validation needs to be documented. As the FDA is known for saying, "If it isn't documented, it didn't happen". It is best practice[BP1] and industry standard (and expected by the FDA) to use a pre-approved validation protocol and a post approved report (results) as diagramed in Figure 41. Pre-approval of the protocol before executing validation ensures that questionable results are not considered after the validation was performed. The FDA realizes that developers are more likely to be less bias and will make decisions more objectively about acceptance criteria if determined, documented and approved **prior** to performing and seeing the results of the validation.

FIGURE 41

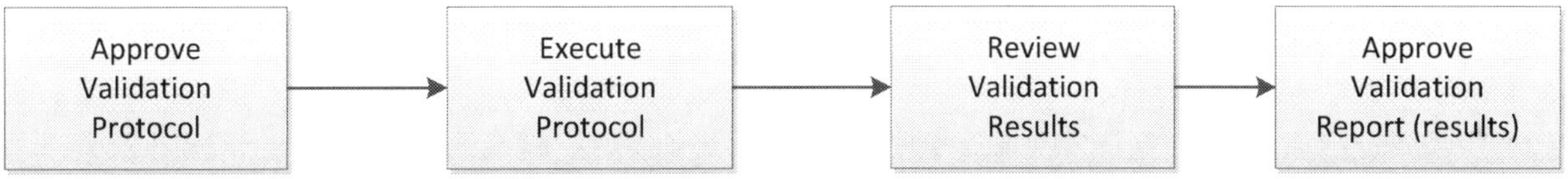

| Approve Validation Protocol | → | Execute Validation Protocol | → | Review Validation Results | → | Approve Validation Report (results) |

#1 Best Practice – Use a pre-approved validation protocol and a post approved report (results).

FDA expects a pre-approved protocol (including acceptance criteria) **before** validation is executed. A post approval report of the results is also expected which provides objective evidence of the validation pass/fail status. "If it isn't documented, it didn't happen".

8.9. Design Verification vs. Design Validation (*V&V*)

See the Design Verification chapter for a detailed explanation of the difference between design verification and validation.

8.10. Step by Step Process for Planning and Executing Design Validation (*V&V*)

See the Design Verification chapter for detailed steps for performing design verification and validation.

8.11. Design Validation Methods

The FDA Design Control Guidance states (FDA D.C. Guidance, 2015)**:**

> *"**VALIDATION METHODS.** Many medical devices do not require clinical trials. However, all devices require clinical evaluation and should be tested in the actual or simulated use environment as a part of validation. This testing should involve devices which are manufactured using the same methods and procedures expected to be used for ongoing production. While testing is always a part of validation, additional validation methods are often used in conjunction with testing, including analysis and inspection methods, compilation of relevant scientific literature, provision of historical evidence that similar designs and/or materials are clinically safe, and full clinical investigations or clinical trials.* (FDA D.C. Guidance, 2015)

Just as with design verification, development teams have different avenues in which they can take to validate a device. In addition to the three methods stated in the design verification guidance (testing, inspection and analysis), the design validation guidance includes: compilation of relevant scientific literature, historical evidence of similar designs and/or full clinical investigations or clinical trials.

Validation activities can include the following activities: Clinical trial studies through an IRB review board, 510k/PMA historical database search for predicate devices, stability studies on both the packaging and product, literature search (journal reviews), review of labeling, labels, packaging and product history, simulated testing, performance tests, functional tests, biocompatibility tests.

Important Points

- Design validation should be performed for each relevant party (patient, health care worker, etc) and for each intended use. Design validation should address the design outputs of labeling and packaging

- Risk analysis must be performed during the validation phase as well as the verification phase to make sure the solutions/ design controls actually worked to mitigate risk and did not cause additional risk.

- Software used to control manufacturing processes (and device) needs to be validated. It may start in parallel with other development activities but should finish up in validation.

Medical Device Regulation Consulting and Training – www.Procenius.com

- Design validation is complete when clinical validations is completed. Clinical validation is not just a clinical trial. It may include safety and effectiveness testing, 510k reviews, literature searches,

- Design validation may expose deficiencies in original assumptions regarding user needs or intended uses, if so, discrepancies must be addressed and outputs should be changed to address the discrepancy.

IMPORTANT
Risk vs. Resource Trade Off

It is often assumed that the "best method" for performing design validation is an extensive clinical trial that is performed in the actual use conditions by the intended users. While in theory this may seem like the "best" method most of the time, in practice it may not be. The key thing to remember about either design validation or design verification is that there is always a risk and resource/time trade off when determining what validation or verification method should be used. Some may say that to minimize risk a clinical trial should always be performed but what would be the consequence of the trial? Could it delay launch of the product? Would it therefore delay patient access to new life saving technology that would have others come to market sooner if an alternative, yet safe and effective validation method was chosen? Would unnecessary clinical trials drive up the cost of the device and limit what patients have access to the technology or prevent the manufacturer from marketing the device? These are all questions that should be considered when determining the best validation method.

The biocompatibility requirement from the Design Verification chapter is a clear example where previous documented literature can be used to justify not having to include biocompatibility testing during design verification or validation. In this case the scalpel was designed to use a specific stainless steels that has been thoroughly proven through many prior clinical trials to be biocompatible. As in this case and in many other cases, developers should always consider the risk versus benefits[BP2] when deciding which validation methods should be used to bring new life saving technology to patients as soon as possible yet ensuring its safety and effectiveness.

> **#2 Best Practice – Validation and Verification Method Decisions Require Risk vs. Benefit Analysis**
>
> Developers should always consider the risk versus benefits when deciding which validation methods should be used to bring new life saving technology to patients as soon as possible yet ensuring its safety and effectiveness.

Compilation of Relevant Scientific Literature

A compilation of relevant scientific literature can make a strong case for not having to perform clinical trials or validation testing when the user needs being validated are relatively straight forward (e.g. previously validated materials). If scientific literature is cited, there should be sufficient evidence to truly validate the device. The stronger the similarities between the device being validated and the reference literature, the stronger the case will be for justifying this method to the FDA during an inspection.

Additional Validation Methods (*V&V*)

See the Design Verification chapter where these methods are discussed in greater detail. The principles and implementation practices apply to both design verification and validation.

- Validation by Inspection
- Validation by Analysis
- Validation by Test
- Rationale

8.11.1. Design Validation Examples

Ultimately the best way to understand design validation is by example or application. Table 22 gives examples of how the design progresses from user needs all the way through device validation.

The letters and numbers listed in Table 22 are defined in Table 23 below

TABLE 22

User Needs	Design Input Requirements	Design Process	Design Output	Verification Method	Design Verification Examples	Validation Method Examples
A	1	11	17	23	33	J
B	2	12	18	24	34	K
C	3	13	19	25	35	L
D	4	14	20	26	36	M
E	5	15	21	27	37	N
F	6			28	38	O
	7			29	39	
G	8	16	22	30	40	P
H	9			31	41	Q
I	10			32	42	R

TABLE 23

A	The MRI machine shall operate using a standard 120V outlet.
B	The MRI machine shall be able to be transported through standard hospital doors and operating suites. Doors (6'8" H X 96" W); Aisles: 5' W
C	The catheter shall allow an industry standard dialysis machine to pump 6 pints of blood in 4 hours.

D	The x-ray machine shall provide direct user access from the main display screen for the three most frequently used features.
E	The x-ray machine shall not require maintenance or repair for 1 year.
F	The scalpel shall be able to cut through muscle, tendons, and ligaments without causing damage to the scalpel.
G	The scalpel shall be able to be reused after cleaning and sterilization.
H	The scalpel shall not cause any adverse effects when in contact with internal or external body tissue.
I	A surgical scalpel shall weigh more than 0.5 but no more than 2 ounces.
J	The system is validated by having a clinician plug in the machine, turn on the power and take an MRI.
K	The system is validated by having a clinician transport the MRI machine through the halls of a hospital and into the operating suite with <u>Doors</u> (6'8" H X 96" W) and <u>Aisles:</u> 5' W.
L	The catheter is validated by identifying the most frequently used dialysis machines and having a clinician execute numerous dialysis cycles. Confirmation of the time and amount of blood will be measured.
M	Validation in this case is simply documenting that the device has the three specified features on the main interface page as indicated by the market research and user needs.
N	For practicality sake, validation will rely upon the results from verification testing. A rationale will be written to explain how the accelerated reliability testing as demonstrated in verification is adequate to fulfill validation. Even though this is not executed in a real clinical environment, it is in a simulated environment and could be considered design validation.
O	A clinician will use the scalpel on a cadaver or during animal trials.
P	Validation will leverage previously performed cleanliness verification.
Q	Validation will leverage previously performed biocompatibility verifications performed on the same material (440C).

Medical Device Regulation Consulting and Training – www.Procenius.com

R	Validation in this case is simply weighing the scalpel and confirming that the weight is acceptable to the user.
1	The MRI machine's electrical system shall operate at 120V at less than 16 amps.
2	The overall size of the MRI machine shall be less than 9.5'(long) X 4' 8" (wide) X 6' 6"ft (high)
3	The dialysis catheter shall have a flow rate of 400 ml per minute at 10psi.
4	The x-ray machine's software system shall display options to operate fluoroscopy, still image and deep tissue images from the main interface screen.
5	The x-ray machines articulating arm shall function as intended through 10,000 cycles at 360 degree rotations.
6	A surgical scalpel shall support a bending load greater than 20 lbs. force.
7	A surgical scalpel shall support an axial load (resistance to buckling) greater than 10 lbs. force.
8	A surgical scalpel shall be made from materials that can conform to ASTM E2314 (cleanliness standards).
9	A surgical scalpel shall be made from materials that are biocompatible as determined by ISO-10993.
10	A surgical scalpel shall weigh more than 0.5 ounces but no more than 4 ounce lbs.
11	Components such as motors, actuators and LEDs rated for 120V that will meet functional requirements will be specified but will not exceed a total of 16 amps during operation. The design process will include design iterations, informal bench testing, research and prototyping.
12	A 3D design envelope that will be no greater than 9.5' (long) X 4' 8" (wide) X 6' 6"ft (high) will be defined in a CAD system. The sub-systems and components will be designed and specified to operate within the required maximum design envelope.

13	An iterative flow analysis to determine the minimum internal cross sectional area required to meet the flow requirement will be performed. Other requirements will also have to be considered that will drive material type, the external diameter and profile of the catheter extrusion.
14	The software developers will develop the code for the main interface page of the software such that all required image types are available from the main page.
15	Components and materials that are rated for high reliability (high cycles) applications to meet the design requirement will be identified and integrated as part of the design.
16	Multiple design iterations are evaluated with various combinations of materials, features, components, and geometries. All compounding requirements are considered during design: weight, strength (axial and bending loads), biocompatibility and cleaning. A 0.25 in. diameter cylindrical shafted design using 440C stainless steel has been determined to be the optimal design.
17	Once a viable design has been identified, the components and configuration of the design will be documented. A bill of materials (list of all components) and an electrical schematic (defines the configuration and layout of the components and wiring) are the design outputs.
18	The design envelope will be defined in a 3D CAD system and will be electronically stored as a 3D model. The detail of the design will be stored as a 2D drawing and bill of materials. The CAD files, drawings and bill of materials are the design outputs.
19	The final cross sectional geometry and material will be defined in a 3D CAD system and will be electronically stored as a 3D model. The detail of the design will be stored as a 2D drawing and bill of materials. The CAD files, drawings and bill of materials are the design outputs.
20	The software code will define the image display information that will meet the image requirement. The software code is therefore the output of the software design effort. Any documentation that supports the software code will also be part of the design output.
21	The design of the articulating arm using the high cycle components and materials will be documented in a 3D CAD system or on drawings.
22	The design of the scalpel and material will be documented in a 3D CAD system or on drawings.

23	Test
24	Analysis
25	Test
26	Inspection
27	Test
28	Analysis
29	Analysis
30	Inspection
31	Inspection
32	Analysis
33	The system is tested by measuring the power draw by the system during operation. Verification passes if the power draw is less than 16 amps @ 120V.
34	For simplicity, verification can be performed by analysis. The drawings or 3D model can be used to evaluate if the design will meet this requirement. (This could also be performed by testing (measuring) the actual system.)
35	Even though modern fluid dynamic analysis software is very advanced, there is sufficient variability in fluid viscosity, extrusion friction forces and variability in extrusion geometry to warrant testing the catheter. The catheter is flow tested to ensure the catheter can meet the 400 ml flow requirement at 10psi.
36	Verification is executed by confirming that the main interface screen displays options for operating fluoroscopy, still images and deep tissue images.
37	Verification should be performed by testing. Most moderate to complex designs with reliability requirements should be tested. Interaction between unique materials, components, and the intended design application make it very difficult if not impossible to accurately predict the end of the design's functional life due to

Medical Device Regulation Consulting and Training – www.Procenius.com

	wear, creep, corrosion or fatigue.
38	Verification by analysis can be easily justified because the geometry of a standard cylindrical shaped scalpel can be easily and accurately analyzed using a thoroughly proven moment formula for loads causing stress from bending.
39	Verification by analysis can be easily justified because the geometry of a standard cylindrical shaped scalpel can be easily and accurately analyzed using a thoroughly proven buckling formula for axial loads.
40	Verification by inspection can be easily justified because 440C stainless steel is a common material that has been previously proven to meet ASTM E2314 cleanliness standards.
41	Verification by inspection can be easily justified because 440C stainless steel is a common material that has been previously proven to meet ISO 10993 biocompatibility standards.
42	Verification by analysis can be easily justified because the geometry of a standard cylindrical shaped scalpel can be easily and accurately analyzed using a simple density to weight derivation or by using a validated CAD software to verify the weight.

8.12. Design Validation Planning

The FDA Design Control Guidance states:

"Planning for validation should begin early in the design process. The performance characteristics that are to be assessed should be identified, and validation methods and acceptance criteria should be established. For complex designs, a schedule of validation activities and organizational or individual responsibilities will facilitate maintaining control over the process. The validation plan should be reviewed for appropriateness, completeness, and to ensure that user needs and intended uses are addressed." (FDA D.C. Guidance, 2015)

As mentioned in the Design Verification chapter, a validation master plan is typically the document used to plan all verification and validation activities which will typically include the elements listed in the guidance.

8.13. Design Validation Includes Process Validation

The concept of process validation being a part of design validation may seem foreign to some developers. After all, they are in separate sections of the regulation, right? One validates the design requirements to user needs and process validation ensures that a process (usually manufacturing the device) can be performed "with a high degree of assurance".

The FDA Design Control Guidance states:

"... design validation is a <u>cumulative summation</u> of all efforts to assure that the design will conform with user needs and intended use(s), <u>given expected variations in components, materials, manufacturing processes</u>, and the use environment. (FDA D.C. Guidance, 2015)

The key phrases here are "cumulative summation" ..."given expected variations in components, material, manufacturing processes"..... . So this can clearly be interpreted as process validation being one of those "efforts" to show that the design *"will conform with user needs and intended use(s), <u>given expected variations in components, materials, manufacturing processes,</u>...".* So from this interpretation the process validation is clearly a sub-activity of design validation.

There is additional evidence to support this from the regulation which states, *"Design validation shall ensure that devices conform to defined user needs and intended uses and shall <u>include testing of production units</u> under actual or simulated use conditions".*

And,

"Design validation shall be performed under defined operating conditions on <u>initial production units, lots, or batches,</u> or their equivalents."

So these excerpts from the design validation regulation indicate that design validation should be performed using "production units" and since production processes should be validated, this

Medical Device Regulation Consulting and Training – www.Procenius.com

inherently implies that devices used for design validation should have been produced by a process which has been validated. The only way manufacturers can avoid having to use design validation devices from a process which has been validated is by invoking the *"...or equivalents"* clause from the regulation as previously explained in this chapter under the *Interpretation and Application* section.

The relationship between design validation and process validation is further illustrated by Figure 42. In this figure, inputs to process validation include the typical installation qualification (IQ), operational qualification (OQ) and process performance qualification (PQ) but another input that should not be forgotten is the *product performance qualification (PPQ)*. IQ, OQ and PQ will be discussed in more depth in the process validation chapter, but it is important at this point to understand the difference between process qualification and product performance qualification. The following excerpts from FDA's "Medical Device Quality Systems Manual: A Small Entity Compliance Guide" (FDA QS Manual, 2013) best defines the differences and relationship between these two activities.

Process Performance Qualification (PQ)

The purpose of process performance qualification is to rigorously test the process to determine whether it is capable of consistently producing an output or in-process or finished devices which meet specifications. (FDA QS Manual, 2013)

Product Performance Qualification (PPQ)

The purpose of product performance qualification is to demonstrate that the process has not adversely affected the finished product and that the product meets its predetermined specifications and quality attributes. Product performance qualification and design validation of initial finished devices are closely related. According to the design control requirements, design validation shall be performed under defined operating conditions on initial production units, lots, or batches, or their equivalents [820.30(g)]. Products used for design validation should be manufactured using the same production equipment, methods and procedures that will be used in routine production. Otherwise, the product used for design validation may not be representative of production units and cannot be used as evidence that the manufacturing process will produce a product that meets pre-determined specifications and quality attributes.

Design validation can be conducted using finished products made during process validation studies and will satisfy the need for product performance qualification. Design validation shall ensure that devices conform to defined user needs and intended uses and shall include testing production units under actual or simulated use conditions [820.30(g)]. (FDA QS Manual, 2013)

It is clear from these descriptions that process performance qualification and product performance qualification have two separate distinct purposes yet are both used to support process validation. It is important to take note that *product performance qualification* can be satisfied by design validation if product from a validated process (IQ, OQ, PQ) is used during design validation, otherwise if "equivalents" are used, product performance qualification will be required after IQ, OQ and PQ are completed.

FIGURE 42

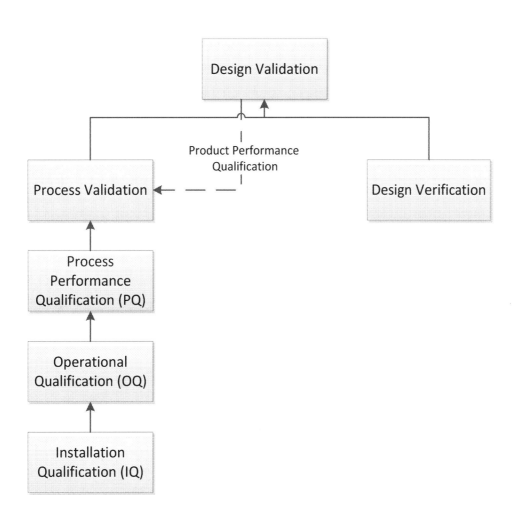

Figure 42 shows that process validation (IQ, OQ, PQ) is an input to design validation but to completely validate a processes, product performance qualification should be performed through design validation or independently as applicable.

Figure 43 illustrates the decision tree for determining if product performance qualification is required. The requirement for performing product performance qualification is determined by whether or not design validation is using product from initial production lots after design transfer (including process validation).

FIGURE 43

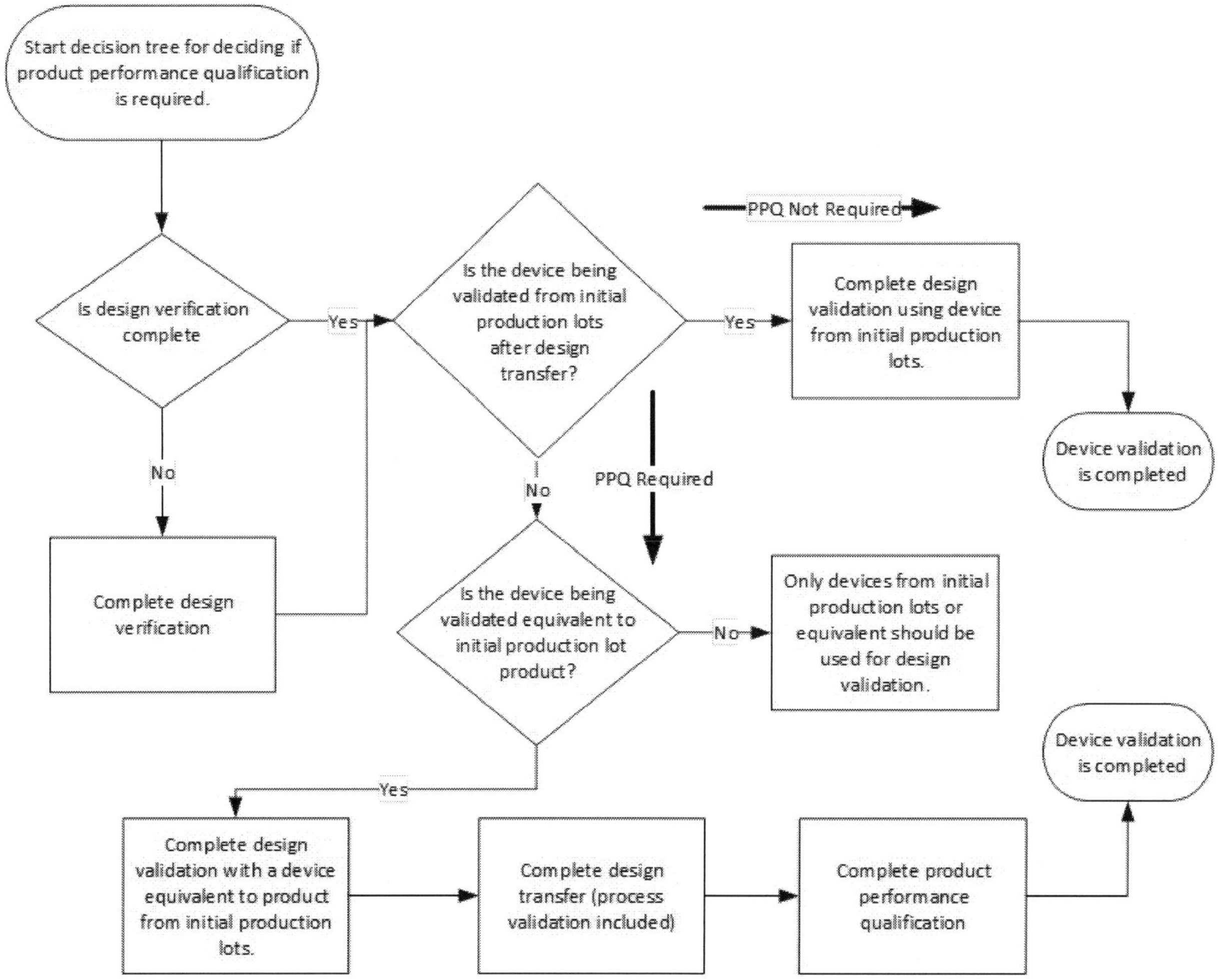

8.14. Templates

Visit *Procenius.com* to download design validation protocol/report templates.

9.0 Design Transfer

9.1. Overview

The purpose of design transfer is to ensure that the device is properly manufactured in a production environment. Early in the development process, device prototypes are often built by skilled technicians or even engineers. These technicians and engineers are very close to the design and understand the critical aspects of the design which may need special attention during fabrication or assembly. They may take great care in building their prototypes to ensure the critical features are fabricated or assembled correctly in preparation for design verification.

After the design is transferred to a high volume production environment, this tribal knowledge of critical design features or manufacturing processes may easily be lost. The design transfer regulation is intended to avoid this tribal knowledge from being lost by ensuring that everything required to reliably and consistently manufacture a medical device in a production environment has been completed, approved and validated as applicable. The accurate manufacture of the device is no longer dependent upon the expertise of development technicians or engineers, but now relies on validated processes and established inspection procedures that can be sustainable throughout the life of the device which is independent of individual product experience or knowledge.

9.2. Quick Reference Summary

TABLE 24

Purpose	The purpose of design transfer is to ensure that everything required to reliably and consistently manufacture a medical device in a production environment has been completed, approved and validated as applicable.
Regulation	21 CFR 820.30 (h): Each manufacturer shall establish and maintain procedures to ensure that the device design is correctly translated into production specifications. (FDA D.C. Guidance, 2015)

Medical Device Regulation Consulting and Training – www.Procenius.com

Standard(s)	ISO 13485 (7.3.1) (ISO 13485, 2007)	
Guidance	21 CFR 820.30 (h) (FDA)	FDA Design Control Guidance for Medical Device Manufacturers (FDA D.C. Guidance, 2015)
	ISO 13485 (7.3.1)	Medical Devices – Quality Management Systems – Guidance on the Application of ISO 13485:2003 (ISO 14969, 2004)
Timing of Design Transfer Relative to Research and Development Cycle	Figure 44 The two humps in Figure 44 depict the relationship and the relative amount of research and development activities during the design and development cycle. The shaded area is the typical time when the design transfer process is implemented.	
Deliverables	• **All deliverables on the Design Transfer Checklist** o **Revision 1 (Planning)** o **Revision 2 (Execution)** o **Revision 3 (PQ)**	

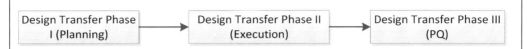

Design Transfer Process	### Design Transfer Phase I (Planning)

The purpose of Phase I (planning) is to thoroughly plan when, what, who and how design transfer activities and deliverables will be completed. Effective planning initiated during early to mid-term development stages provides the design transfer team time to schedule and allocate necessary resources for executing design transfer activities.

Phase I is completed when a design transfer review is performed and the design transfer checklist is approved for all phase I deliverables.

Design Transfer Phase II (Execution)

The purpose of Phase II (execution) is simply to execute the design transfer plan. Typically these activities will be completed in parallel with design verification activities but before design validation is initiated. Essentially all design transfer activities are completed in this phase except process performance qualification.

Phase II is completed when a design transfer review is performed and the design transfer checklist is completed and approved for all phase II deliverables.

Design Transfer Phase III (PQ)

Phase III (PQ) is the culmination of the design transfer process. All design transfer deliverables should have been completed and approved and ready to be used during the final process performance qualification (PQ). PQ is the final and comprehensive validation of all of the production processes, systems, specifications, equipment, materials, tooling, etc. The PQ should provide objective evidence that all of the design transfer activities are working in harmony with each other to consistently produce a reliable product. (PQ will be discussed in greater detail in the process validation chapter)

Phase III is completed when: the PQ report is approved, a design transfer review is performed and the design transfer checklist is completed and approved. Completion of phase III indicates that design transfer has been completed. |

Medical Device Regulation Consulting and Training – www.Procenius.com

Design Transfer Checklist	The design transfer checklist is one of the most common tools used by developers and is an industry best practice. A checklist can provide a convenient format for making assignments, tracking completion dates, referencing deliverable documents and recording plans/rationales/status.
Design Transfer Checklist Approval	The FDA does not specify who should approve design transfer but depending on the manufacturer and the scope of design transfer, it may be appropriate for some of the following team members to approve: • Project Manager/Engineer • Process Validation Specialist/Engineer • Manufacturing Quality Engineer • Supplier/Vendor Manager • Facilities Representative • Engineering/R&D (or Product Expert) • Production Equipment/Tooling Engineer • Operations Manager/Representative
Examples of Design Transfer Deliverables on the Checklist	• Manufacturing quality plan • Equipment procurement plan • Process validation plan • Personnel Plan • Process control requirements • Process validation reports (IQ,OQ,PQ) • Process procedures approved • Manufacturing equipment software validation reports • Tooling drawings approved and tooling validated • Manufacturing component, sub-assembly and final assembly drawings • Operator/technician training records to production procedures are approved (manual assembly, machine operation etc.) • Inspectors trained to quality control procedures (in process, incoming inspection, etc.) • Quality control criteria and acceptance procedures are approved (in process and incoming inspection) • Process Risk assessment approved and controls implemented • Standard specifications for off the shelf parts are available • Design specifications (drawings, schematics, etc.) used for manufacturing or inspections

	- Approved vendor list - Bill of materials - Identification of vendor requirements have been identified - Incoming inspection plan; Including inspection requirements and acceptance criteria - Production forecast available - Capital equipment and labor plan to support production forecast is available - Labeling and packaging acceptance criteria and procedures - Product servicing procedures - Device History forms - Material handling and control procedures - Materials receiving and inspection procedures - And more…
Design Transfer Team	In general the following design transfer specialists (or sub-teams) make up the design transfer team: - Project Manager/Engineer - Process Validation Specialist/Engineer - Manufacturing Quality Engineer - Supplier/Vendor Manager - Facilities Representative - Engineering/R&D (or Product Expert) - Production Equipment/Tooling Engineer - Operations Manager/Representative
Design Transfer Reviews	A design transfer review should be held to close out each design transfer phase. The review is intended to be used as a forum to ensure: - All design transfer requirements, deliverables and activities have been identified - The design transfer plan is approved by the design transfer team - All items required to close each phase are completed Just as with traditional design reviews, design transfer reviews should be documented with meeting minutes and actions should be tracked until completed.

Best Practices	• Plan and execute design transfer activities into phases to ensure design transfer activities and deliverables are effectively planned in the appropriate sequential order. • Poor design transfer planning will lead to delayed product launch, increased design transfer costs, and impact product quality. Detail design transfer planning can be included as part of the design and development plan but it often is more effective and an easier transition if included as part of the design transfer checklist/protocol. • Use a checklist to plan, execute and verify design transfer deliverables.
Templates	Visit *Procenius.com* to download design transfer checklist/protocol templates.

9.3. Regulation (21 CFR 820.30 (h)) - Design Transfer

Each manufacturer shall establish and maintain procedures to ensure that the design is correctly translated into production specifications. (FDA QS Regulation, 2015)

9.4. Design Control Guidance Document (for 21 CFR 820.30 (h))

Production specifications must ensure that manufactured devices are repeatedly and reliably produced within product and process capabilities. If a manufactured device deviates outside those capabilities, performance may be compromised. Thus, the process of encapsulating knowledge about the device into production specifications is critical to device quality.

The level of detail necessary to accomplish this objective varies widely, based on the type of device, the relationship between the design and manufacturing organizations, and the knowledge, experience, and skills of production workers. In some cases, devices are produced by contract manufacturers who have no involvement in the development and little or no contact with the designers. At the other extreme, some devices are hand-crafted by skilled artisans with extensive knowledge about the use of the product.

One normally associates the term "production specifications" with written documents, such as assembly drawings, component procurement specifications, workmanship standards, manufacturing instructions, and inspection and test specifications. While these types of documents are widely employed in medical device production, other equally acceptable means of conveying design information exist, and manufacturers have the flexibility to employ these alternate means of communication as appropriate. For example, each of the following could constitute "production specifications" within the meaning of the quality system requirements:

- documentation (in electronic format as well as paper)

- training materials, e.g., manufacturing processes, test and inspection methods

- digital data files, e.g., programmable device files, master EPROM, computer-aided manufacturing (CAM) programming files

- manufacturing jigs and aids, e.g., molds, sample wiring harness to be duplicated

Historically, shortcomings in the production specifications tend to be manifested late in the product life cycle. When the design is new, there is often intensive interaction between the design and production teams, providing ample opportunity for undocumented information flow. Later, as production experience is gained, some decoupling often occurs between design and production teams. In addition, key personnel may leave, and their replacements may lack comparable training, experience, or institutional knowledge.

Particular care should be taken when the product involves new and unproved manufacturing processes, or established processes which are new to the manufacturer. It may not be possible to determine the adequacy of full-scale manufacturing on the basis of successfully building prototypes or models in a laboratory and testing these prototypes or models. The engineering feasibility and production feasibility may be different because the equipment, tools, personnel, operating procedures, supervision and motivation could be different when a manufacturer scales up for routine production.

No design team can anticipate all factors bearing on the success of the design, but procedures for design transfer should address at least the following basic elements.

- First, the design and development procedures should include a qualitative assessment of the completeness and adequacy of the production specifications.

- Second, the procedures should ensure that all documents and articles which constitute the production specifications are reviewed and approved.

- Third, the procedures should ensure that only approved specifications are used to manufacture production devices.

The first item in the preceding list may be addressed during design transfer. The second and third elements are among the basic principles of document control and configuration management. As long as the production specifications are traditional paper documents, there is ample information available to guide manufacturers in implementing suitable procedures. When the production specifications include non-traditional means, flexibility and creativity may be needed to achieve comparable rigor. (FDA D.C. Guidance, 2015)

9.5. Timing of Design Transfer Activities and Development

The following graphical models give some clarity as to when design transfer typically begins and ends relative to research and development activities.

The two humps in this Figure 45 depict the relationship and the relative amount of research and development activities during the design and development cycle. The shaded area is the typical time when design transfer is planned and executed.

FIGURE 45

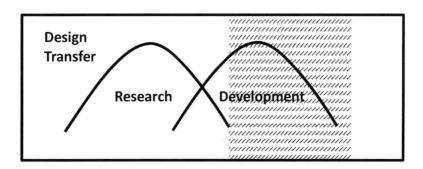

9.6. Interpretation & Application (21 CFR 820.30 (h))

The concept of design transfer is really straight forward but unfortunately it is often misunderstood. In simple terms, design transfer is ensuring that everything required to reliably and consistently manufacture a medical device in a production environment has been completed, approved and validated as applicable.

The best way to explain the principle of design transfer implementation is by example. The following is a typical list of design transfer deliverables:

- Device Master Record (DMR)
- Manufacturing quality plan
- Equipment procurement plan
- Process validation plan
- Personnel Plan
- Process control requirements
- Process validation reports (IQ,OQ,PQ)
- Process procedures approved
- Manufacturing equipment software validation reports
- Tooling drawings approved and tooling validated
- Manufacturing component, sub-assembly and final assembly drawings
- Operator/technician training records to production procedures are approved (manual assembly, machine operation etc.)
- Inspectors trained to quality control procedures (in process, incoming inspection, etc.)
- Quality control criteria and acceptance procedures are approved (in process and incoming inspection)
- Process Risk assessment approved and controls implemented
- Standard specifications for off the shelf parts are available
- Design specifications (drawings, schematics, etc.) used for manufacturing or inspections
- Approved vendor list
- Bill of materials
- Identification of vendor requirements have been identified
- Incoming inspection plan; Including inspection requirements and acceptance criteria
- Production forecast available
- Capital equipment and labor plan to support production forecast is available
- Labeling and packaging acceptance criteria and procedures
- Product servicing procedures
- Device History forms
- Material handling and control procedures
- Materials receiving and inspection procedures
- And more…

A common misconception about design transfer is that it is a <u>point in time</u> when production takes over the engineering design into a production environment. On the contrary, design transfer is not a point in time, but is often a long and sometimes complex process. A second misconception is that design transfer occurs only at the end of the development cycle. While in practice this may often be the case, it is by no means the best case scenario. Ideally design transfer will begin during early to intermediate development phases.

When the FDA says design procedures are required, "…**to ensure that the design is correctly translated into production specifications**", what they are really saying is that all of the engineering and R&D documents, equipment, tooling, process etc. that was used to develop the design needs to be effectively translated into a robust manufacturing system that can reliably produce the medical device in a production environment (typically high volume manufacturing). This should also include personnel being adequately trained, quality control inspection criteria being established and process validations being performed.

9.7. Three Key Components of Effective Design Transfer Procedures

9.7.1. Design Transfer Checklist

"First, the design and development procedures should include a qualitative assessment of the completeness and adequacy of the production specifications." (FDA D.C. Guidance, 2015)

The most common industry excepted method for quantitatively assessing the completeness and adequacy of the production specifications is to use a design transfer checklist. An example of a design transfer checklist is provided later in this chapter. This checklist allows for the design transfer team to effectively identify, plan and execute all design transfer activities prior to the device being manufactured.

9.7.2. The Design Transfer Checklist Should Be Reviewed and Approved

"Second, the procedures should ensure that all documents and articles which constitute the production specifications are reviewed and approved." (FDA D.C. Guidance, 2015)

A design transfer review of the planned and completed design transfer checklist should be reviewed and approved. Usually these reviews are similar to design reviews in respect to cross functional reviewers appropriate for the design transfer process. Design transfer reviews are discussed more later in this chapter.

Medical Device Regulation Consulting and Training – www.Procenius.com

---

IMPORTANT CONCEPT

Final Design Outputs Should Be Approved By Product Experts

During the final stages of development and during design transfer, design transfer teams may be assigned the responsibility of finalizing design outputs to make them production ready. While these teams may be expert in the design transfer process, they are not the product experts. To mitigate the risk of design intent or critical design features being lost during design transfer, the final design outputs which define the design definition such as mechanical drawings, electrical schematics or software code, should be reviewed and approved by the product development experts.

9.7.3. Approved Specifications Shall Be Used to Mfg. Production Devices

"Third, the procedures should ensure that only approved specifications are used to manufacture production devices." (FDA D.C. Guidance, 2015)

This suggestion from the guidance is straightforward; production specifications should be approved by qualified personnel prior to using to produce production devices.

9.8.   The Design Transfer Process – A Phased Approach

Like all other elements of design control regulation, the FDA does not specify how design transfer should be executed but industry best practice[BP1] typically involves a phased approach to ensure design transfer activities and deliverables are effectively planned in the appropriate sequential order and to coincide with the associated design deliverables.

#1 Best Practice – Use a phased approach for design transfer planning & execution

Plan and execute design transfer activities into phases to ensure design transfer activities and deliverables are effectively planned in the appropriate sequential order.

The following is one example of a proven design transfer process.

9.8.1. <u>Design Transfer Phase I (Planning)</u>

The purpose of Phase I (planning) is to thoroughly plan when, what, who and how design transfer activities and deliverables will be completed. Effective planning initiated during early to intermediate development stages provides the design transfer team sufficient time to schedule and allocate necessary resources for executing design transfer activities.

Phase I is completed when a design transfer review is performed and the design transfer checklist is approved for all design transfer deliverables. Planning should begin near the beginning to middle of the development stage(s) (see Figure 46).

FIGURE 46

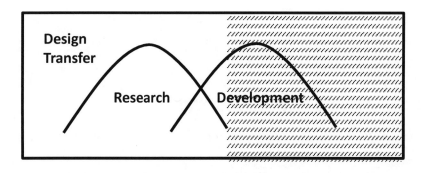

Medical Device Regulation Consulting and Training – www.Procenius.com

Lack of design transfer planning will lead to delayed product launch, increased design transfer costs, and reduced product quality[BP2].

#2 Best Practice – Plan design transfer activities during early development to reduce project risk

Poor design transfer planning will lead to delayed product launch, increased design transfer costs, and impact product quality. Detail design transfer planning can be included as part of the design and development plan but it often is more effective and an easier transition if included as part of the design transfer checklist/protocol.

9.8.1.1. Why Planning is Part of Design Transfer

Some developers may consider planning design transfer activities a project management activity and not a design control requirement. It is true that in the strictest sense of the word "planning" for design transfer may not be required to be compliant to design transfer regulation, on the other hand poor planning can highly impact regulatory compliance and meeting target launch dates.

Poor planning will result in unintended consequences as demonstrated in the scenario below:

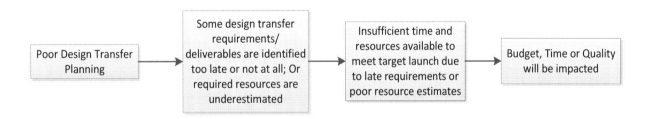

At the end of the day, the budget, time or quality will be impacted by poor planning. Unfortunately many companies take the high risk route and compromise quality over increasing budgets or delaying launch. This decision is not only a regulatory compliance risk, but also potentially a risk to the user/patient that uses the device.

9.8.2. Design Transfer Phase II (Execution)

The purpose of Phase II (execution) is simply to execute the design transfer plan. Typically these activities will be completed in parallel with design verification activities but before design validation is initiated. Essentially all design transfer activities are completed in this phase except process performance qualification.

Phase II is completed when a design transfer review is performed and the design transfer checklist is completed and approved for all phase II deliverables.

9.8.3. Design Transfer Phase III (PQ)

Phase III (PQ) is the culmination of the design transfer process. All design transfer deliverables should have been completed and approved and ready to be used during the final process performance qualification (PQ). PQ is the final and comprehensive validation of all of the production processes, systems, specifications, equipment, materials, tooling, etc. The PQ should provide objective evidence that all of the design transfer activities are working in harmony with each other to consistently produce a reliable product. (PQ will be discussed in greater detail in the process validation chapter)

Phase III is completed when: the PQ report is approved, a design transfer review is performed and the design transfer checklist is completed and approved. Completion of phase III indicates that design transfer has been completed.

9.8.3.1. Design Transfer Phase Activities and Deliverables

While the activities and deliverables in Table 25 are a thorough compilation of all activities which are appropriate to ensure a robust design transfer process, minimal deliverables which are typically used for being compliant to design transfer regulation are indicated with "*" which may be preferred by some manufacturers to lower the non-compliance risk during an FDA inspection. Other non-essential aspects of these activities may be implemented as guidance when performing design transfer but not requirements.

TABLE 25

	Phase I (Planning)	Phase II (Execution)	Phase III (PQ)
*Design Transfer Checklist	Develop and approve design transfer checklist to be reviewed in design transfer review	Execute Phase II design transfer activities and approve executed checklist for Phase II deliverables	Execute Phase III design transfer activities and approve executed checklist for Phase III deliverables
*Design Transfer Reviews	Review initial design transfer checklist (list of required design transfer activities)	Review completion of executed Phase II activities & deliverables	Review completion of all executed Phase III activities & deliverables; Approval of review meeting minutes will indicate completion of design transfer
Personnel	Develop staffing plan to support production forecast; Propose budget for new hires and training; Plan training	Hire and train personnel to support production activities; Training records required	Trained personnel execute production activities during Process Performance Qualification (PQ)
Production Equipment	Identify and plan procurement of production equipment based on production forecast;	Install equipment; Program equipment software and perform software validation	Execute Process Performance Qualification (PQ)
*Production Processes	Develop high level process validation plan	Draft, review and approve process validation protocols (IQ,OQ,PQ); Perform installation and operational qualification (IQ/OQ)	

*Production Facilities	Identify production facility requirements; Identify production facility location; Plan design of production environment (infrastructure: walls, utilities, temperature, clean room level, etc); Plan facilities validation plan	Build/install facility infrastructure; Perform facilities validation	PQ should be performed in validated facility
*Production Specifications	Determine what type of production specifications will be required (assembly drawings, process procedures, inspection criteria, DHR forms, etc.)	Draft, review and approve production specifications (assembly drawings, process procedures, etc.)	Use approved production specifications to perform PQ
*Product Acceptance Criteria	Identify critical "in process" and "final product" acceptance criteria	Draft, review and approve "in process" and "final product" acceptance documents	Use product acceptance criteria for evaluating acceptance of PQ lots
Supplier/Vendor Specifications and Production Forecast	Identify and allocate resources for developing supplier specifications; Initiate communications with supplier about production forecasts	Draft, review and approve supplier component (or service) production specifications; Provide supplier with production forecasts; Supplier to provide first piece samples for component qualification	Supplier to provide controlled and traceable components/services required for PQ lots
Approved Supplier/Vendor List	Identify suppliers for device components or manufacturing services; Plan activities for getting supplier on approved supplier list	Approval of supplier on approved supplier list;	Components from suppliers/vendors used during PQ should be from the approved supplier/vendor list

*Materials	Identify and plan procurement of materials needed for PQ and initial production lots	Purchase and qualify material needed for PQ and initial production lots	Use qualified material for PQ and initial production lots
*Quality Control	Identify and plan quality control activities based on critical design specifications and process risk	Draft, review and approve quality control procedures (in process/incoming inspection) based on critical design specifications and process risk	Use quality control procedures and specifications during execution of PQ
*Tooling	Identify and plan required tooling to support PQ and production	Design, build and validate required tooling to support PQ and production	Use validated tooling for PQ
*Process Risk Assessment	Perform and approve initial process risk assessment to identify patient risk from process hazards; Identify controls to mitigate process risk to as low as reasonably practical	Implement required controls into process design to mitigate process risk; Revise process risk assessment with residual risk after controls have been implemented	Perform PQ using revised process with required controls
*Device Master Record (DMR)	Identify scope of device, mfg procedures, bill of material (BOM) etc. to be defined in DMR (Hardware, software, labeling, etc.)	Draft, review and approve DMR.	Production procedures, inspection procedures, BOM, etc. approved in DMR should be used to perform PQ.

9.8.3.2. Design Transfer Checklist Example

The design transfer checklist is one of the most common tools used by developers and is an industry best practice[BP3]. The following checklist (Table 26, Table 27 and Table 28) is divided into the three design transfer phases. The checklist also provides a convenient format for making assignments, tracking completion dates, referencing deliverable documents and recording plans/rationales/status.

> **#3 Best Practice – Use a checklist in each design transfer phase**
>
> Use a checklist to plan, execute and verify design transfer deliverables.

TABLE 26

Phase I (Planning)				
Deliverable	**Assigned To**	**Date Completed**	**Deliverable Document Reference** (Document #)	**Plan/Rational/ Status**
Design Transfer Review Meeting Minutes (Planning Phase)				
Staffing Plan				
Training Plan				
Production Equipment Procurement Plan				
Process Validation Master Plan				

Facility Validation and Development Plan			
Identification of required production specifications (assembly drawings, process procedures, etc.)			
Identification of required in process inspection criteria			
Vendor and component (purchased) qualification plan			
Material procurement plan			
Quality Control Plan			
Tooling Plan			
Process Risk Assessment (Initial Risks)			

TABLE 27

Phase II (Execution)				
Deliverable	**Assigned To**	**Date Completed**	**Deliverable Reference** (Document #)	**Plan/Rational/Status**
Design Transfer Review Meeting Minutes (Execution Phase)				
Hire required staff/operators				
Training Records				
Equipment Purchased				
Process Validation Reports (IQ/OQ)				
Facility validation report				
Approved production specifications (assembly drawings, process procedures, etc.)				
Approved "in process" inspection criteria				
Vendor and component (purchased) qualification				
Material procured				

Approved quality control procedures				
Tooling validation report				
Updated process risk assessment (Control Implementation)				

TABLE 28

Phase III (PQ)				
Deliverable	**Assigned To**	**Date Completed**	**Deliverable Reference** (Document #)	**Plan/Rational/Status**
Process performance qualification (PQ) report				

9.9. Challenges During Design Transfer

Even the best planned design transfer projects will not be successful if they are not properly supported and executed. Some of the typical problems that arise during design transfer include the following:

- The purchasing department does not have enough time to identify and approve new vendors, verify component specifications, and update the manufacturing planning system.

- The process flow of the manufacturing organization is interrupted by having to wait for released materials, procedures, and tooling.

- Product experts and managers do not understand the scope of the design transfer effort and underestimate the amount of time and effort required.

- Manufacturing processes have not been developed, documented, or validated.

- Supply chain vendors are not on the approved vendor list.

- Delays occur even after all the documentation is approved, because manufacturing must receive, inspect, and finally release parts for production.

- Developers bring unresolved cost, reliability, or safety issues to the manufacturer.

- Developers have not completed the final design.

- Execution of design transfer activities is ineffectively executed due to team inexperience.

These challenges can ultimately cripple a product launch if adequate planning and resources are not effectively allocated to mitigate these risks. The following three things are essential for effectively over coming these challenges:

An experienced design transfer team
Experienced design transfer teams will enable the design transfer process to occur with efficiency and timeliness. Teams which lack necessary experience will lead to incomplete and delayed design transfer deliverables.

A proven design transfer process
A robust, proven design transfer process and procedures is required to ensure that design transfer occurs consistently and effectively. The process should be designed to meet the unique needs of the organization, refined for efficiency and validated prior to implementation.

Adequate resources and time
This may seem obvious but if sufficient time and resources are not identified, allocated, and budgeted, design transfer will not be successful. In some cases relatively little planning is required for simple designs. On the opposite side of the spectrum design transfer may take months or even years for complex devices.

9.10. The Design Transfer Team

The scope and size of the design transfer team's activities will heavily depend upon the size of the organization and the complexity of the medical device. Small organizations that manufacture simple medical devices may only have a one or two person design transfer team. Large organizations that manufacture complex devices may have a team with 20+ people or multiple sub-team specialists.

Medical Device Regulation Consulting and Training – www.Procenius.com

In general the following design transfer specialists (or sub-teams) make up the design transfer team:

- Project Manager/Engineer
- Process Validation Specialist/Engineer
- Manufacturing Quality Engineer
- Supplier/Vendor Manager
- Facilities Representative
- Engineering/R&D (or Product Expert)
- Production Equipment/Tooling Engineer
- Operations Manager/Representative

TABLE 29

Design Transfer Specialist (or sub-team)	Responsibilities, Activities, and Deliverables
Project Manager/Engineer	Assembles an effective design transfer team and ensures design transfer activities are adequately planned and executed to support project milestones
Process Validation Specialist/Engineer	Develops production processes; Executes/leads all process validation activities (IQ, OQ, PQ etc.); Develops validation protocols and reports
Manufacturing Quality Engineer	Leads and executes process risk assessment; Reviews and approves design transfer documents to ensure compliance to internal procedures and regulations.

Supplier/Vendor Manager	Leads and executes all activities to establish a solid supply chain, ensure that supplier components are qualified, ensure suppliers are on the approved supplier list, etc.
Facilities Representative	Prepares facility infrastructure for production equipment, process validation, facility validation, (e.g. ventilation, water, air, power, space)
Engineering/R&D (or Product Expert)	Ensures that the device design (and it's intent) is accurately translated into production specifications
Production Equipment/Tooling Engineer	Develops equipment/tooling requirements; Designs, builds and validates equipment/tooling;
Operations Manager/Representative	Schedules equipment and personnel for validation runs; Ensures production operators are trained in preparation for initial production and process validation (PQ); Provide estimation of needed personnel to support production forecast

9.11. Design Transfer Reviews

A design transfer review will be held to close out each design transfer phase. The review is intended to be used as a forum to ensure:

- All design transfer requirements, deliverables and activities have been identified
- The design transfer plan is approved by the design transfer team
- All items required to close each phase are completed and approved
- All non-conformances are addressed

Medical Device Regulation Consulting and Training – www.Procenius.com

Just as with traditional design reviews, design transfer reviews should be documented with meeting minutes and actions should be tracked until completed.

9.12. Design Transfer by Contract Manufacturers

There are both pros and cons to using contract device manufacturers. Depending on the contractor's experience and resources, developers can effectively off load some, if not all, of the design transfer process to the contractor. Developers will obviously need to give some guidance as to the criticality of design features that will drive inspection criteria and risk assessments etc., but in many cases the contractor takes on the burden of developing the design transfer documents, performing process validation and other resource intensive activities.

Even though using contract manufacturers may seem enticing, they don't come without their problems. To minimize problems that may occur during design transfer, the following guidelines should be followed:

- Involve the contractor early in the planning phase of design transfer
- Critical design specifications should be provided to the contractor as soon as possible
- Developers should track the contractors design transfer progress
- Developers should approve major design transfer deliverables to ensure quality metrics are achieved
- Developers should communicate clearly and often
- Critical decisions, expectations and communications should be in writing to minimize miscommunication

9.13. Quality Systems Manual: Design Transfer

DESIGN TRANSFER

Excerpt from the "Quality Systems Manual: A Small Entity Compliance Guide"
(Withdrawn from FDA website 12 December 2013)
(FDA QS Manual, 2013)

The design controls require that each manufacturer shall establish and maintain procedures to ensure that the device design is correctly translated into production specifications.

It is common practice for sections of a design to be transferred before the entire design is completed. The QS regulation does not prevent such split or multiple transfers. Transfer is to be performed only for completed elements of the design -- multiple transfers may not be used to bypass any design, labeling or other GMP requirements.

A significant part of the transfer requirement is met when the design output is being created. That is, some of the design output documents are part of the DMR and are used directly for production. The remaining DMR documents are based on design output information. A procedure is needed to cover the generation of the remaining device master record documents based on information in the design output documents.

Design transfer should assure that the section of the design being transferred:

- meets input requirements;
- contains acceptance criteria, where needed;
- contains design parameters which have been appropriately verified;
- is complete and approved for use;
- is fully documented in the DMR or contains sufficient design output information to support the generation of remaining DMR documents; and
- is placed under change control if not already done.

Design transfer may include training of production, installation and service employees and such training should be covered by or referenced by the transfer procedure.

9.14. Templates

Visit **Procenius.com** to download design transfer checklist/protocol templates.

Medical Device Regulation Consulting and Training – www.Procenius.com

10.0   Design Changes

10.1. <u>Overview</u>

The purpose of the design change regulation is to ensure the device remains safe and effective after the design change is implemented. The concept of design change encompasses *document control* and *change control* to ensure appropriate tasks, reviews and activities are completed and appropriately documented prior to making changes to a design.

10.2. <u>Quick Reference Summary</u>

TABLE 30

Purpose	The purpose of design change control is to ensure the device remains safe and effective after the design change is implemented.	
Regulation	21 CFR 820.30 (i): Each manufacturer shall establish and maintain procedures for the identification, documentation, validation or where appropriate verification, review, and approval of design changes before their implementation. (FDA QS Regulation, 2015)	
Standard(s)	ISO 13485 (7.3.7) (ISO 13485, 2007)	
Guidance	21 CFR 820.30 (i) (FDA)	FDA Design Control Guidance for Medical Device Manufacturers (FDA D.C. Guidance, 2015)

Medical Device Regulation Consulting and Training – www.Procenius.com

	ISO 13485 (7.3.7)	Medical Devices – Quality Management Systems – Guidance on the Application of ISO 13485:2003 (ISO 14969, 2004)
Timing of Design Changes Relative to the Research and Development Cycle	FIGURE 47 The two humps in Figure 47 depict the relationship and the relative amount of research and development activities during the design and development cycle. The shaded area is the typical time when documented formal design changes are implemented.	
Objectives of a Design Change Process	• To track corrective actions to completion; • To ensure changes are implemented in such a manner that the original problem is resolved and no new problems are created; or if new problems are created, they are also tracked to resolution; and • To ensure design documentation is updated to accurately reflect the revised design. • To communicate the design change to all applicable stakeholders (FDA D.C. Guidance, 2015)	

FDA Expectations for Design Change	<ul><li>A formal, documented and well controlled design change control process should be established.</li><li>The review and approval process must be effectively communicated to all affected departments.</li><li>Changes should be reviewed and approved before and after the change is made.</li><li>All design changes (including software) should be performed through the change control process.</li><li>Impact assessment of design change (especially to risk, verification and validation) should be performed</li><li>The impact of how the change may cause additional risk should be evaluated so there is no unintended risks/ consequences, etc.</li><li>Evaluation of evidence that the change was approved and implemented correctly.</li></ul>
Elements of Effective Design Change	<ul><li>Impact Assessment</li><li>Assessment of Re-Verification or Re-Validation</li><li>Design Change Plan</li><li>Risk Assessment Review</li><li>Cross Functional Team Review</li><li>Design Change Approvals (Pre and Post)</li><li>Regulatory Review of Design Changes</li><li>Multi-Level Design Change Categories</li><li>Design Change Implementation Assessment</li></ul>
Typical Design Change Process	1. *Design Change Request Initiated* 2. *Design Change Pre-Approved* 3. *Design Change Executed* 4. *Design Change Post Approval* 5. *Design Change Implemented*

Medical Device Regulation Consulting and Training – www.Procenius.com

Design Change Review and Approval	The FDA requires that design changes are approved prior to "implementation", but does not require a "pre-approval" before the changes are made in a draft or unreleased state. In a production environment it often makes good business sense to have a "pre-approval" because changes are often costly and require significant resources. The operations manager does not want to pay for a potential change before it has been thoroughly reviewed. Normally a full cross functional change control committee would make a pre-approval decision before extensive resources are committed. During development the same "pre-approved" requirement may exist but instead of requiring a change control committee to review and approve; a project manager, technical expert and quality representative may be the only approvals required. For smaller companies with simple devices and design changes "pre-approval" may not be needed or practical. "Post approval" of a design change is also an effective practice especially in a production environment. The "post approval" is a method of ensuring the quality of the design change as originally planned. This is the last check before the change is implemented into production which could have a significant and immediate impact on the safety and effectiveness of the device. Post approval can be performed by the same team that pre-approved the change. An alternative to having the entire team post approve the change is to have a quality representative approve the change instead with the purpose of verifying that all design change tasks were executed. **Typical Reviewers/ Committee Members** Cross Functional Committee Quality Assurance Regulatory Affairs R&D / Engineering Marketing Project Management Other Stake Holders

Best Practices	• Product experts should review and approve complex or high risk design changes • Design change procedure requirements should be customized for the environment for which it will be used and in proportion to the significance of the change. • Establish separate (or modified) processes for assessing risk during product development and during design change • Change control committee meetings should be held frequently • Design changes should be reviewed by a regulatory representative
Other General Best Practices	• Contractors should provide formal notification to device manufacturer of proposed changes to components or devices. • Supporting documentation of design change orders should be referenced or attached. • Redlines of proposed changes (electronically or paper) should be provided during pre-approval of design change. Final approval (post approval) should include review of the changed design element. (redlines should not be used as final approval). • The design change procedure should require timely follow up of design change requests and orders in a reasonable time (typically no more than three months). (Timely follow up seems to be problematic in the industry). • Publish report of change requests and open assignments and summary of how long the change request has been open should be provided to the change control committee. A list with people assigned to action items will usually motivate them to get their name off the list. • Describe expectations for temporary changes. Any temporary changes that repeat should be made permanent.

	• The design change control process should be assigned to personnel at a managerial level; it is not just an administrative activity. • Change control committee should have specific assignments for what things to look for during design change review.
Templates	Visit **Procenius.com** to download design change templates.

10.3. Design Change Definitions

Change Request: A proposal to make a design change; if approved, a change request will become a change order and the change will be implemented

Change Order: An approved directive to implement a design change initiated by a change request

Design Changes: Changes made to design inputs or outputs

Temporary Changes: Changes which are only intended to be valid for a short time period to address a temporary situation

Pre-Approval: Approval of proposed design change plans, tasks, activities and deliverables prior to executing

Post Approval: Approval of the results or completeness of the design change tasks, activities and deliverables after completion

Redlines: Draft version of documents which are used to propose changes to existing design documents. (the name "redlines" originates from documents being marked with red pen to propose changes)

Change Control Committee: Cross functional committee which participates in design change reviews

Design Change Reviews: Review of design changes used to determine cross functional impact and to identify required tasks, activities and deliverables required prior to implementing the design change

10.4. Regulation (21 CFR 820.30 (I)) - Design Changes

Each manufacturer shall establish and maintain procedures for the identification, documentation, validation or where appropriate verification, review, and approval of design changes before their implementation. (FDA QS Regulation, 2015)

10.5. Design Control Guidance Document (for 21 CFR 820.30 (i))

10.5.1. Design Change: Document Control and Change Control

There are two principal administrative elements involved in controlling design changes:

- **Document control**-enumeration of design documents, and tracking their status and revision history. Throughout this section, the term "document" is used in an inclusive sense to mean all design documents, drawings, and other items of design input or output which characterize the design or some aspect of it.

- **Change control**-enumeration of deficiencies and corrective actions arising from verification and review of the design, and tracking their resolution prior to design transfer.

For a small development project, an adequate process for managing change involves little more than documenting the design change, performing appropriate verification and validation, and keeping records of reviews. The main objectives are ensuring that:

- corrective actions are tracked to completion;

- changes are implemented in such a manner that the original problem is resolved and no new problems are created; or if new problems are created, they are also tracked to resolution; and

- design documentation is updated to accurately reflect the revised design.

For projects involving more than two persons, coordination and communication of design changes become vitally important. In other words, manufacturers should take steps to avoid the common situation where, for example, Jon and Marie agree to a make a change but neglect to inform Pat of their decision.

Medical device manufacturers are usually quite comfortable with the processes of document control and change control with respect to managing manufacturing documents. The principles of these processes are reviewed in the following paragraphs. Subsequently, we will explore how these may be applied to design activities.

10.5.2. Document Control

The features of a manufacturing document control system typically include the following:

- Documents should be identified (i.e., named and numbered) in accordance with some logical scheme which links the documents to the product or component they describe or depict and illuminates the drawing hierarchy.

- A master list or index of documents should be maintained which presents a comprehensive overview of the documentation which collectively defines the product and/or process.

- Approval procedures should be prescribed which govern entry of documents into the document control system.

- A history of document revisions should be maintained.

- Procedures for distributing copies of controlled documents and tracking their location should be prescribed.

- Files of controlled documents should be periodically inventoried to ensure that the contents are up to date.

- A person or persons should be assigned specific responsibility to oversee and carry out these procedures. It is desirable that the document control system be administered by a person who is not directly involved with developing or using the documents. For a small manufacturer, document control might be a part-time job for a technician or clerical staff person. More typically, one or more librarians or full-time clerical or paraprofessional employees are required to administer the system.

- There should be a procedure for removal and deletion of obsolete documents.

10.5.3. Change Control

Manufacturing change control is usually implemented using a set of standardized procedures similar to the following:

- A change request might be originated by a developer, manager, reviewer, marketing representative, user, customer, quality assurance representative, or production personnel, and identifies a design problem which the requester believes should be corrected. Change requests are typically reviewed following the manufacturer's prescribed review process, and the request might be rejected, deferred, or accepted.

- If a change request is accepted and corrective action is straightforward, a change order might be issued on the spot to implement the change. The change order pertains to an explicitly identified document or group of documents, and specifies the detailed revision of the document content which will fix the identified problem.

- Often, the change request results in an assignment to developers to further study the problem and develop a suitable corrective action. If the change is extensive, wholesale revision of affected documents may be warranted in lieu of issuing change orders.

- Change requests and change orders should be communicated to all persons whose work might be impacted by the change.

- It may not be practical to immediately revise documents affected by a change order. Instead, the common practice is to distribute and attach a copy of the change order to each controlled copy of the original document.

- Change control procedures should incorporate review and assessment of the impact of the design change on the design input requirements and intended uses.

- A mechanism should be established to track all change requests and change orders to ensure proper disposition.

- Change control procedures are usually administered by the document control staff.

10.5.4. Application of Document and Change Controls to Design

The design control system has to be concerned with the creation and revision of documents, as well as the management of finished documents. Additional mechanisms are required to provide needed flexibility while preserving the integrity of design documentation. These additional mechanisms are embodied in the procedures for review and approval of various documents.

It is important that the design change procedures always include re-verifying and re-validating the design. Fortunately, most design changes occur early in the design process, prior to extensive design validation. Thus, for most design changes, a simple inspection is all that is required. The later in the development cycle that the change occurs, the more important the validation review becomes. There are numerous cases when seemingly innocuous design changes made late in the design phase or following release of the design to market have had disastrous consequences.

For example, a manufacturer encountered problems in the field with a valve sticking in a ventilator due to moisture in the breathing circuit. The problem was resolved by slightly increasing the weight of the disc. Since the change was minor, minimal testing was performed to verify the change. Subsequently, when the revised valves entered production, significant numbers of valves began failing. Investigation revealed that the heavier disc was causing the valve cage to separate due to higher inertia. This failure mode was more serious than the original sticking problem, and resulted in a safety recall. (FDA D.C. Guidance, 2015)

10.6. When Should Design Change Begin?

The FDA does not specify in the regulation at what point in the design and development process when design changes need to be documented but the QSR preamble indicates that design changes should be formalized after the initial design inputs are approved:

The Quality Systems Regulation Preamble states:

Comment 87

"Manufacturers are not expected to maintain records of all changes proposed during the very early stages of the design process. However, all design changes made after the design review that approves the initial design inputs for incorporation into the design, and those changes made to correct design deficiencies once the design has been released to production, must be documented." (FDA Preamble, 2015)

Comment 88

"... Again, manufacturers are not expected to maintain records of changes made during the very early stages of product development; only those design changes made after the approval of the design inputs need be documented." (FDA Preamble, 2015)

The two humps in Figure 48 depict the relationship and the relative amount of research and development activities during the design and development cycle. The shaded area is the typical time when design changes are generated, reviewed, approved and implemented.

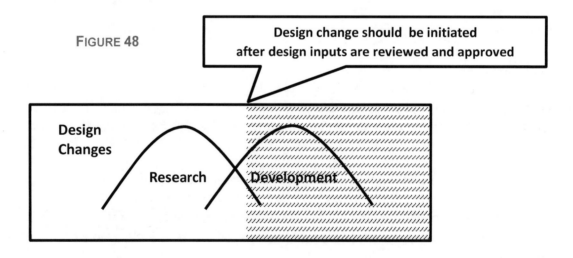

FIGURE 48

Design change should be initiated after design inputs are reviewed and approved

Design Changes

Research Development

10.7. Interpretation & Application (21 CFR 820.30 (I))

When the FDA states *"Each manufacturer shall establish and maintain procedures....* "they are saying that "*establish*" means to define, document (in writing or electronically), and implement.

They are also saying that the manufacturer must have a documented procedure(s) that defines the "what, who, how, why and when" of how design changes are created and applied. The FDA wants to ensure that a standard design change procedure has been created, vetted, reviewed and approved. The procedure must be "maintained" (in other words revised and updated) as required to be current with the intended and approved design change activities. Typically this procedure is assigned to the document control department.

The regulation also states that the manufacturer shall maintain procedures for the "*identification, documentation, validation or where appropriate verification, review, and approval of design changes before their implementation.*"

In this case, **"identification"** should be interpreted as meaning the design change procedure must specify the design that is being changed and what aspect (feature, component, etc) of the design that is changing.

"Documentation" should be interpreted as meaning the procedure must specify what documentation is required to record and approve the design change.

When the FDA says **"*validation or where appropriate verification*"** it should be interpreted as meaning the procedure must specify how to determine if and when validation or verification is required before implementing a design change. The FDA wants the manufacturer to evaluate if the design change will invalidate a previous validation or verification, or if new requirements are created which will require additional verification or validation.

FDA Design Control Guidance states this about re-verification and validation for design changes:

"*...It is important that the design change procedures always include re-verifying and re-validating the design....*" (FDA D.C. Guidance, 2015)

The intent of the **"review"** is to have qualified personnel understand the proposed design change and its impact to the design and to development activities performed up to that point in the development process.

"*...before their implementation.*" This phrase of the regulation requires that the change request is approved prior to the change being introduced into a production environment or into the controlled design configuration during development.

10.8. Objectives of a Change Control (Design Change) Process

A change control process should have the following objectives:

- To track corrective actions to completion;

- To ensure changes are implemented in such a manner that the original problem is resolved and no new problems are created; or if new problems are created, they are also tracked to resolution; and

- To ensure design documentation is updated to accurately reflect the revised design.

- To communicate the design change to all applicable stakeholders

10.9. What Documents Should be Under Change Control vs. Document Control

As quoted from the design control guidance, there two aspects to design change:

- ***"Document Control**-enumeration of design documents, and tracking their status and revision history. Throughout this section, the term "document" is used in an inclusive sense to mean all design documents, drawings, and other items of design input or output which characterize the design or some aspect of it.*

- ***Change Control**-enumeration of deficiencies and corrective actions arising from verification and review of the design, and tracking their resolution prior to design transfer."*

The application of document control is very straightforward. Any formal document that is required to support the design or development process should be controlled by document controls as specified in 21 CFR 820.40.

Change Control may not be as obvious. Often there is confusion about what documents (or software) need to be controlled through simple document control vs. change control. Most manufacturers only interpret the "design" to consist of design inputs and outputs. Therefore it is commonly accepted in industry that change control only applies when design inputs and outputs are changed.

In practice this logic makes a lot of sense. Change control is only intended to track corrective actions, ensure design problems are resolved and to ensure updates are accurately reflected in the design inputs and outputs. Changes to other standard development documents such as development plans, verification protocols, or verification reports do not require this same level of change control and therefore only document controls are applicable for these documents.

Medical Device Regulation Consulting and Training – www.Procenius.com

10.10. Why Effective Design Change Control is Important

Effective change control is very important because it provides a change history of the evolution of the design and ensures design changes are adequately evaluated to maintain the safety and effectiveness of the device.

10.10.1. Change Control Provides a Change History of the Design Evolution

The Quality Systems Regulation Preamble states the following about change history being recorded through design change:

Comment 87

"The records of these changes create a history of the evolution of the design, which can be invaluable for failure investigation and for facilitating the design of future similar products. Such records can prevent the repetition of errors and the development of unsafe or ineffective designs." (FDA Preamble, 2015)

10.10.2. Change Control Maintains Device Safety and Effectiveness

The Quality Systems Regulation Preamble states the following about device safety and effectiveness being controlled through design change.

Comment 87

"The safety and effectiveness of devices cannot be proven by final inspection or testing. Product development is inherently an evolutionary process. While change is a healthy and necessary part of product development, quality can be ensured only if change is controlled and documented in the development process, as well as the production process." (FDA Preamble, 2015)

Design change is a critical part of the development process. A thorough and robust design change process is essential for ensuring a device remains safe and effective. If performed improperly, one poor design change decision could effectively invalidate years of product development effort or seriously compromise the safety of a device.

As an example, years ago the manufacturer of an MRI medical device experienced a failure which almost resulted in a patient fatality that was due to a poor design change decision. The product design included two monitors that were suspended above the patient by an articulating arm that the physician would maneuver during a procedure. There were a few reports that the rotating joint on the articulating arm failed which caused the two monitors to drop just above the heads of the patients which only avoided contact because the power cable prevent the monitors from full disengagement.

The failure was investigated and it was determined that the failure was caused by a fractured shoulder bolt. It turns out that the original design required two .025" thick washers to be used on one end of the bearing to allow the shoulder bold to rotate freely on the needle bearings. Somewhere during the course of the production life of the product, a design change was made to remove one of the bearing washers. The reason for the design change and the projected impact and risk of the change, including verification testing, was not adequately documented or well understood.

It turns out that the removal of the second washer restricted the rotation of the articulating arm. Over time extreme torque was applied to the shoulder bolt which eventually caused it to fracture. The fracture led to the complete failure of the articulating arm.

This is just one of many real life examples where an insufficient change control process resulted in an unidentified patient risk.

As in this example, design change can introduce additional patient risk if not effectively implemented. In most organizations design change post design transfer has inherent risk because in many cases design changes are not reviewed and approved by the original developers of the design. The engineers or scientists that originally developed the design understand the minute details of each feature and function of the device. They went through endless design iterations during development and they know the design like no one else. For this reason they are the best resource to evaluate design change requests. Unfortunately they are often transitioned off of the project after design transfer occurs and someone with less knowledge (if any) about the design is assigned to review design changes. This gap in knowledge may lead to higher risk design changes if robust design change procedures are not effectively documented and implemented.

It is best practice[BP1] to rely on the original developers or the product experts to review and approve complex or high risk design changes. On the other hand, sustaining production engineers should be able to support minor, low risk design changes. The design change procedure should specify the functional group assigned to each level of change (i.e. – Complex, high risk changes = Product Experts; Simple, low risk changes = Sustaining Engineering)

> **#1 Best Practice – Product experts should review and approve complex or high risk design changes.**

10.11.   Design Change During Development vs. Production

The FDA does not specify that a manufacturer's design change process be the same for development and production environments, they only state that design change should include the same minimum requirements as explained below in the QSR Preamble.

The Quality Systems Regulation Preamble states:

Comment 87

"Procedures must ensure that after the design requirements are established and approved, changes to the design, both pre-production and post-production are also reviewed, validated (or verified where appropriate), and approved." (FDA Preamble, 2015)

For practicality sake, all requirements to perform design changes during development should not be the same for a design in production. As an example, most change control procedures require at least the following basic steps.

In a production environment each of these steps may require extensive documentation and multiple reviewers and approvers to complete a simple design change. In contrast, design changes which occur in development may use this same basic process but may only require minimal documentation and minimal reviewers and approvals.

The FDA supports this approach in the Quality System Preamble:

Comment 87

"The evaluation and documentation should be in direct proportion to the significance of the change." (FDA Preamble, 2015)

Design change procedures should be customized for the environment for which it will be used (development vs. production; simple vs. complex devices)[BP2]. In the real world design change control procedures that are complicated or are too laborious to follow will most likely not be followed accurately which will lead to compliance issues.

To clearly distinguish between development and production changes, some manufacturers will use alphabetic letters for development revision control and numeric for production revision control. This method (or similar methods) can significantly reduce confusion when determining what design change control procedure is required (development or production).

Medical Device Regulation Consulting and Training – www.Procenius.com

> **#2 Best Practice – Design change procedure requirements should be customized for the environment for which it will be used and in proportion to the significance of the change.**

10.12. Design Changes During the Product Life Cycle

Experienced product developers understand that design changes during development are frequent and often significant, especially during early design stages. As the design matures, the number of design changes will vary greatly. Figure 49 is a representation of the relative quantity of design changes over time during the product life cycle.

FIGURE 49

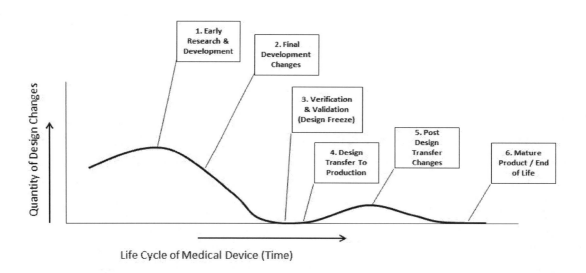

Medical Device Regulation Consulting and Training – www.Procenius.com

10.12.1.   Early Research and Development Changes

During early stages of development, there are often significant and frequent changes. Frequent and numerous design changes are advantageous for developers because it is significantly less costly to fail and make changes early in the development process than during later phases of development. Typically formal design change control is not required during early development until design input requirements and design output specifications have been approved.

10.12.2.   Final Development Changes

As the design becomes solidified, the rate of design changes starts rapidly decreasing heading into design verification and validation. During this phase, design changes are formally controlled. At this point in the development cycle additional resources have been allocated to the project so any significant change is typically costly and impactful to the project schedule.

10.12.3.   Design Verification and Validation (Design Freeze)

Before going into design verification and validation the device design should be solidified (frozen). Design verification and validation (V&V) should not be performed on a moving target. Design changes should end prior to initiating V&V. Any changes that occur post V&V should be evaluated through the design change procedure which should assess the impact on the validity of the results of the V&V activities. A verification and validation assessment should be performed to determine if the previously executed verification and validation is still valid if the change were to be implemented.

10.12.4.   Post Design Transfer Changes

A majority of design changes after design transfer are typically initiated due to cost reduction activities or design improvement changes instigated by constomer feedback. Shortly after design transfer, manufacturers are highly motivated to reduce costs by making supplier changes and by reducing costs associated with manufacturing processes and materials. These changes will eventually taper off as the commercialized product matures. Even though the device is in production, a cross functional team that is qualified to assess the impact of changes should provide sustaining support. This team is usually referred to as a change control board. The level of scrutiny of the design change is significantly higher than those changes made in early development. There are typically more approvers and more documentation associated with evaluating and recording the change due to the direct impact and immediate risk a design change could have on the safety and effectiveness of the device.

Medical Device Regulation Consulting and Training – www.Procenius.com

10.12.5.   Mature Product / End of Life

As the product matures, cost reduction and design improvement changes will become minimal, and the product will eventually be discontinued.

10.13. FDA Expectations for Design Change

- A formal, documented and well controlled design change control process should be established.
- The review and approval process must be effectively communicated to all affected departments.
- Changes should be reviewed and approved before and after the change is made.
- All design changes (including software) should be performed through the change control process.
- Impact assessment of the design change (especially to risk, verification and validation)
- The impact of how the change may cause additional risk should be evaluated so there is no unintended risks/ consequences, etc.
- Evaluation of evidence that the change was approved and implemented correctly.

10.14. Elements of Effective Design Change

10.14.1.   Impact Assessment

An impact assessment of how the design change will affect patient risk (safety), product performance, costs and design outputs/inputs should be performed. A significant amount of time may need to be invested in this process to ensure that all possible impact scenarios are considered. Unfortunately design changes can be a major source of introducing unintended risks to the design's function or performance if not thoroughly vetted.

10.14.2.   Evaluate Risks During Design Changes

For most significant changes, the design risk assessment should be evaluated to determine if the change impacts the previously assigned risk level. In addition to considering the impact to the currently identified hazards and risks, it is also necessary to evaluate if additional hazards have been introduced into the design due to the design change. If a risk assessment is currently not available which addresses the design element being changed, the risk assessment should be updated with the new potential risk.

Manufacturers should be careful not to overburden developers with design change procedures which require extensive and unnecessary risk assessments during design change. An effective, streamlined process of evaluating risk should be established for design change that does not

Medical Device Regulation Consulting and Training – www.Procenius.com

cripple the development process or product production yet ensures that the device is still safe and effective. It is best practice to establish separate (or modified)[BP3] processes for assessing risk during product development vs. those assessments performed for specifically for design changes during production. Manufacturers often try to use the same design change process for both environments and they end up shutting down the development process or production lines because they try to use a "one size fits all" design change process that is ineffective in both cases.

#3 Best Practice – Establish separate (or modified) processes for assessing risk during product development and during design change

It is best practice to establish separate (or modified) processes for assessing risk during product development and for design change to avoid hindering product development or production/manufacturing when making design changes.

10.14.3. Assessment of Re-Verification or Re-Validation

The design change regulation (21 CFR 820.30(i)) specifically requires that verification and validation be addressed as part of the design change process. As part of the impact assessment, the cross functional team should assess how the design change will affect the validity of previously performed verifications or validations. Usually the impact to verification or validation falls into one of these three categories:

- The design change invalidates the validity of the verification/validation results so verifications/validations will have to be fully executed again.

- The design change invalidates specific independent parts (sub-parts) of the verification/validation results that can be independently verified/validated without re-performing the entire verification/validation testing.

- The design change has no impact on the validity of previously performed verifications or validations testing therefore no additional verification or validation testing is required. A justification of why the change does not impact the verification/validation results should be documented with the change control documentation.

10.14.4. Design Change Plan

Once an impact assessment is performed, a plan should be developed to specify how the change should be executed and implemented. Design change plans will typically include the following activities and deliverables:

- Change requirements
- Who is going to make the change to the design element(s)
- Effective Date
- Expected change initiation date
- Expected change completion date
- Document design element being changed
- What feasibility, validation or verification testing will be performed as a result of making the change
- Who should be notified of the change
- Who is going to implement the change into the device
- Reference to the change request number
- Design Verification Plan (if required by the impact assessment)
    - Include reasoning for choosing design verification instead of design validation.
- Design Validation Plan (if required by the impact assessment)
    - Include reasoning for choosing design validation instead of design verification.
- Training requirements:
    - Description of training that should be completed
    - Identification of people, departments, and/or roles that should be trained
    Design change procedures should specify the extent to how many of these activities or deliverables are required. These requirements should be based on the relative complexity of the device and whether or not the design is in development or in production.

10.14.5. Cross Functional Team Review

A cross functional team (e.g. change control committee) review should be performed by all potential impacted departments or cross functional team members prior to approving the change. Even after the design is transferred to production, a cross functional team with sufficient expertise should review and approve the design changes. It is best practice to hold a change control committee meeting frequently[BP4] to ensure changes can continuously flow through the organization. In medium to large organizations it is typical for the change control committee to meet weekly to address weekly proposed changes.

Medical Device Regulation Consulting and Training – www.Procenius.com

> **#4 Best Practice – Change control committee meetings should be held frequently**
>
> It is best practice to hold a change control committee meeting frequently to ensure changes can continuously flow through the organization. In medium to large organizations it is typical for the change control committee to meet weekly to address weekly proposed changes.

10.14.6.   Design Change Approvals (Pre and Post)

The FDA requires that design changes are approved prior to "implementation", but does not require a "pre-approval" before the change is initiated. In a production environment it often makes good business sense to have a "pre-approval" because changes are often costly and require significant resources. The operations manager does not want to pay for a potential change before it has been initially reviewed. Normally a full cross functional change control committee would make a pre-approval decision before extensive resources are committed to evaluating the details of the change.

During development, the same "pre-approved" procedural requirement may exist but instead of requiring a change control committee to review and approve, a project manager, technical expert and quality representative may be the only approvals required. For smaller companies with simple devices and design changes "pre-approval" may not be needed or practical.

"Post approval" of a design change is also an effective practice especially in a production environment. The "post approval" is a method of ensuring that all actions of the design change were completed as originally planned. This is the last check before the change is implemented into production which could have a significant and immediate impact on the safety and effectiveness of the device. Typically post approvals should be performed by the same team that pre-approved the change. In a development environment, the impact of a change is lower and therefore a post approval may only require the confirmation of a quality assurance representative to ensure all of the planned actions/tasks were implemented as part of the change.

10.14.7.   Regulatory Review of Design Changes

It is best practice to have a regulatory representative on the cross functional change control committee to adequately evaluate the impact of the change to the regulatory path[BP5].

Medical Device Regulation Consulting and Training – www.Procenius.com

The Quality Systems Regulation Preamble states:

Comment 87

"Note that when a change is made to a specification, method, or procedure, each manufacturer should evaluate the change in accordance with an established procedure to determine if the submission of a premarket notification (510(k)) under Sec. 807.81(a)(3) (21 CFR 807.81(a)(3)), or the submission of a supplement to a PMA under Sec. 814.39(a) (21 CFR 814.39) is required. Records of this evaluation and its results should be maintained." (FDA Preamble, 2015)

During development a design change may cause a planned 510k notification into a required PMA submission. During production, a design change may turn a simple annual report change into a required 30, 90, or 120 day change or even a PMA supplement. The distinction between these regulatory paths and requirements is significant in both cost and time.

Design changes that could potentially have significant effects on safety or performance must be reviewed to determine if a new 510k or a supplemental to a PMA application will be required. The potential resulting consequences of design changes on regulatory requirements should not be taken lightly.

The FDA has two resources which help device manufacturers determine when a new 510(k) or PMA supplement is required during design changes:

- "Modifications to Devices Subject to Premarket Approval" (PMA) (March 2007)
- "Deciding When to Submit a 510(k) for a change to an Existing Device" (January 1997).

#5 Best Practice – Design changes should be reviewed by a regulatory representative

It is best practice to have a regulatory representative on the cross functional change control committee to adequately evaluate the impact of the change on the regulatory path.

Medical Device Regulation Consulting and Training – www.Procenius.com

10.14.8. Multi-Level Design Change Categories

Medical device manufacturers will typically bucket design changes into multiple levels based on the scope of the change. Three levels that are often used are: *Minor, Moderate and Major.* These three pre-defined levels allow manufacturers to effectively and consistently address design changes based on various levels of risk and scope.

The FDA QSR Preamble indicates that multi-level change control categories (i.e. Minor, Moderate, Major) which dictate the amount of documentation, review and approval of the change are appropriate and should be in direct proportion to the significance of the change.

The Quality Systems Regulation Preamble states:

Comment 87

"The evaluation and documentation should be in direct proportion to the significance of the change." (FDA Preamble, 2015)

Minor changes are often characterized as those that are only document correction, misspellings, name changes, typos, missed fields, formatting etc. The changes would not change the device performance, labeling instructions or any other technical aspects of the device. These design changes should only require a minimum number of approvers and reviewers.

Moderate changes are often characterized as those that may change non-critical design features and do not affect the functionality or safety of the device. These design changes will require more scrutiny than minor changes but not as much as major changes.

Major changes are often characterized as those that may directly impact the performance of the device which typically requires re-verification or re-validation. These changes should require the most scrutiny including impact assessment, risk analysis, design change planning and design reviews.

For a multi-level design change system to be effective, it is critical for the initial reviewers to be highly experienced. They have to have sufficient breadth and depth about the product to allow them to make rational decisions for making the design change level assignments.

10.15. Typical Design Change Process

There are an endless number of design change processes in the medical device industry but many of them have the same basic process steps:

1. Design Change Request Initiated

The design change request is the first step in the process. This process typically consists of the initiator providing a brief description of the change, reason for change, name of initiator and for which product the change is being requested.

2. Design Change Pre-Approved

The design change request should be evaluated and pre-approved (or rejected) by a cross functional team. The cross functional team should be qualified to review design change requests in all functional areas such as, but not limited to: technical, quality, marketing, regulatory and clinical areas of expertise. During this step in the process the following activities typically are performed:

- Impact Assessment
- Risk Evaluation
- Design Change Plan Created
  - Tasks required to complete the change are identified and task owners are assigned
- Regulatory, Technical, Quality, Marketing, and Clinical Review
- Change Requested Approved and Change Order Initiated

The design change request becomes a design change order after the design change request is approved.

3. Design Change Executed

The change order will be executed according to the design change plan. The plan should contain the "who, what, how, and when" the design change should be made. This will usually involve revising documents, CAD models or software code (design outputs or inputs) which define the device in some way. Execution of the design changes will occur in draft form or under a "validation" state depending how the design change process is structured. This is the intermediate environment where design outputs or inputs are changed but not put into production or in some cases in development prototypes. Implementation into these formal environments should not occur until post approval occurs.

For a design change for a device in production, this step would involve testing, verification, validation or other evaluation activities that would be needed to show compliance to design inputs and conformance to user needs.

Medical Device Regulation Consulting and Training – www.Procenius.com

4. Design Change Post Approval

The purpose of design change post approval is to ensure the design changes were actually made as originally intended by the cross functional team. Unfortunately some things are often lost in translation from the design change order to the actual execution of the design change. In more experienced design change control systems the entire cross functional team may not be required. A quality assurance team member may be sufficient to confirm that all actions on the change order were effectively completed.

5. Design Change Implemented

The final implementation step is the point in time that the input or output being changed is "released" into production.

10.16. <u>Design Change Request Owner</u>

The person initiating the change is typically the person responsible for owning the change including ensuring all documentation is completed and submitted to the appropriate reviewers. It is typically best practice to have the design change requester be the owner of the change because the person submitting the change often has the most vested interest in making sure the change happens. Other than the initiator, change coordinators also serve the role of "bird dogging" changes and ensuring they are followed through to completion.

10.17.   <u>Design Change Process Owner</u>

The actual design change process is typically owned by quality assurance. They are usually the ones that make sure the process is accurately maintained and controlled. A quality representative should be a required approver and someone from quality should lead the change control committee (cross functional approval committee) as applicable. The quality assurance representative also acts as the "check" that rationales for changes are reasonable and based on objective evidence.

10.18.   <u>Design Changes Shall Not Be Made Prior to Approval</u>

Some device manufacturers have a bad habit of making design changes first and then following up with documenting the change that was already implemented. This may be tempting when production or development schedules are tight but this practice is not acceptable to the FDA. The regulation is clear; "*...review, and approval of design changes **before** their implementation...".* If changes are implemented before review and approval, a non-conformance record should written to document and approve the change post implementation (This should be the exception and not the rule).

Medical Device Regulation Consulting and Training – www.Procenius.com

10.19. General Best Practices For Design Change Control

- Contractors should provide formal notification to device manufacturers of proposed changes to components or devices. Contracts should include details of when and how design changes are communicated from the contractor to the manufacturer and vice versa.
- Supporting documentation of design change orders should be referenced or attached.
- Redlines of proposed changes (electronically or paper) should be provided during pre-approval of the design change. Final approval (post approval) should include review of the changed design element. (redlines should not be used as final approval).
- The design change procedure should require timely follow up of design change requests and orders (typically no more than three months). (Timely follow up seems to be problematic in the industry).
- A report of change requests, open assignments and of how long the change requests have been open should be provided to the change control committee. A list with people assigned to action items will usually motivate them to get their name off the list.
- Describe expectations for temporary changes. Any temporary changes that repeat should be made permanent.
- The design change control process should be assigned to personnel at a managerial level; it is not just an administrative activity.
- The Change control committee should have specific assignments for what things to look for during design change review.

10.20. Quality Systems Manual: Design Change

DESIGN CHANGE

Excerpt from the "Quality Systems Manual: A Small Entity Compliance Guide"
(Withdrawn from FDA website 12 December 2013)
(FDA QS Manual, 2013)

Changes to a design element are controlled per 820.30(i) Design Changes which states that: each manufacturer shall establish and maintain procedures for the identification, documentation, validation or where appropriate verification, review, and approval of design changes before their implementation.

The original design activities and subsequent change control activities for the design are both done under the full set of the quality system design controls. A manufacturer may not use a design change control procedure to bypass part of the design controls. Thus, it is difficult to describe change control before design transfer because both activities are done under design controls.

Medical Device Regulation Consulting and Training – www.Procenius.com

Most of the details of the change control system are left to the manufacturer to develop, document and implement. As the design activity progresses toward the final stage, it is expected that the degree of change control will increase.

Those elements of the design that have been verified and accepted obviously should be under change control. A design that has been submitted to FDA for marketing clearance should be under change control. A design undergoing clinical trials should be under change control or the clinical data may not be accepted by FDA. A design that is released for production should be under design and general change control.

After design activities are begun and the physical design evolves into an accepted entity, subsequent changes to the device specification(s) are proposed, evaluated, reviewed, approved, and documented per all of 820.30. The revised specification(s) becomes the current design goal in accordance with the manufacturer procedures for: design control, design change control, and document control.

A design change control procedure should at least cover:

- under what conditions change control is required;

- documenting the reason for the change;

- any differences in the change control process when outside parties are involved;

- analysis of the design to identify other elements that are impacted by the change; and

- for significant changes which includes any change requiring verification and/or validation, placing the reason for the change in the design history file along with the required design verification, validation and review documentation.

10.21. Templates

Visit **Procenius.com** to download design change templates.

11.0   Design History File

11.1. <u>Overview</u>

The purpose of the design history file regulation is to ensure manufacturers maintain a record of how the device was developed. The FDA wants to make it clear that the history of how the device was developed is critical in supporting and maintaining the device during development and throughout its life. Not only does it allow manufacturers and FDA inspectors to verify that the device meets intended requirements and development plans, it also is an invaluable resource when making design change decisions and when investigating device defects.

11.2. <u>Quick Reference Summary</u>

TABLE 31

Purpose	• To provide evidence that the device was developed according to the design and development plans and to all requirements. • To provide manufacturers a history of how the device was developed in order to aid in making future decisions during design change or when investigating device defects.
Regulation	21 CFR 820.30 (j): Each manufacturer shall establish and maintain a DHF for each type of device. The DHF shall contain or reference the records necessary to demonstrate that the design was developed in accordance with the approved design plan and the requirements of this part. (FDA QS Regulation, 2015)
Standard(s)	ISO 13485 does not specify requirements for a design history file.

Guidance	21 CFR 820.30 (j) (FDA)	FDA Design Control Guidance for Medical Device Manufacturers (FDA D.C. Guidance, 2015)
	ISO 13485 does not specify requirements for a design history file.	ISO 13485 does not specify requirements for a design history file.
Timing of the Design History File Relative to the Research and Development Cycle	FIGURE 50 The two humps in Figure 50 depict the relationship and the relative amount of research and development activities during the design and development cycle. The shaded area is the typical time when the design history file is created and approved. Initial approval may occur at the end of some development phases and at product launch. The design history file will continue to be updated throughout the life of the product.	

Deliverables	**Design History File Record (DHFR)** Traditionally design history files would often be a physical compilation of all of the design documents in a file cabinet or in large binders. As devices have become more complex and as electronic records have become the standard, DHF's are now most often a "reference" file or a record of document numbers which point or reference the document name and number. This is often referred to as the *Device History File Record (*DHFR*)*. The DHFR is typically segregated into easily retrievable design control sub-parts.
Examples of Design History File Content	<ul><li>Inputs</li><li>Outputs</li><li>Design and Development Plan (or all plans)</li><li>Verification protocols and reports</li><li>Validation protocols and reports (Design, process, etc.)</li><li>Design transfer checklist/protocol</li><li>Design review meeting minutes</li><li>Design change records</li><li>Risk assessments & reports</li><li>Process validation protocols and reports</li><li>Software validation plans, protocols, and reports</li><li>Other development documents</li></ul>
Review	Not required to be reviewed in a formal design review.
Approval	**Typical approvers of the DHF (or DHFR) may include:** Quality Assurance R&D / Engineering Operations Project Engineer/Manager Document Control (To ensure all documents have been released/approved)

Best Practices	Create a DHFR revision at each major phase during development to ensure that design documents are tracked and not inadvertently missed during subsequent design phases. A DHFR revision should be approved and released prior to design transfer. As design changes occur after design transfer, the DHFR should be updated and approved to ensure the DHF is continuously updated as the design changes over time.
Templates	Visit *Procenius.com* to download design history file record templates.

11.3. Regulation (21 CFR 820.30 (j)) - Design History File

Each manufacturer shall establish and maintain a DHF for each type of device. The DHF shall contain or reference the records necessary to demonstrate that the design was developed in accordance with the approved design plan and the requirements of this part. (FDA QS Regulation, 2015)

11.4. Definition 21 CFR 820.3 (e) – Design History File

Design history file (DHF) means a compilation of records which describes the design history of a finished device.

11.5. Design Control Guidance Document (for 21 CFR 820.30 (j))

There is no specific requirement in ISO 9001 or ISO 13485 for a design history file. However, in order to market a medical device in the United States, a manufacturer must comply with the U. S. Food and Drug Administration (FDA) quality system regulation, which requires a design history file. For this reason, some guidance is provided on the U.S. FDA design history file.

Other national regulations require some form of documentation and records. Product documentation required by Canada, Europe, and Japan contain certain elements of the U. S. FDA design history file requirements without requiring all the elements to be compiled in a file.

Virtually every section of the design control requirements specifies information which should be recorded. The compilation of these records is sometimes referred to as the design history file.

Throughout this guidance document, suggestions are made when warranted as to the form and content of documents contained in the design history file.

The primary beneficiary of the device history file is the device manufacturer. For example, in one case, a microprocessor-controlled enteral feeding pump was reported to be behaving erratically in the field. Some of the symptoms pointed to software problems. But the manufacturer admitted that they did not possess a copy of the software source code for the product. The software had been developed by a contractor who had delivered only a master EPROM (memory chip) which was duplicated by the manufacturer to install the software in each machine. The contractor had subsequently withdrawn following a contractual dispute, leaving the manufacturer with no rights to the source code developed by the contractor, and no practical way to maintain the software. For this and other reasons, the product was the subject of a mandatory recall and all known units were collected and destroyed.

This is admittedly an extreme case, but many similar cases have been documented in which the manufacturer lacked design information necessary to validate a design and maintain it throughout the product life cycle. This occurs for the most innocent of reasons-contracts expire, companies reorganize, employees move on to new projects or new jobs. Even when the designer is available, he or she may forget why a particular decision was made years, months, or even weeks before. Since design decisions often directly affect the well-being of device users and patients, it is to the manufacturer's benefit to maintain the knowledge base which forms a basis for the product design.

Except for small projects, it is unusual for all design history documents to be filed in a single location. For example, many design engineers maintain laboratory notebooks which are typically retained in the engineers' personal files. In addition, the design history may include memoranda and electronic mail correspondence which are stored at various physical locations. Quality system plans applicable to a development project may reside in the quality assurance department, while the chief engineer may be responsible for maintaining design and development plans. These diverse records need not be consolidated at a single location. The intent is simply that manufacturers have access to the information when it is needed. If a manufacturer has established procedures for multiple filing systems which together satisfy that intent, there is no need to create additional procedures or records.

As an example of the level of detail which may be entailed, some manufacturers have policies covering laboratory notebooks. Manufacturers typically find that without such written procedures, a breakdown in communications eventually occurs, resulting in a loss of control. These procedures might address the following points.

- Laboratory notebooks are the property of the manufacturer, not the individual.

- A separate notebook is to be maintained for each project, and surrendered to the engineering librarian at the conclusion of the engineer's active participation in the project.

- Laboratory notebooks are to be surrendered if the employee leaves the company.

Medical Device Regulation Consulting and Training – www.Procenius.com

- Product development supervisors shall review employees' laboratory notebooks at specified intervals to ensure that records are complete, accurate, and legible.

There are no requirements on the location or organization of the design history file. In some cases, especially for simple designs, the designer will assemble and maintain the entire design history file. For larger projects, a document control system will likely be established for design documents, and these files will likely be maintained in some central location, usually within the product development department.

Based on the structure (or lack thereof) of the product development organization, more or less extensive controls will be required. For example, company policy should state unequivocally that all design history documentation is the property of the manufacturer, not the employee or contractor. Design and development contracts should explicitly specify the manufacturer's right to design information and establish standards for the form and content of design documentation. Finally, certain basic design information may be maintained in a single project file in a specified location. This may include the following:

- Detailed design and development plan specifying design tasks and deliverables.

- Copies of approved design input documents and design output documents.

- Documentation of design reviews.

- Validation documentation.

- When applicable, copies of controlled design documents and change control records.

11.6. Timing of the Design History File

The FDA does not specify when the design history file needs to be compiled, but best practice is to create a revision of the design history file record (if applicable, see section 11.7) at each major phase in development to ensure that design documents are adequately tracked and not inadvertently missed during subsequent design phases. For development projects that take multiple years it can be challenging to keep track of these documents unless they are periodically compiled (or referenced) in a common location such as the design history file record. With the advancement in document control software there are many methods of tracking documents such as a traditional electronic file/directory system or by "tagging" electronic documents with a unique identifier which ties the documents to the design history file record.

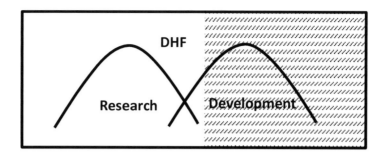

11.7.   Interpretation & Application (21 CFR 820.30 (j))

When the FDA says to "*establish*" a DHF, they mean that the design history file should be defined, documented (in writing or electronically), and implemented. The FDA also says the DHF must be "maintained" or in other words revised and updated as new design documentation is created.

The FDA states that the DHF "**shall contain or reference the records**....". Traditionally design history files would often be a physical compilation of all of the design documents in a file cabinet or in large binders. As devices have become more complex and as electronic records have become the standard, DHF's are now most often a reference file or a record of document numbers which point to (or reference) the document name and number. This is often referred to as the *Device History File Record* (DHFR). The DHFR is typically segregated into easily retrievable design control sub-parts as shown in Table 32.

The Quality Systems Regulation Preamble states:

Comment 91

"*...The intent of the DHF is to document, or reference the documentation of, the activities carried out to meet the design plan and requirements of Sec. 820.30. A DHF is, therefore, necessary for each type of device developed. The DHF must provide documentation showing the actions taken with regard to each type of device designed, not generically link devices together with different design characteristics and give a general overview of how the output was reached...*"

Medical Device Regulation Consulting and Training – www.Procenius.com

TABLE 32

Design and Development Plan		
Document Description	**Document Number**	**Date Approved**

Design Inputs		
Document Description	**Document Number**	**Date Approved**

Design Outputs		
Document Description	**Document Number**	**Date Approved**

Design Reviews		
Document Description	**Document Number**	**Date Approved**

Design Transfer		
Document Description	**Document Number**	**Date Approved**

Verification		
Document Description	**Document Number**	**Date Approved**

Validation		
Document Description	**Document Number**	**Date Approved**

Design Changes		
Document Description	**Document Number**	**Date Approved**

Miscellaneous Documents, Records, Memos etc.		
Document Description	**Document Number**	**Date Approved**

Medical Device Regulation Consulting and Training – www.Procenius.com

---

#1 Best Practice – Create a DHFR revision at each major design phase

Create a DHFR revision at each major phase in development to ensure that design documents are adequately tracked and not inadvertently missed during subsequent design phases. A DHFR revision should be approved and released prior to design transfer. As design changes occur after design transfer, the DHFR should be updated and approved to ensure the DHF is continuously updated as the design changes over time.

In recent years advanced document control software applications have been developed that create virtual DHFR's that are much easier to maintain. Users are able to program pre-defined search queries that enable quick retrieval of design documents into pre-defined files folders such as: design and development plan, design inputs, design outputs, verification, validation, etc.

The DHF should be product focused. Each product should have its own DHF and will not typically be linked to other products. As a general rule, there should be a separate DHF for each commercialized product.

The only typical exceptions to this are when the device design is exactly or almost exactly the same such as in these examples:

- New product designs that are only line extensions where only a few features (for higher end models) are different but the base design is the same (e.g. hard drive with faster processor or more memory etc.)
- New products that only have a few physical characteristics that are different (e.g. different catheter lengths)
- Products that have the exact same design but are sold under different commercial names and only have labeling differences

11.8. Maintaining Ownership of the Design

The FDA wants to make sure that device manufacturers maintain ownership of the device design during development, during production, and until the product is retired. In many instances the ownership of the device may change hands throughout the life of the product. The manufacturer taking new ownership should ensure the design history file is also transferred to them as part of the owner transfer transaction. The new manufacturer will be responsible for maintaining the design and supporting design changes, device investigations, recalls, MDR's, etc.

The Quality Systems Regulation Preamble stated below makes it clear that the device manufacturers need to maintain DHF's so they can "maintain and be accountable for the design process".

Comment 91

…..."The DHF... contains or references all the records necessary to establish compliance with the design plan and the regulation, including the design control procedures. The DHF illustrates the history of the design, and is necessary so that manufacturers can exercise control over and be accountable for the design process, thereby maximizing the probability that the finished design conforms to the design specifications..." (FDA Preamble, 2015)

11.9. DHF vs. DMR vs. DHR

Developers that are just learning design control regulation often find all of the similar acronyms quite confusing. The relationships between the design history file (DHF), device master record (DMR) and device history record (DHR) are often some of the most misunderstood acronyms in the regulation.

Design History File (DHF): In layman's terms, the DHF is a compilation or reference to documents or electronic files that were used during the development of the device that show that the device was developed according to the development plans and requirements.

In the original draft of the design control regulation the FDA stated that "all" records must be contained in the DHF. After considering industry feedback, the FDA removed the word "all" but they clearly caution manufacturers that the "complete history of the design process should be documented in the DHF" as stated in the Quality Systems Preamble, Comment 92:

Comment 92...

"...The proposed requirement does not state that all records must be contained in the DHF, but that all records necessary to demonstrate that the requirements were met must be contained in the file. FDA has deleted the word "all" but cautions manufacturers that the complete history of the design process should be documented in the DHF. Such records are necessary to ensure that the final design conforms to the design specifications. Depending on the design, that may be relatively a few records. Manufacturers who do not document all their design efforts may lose the information and experience of those efforts, thereby possibly requiring activities to be duplicated..." (FDA Preamble, 2015)

So this can be interpreted that the FDA will not hold manufacturers responsible if some inconsequential records are not available, but the implied expectation from the preamble is that the history should be complete and comprehensive.

Medical Device Regulation Consulting and Training – www.Procenius.com

Examples of contents in DHF (will include but not limited to)

- Inputs
- Outputs
- Design and Development Plan (or all plans)
- Verification protocols and reports
- Validation protocols and reports
- Design transfer checklist/protocol
- Design review meeting minutes
- Design change records
- Risk assessments & reports
- Process validation protocols and reports
- Software validation plans, protocols, and reports

Device Master Record (DMR): The easiest way to understand the DMR is to think of it as a "recipe" for the device. A recipe for a cake typically describes the required ingredients and how to cook it. The DMR is very much the same, it will typically specify the raw materials, component / assembly drawings, labeling, manufacturing instructions, process instructions, inspection instructions, device history record forms, etc. In simple terms the DMR can be thought of as the documents (or electronic files) that define what materials, components, software, and labelling needed to make the device and instructions for how the device is manufactured, processed, packaged and inspected.

The Quality Systems Regulation Preamble comments 76 and 90 describe outputs and the device master record:

Comment 76…

…"The output includes the device, its labeling and packaging, associated specifications and drawings, and production and quality assurance specifications and procedures. These documents are the basis for the device master record (DMR). The total finished design output consists of the device, its labeling and packaging, and the DMR." (FDA Preamble, 2015)

Comment 90…

…"The DMR contains the documentation necessary to produce a device. The final design output from the design phase, which is maintained or referenced in the DHF, will form the basis or starting point for the DMR. Thus, those outputs must be referred to or placed in the DMR. The total finished device design output includes device specifications and drawings, as well as all instructions and procedures for production, installation, maintenance, and servicing."

Medical Device Regulation Consulting and Training – www.Procenius.com

Examples of contents in DMR (will include but not limited to)

- Component and assembly drawings
- Labeling
- Manufacturing instructions
- In process and incoming inspection
- Bill of materials
- Software code
- Manufacturing equipment
- Anything else that defines the device or the process of how the device is manufactured

What is NOT included in the DMR (these are development documents, they are not the device "recipe")

- Design and development plan (or any plans)
- Risk Assessments
- Verification / Validation protocols or reports
- Design requirements (or any inputs)
- Meeting Minutes
- Design change records
- Anything else that DOES NOT define the device or the process of how the device is manufactured and/or how quality control of the device is implemented

All of the items in Figure 51 are contained in the design history file but only those outputs connected by a dotted line arrow are part of the DMR. It is important to realize that the DMR is a subset of items within the DHF, or in other words the DHF contains the DMR but not the other way around. The DMR is usually categorized in the output section of the DHF.

Relationship between Design Outputs and DMR

FIGURE 51

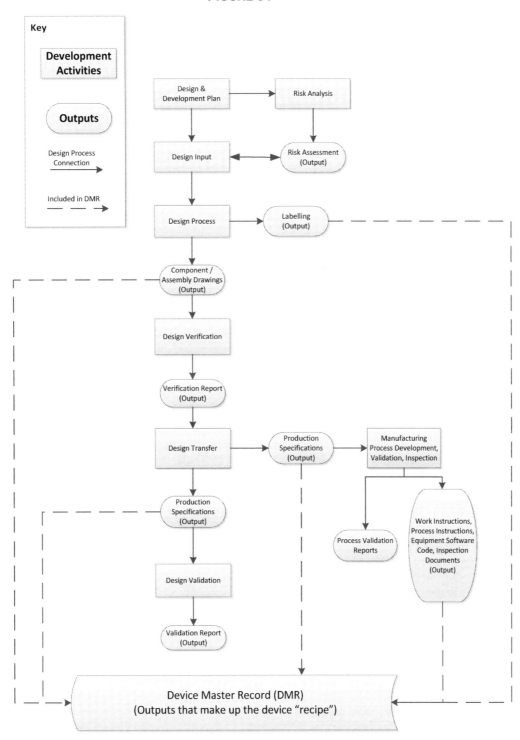

Medical Device Regulation Consulting and Training – www.Procenius.com

Device History Record (DHR) (not part of design control regulation): A compilation of records containing the production history of a finished device. (FDA QSR , 2014)

The DHR consists of all of the records used to produce, inspect or package a specific device (unique unit). Previous discussions of the DMR and DHF focus on the "design and development" of the device. The DHR is specific to a particular serialized device. The DHR may consist of batch records which contain information such as material lot numbers, device serial numbers, process parameters, or results from in process or final inspection. The DHR should be able to be used to trace exactly how and when and by whom a specific device was manufactured and inspected. The records should also provide a traceability trail back to the raw materials used or the supplier manufacturer.

In some cases where devices are serviced in the field, records of upgrades or repairs should be recorded as part of the DHR also.

11.10.   Quality Systems Manual: Design History File

DESIGN HISTORY FILE

Excerpt from the "Quality Systems Manual: A Small Entity Compliance Guide"
(Withdrawn from FDA website 12 December 2013)
(FDA QS Manual, 2013)

Design history file (DHF) means a compilation of records which describes the design history of a finished device [820.3(e)].

The DHF covers the design activities used to develop the device, accessories, major components, labeling, packaging and production processes.

The design controls in 820.30(j) require that each manufacturer shall establish and maintain a DHF for each type of device. Each type of device means a device or family of devices that are manufactured according to one DMR. That is, if the variations in the family of devices are simple enough that they can be handled by minor variations on the drawings, then only one DMR exists. It is common practice to identify device variations on drawings by dash numbers. For this case, only one DHF could exist because only one set of related design documentation exists. Documents are never created just to go into the DHF.

The QS regulation also requires that the DHF shall contain or reference the records necessary to demonstrate that the design was developed in accordance with the approved design plan and the requirements of this part. As noted, this requirement cannot be met unless the manufacturer develops and maintains plans that meet the design control requirements. The plans and subsequent updates should be part of the DHF. In addition, the

Medical Device Regulation Consulting and Training – www.Procenius.com

QS regulation specifically requires that:

- the results of a design review, including identification of the design, the date, and the individual(s) performing the review, shall be documented in the DHF.

- design verification shall confirm that the design output meets the design input requirements.

The results of the design verification, including identification of the design, method(s), the date, and the individual(s) performing the verification, shall be documented in the DHF.

Typical documents that may be in, or referenced in, a DHF are listed below:

- design plans;
- design review meeting information;
- sketches;
- drawings;
- procedures;
- photos;
- engineering notebooks;
- component qualification information;
- biocompatibility (verification) protocols and data;
- design review notes;
- verification protocols and data for evaluating prototypes;
- validation protocols and data for initial finished devices;
- contractor / consultants information;
- parts of design output/DMR documents that show plans were followed; and
- parts of design output/DMR documents that show specifications were met.

The DHF contains documents such as the design plans and input requirements, preliminary input specs, validation data and preliminary versions of key DMR documents. These are needed to show that plans were created, followed and specifications were met.

The DHF is not required to contain all design documents or to contain the DMR, however, it will contain historical versions of key DMR documents that show how the design evolved.

Does the DHF have value for the manufacturer? Yes, when problems occur during re-design and for new designs, the DHF has the "institutional" memory of previous design activities. The DHF also contains valuable verification and validation protocols that are not in DMR. This information may be very valuable in helping to solve a problem; pointing to the correct direction to solve a problem; or, most important, preventing the manufacturer from repeating an already tried and found-to-be-useless design.

12.0   Risk Management

12.1. Overview

The FDA has this to say about risk management in the Design Control Guidance (FDA D.C. Guidance, 2015):

> **"RISK MANAGEMENT AND DESIGN CONTROLS**. Risk management is the systematic application of management policies, procedures, and practices to the tasks of identifying, analyzing, controlling, and monitoring risk. It is intended to be a framework within which experience, insight, and judgment are applied to successfully manage risk. It is included in this guidance because of its effect on the design process.
>
> Risk management begins with the development of the design input requirements. As the design evolves, new risks may become evident. To systematically identify and, when necessary, reduce these risks, the risk management process is integrated into the design process. In this way, unacceptable risks can be identified and managed earlier in the design process when changes are easier to make and less costly."

Most of the risk management framework as outlined in this chapter is based on ISO 14971:2007 as referenced. (ISO 14971, 2007)

12.2. Quick Reference Summary

TABLE 33

Purpose	Risk management is the systematic application of management policies, procedures, and practices to the tasks of identifying, analyzing, controlling, and monitoring risk. It is intended to be a framework within which experience, insight, and judgment are applied to successfully manage risk. (FDA D.C. Guidance, 2015)
Regulation	21 CFR 820.30 (g): …Design validation shall include software validation and **risk analysis**, where appropriate…

Standard(s)	ISO 14971:2007	
Guidance	21 CFR 820.30 (g) (FDA)	FDA Design Control Guidance for Medical Device Manufacturers (FDA D.C. Guidance, 2015)
Timing of Risk Management Relative to the Research and Development Cycle	FIGURE 52 The two humps in Figure 52 depict the relationship and the relative amount of research and development activities during the design and development cycle. The shaded area is the typical time when risk management is performed.	

Deliverables	1) **Risk Assessment**
	  • <u>Risk Analysis-</u> Systematic use of available information to identify hazards and to estimate the risk
	
	  • <u>Risk Evaluation -</u> Process of comparing the estimated risk against given risk criteria to determine the acceptability of the risk
	
	2) **Risk Management Report**
	    Summary of final results from the risk management process
	
	                (ISO 14971, 2007)	

Types of Risk Assessments	**Design Risk Assessment** Risk assessments which evaluate the risk to device users, patients or the environment which are caused by design features failing, performing or functioning as intended. **Process Risk Assessment** Risk assessments which evaluate the risk to device users, patients or the environment which are caused by a process (typically manufacturing) failing, performing or functioning as intended.
Risk Management Process	1. Risk Assessment (Risk Analysis & Evaluation) 2. Risk Control 3. Residual Risk Reduction 4. Risk Management Report 5. Production and Post-Production Information (ISO 14971, 2007)
Approval	A cross functional team typically approves risk management reports. The cross functional team should have the expertise to understand the various risks identified in the risk assessment and report. Management's approval indicates that they agree and accept the risk levels indicated in the risk management report. Approvals should be documented manually with signature and date or electronically to be in compliance with 21 CFR part 11.

	Typical Approvers:
	Cross Functional Team Management
	Quality Assurance VP of Quality Assurance
	Operations VP of Medical Affairs
	R&D / Engineering VP of R&D /Engineering
	Clinicians
Revisions	The risk management plan and report are living documents and should be updated and revised as risks are discovered and mitigated as the design evolves. The plan and report may be revised as necessary throughout the design process and should follow the same review and approval process which was required for the initial version.
Best Practices	Use a standard operating procedure for risk management
Templates	Visit **Procenius.com** to download risk management assessments, plans, and report templates.

12.3. Regulation (21 CFR 820.30) - Risk Management

The regulation only briefly mentions risk analysis (risk management) in the design validation section (21 CFR 820.30 (g)).

Design validation shall include software validation and <u>risk analysis</u>, where appropriate.

Other than this mention of risk analysis in the regulation, the only other place it is mentioned is in the FDA quality system preamble and in the design control guidance as provided in the overview section at the beginning of this chapter.

12.4. Timing of Risk Management Activities

In the Design Controls Guidance the FDA indicates that risk management should begin as the design input requirements are being developed. The following graphical models give some clarity as to when risk management typically begins and ends relative to research and development activities. In reality risk management of a device will never end until the device is retired. Even after development, design changes and failures will occur which should instigate a review and update of the risk assessment.

The two humps in Figure 53 depict the relationship and the relative amount of research and development activities during the design and development cycle. The shaded area is the typical time when risk management is performed.

FIGURE 53

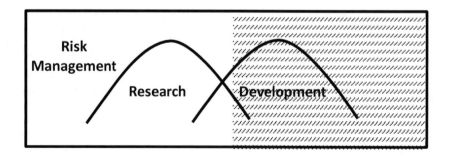

Medical Device Regulation Consulting and Training – www.Procenius.com

12.5. ISO 14971 – Industry Standard and FDA Expectations

Even though the FDA does not have significant guidance addressing risk management, they do recognize and expect medical device manufacturers to follow industry standard risk management definitions, principles and techniques such as those found in ISO 14971. The following sections are not intended to be comprehensive, but is intended to complement the use of ISO 14971 and clarify the standard which is already quite comprehensive. (ISO 14971, 2007)

FDA Quality System Preamble states:

"FDA believes that sufficient domestic and international guidelines are available to provide assistance to manufacturers for the validation of software and risk analysis." (FDA Preamble, 2015)

12.6. Key Risk Management Terms and Definitions (ISO 14971:2007)

Harm: Physical injury or damage to the health of people or damage to property of the environment

Hazard: Potential source of harm

Hazardous Situation: Circumstance where people, property or the environment are exposed to one or more hazard(s)

Intended Use: Use for which a product, process or service is intended according to the specifications, instructions and information provided by the manufacturer

Residual Risk: Risk remaining after risk control measures have been taken

Risk: Combination of the probability of occurrence of harm and the severity of that harm

Risk Analysis: Systematic use of available information to identify hazards and to estimate the risk

Risk Assessment: Overall process compromising risk analysis and risk evaluation

Risk Control: Process in which decisions are made and measures implemented by which risks are reduced to, or maintained within specified levels

Risk Estimation: Process used to assign values to the probability of occurrence of harm and the severity of that harm

Risk Evaluation: Process of comparing the estimated risk against given risk criteria to determine the acceptability of the risk

Risk Management: Systematic application of management policies, procedures, and practices to the task of analyzing, evaluating, controlling and monitoring risk

Severity: Measure of the possible consequences of a hazard

12.7.   How to Implement Risk Management

12.7.1.   Risk Management Plan

Like every other development activity, the FDA expects risk management activities to be planned. The plan can take many different forms depending on the organization where it is being utilized. Experienced medical device manufacturers may have a standard risk management operating procedure in place that has pre-established how risk management should be performed. In most cases using a standard risk management procedure[BP1] is best practice because consistency of how risk management is performed between multiple products or between the same product throughout its life cycle is not only important to the FDA but will also encourage compliance.

#1 Best Practice – Use a standard operating procedure for risk management

Using a standard risk management procedure will allow for consistency during the risk management process between product development cycles. Without a standard operating procedure, the subjectivity involved in the risk assessment process may vary greatly over time.

The risk management procedure will typically contain general procedures pertaining to how risk management should be executed at a high level as illustrated in Figure 54. When at all possible, the plan should reference the risk management procedure as well as other standard quality management system documents which will encourage consistency during the development process. Even though a risk management procedure is available, a plan still needs to be developed to explain how those general procedures will be specifically applied for the device that is being developed.

The risk management plan should include "what" and "how" risk management activities will be performed and "who" is assigned to perform them. The typical outline of a risk management plan will include the following sections:

Medical Device Regulation Consulting and Training – www.Procenius.com

- Purpose
- Scope
- Responsibility and Authority
- Risk Management Requirements
- Risk Acceptability Criteria
- Risk Verification
- Production Activity Data Collection and Review
- Post Production Activity Collection and Review

The contents of what should be included in these sections of the risk management plan will be become more evident during the following explanation of the risk management process.

12.7.2.   Risk Management File

The risk management file is simply a compilation (or reference to) the following risk management records:

- Risk Analysis
- Risk Evaluation
- Evidence of Implementation and verification of risk controls
- Assessment of the acceptability of residual risk

12.7.3.   Risk Management Process

The risk management process is a systematic method of analyzing, evaluating, reducing, controlling, and monitoring risks. ISO 14971 (ISO 14971, 2007) defines the risk management process as shown in Figure 54.

FIGURE 54

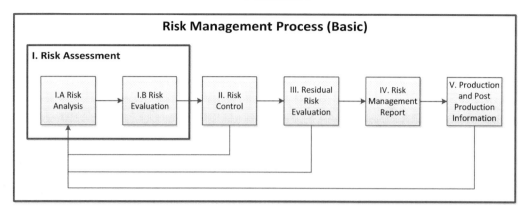

FIGURE 54

12.7.3.1. I. Risk Assessment

The risk assessment is a sub-process of the overall risk management process comprised of risk *analysis* and *risk evaluation*.

FIGURE 55

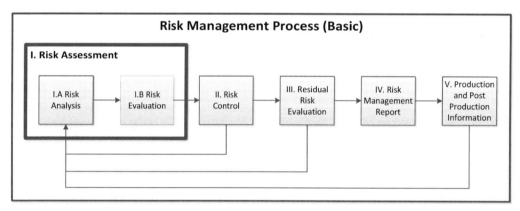

I.A Risk Analysis

In basic terms, a risk analysis is the method medical device developers use to try and predict or foresee what risks medical devices may potentially pose. In many respects, initial risk analyses for new devices are often very subjective, educated guesses. Even though they may be subjective evaluations, they are a solid starting point in an effort to make the device as safe as possible.

Even the most thorough risk analysis will not be able to predict the potentially endless number of possible risks, but as a natural consequence of mitigating as many risk as practically possible, the design will be improved with the addition of safety controls and increased robustness that will mitigate even unforeseen risks.

<u>Risk Analysis Process Steps</u>

1. **Determine Intended Use and Identify Characteristics Related to the Safety of the Medical Device**
    a. Intended use and foreseeable misuse of the device should be documented
    b. Characteristics that could affect the safety of the device should be identified and documented.

2. **Identify Hazards**

    <u>Hazard:</u> Potential source of harm

    To identify all known and foreseeable hazards, all possible internal and external expert resources should be tapped such as: technical experts, product managers (marketing), customer service representatives, account managers (sales), clinical specialist (i.e. physicians), etc. Additional resources should also include data from similar devices in the field to ensure real life hazards and hazardous situations are integrated back into the development risk analysis.

    It is very important to consider possible hazards in both the normal and fault conditions. In other words, hazards that may occur from the device failing or when hazards may occur during normal use due to user error or unintended use.

IMPORTANT

It is very important to consider possible hazards in both the normal and fault conditions. In other words, hazards that may occur from the device failing or when the device is functioning properly with consideration of user error or unintended use.

The Quality Systems Regulation Preamble States:

Comment 83

…*"When conducting a risk analysis, manufacturers are expected to identify possible hazards associated with the design in both normal and fault conditions. The risks associated with the hazards, including those resulting from user error, should then be calculated in both normal and fault conditions."* (FDA Preamble, 2015)

3. **Estimate Risk(s) for Each Hazardous Situation**

   <u>Hazardous Situation:</u> Circumstance where people, property or the environment are exposed to one or more hazard(s)

   a. **Identify Initiation and Intermediate Events that Lead to Hazardous Situations (Causes)**

   There may be numerous causes or events which lead to hazardous situations. Events should be described in general terms and then expanded to more detail conditions. All initial events and those intermediate events which cause a domino effect that eventually lead to a hazardous situation should be identified as part of this analysis.

   b. **Identify the Harm(s)**

   <u>Harm:</u> Physical injury or damage to the health of people or damage to property of the environment

   In many instances a clinical specialist such as a physician or nurse is most qualified to understand the harm that a patient or user may experience when exposed to a hazardous situation.

   c. **Estimate the Severity and Probability of Harm (Risk)**

   <u>Severity:</u> Measure of the possible consequences of a hazard

   <u>Risk:</u> Combination of the probability of occurrence of harm and the severity of that harm

   The heart of a risk analysis is determining the severity level and probability of harm. Just as understanding the harm requires a clinical specialist, so does determining the severity of the harm that a patient may experience when exposed to a hazardous situation. The probability of occurrence of harm will often need to be determined by a cross functional team that is qualified to understand the causes and events which lead to a hazardous situation. This team may include clinical specialists, engineers, product managers (marketing), sales or other team members that have knowledge of the device and its intended use.

   Severity tables like the one below (Table 34) are often established in risk management plans or in standard operating procedures. Using a severity of harm table allows consistency for risk analyses for multiple devices analyzed.

TABLE 34

Severity Levels of Harm	
Level	**Description**
Catastrophic (Ca)	Results in Death
Critical (C)	Results in permanent impairment to life-threatening injury
Serious (S)	Results in injury or impairment requiring medical intervention
Minor (M)	Results in injury or impairment not requiring medical intervention
Negligible (N)	Inconvenience or temporary discomfort

Probability of occurrence tables like the one below (Table 35) are often established in risk management plans or in standard operating procedures. Using a probability of occurrence table allows consistency for risk analyses for multiple devices analyzed.

TABLE 35

Probability of Occurrence	
Level	**Description**
Frequent (F)	Happens often
Probable (P)	Likely to happen
Occasional (O)	Can happen, but not likely
Remote (R)	Unlikely to happen
Improbable (I)	Highly unlikely to happen

d. Calculate the Risk

Risk: Combination of the probability of occurrence of harm and the severity of that harm

Therefore risk can be calculated by (ISO 14971, 2007) where:

$$\text{Risk} = (P^1 \times P^2) \times SL$$

P^1 = Probability of Hazardous Situation Occurring

P^2 = Probability of Hazardous Situation Leading to Harm

SL = Severity of Harm

There is an important distinction between P^1 and P^2 that should be thoroughly understood when determining this probability. P^1 is the probability of the cause(s) or sequence of events that may lead to a hazardous situation. P^2 on the other hand is the probability of harm occurring once the hazardous situation occurs.

As an example:

A medical device has a power cord that has a worn outer cover (insulation and grounding material) which has bare metal wires exposed (the hazard). Hazardous situations would include the power cord being plugged in and the user coming in contact with the bare wires with his shoe, hand, arm, leg or other body parts. Other hazardous situations include the bare metal wires coming in contact with equipment or other items in the environment. Each hazardous situation would have its own probability of occurring (P^1).

The resulting harms from those hazardous situations would vary: burns, ventricular fibrillation, neurological effects, and death. Each possible harm would have its own probability (P^2) of occurrence based on the body parts exposed and other environmental factors such as the presence of an insulator (i.e. clothes, shoes, gloves, carpet)

The combination of P^1 and P^2 should be considered as the overall probability for each hazardous situation. This example is explained in detailed in a risk analysis example at the end of the chapter.

Medical Device Regulation Consulting and Training – www.Procenius.com

IMPORTANT

Determining Overall Probability of Occurrence of Hazardous Situations Using Fault Tree Analysis

A fault tree analysis is a very useful and simple evaluation tool to effectively assess the overall probability of each hazardous situation. This type of analysis identifies hazardous situations which are a result of single or multiple fault scenario(s). Single fault scenarios have much higher probabilities of occurrence relative to multiple fault conditions as illustrated in Figure 56 and Figure 57 below. Therefore it is best practice to increase the number of fault conditions which must occur for a given hazardous situation based on the results of the risk analysis.

The Quality Systems Regulation Preamble States:

Comment 83

..." Tools for conducting such analyses [risk analysis] include Failure Mode Effect Analysis and Fault Tree Analysis, among others."

Medical Device Regulation Consulting and Training – www.Procenius.com

FIGURE 56

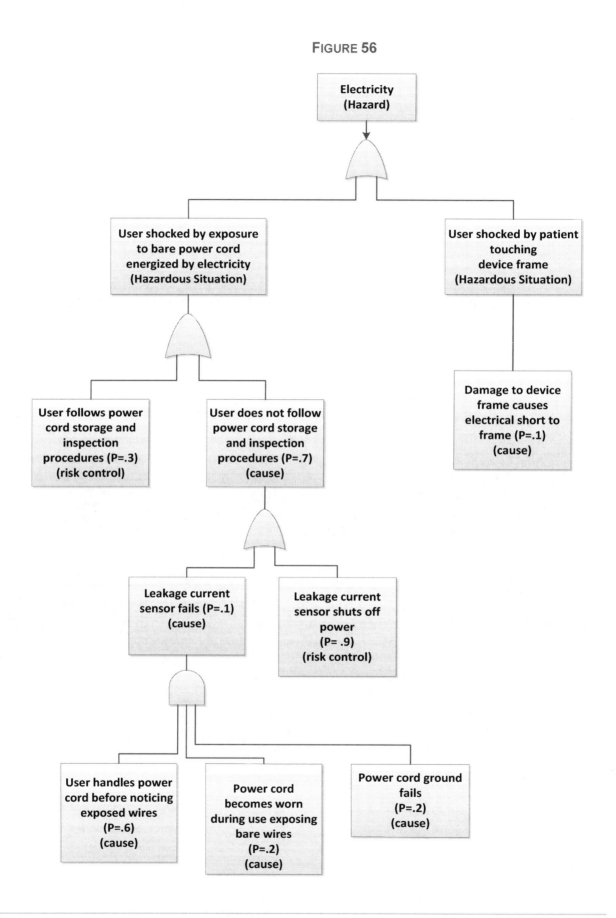

Medical Device Regulation Consulting and Training – www.Procenius.com

This example clearly illustrates that multiple fault conditions have a significantly lower probability of harm than a single fault condition.

Probability of shock caused by touching the device frame: .1 X 100 = 10%

Probability of shock caused by exposure to bare power cord: .7 X .1 X .6 X .2 X .2 X100 = 0.17%

Medical Device Regulation Consulting and Training – www.Procenius.com

FIGURE 57

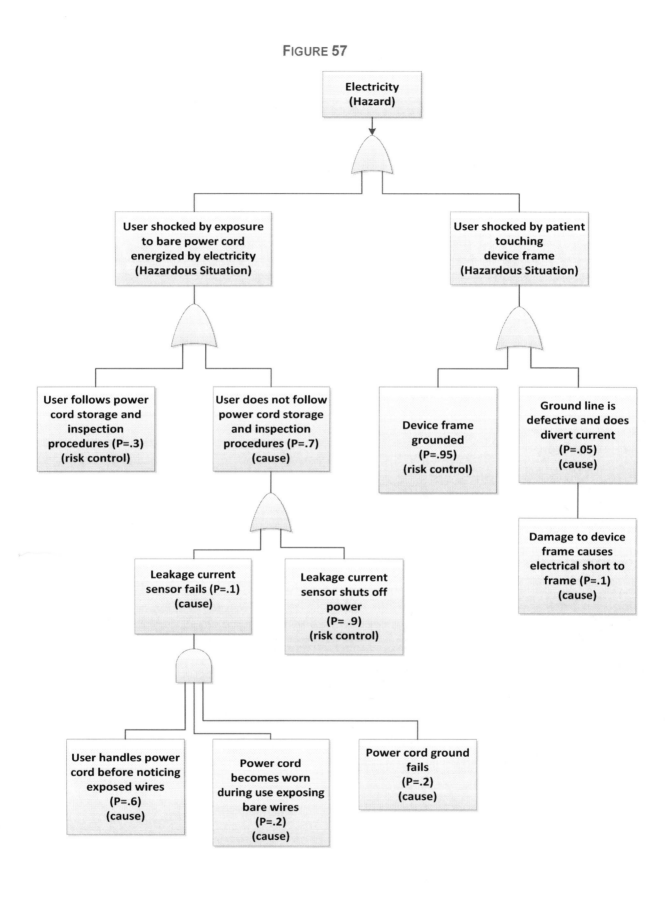

Medical Device Regulation Consulting and Training – www.Procenius.com

By adding a risk control to reduce the probability of shock from touching the device frame, the single fault condition is converted to a multiple fault condition.

The probability of shock caused by touching the device frame went from 10% to 0.5% (.05 X .1 X 100 = 0.5%).

I.B Risk Evaluation

<u>Risk Evaluation:</u> Process of comparing the estimated risk against given risk criteria to determine the acceptability of the risk

The risk evaluation is the second part of the risk assessment (risk analysis being the first). The risk evaluation is often performed using a table which provides a risk level for a given severity level and probability of occurrence.

The following table is an example of how a risk evaluation is performed. Tables such as this are often developed in a risk management plan or a standard operating procedure. The R1, R2 and R3 represent three risk levels that have been pre-determined in the plan or procedure. The plan or the procedure may require different levels of scrutiny for each resultant risk level (R1, R2, R3).

For example, level R1 risks may only require the development team's approval with no required actions. Level R2 risk may require mitigation of risks through implementation of design controls. The procedure may also require additional approval for R2 level risks such as executive management. If residual risks end up being a R3 level, the procedure may require a risk vs. benefit analysis as explained by ISO 14971. The analysis can be performed to determine if the availability of the medical device to the public ("the benefit") outweighs the risk to the patient. The risk vs. benefit analysis should typically be approved by a cross functional team which should include a qualified clinician such as a physician.

R1= Acceptable Risk

R2= As low as reasonably practicable (ALARP)

R3= Unacceptable

Risk Evaluation (Example 1)

TABLE 36

		Severity of Harm Levels				
		Negligible	Minor	Serious	Critical	Catastrophic
Probability of Occurrence	**Frequent**	R2	R2	R3	R3	R3
	Probable	R2	R2	R2	R2	R3
	Occasional	R2	R2	R2	R2	R3
	Remote	R1	R1	R2	R2	R3
	Improbable	R1	R1	R2	R2	R3

The previous table is just one configuration that device manufacturers may use to evaluate risk. The risk evaluation table may vary depending on the device being manufactured. The following examples are additional examples of risk evaluation tables that may be used.

Risk Evaluation (Example 2)

TABLE 37

		Severity of Harm Levels				
		Negligible	Minor	Serious	Critical	Catastrophic
Probability of Occurrence	**Frequent**	R2	R2	R3	R3	R3
	Probable	R2	R2	R3	R3	R3
	Occasional	R1	R2	R2	R3	R3
	Remote	R1	R1	R2	R2	R3
	Improbable	R1	R1	R2	R2	R2

Risk Evaluation (Example 3)

TABLE 38

		Severity of Harm Levels				
		Negligible	Minor	Serious	Critical	Catastrophic
Probability of Occurrence	Frequent	R2	R2	R3	R3	R3
	Probable	R2	R2	R3	R3	R3
	Occasional	R1	R2	R2	R3	R3
	Remote	R1	R1	R2	R2	R2
	Improbable	R1	R1	R1	R2	R2

12.7.3.2. II. Risk Controls

Risk Control: Process in which decisions are made and measures implemented by which risks are reduced to, or maintained within specified levels

FIGURE 58

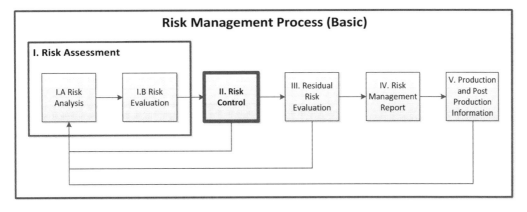

After the initial risk assessment (risk analysis and evaluation) is performed, risk controls should be implemented for all risks that are not acceptable by the manufacturer. Ideally an

initial risk assessment should be performed early in the development cycle to allow for adequate time and resources to be dedicated to mitigating the identified risks. At times risk controls include redesign aspects of the device that may be very cost prohibitive if introduced late in the development cycle. If risk assessments are performed early in the development cycle the design is often at the prototype level or just a design concept that can easily be changed with little cost.

The Quality Systems Regulation Preamble States:

Comment 83

…"If any risk is judged unacceptable, it should be reduced to acceptable levels by the appropriate means, for example, by redesign or warnings [Risk Controls]. An important part of risk analysis is ensuring that changes made to eliminate or minimize hazards do not introduce new hazards…."

Risk controls usually take at least of one of the following forms:

- Safety by design
- Protective design or manufacturing measures
- Information for safety; labeling, warnings, etc.

Safety by Design: The safety by design approach should be attempted first when trying to mitigate risks. This approach typically involves designing device features that prevent hazardous situations from occurring. This approach is the most robust because it gets to the heart of the condition that causes the hazard in the first place. As previously mentioned, risks identified early in the design process can be mitigated by implementing "safety by design" improvements.

Protective Measures: Protective measure should be the second priority of design measures used to mitigate risks. In theory most protective measures will be additional or backup safety features that will be used to protect device users, but in reality this approach often ends up being a "band aid" approach that is used because the risk was identified too late in the design cycle and it is less expensive to implement a protective measure (or band aid) instead of re-designing safety into the design.

Information for Safety: This is by far the least preferred risk prevention method of the three approaches. This approach uses labeling such as instructions for use or warning labels to mitigate risks. This approach is least preferred because of the inherent ineffectiveness of this method. The premise of this approach relies on potentially multiple unreliable human factors. First, the assumption is that the user will actually see and read the information. Second, the user actually understands the information. Third, the user will actually follow the information directions or warnings. The "information for safety" approach is often the most abused

Medical Device Regulation Consulting and Training – www.Procenius.com

because it is the quickest and least expensive "band aid" of them all. In many instances device manufacturers will discover risks late in development when designs have already been verified and validated and any change would greatly increase design costs or delay product launch. As an unethical compromise device manufacturers will mitigate the risk by providing additional labeling that may or may not effectively mitigate the risk.

The "information for safety" approach should only typically be used under the following conditions:

- When it is used as a backup risk mitigation method where "safety by design" and "protective measures" are the first line of defense.

- When the "information" being used to mitigate risk is validated to be effective through human factors studies or other validation studies.

Risk Controls Examples

TABLE 39

Hazard	Hazardous Situation	Cause	Type of Risk Control	Example of Risk Control
Device power cord is energized with high voltage/amps.	The energized wires within the device power cord are exposed to the user.	Outer sheath of power cord becomes worn due to dragging cord on floor and across abrasive and sharp objects	Safety by Design	1) The outer sheath is designed with a highly durable material such as braided metal or highly wear resistant plastic. A design requirement is established which requires a design which will resist wear and / or 2) The device is designed with low voltage and amperage that will not cause serious harm to patient if exposed to bare wires.
			Protective Measures	The power cord is designed with a grounding sheath and is connected to a ground fault circuit interrupt to protect the user if exposed to high voltage and amps
			Information for Safety	A warning label is fixed to the power cord which warns users of possible electric shock if bare wires are exposed.

The most effective risk control is "safety by design" #2. Ideally if the design can be changed such that low voltage and amperage can be used; the severity of harm and therefore the overall risk will be reduced. In the early stages of development changing the required line power may be insignificant. If this change was implemented at the end of the design phase, the entire electrical design including components, power supplies, motors etc. would need to be revamped. In most instances device manufacturers would go with the path of least resistance and implement protective measures or provide information for safety to mitigate the risk. While using the latter two approaches may be the easiest to rationalize, it is most likely not the safest approach. Ideally all three risk controls could be implemented if needed to reduce the risk to acceptable levels.

Risk Controls Verification

After a risk control is identified, the implementation and effectiveness of the risk control must be verified. There are two types of verification that should be performed when implementing risk controls.

1. Verify that the risk control was actually implemented as part of the device design

2. Verify that the risk control was effective

There are numerous ways to implement this verification, but as outlined in the design inputs chapter, one typical way is to let the risk control be an input to the design input requirements. This approach will kill two birds with one stone. During design verification the risk controls will be verified along with all of the other design input requirements. As a natural consequence of including it in the design input requirements, verification will require an approved method and adequate sample size to give developers confidence that the device meets it's input requirements which in this case are the risk controls. Therefore the design verification will document that the risk control was actually implemented as part of the device and that it is an effective risk control.

Medical Device Regulation Consulting and Training – www.Procenius.com

12.7.3.3. III. Residual Risk Evaluation

Residual Risk: Risk remaining after risk control measures have been taken

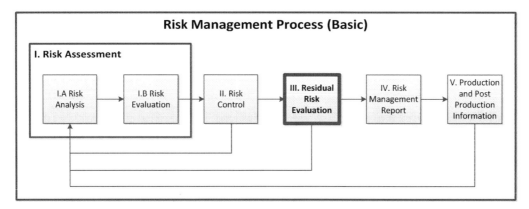

FIGURE 59

After implementation of risk controls, risks should be reanalyzed (reassess probability of hazardous situation occuring) and re-evaluated using a risk evaluation table to determine if the risk controls impacted the risk level. In most instances after risk controls are implemented it is assumed that the risk level will be reduced or at least stay the same depending on the effectiveness of the control. Unfortunately this is not always the case, in some instances implementing risk controls may unintentionally increase the risk level for some design features. If this is the case, the new elevated risk should be addressed through the risk management process as previously described. Ideally the risk levels would be reduced to an acceptable level or at least as low as reasonably practicable (ALARP). If the risk levels are not adequately reduced, additional risk control measures should be pursued or a risk vs. benefit analysis should considered as possible next steps.

Medical Device Regulation Consulting and Training – www.Procenius.com

12.7.3.4. IV. Risk Management Report (Key Stages of Product Development)

FIGURE 60

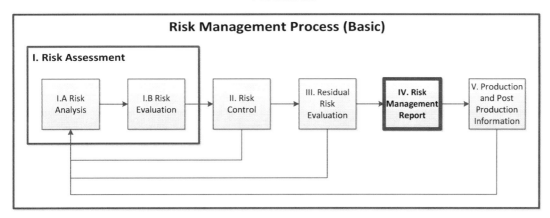

The final risk management report should contain the following:

- Results from all risk assessment(s) revisions
- Evidence of risk controls being implemented
- Evidence of risk controls effectiveness
- Results from residual risk evaluation and acceptability (approval)
- Risk vs. medical benefit analysis (if applicable)
- Method of how production and post-production information will be collected

The risk management report should be created, revised and approved at key stages during product development.

Risk Management Report (Revision I; Risk Assessment)

The initial revision of the report typically includes the results and documentation of the risk assessment activities (risk analysis and risk evaluation). Typically the risk assessment activities will identify the need to update the design input requirements with "safety requirements" which will be used to mitigate risk. Therefore the design input requirements document is typically developed in parallel with the initial version of the risk management report. Ideally this revision will be approved prior to a majority of the design work and design verifications being performed to allow risk controls to be implemented concurrently into the design instead of post design or verification.

The initial revision of the risk management report should include:

- A description and identification of the medical device being analyzed
- Identification of the persons and organization who carried out the risk analysis
- Scope and date of the risk analysis

- Results of the initial risk analysis and evaluation
- Approval of the report including results and conclusion

Risk Management Report (Revision II; Risk Controls Implementation and Residual Report)

The second revision of the risk management report will document evidence of the risk controls implementation, evidence of risk controls effectiveness, the residual risk and risk vs. benefit analysis (if applicable). If the risk controls are determined to be insufficient after evaluating the residual risk, the design should be iterated to implement additional risk controls as illustrated in Figure 59. If the risk controls are not able to reduce the risk to a level that is "As Low As Reasonably Practicable", a risk vs. benefit analysis should be considered.

The final revision of the risk management report should include:

- A description and identification of the medical device being evaluated

- Identification of the persons and organization who carried out the risk management plan

- Scope and date of completion of the risk management plan (as applicable to the status of the plan)

- Results of the risk analysis and evaluation (at that sate in development or final version)

- Approval of the report including results and conclusion

FIGURE 61

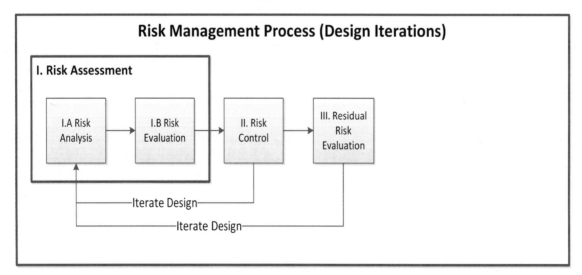

Medical Device Regulation Consulting and Training – www.Procenius.com

12.7.3.5. V. Production and Post-Production Information

As new devices are developed and used in the field, new hazardous situations will be discovered that were not able to be predicted in the original risk assessment.

Therefore, after a medical device becomes commercialized (product launch into the field), a process should be developed to collect data from device non-conformances, failures, injury, or death. The resultant collected data should include a minimum of the following categories:

- Device failures during use (including features that failed)
- Non-conformances (production environment)
- Harm caused to user or patients (Injury or death from failure)
- Root cause of failure
- Events leading up to failure
- Frequency of failure

Production and post-production information is a valuable source for field assurance representatives and medical device developers. Field assurance representatives should be tracking device failures and harm to users or patients which are captured through the complaint system. Statistical tracking of device failures should be monitored for trends that may indicate that there is a systematic problem that should be addressed.

New product development teams also highly value this data. Frequently new products are based off of similar previous designs from which field assurance device data can be used to predict risks in new products. (See Figure 62)

FIGURE 62

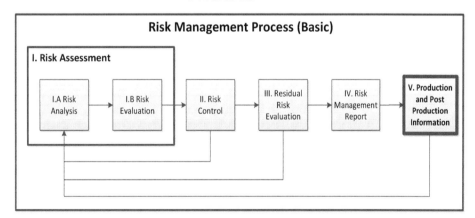

Medical Device Regulation Consulting and Training – www.Procenius.com

12.8. Risk Analysis Process Example (portable MRI machine)

The following example represents a risk analysis of a portable MRI machine. In this complex machine there will be a significant number of potential hazards ranging from electrical, mechanical, electromagnetic, etc.

Table 40 below shows how a risk analysis table can become very in depth and extensive. This example only contains two types of hazard and one hazardous situation associated with each hazard. This example will walk through the detail steps of how to perform a risk analysis.

Step 1 - Determine intended use and identify characteristics related to the safety of the medical Device

Intended use of the portable MRI machine is an imaging device which allows clinicians the ability to non-invasively determine clinical and anatomical patient information by detecting magnetic resonance (MR) signals from the body. The images produced from the MR reflect the spatial distribution of protons which exhibit magnetic resonance. When interpreted by a trained clinician, these images provide information that can be useful in diagnosis determination.

Safety Related Device Characteristics Identify device characteristics (or features) which could affect the safety of the device. In this example - electrical, mechanical and electromagnetic hazards were identified.

Step 2 - Identify all known and foreseeable hazards (hazard analysis)

For the portable MRI machine, three initial hazards have been identified:

- Device power cord is energized with high voltage/amps

- Access door to patient platform

- MRI generates high power electromagnetic energy

Step 3 - Risk of hazardous situations should be estimated with associated hazards and causes

The following table is an example of three hazards with associated hazardous situations and causes which led to the hazardous situations.

Hazard Analysis

TABLE 40

Hazard	Hazardous Situation	Causes / Chain of Events
Device power cord is energized with high voltage/amps	Cord has exposed bare wires and is handled by user or patient	Cord is dragged through hall way when machine is moved which causes the sheath to become damaged
		Environmental conditions cause sheath to crack and cause exposure (heat, chemicals, etc.)
		Wrapping of cord around machine causes excessive stress to wire sheath
Access door to patient platform	The access door closes on patient/users fingers, arms, legs or head.	User inadvertently closes access door on patient
		Access door hinge fails due to material fatigue or wear
		Access door closes on door due to door being bumped and force of gravity

MRI generates high power electromagnetic energy	Electromagnetic energy attracts ferrous metal objects when patient is on platform	Ferrous metal objects are brought into close proximity to MRI machine
		Ferrous metal objects in patient are not identified
		Combination of inputs to MRI software induces unintended and excessive electromagnetic energy.

The culmination of the risk assessment and risk controls implementation is defined in Table 42 in a Failure Modes Effects "like" Analysis (FMEA). The elements of the risk assessment are defined below and are indicated by letters (A-K) in Table 42.

The Quality Systems Regulation Preamble States:

Comment 83

…"If any risk is judged unacceptable, it should be reduced to acceptable levels by the appropriate means, for example, by redesign or warnings. An important part of risk analysis is ensuring that changes made to eliminate or minimize hazards do not introduce new hazards. Tools for conducting such analyses include Failure Mode Effect Analysis and Fault Tree Analysis, among others." (FDA Preamble, 2015)

The following terms are referenced by letters in () in Table 42 and Table 44

A. – Hazard - Potential source of harm. Hazards from the hazard analysis should be used to populate this section.

B. – Hazardous Situation – Circumstance where people, property or the environment are exposed to one or more hazard(s). Hazardous situations from the hazard analysis should be used to populate this section.

C. – Cause/Chain of Events – The chain of events which may potentially cause the hazard should be identified by subject matter experts. Causes from hazard analysis should be included in this section.

D. – P - Overall probability of harm occurring (P^1 X P^2)

P^1 = Probability of Hazardous Situation Occurring

P^2 = Probability of Hazardous Situation Leading to Harm

E.- Harm - Physical injury or damage to the health of people or damage to property of the environment. Typically a clinician such as a physician should provide input to the risk analysis to determine harm caused by identified hazards.

F.- Severity Level - Measure of the possible consequences of a hazard. Typically a clinician such as a physician should provide input to the risk analysis to determine the severity of harm caused by identified hazards.

G. – Risk Level - The risk level is determined by using the overall probability of harm and severity level as inputs for using a risk evaluation table.

H. – Recommended Actions – As a result of the risk evaluation process, recommendations for additional design controls should be identified for unacceptable risks (R3) or in some cases for those identified as "As Low As Reasonably Practicable (ALARP)" (R2).

I.- Controls Implemented – The recommended actions (risk controls) that are actually implemented should be identified in this section. The intent of implementing these controls is to reduce the probability of overall harm of its associated hazard.

J. – RRP – The residual risk probability (RRP) is the overall probability of the risk after the risk controls were implemented.

K.- RRL – The residual risk level (RRL) is the resulting risk level after adjusting the risk for the reduced residual risk probability (RRP).

Medical Device Regulation Consulting and Training – www.Procenius.com

Risk Evaluation Table

TABLE 41

Probability of Occurrence		Severity of Harm Levels				
		Negligible	Minor	Serious	Critical	Catastrophic
	Frequent	R2	R2	R3	R3	R3
	Probable	R2	R2	R3	R3	R3
	Occasional	R1	R2	R2	R3	R3
	Remote	R1	R1	R2	R2	R2
	Improbable	R1	R1	R1	R2	R2

Key for Table 42 & Table 44

SL = Severity Level
P = Overall probability of harm (P^1 X P^2)
RL = Risk level (see Risk Evaluation Chart)
RRP = Residual risk probability after implementing controls
RRL = Residual risk level (see Risk Evaluation Chart)

*P = Probability of Occurrence (Overall probability of harm (P^1 X P^2))

F = Frequent
P = Probable
O = Occasional
R = Remote
I = Improbable

†SL = Severity of Harm Levels

N = Negligible
M = Minor
S = Serious
C = Critical
Ca = Catastrophic

Medical Device Regulation Consulting and Training – www.Procenius.com

Risk Level Acceptance Criteria

R1= Acceptable Risk

R2= As low as reasonably practicable (ALARP)

R3= Unacceptable Risk

The numbers listed in Table 42 are defined in Table 43. The letters enclosed in ( ) are referenced in Table 42 and have been previously defined above.

TABLE 42

Risk Analysis (Step 1.A.) The risk analysis includes identifying: Hazards, Hazardous Situations, Causes, Probability of Hazardous Situation & Hazardous Situations Leading to Harm, Harm and Severity of Harm.						Risk Evaluation (Step 1.B.) Use risk acceptance criteria from risk management plan/ SOP to determine if risk reduction is required. (e.g. risk evaluation table)		Risk Controls (Step 2) When risk reduction is required, risk control measures should be identified to reduce risk.	Residual Risk (Step 3) Residual risks should be evaluated after implementation of controls.	
Risk Analysis						**Risk Evaluation**		**Risk Controls**	**Residual Risk**	
Hazard (A)	Hazardous Situation (B)	Cause/ Chain of Events (C)	P* (D)	Harm (E)	SL† (F)	RL** (G)	Action/ Controls (H)	Controls (I)	RRP (J)	RRL (K)
1	2	3	4	5	6	7	8	9	10	11
		12	13			14	15	16	17	18
		19	20			21	22	23	24	25

Medical Device Regulation Consulting and Training – www.Procenius.com

TABLE 43

1	Device power cord is energized with high voltage/amps
2	Cord has exposed bare wires and is handled by user or patient
3	Cord is dragged through hall way when machine is moved which causes the sheath to become damaged
4	F- Frequent Probability
5	Death due to cardiac arrest (heart failure) (C); Tissue damage or burns(S);
6	C – Critical Severity
7	R3 – Unacceptable Risk Level
8	Redesign sheath material to resist and extend life of power cord.
9	Sheath material has been redesigned with wear resistant material. See results from verification (*document #*).
10	R – Remote Probability
11	R2 – As low as reasonably practicable (ALARP) Risk Level
12	Environmental conditions cause sheath to crack and cause exposure (heat, chemicals, etc.)
13	R- Remote Probability
14	R2 – As low as reasonably practicable (ALARP) Risk Level
15	Redesign sheath material to resist typical heat and chemical exposure.
16	Sheath material has been redesigned with heat and chemical resistant material. See results from verification (*document #*).
17	I – Improbable Probability
18	R2 – As low as reasonably practicable (ALARP) Risk Level
19	Wrapping of cord around machine causes excessive stress to wire sheath
20	O – Occasional Probability
21	R2 – As low as reasonably practicable (ALARP) Risk Level
22	Redesign sheath and internal conductor materials to resist typical expected bending conditions.
23	Sheath and conductors have been redesigned with fatigue resistant material. See results from verification (*document #*).
24	R – Remote Probability
25	R2 – As low as reasonably practicable (ALARP) Risk Level

The numbers listed in Table 44 are defined in Table 45. The letters enclosed in ( ) are referenced in Table 44 and have been previously defined above.

TABLE 44

Risk Analysis (Step 1.A.) The risk analysis includes identifying: Hazards, Hazardous Situations, Causes, Probability of Hazardous Situation & Hazardous Situations Leading to Harm, Harm and Severity of Harm.					Risk Evaluation (Step 1.B.) Use risk acceptance criteria from risk management plan to determine if risk reduction is required. (e.g. risk evaluation table)			Risk Controls (Step 2) When risk reduction is required, risk control measures should be identified that are appropriate for reducing risk to an acceptable level.	Residual Risk (Step 3) Residual risks should be evaluated after implementation of controls.	
Risk Analysis					Risk Evaluation			Risk Controls	Residual Risk	
Hazard (A)	Hazardous Situation (B)	Cause/ Chain of Events (C)	P* (D)	Harm (E)	SL† (F)	RL** (G)	Action/ Control (H)	Controls (I)	RRP (J)	RRL (K)
1	2	3	6	9	10	11	14	17	20	23
		4	7			12	15	18	21	24

Medical Device Regulation Consulting and Training – www.Procenius.com

TABLE 45

1	Access door to patient platform
2	The access door closes on patient/users fingers.
3	User inadvertently closes access door on patient
4	Access door hinge fails due to material fatigue or wear
5	Access door closes on door due to door being bumped and force of gravity
6	I^t - Improbable Probability
7	P – "Probable" Probability
8	R – Remote Probability
9	Broken finger (S); Bruising (M)
10	S - Serious
11	R1 – Acceptable Risk
12	R3 – Unacceptable Risk
13	R2 – As low as reasonably practicable (ALARP) Risk Level
14	R1 level risk is acceptable according to risk management procedure, no action recommended.
15	Redesign access door hinge with fatigue resistant material. Design a mechanical stop to prevent access door from closing completely.
16	Design a mechanical stop to prevent access door from closing completely.
17	Not Applicable
18	Access door hinge was redesigned with fatigue resistant material. See results from verification (*document #*).
19	The access door design was modified to include a mechanical stop to prevent access door from closing completely. See results from verification (*document #*).
20	I^t - Improbable Probability
21	R – Remote Probability
22	I – Improbable Probability
23	R1 – Acceptable Risk
24	R2 – As low as reasonably practicable
25	R1 – Acceptable Risk

12.9. Templates

Visit **Procenius.com** to download risk management assessments, plans, and report templates.

13.0   Compliance to Design Control Regulation

To those new to design controls regulation, compliance may seem like a daunting task. Being compliant to design controls regulation is not rocket science. The best way for manufacturers to tackle design control compliance is by understanding and applying the following basic key principles.

13.1. Critical Design Control Compliance Principles

- FDA expects manufacturers to demonstrate interaction of the design control elements through document traceability
- FDA does not prescribe how a medical device should be developed to ensure safety and effectiveness
- Procedures should be compliant to the regulation
- Internal procedures must be followed
- Internal audit and CAPA systems must be effective
- Medical Device Manufacturers should:
  - Plan and document what they are going to do
  - Do what they planned
  - Document what they did (*If it isn't documented, it didn't happen*)

13.1.1. Interaction of Design Control Elements Through Document Traceability

FDA inspectors will have a clear indication that device manufacturers know what they are doing in the design control world if there is sufficient evidence that proper interfaces between design control activities are adequately documented and traceable as defined in chapter 1, under "Design Control Activities Interfaces, Key Relationships, and Traceability". This traceability is created by referencing document numbers from other design documents where information needs to be referenced to indicate the source of plans, decisions or device definition (i.e. design inputs or design outputs). Creating this effective documentation traceability web gives the FDA a clear picture of the effectiveness of the device manufacturer's design control process.

As an example, the development of effective design verification protocols and reports require interfacing with many other design documents as explained below:

- The protocol should reference the design input document number and the specific design input ID# to show traceability to the requirement which is being met by verification of the applicable design output.

- The protocol should also reference the risk assessment to indicate how the level of risk associated with the design output being verified was used to develop the appropriate verification method, sample size and acceptance criteria. (i.e. outputs associated with higher risks should have more stringent verification strategies).

- The protocol should reference the document number of the design output being verified.

- If the verification is the result of a design change, the change control number should be referenced in the protocol.

- The protocol should include a reference to the DHF # for which the verification protocol will be included.

- The DHF should be updated to include a reference to the protocol and report document numbers.

- The results from executing the verification protocol should be documented in a verification report which should reference the protocol document number.

- The results from the verification should be reviewed in a design review and the document number for the meeting minutes documenting the design review should be referenced in the report. The meeting minutes from the design review should include a document # reference to the executed protocol.

- If a deviation or non-conformance occurred during verification; as part of the deviation or non-conformance evaluation, the risk assessment should be referenced and the decision made by reviewing the risk assessment should be traceable back to the final disposition of the deviation or non-conformance record.

13.1.2. FDA Does Not Prescribe How a Medical Device Should be Developed

It is true that the FDA specifies general requirements of how designs should developed (i.e. plan, develop design requirements, verify and validation etc.), but the methods used to follow the regulation is left up to the manufacturer. The manufacturer is given freedom of how to plan, what requirements are needed, and what verifications and validations are required etc. but an important concept to remember is that the device manufacturer is the product expert, the FDA is not. It is true that the FDA may question methods, requirements, designs etc. but if sufficient rational evidence is provided (ideally prior to the question being asked), FDA will in most case be satisfied. The FDA is looking for evidence that the manufacturer has thoroughly thought through what they are doing and have made critical design decisions based on data, logic and expertise that will result in a safe and effective design.

The FDA may determine that there is insufficient evidence to support safety and effectiveness but in most cases will not specify requirements, verification or validation methods. The FDA's

Medical Device Regulation Consulting and Training – www.Procenius.com

main focus is to ensure that manufacturer's procedures are compliant to the regulation and that they are following their own procedures.

13.1.3. <u>Procedures Should be Compliant to the Regulation</u>

This may seem obvious to most people but it is surprising how often non-compliance issues arise because manufacturers have not established procedures which prescribe how their organization will be compliant to regulations. The FDA states numerous times in the design control that procedures must be "established". 21 CFR 820.3 (Definitions) defines "establish" as: *to define, document (in writing or electronically), and implement*. So the first step is to write a procedure and then it should be approved by the appropriate people in the manufacturer's organization. Procedures are often initially written with all of the best intentions but somewhere along the way compliance gets lost.

Non-compliance typically occurs because of one of two circumstances (or both): (1) either authors of the procedures do not understand the regulation (or they do not know how to apply it in their organization) and/or (2) those using the procedures do not adequately understand the procedures. The best method of conveying the medical device regulation intent is to implement effective work instructions, procedures and policies. Before elaboration on this topic, clarification between the different document types is provided below by the following definitions and figures.

Policy: A policy is a deliberate system of principles to guide decisions and achieve rational outcomes. A policy is a statement of intent, and is implemented as a procedure or protocol. Policies are generally adopted by a senior governance body within an organization whereas procedures or protocols would be developed and adopted by senior executive officers.

<u>Policy Example:</u> Company ABC shall be compliant to all FDA Quality System Regulations

This maybe one of many policies found in a medical device manufacturer's quality manual.

Procedure: A procedure is a document written to support a "Policy Directive". A Procedure is designed to describe Who, What, Where, When, and Why by means of establishing corporate accountability in support of the implementation of a "policy". The "How" is further documented by each organizational unit in the form of "Work Instructions" which aims to further support a procedure by providing greater detail. For example, a manufacturing facility established a policy that all overtime shall be approved. A procedure can be created to establish "Who" can approve overtime (ranks, roles & responsibilities), "What" forms/systems need to be used, "Where" they are located, "When" overtime is applicable. And the "Why" refers to the management directive established via a "Policy".

Work Instruction: The work instruction is the output of a procedure and is the step by step process of describing the details of how the procedure should be implemented. (i.e. – 1. Upload the document into the document control system, 2. Select the document approvers 3. Submit the document for approval)

Medical Device Regulation Consulting and Training – www.Procenius.com

Form: A form is a document with blank spaces for information to be inserted. A form is a very powerful document that can be used to encourage compliance. Forms have the ability to prompt users to know what type of information is required and how it should be recorded on a consistent basis. In many cases even though someone may not exactly understand how to follow the work instructions, the form will prompt them to execute the activity correctly. On the other hand forms can back fire during an inspection if not properly filled out. The FDA assumes that an approved form is meant to be filled out. So if certain areas of a form are left blank than it is assumed the information should have been provided according to the procedure or work instructions. To mitigate this risk, *good documentation practices (GDP)* should be followed (i.e. – Fill in all blank fields with N/A, initial and date, if not applicable).

Record: A record is exactly what it sounds like, it is a document (or electronic file) that provides evidence (or a "record") of something. A filled out form is an example of a record.

Record Example: A report providing evidence of results from design verification or from an audit.

Medical Device Regulation Consulting and Training – www.Procenius.com

Figure 63 and Figure 64 illustrates the relationships between policies, procedures, work instructions, forms and records.

Document Triangle

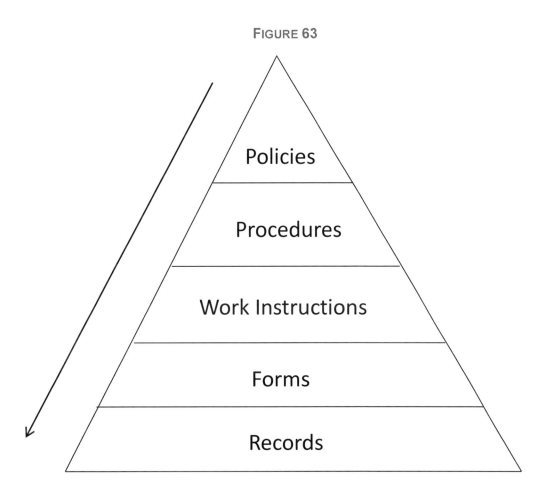

FIGURE 63

Medical Device Regulation Consulting and Training – www.Procenius.com

FIGURE 64

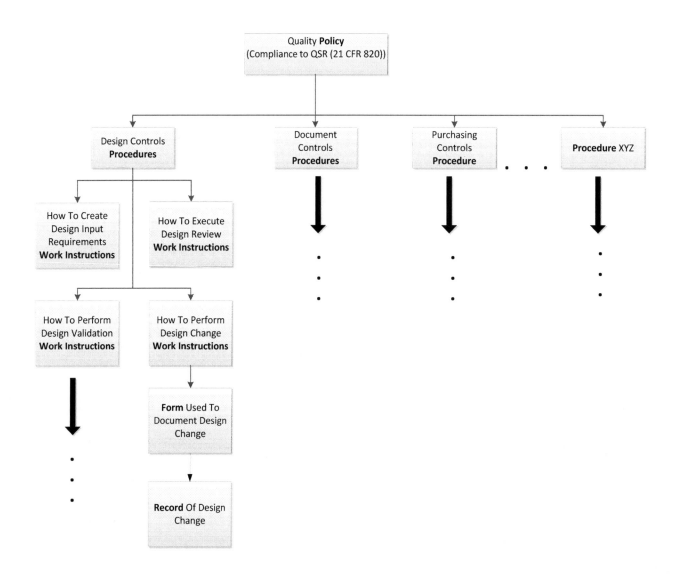

Medical Device Regulation Consulting and Training – www.Procenius.com

When manufacturers don't understand the relationships between these types of documents, intermingling of document types tend to creep into the documentation process. Ideally requirements at the procedure level will align directly with compliance to FDA regulation. Because procedures that define the "Who, What, Where, When, and Why" (5 W's) are typically not over complex, it is very easy to develop and maintain compliant procedure to FDA regulation. Manufacturers run into noncompliance issues when procedures and work instructions are combined as one document. So in this situation the procedure would not only include the 5 W's, but also the "How". The "How" (or work instruction) is often very detailed and lengthy. Manufacturers have a tendency to over complicate their procedures/work instructions intermingling the step by step "How" with the 5 W's. Combining these document types is asking for trouble. The combined document makes it difficult to clearly show compliance to regulation both internally and to FDA inspectors. Over time the problem becomes worse. Processes change and therefore work instructions will also. These changes in the "How" may also inadvertently change the procedure requirements which are supposed to ensure compliance. So it is best practice to separate procedures from work instructions and to establish a document control system which requires all elements from the document triangle.

#1 Best Practice – Document Control Policies Should Require Quality System Policies, Procedures, Work Instructions and Records (Document Triangle)

Using all elements of the document triangle will build in clarity and document organization in the document control system which will encourage and facilitate compliance.

13.1.4. Internal Procedures Must Be Followed

There are four basic reasons employees do not follow internal procedures:

- Management does not make them aware of the procedures (no training or communication that procedures are available)
- Management does not motivate employees to follow the procedures
- Management does not provide time and resources to allow procedures to be followed
- Employees do not understand the procedures (inadequate training or unclear procedures)

It is obvious from this list that inadequate management support is can easily be the potential root cause of non-compliance issues. Management must make compliance to procedures a priority to ensure compliance to FDA regulations.

Training

Since the lack of training (or ineffective training) is at the heart of two of the reasons why employees don't follow procedures, it is obvious that effective training must be implemented to ensure compliance.

Effective training will have the following elements:

- Content presented with the correct depth versus content level (balance the amount of details with the training time available)
    - Too much content is unable to be absorbed if there is too little time

- Principles and background should be communicated (the what, who, and why; not just the how)
    - Teaching principles and background will give depth of understanding, will enable better decision making and application, and will more likely be retained
    - Teaching principles and background encourages conceptual learning

- Provide concrete examples where principles can be applied
    - Concrete examples encourage application learning and retention

- Training Assessment
    - An assessment of training effectiveness should be required to help solidify understanding and encourage information retention

13.1.5. Internal Audit and CAPA Systems Must Be Effective

Manufacturer's audit and CAPA (Corrective Action and Preventative Action) systems are the life blood of a compliant design controls process (and a quality system for that matter). If audit and CAPA systems are the lifeblood, then management is the brain, heart and muscle (makes decisions, ensures audit and CAPA's are functioning, keeps the quality system working). CAPA and audit reports feed into management reviews. They are the "collectors" of non-compliance issues. It is then management's responsibility to take action by setting clear priorities and allocating appropriate resources to correct and prevent non-compliance issues.

Figure 65 illustrates how audit results and CAPA's should drive change and improvement toward greater compliance.

Medical Device Regulation Consulting and Training – www.Procenius.com

FIGURE 65

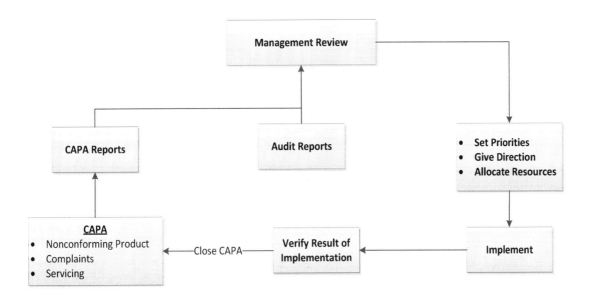

This figure illustrates how audits and CAPAs are inputs into the management review. Management review should establish priorities, guidance and allocate resources to allow corrections and improvements to be implemented to ensure quality compliance. Implementation of management guidance should be verified and used to close the CAPA. Any broken link in the process may result in non-compliance.

13.1.6. Plan, Do & Report (if it isn't documented, it didn't happen)

The "Plan, Do & Report" model is an underlying theme across all design control elements.

Plan

The FDA is big on planning! The FDA has long since realized that a significant cause of poor device development stems from poor planning. Without design control regulations, many manufacturers have a tendency to develop products by "shooting from the hip". They are very reactive by changing course too quickly during development without considering the consequences. They also make unrealistic product launch date decisions without properly evaluating the resources needed to support the date. As a result they are still committed to meet "the date" and will at times take unwise risks and compromises during development to meet those dates. FDA believes that proper planning will reduce the risk of unrealistic development milestones and will promote constructive planning discussions and resource allocation.

In addition to the overall development plan for the project, planning verification and validation activities is also expected. The FDA wants to ensure that high level and low level verification and validation planning occurs. High level planning is typically performed in a validation master plan which highlights the overall verification and validation strategy and execution activities.

Lower level verification and validation protocols are used to plan specific verification and validation testing or analyses activities. Protocols will typically include (methods, samples size, acceptance criteria, design being verified; see verification and validation chapters for more details)

Plans are not set in stone. Many developers that are new to design controls think that planning documents cannot change and if it does, they think the FDA might have a problem with it. The FDA understands that plans change during development. Change is expected, so planning documents should change also. The key is to update planning documents when the plans change prior to implementing the plans. Even though the FDA is ok with changing plans, they are <u>not</u> ok if plans are not followed or if plans are not kept up to date.

Do

This is pretty straight forward, the FDA expects manufacturers to execute activities as planned. The closer activities can be executed relative to the plan, the less explaining and rationales that have to be written and therefore the higher opportunity for compliance to FDA expectations.

Report

The FDA expects the results of executed plans to be documented in an approved report. This is the official record that the device was developed as planned. If executed activities deviated from the plan, an explanation of the deviation should be explained in the report.

If It Isn't Documented, It Didn't Happen

Plain and simple, if there is not record of an event happening then in the FDA's eyes it didn't happen. The extent and formality of documentation required is typically proportional to the phase of the development process. For early concept and feasibility studies, less formal documentation such as lab note books are appropriate. As the final design progresses closer to final validation, the documentation is typically more formal. In any case, documentation should include an approval (written or electronic signature) and date.

Medical Device Regulation Consulting and Training – www.Procenius.com

14.0   Process Validation (GHTF)

Author's Note

The author recognizes that there has been a significant amount of industry accepted guidance on the topic of process validation and therefore has decided to heavily defer to external sources for content on this subject. Essentially all content in this chapter was directly taken from FDA process validation regulation (21 CFR 820.75) and the Global Harmonization Task Force ((GHTF, 2004), now defunct) as noted and referenced in this chapter. FDA recommends using the GTHF document as guidance for following 21 CFR 820.75.

14.1. Regulation (21 CFR 820.75) – Process Validation

a) Where the results of a process cannot be fully verified by subsequent inspection and test, the process shall be validated with a high degree of assurance and approved according to established procedures. The validation activities and results, including the date and signature of the individual(s) approving the validation and where appropriate the major equipment validated, shall be documented.

(b) Each manufacturer shall establish and maintain procedures for monitoring and control of process parameters for validated processes to ensure that the specified requirements continue to be met.

(1) Each manufacturer shall ensure that validated processes are performed by qualified individual(s).

(2) For validated processes, the monitoring and control methods and data, the date performed, and, where appropriate, the individual(s) performing the process or the major equipment used shall be documented.

(c) When changes or process deviations occur, the manufacturer shall review and evaluate the process and perform revalidation where appropriate. These activities shall be documented.

Medical Device Regulation Consulting and Training – www.Procenius.com

14.2. Quality Management Systems – Process Validation Guidance

Reference: Global Harmonization Task Force (GHTF, 2004)

14.2.1. Definitions

For this document [Chapter], the following definitions apply. Terms other than those defined herein may be found in the literature.

Installation qualification (IQ): establishing by objective evidence that all key aspects of the process equipment and ancillary system installation adhere to the manufacturer's approved specification and that the recommendations of the supplier of the equipment are suitably considered.

Operational qualification (OQ): establishing by objective evidence process control limits and action levels which result in product that meets all predetermined requirements.

Performance qualification (PQ): establishing by objective evidence that the process, under anticipated conditions, consistently produces a product which meets all predetermined requirements.

Process validation: establishing by objective evidence that a process consistently produces a result or product meeting its predetermined requirements.

Process validation protocol: a document stating how validation will be conducted, including test parameters, product characteristics, manufacturing equipment, and decision points on what constitutes acceptable test results.

Verification: confirmation by examination and provision of objective evidence that the specified requirements have been fulfilled.

14.2.2. Process Validation Within the Quality Management System

Process validation is part of the integrated requirements of a quality management system. It is conducted in the context of a system including design and development control, quality assurance, process control, and corrective and preventive action.

The interrelationship of design control and process development may, for some technologies, be very closely related. For others the relationship may be remote. The product should be designed robustly enough to withstand variations in the manufacturing process and the manufacturing process should be capable and stable to assure continued

Medical Device Regulation Consulting and Training – www.Procenius.com

safe products that perform adequately. Often this results in a very interactive product development and process development activity.

Daily measuring and monitoring activities are conducted as specified by the process control plan which is often largely developed during process validation.

Corrective actions often identify inadequate processes/process validations. Each corrective action applied to a manufacturing process should include the consideration for conducting process validation/revalidation.

14.2.3.   <u>Process Validation Decision</u>

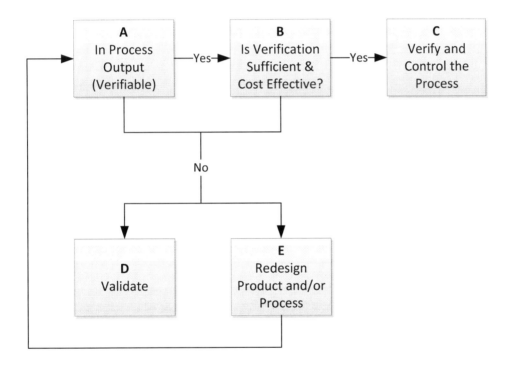

FIGURE 66: PROCESS VALIDATION DECISION TREE

Medical Device Regulation Consulting and Training – www.Procenius.com

The model shown describes a decision tree that a manufacturer can follow when deciding on whether a process needs to be validated. The process under consideration in this model is the simplest possible - many processes may be large and/or a complex set of sub-processes.

Each process should have a specification describing both the process parameters and the output desired. The manufacturer should consider whether the output can be verified by subsequent monitoring or measurement (A). If the answer is positive, then the consideration should be made as to whether or not verification alone is sufficient to eliminate unacceptable risk and is a cost effective solution (B). If yes, the output should be verified and the process should be appropriately controlled (C).

If the output of the process is not verifiable then the decision should be to validate the process (D); alternatively, it may become apparent that the product or process should be redesigned to reduce variation and improve the product or process (E). Also, a change in a manufacturing process may result in the need for process validation even though the process formerly only required verification and control.

The risk or cost may also be reduced by redesigning the product or process to a point where simple verification is an acceptable decision (E).

14.2.4. Examples

The following table is a list of examples of processes which: (1) should be validated, (2) may be satisfactorily covered by verification, and (3) processes which may be verifiable, but for business purposes, validation can be chosen.

(1) Processes which should be validated

- Sterilization processes
- Aseptic filling processes
- Sterile packaging sealing processes
- Lyophilization process
- Heating treating process
- Plating process
- Plastic injection molding processes

(2) Process which may be satisfactorily covered by verification

- Manual cutting processes
- Testing for color, turbidity, total pH for solutions
- Visual inspection of printed circuit boards
- Manufacturing and testing of wiring harnesses

Medical Device Regulation Consulting and Training – www.Procenius.com

(3) Processes by which the above model may be useful in determining the need for validation

- Certain cleaning processes
- Certain human assembly processes
- Numerical control cutting processes
- Certain filling processes

While the output of a process may be verifiable, application of software used in that process should be validated for its intended use.

14.2.5.   Statistical Methods and Tools for Process Validation

There are many methods and tools that can be used in process validation. A primer on statistics and process validation is provided in Annex A as a guide through the basic concepts. Control charts, capability studies designed experiments, tolerance analysis, robust design methods, failure modes and effects analysis, sampling plans, and mistake proofing are some of the examples.

14.2.6. Conduct of a Validation

14.2.6.1.   Getting Started

A consideration should be given to form a multi-functional team to plan and oversee the validation activities. A team approach will help assure the validation processes are well thought out, the protocols are comprehensive and that the final packages are well documented and easy to follow. The team should advise "what could go wrong". The team also provides an opportunity for key functional areas to communicate early about important new and changed products and processes and can foster cooperation.

Members of the validation team could include representatives from or personnel with expertise in:

- Quality Assurance

- Engineering

- Manufacturing

- Others depending on company organization and product types:

  o   Laboratory
  o   Technical Services

- o Research & Development
- o Regulatory Affairs
- o Clinical Engineering
- o Purchasing/Planning

Once the validation team has been formed, the next step is to plan the approach and define the requirements. Many manufacturers develop what is referred to as a master validation plan which identifies those processes to be validated, the schedule for validations, interrelationships between processes requiring validation and timing for revalidations. Once these have been established, and the purpose and scope for validations are clearly stated and known, protocol development can commence.

The following is a list of activities which may be used as a checklist to review validation activity:

- Form multi-functional team for validation

- Plan the approach and define the requirements

- Identify and describe the processes

- Specify process parameters and desired output

- Decide on verification and/or validation

- Create a master validation plan

- Select methods and tools for validation

- Create validation protocols

- Perform IQ, OQ, PO and document results

- Determine continuous process controls

- Control the process continuously

14.2.6.2.   __Protocol Development__

Detailed protocols for performing validations are essential to ensure that the process is adequately validated. Process validation protocols should include the following elements:

- Identification of the process to be validated

- Identification of device(s) to be manufactured using this process

- Objective and measurable criteria for a successful validation

- Length and duration of the validation

Medical Device Regulation Consulting and Training – www.Procenius.com

- Shifts, operators, equipment to be used in the process

- Identification of utilities for the process equipment and quality of the utilities

- Identification of operators and required operator qualification

- Complete description of the process

- Relevant specifications that relate to the product, components, manufacturing materials, etc.

- Any special controls or conditions to be placed on preceding processes during the validation

- Process parameters to be monitored, and methods for controlling and monitoring

- Product characteristics to be monitored and method for monitoring

- Any subjective criteria used to evaluate the product

- Definition of what constitutes non-conformance for both measurable and subjective criteria

- Statistical methods for data collection and analysis

- Consideration of maintenance and repairs of manufacturing equipment

- Criteria for revalidation

For all three phases, IQ, OQ, and PQ, based on product/process requirements:

- Determine what to verify/measure

- Determine how to verify/measure

- Determine how many to verify/measure, i.e. statistical significance

- Determine when to verify/measure

- Define acceptance/rejection criteria

- Define required documentation

Knowing exactly what the product requirements are and what key parameters will be necessary to answer the questions of what to measure. Seal thickness, seal strength, pressure testing and visual defects of samples are examples of measurable parameters.

Utilizing statistically valid techniques such as sampling, design experiments, Taguchi methods, response surface studies and component swapping are statistically valid techniques to answer the questions of how many to measure.

Utilization of standard test methods such as such as those contained in international or national standards will provide guidance in how to measure specific parameters. Also, it is important to ensure test methods replicate actual use conditions.

During the conduct of various phases of validation, the protocol should address the resolution of discrepancies. Some deviations in established protocol may not negate the results. Each deviation should be addressed, evaluated and a conclusion drawn as to acceptance or rejection of the results. As a result, process control procedures may require modification and those modifications should be validated as part of the overall process.

Addressing all product and process requirements and the establishment of specific criteria for each requirement, upper and lower limits based on product specifications and established standards will help define the acceptance/rejection criteria.

14.2.6.3.   Installation Qualification - (IQ)

Simply put, IQ means is it installed correctly? Important IQ considerations are:

- Equipment design features (i.e. materials of construction cleanability, etc.)

- Installation conditions (wiring, utilities, functionality, etc.)

- Calibration, preventative maintenance, cleaning schedules

- Safety features

- Supplier documentation, prints, drawings and manuals

- Software documentation

- Spare parts list

- Environmental conditions (such as clean room requirements, temperature, humidity)

Sometimes activities are conducted at the equipment supplier's site location prior to

Medical Device Regulation Consulting and Training – www.Procenius.com

equipment shipment. Equipment suppliers may perform test runs at their facilities and analyze the results to determine that the equipment is ready to be delivered. Copies of the suppliers' qualification studies should be used as guides, to obtain basic data, and to supplement installation qualification. However, it is usually insufficient to rely solely upon the validation results of the equipment supplier. Each medical device manufacturer is ultimately responsible for evaluating, challenging, and testing the equipment and deciding whether the equipment is suitable for use in the manufacture of a specific device(s). The evaluations may result in changes to the equipment or process.

14.2.6.4.   <u>Operational Qualification - (OQ)</u>

In this phase the process parameters should be challenged to assure that they will result in a product that meets all defined requirements under all anticipated conditions of manufacturing, i.e., worst case testing. During routine production and process control, it is desirable to measure process parameters and/or product characteristics to allow for the adjustment of the manufacturing process at various action level(s) and maintain a state of control. These action levels should be evaluated, established and documented during process validation to determine the robustness of the process and ability to avoid approaching "worst case conditions."

OQ considerations include:

- Process control limits (time, temperature, pressure, line speed, setup conditions, etc.)

- Software parameters

- Raw material specifications

- Process operating procedures

- Material handling requirements

- Process change control

- Training

- Short term stability and capability of the process, (latitude studies or control charts)

- Potential failure modes, action levels and worst-case conditions (Failure Mode and Effects Analysis, Fault Tree Analysis)

- The use of statistically valid techniques such as screening experiments to establish key process parameters and statistically designed experiments to optimize the process can be used during this phase.

14.2.6.5. Performance Qualification - (PQ)

In this phase the key objective is to demonstrate the process will consistently produce acceptable product under normal operating conditions. Please note the guidance for process stability in Annex A "Methods and tools for process validation".

PQ considerations include:

- Actual product and process parameters and procedures established in OQ

- Acceptability of the product

- Assurance of process capability as established in OQ

- Process repeatability, long term process stability

Challenges to the process should simulate conditions that will be encountered during actual manufacturing. Challenges should include the range of conditions as defined by the various action levels allowed in written standard operating procedures as established in the OQ phase. The challenges should be repeated enough times to assure that the results are meaningful and consistent.

Process and product data should be analyzed to determine what the normal range of variation is for the process output. Knowing the normal variation of the output is crucial in determining whether a process is operating in a state of control and is capable of consistently producing the specified output.

One of the outputs of OQ and PQ is the development of attributes for continuous monitoring and maintenance. Process and product data should also be analyzed to identify any variation due to controllable causes. Depending on the nature of the process and its sensitivity, controllable causes of variation may include:

- Temperature

- Humidity

- Variations in electrical supply

- Vibration

Medical Device Regulation Consulting and Training – www.Procenius.com

- Environmental contaminants

- Purity of process water

- Light

- Human factors (training, ergonomic factors, stress, etc.)

- Variability of materials

- Wear and tear of equipment

Appropriate measures should be taken to eliminate controllable causes of variation. Eliminating controllable causes of variation will reduce variation in the process output and result in a higher degree of assurance that the output will consistently meet specifications.

14.2.6.6.   Final Report

At the conclusion of validation activities, a final report should be prepared. This report should summarize and reference all protocols and results. It should derive conclusions regarding the validation status of the process. The final report should be reviewed and approved by the validation team and appropriate management.

14.3.   Maintaining a State of Validation

14.3.1. Monitor and Control

Trends in the process should be monitored to ensure the process remains within the established should be investigated, corrective action may be taken and revalidation considered.

14.3.2.   Changes in Processes and/or Product

Any changes in the process and /or product including changes in procedures, equipment, personnel, etc. should be evaluated to determine the effects of those changes and the extent of revalidation considered.

14.3.3.　Continued State of Control

Various changes may occur in raw materials and/or processes, which are undetected, or considered at the time to be inconsequential. (An example of this type of process is sterilization.) These changes may cumulatively affect the validation status of the process. Periodic revalidation should be considered for these types of processes.

14.3.4.　Examples of Reasons for Revalidation

Revalidation may be necessary under such conditions as:

- change(s) in the actual process that may affect quality or its validation status

- negative trend(s) in quality indicators

- change(s) in the product design which affects the process

- transfer of processes from one facility to another

- change of the application of the process

The need for revalidation should be evaluated and documented. This evaluation should include historical results from quality indicators, product changes, process changes, changes in external requirements (regulations or standards) and other such circumstances.

Revalidation may not be as extensive as the initial validation if the situation does not require that all aspects of the original validation be repeated. If a new piece of equipment is purchased for a validated process, obviously the IQ portion of the validation needs to be repeated. However, most of the OQ aspects are already established. Some elements of PQ may need to be repeated, depending on the impact of the new equipment.

Another example might be if a raw material supplier is changed, the impact of that change on the process and resultant product should be considered. Parts of OQ and PQ might need to be redone, as the interaction between the new raw material and the process may not be fully understood.

14.3.5.　Use of Historical Data for Validation

Validation of a process can be partially based on accumulated historical manufacturing, testing, control, and other data related to a product or process. This historical data may be found in batch records, manufacturing log books, lot records,

Medical Device Regulation Consulting and Training – www.Procenius.com

control charts, test and inspection results, customer feedback, field failure reports, service reports, and audit reports. A complete validation based on historical data is not feasible if all the appropriate data was not collected, or appropriate data was not collected in a manner which allows adequate analysis. Historical manufacturing data of a pass/fail nature is usually not adequate.

If historical data is determined to be adequate and representative, an analysis can be conducted per a written protocol to determine whether the process has been operating in a state of control and has consistently produced product which meets its predetermined requirements. The analysis should be documented.

The terms "retrospective validation", "concurrent validation" and "prospective validation" are often used. Any validation can use historical data in the manner described above, regardless of the term used.

14.4. Summary of Activities

Initial considerations include:

- Identify and describe the processes

- Decide on verification and/or validation

- Create a master validation plan

If the decision is to validate:

- Form multi-functional team for validation

- Plan the approach and define the requirements

- Identify and describe the processes

- Specify process parameters and desired output

- Create a master validation plan

- Select methods and tools for validation

- Create validation protocols

- Perform IQ, OQ, PQ and document results

- Determine continuous process controls

- Prepare final report and secure management approval

- Control the process continuously

Maintaining a state of validation:

- Monitor and control the process continuously

- Revalidate as appropriate

14.5. Templates

Visit *Procenius.com* to download process validation protocol/report templates.

Annex A: Statistical Methods and Tools for Process Validation

A.I   Introduction

Process validation requires that a process is established that can consistently conform to requirements and then studies are conducted demonstrating that this is the case. Process development and optimization may lead directly to the validation of the process. In other words, the methods for developing and optimizing a process may be used (and the data developed) to demonstrate process capability and stability. Thus there is often not a clear distinction between process development and process validation.

However, many processes are well established and subject to routine process validation. Many of the methods and tools described here may already be used for these processes. As validation methods and tools are reviewed for existing processes, some of these may be helpful to improve validation protocols and improve processes.

This annex describes the many contributions that statistical methods and tools can make to validation. Each tool appearing in bold is further described in Annex A.3.

Nonconformities often occur because of errors made and because of excessive variation. Obtaining a process that consistently conforms to requirements requires a balanced approach using both mistake proofing and variation reduction tools. When a nonconformance occurs because of an error, mistake proofing methods should be used. Mistake proofing attempts to make it impossible for the error to occur or at least to go undetected.

However, many nonconformities are not the result of errors, instead they are the result of excessive variation and off-target processes. Reducing variation and proper targeting of a process requires identifying the key input variables and establishing controls on these inputs to ensure that the outputs conform to requirements.

One output of process validation is the development of a control plan. The final phase of validation requires demonstrating that this control plan works, i.e., that it results in a process that can consistently conform to requirements. One key tool here is a capability study. A capability study measures the ability of the process to consistently meet the specifications. It is appropriate for measurable characteristics where nonconformities are due to variation and off-target conditions.

Testing should be performed not only at nominal, but also under worst-case conditions. In the event of potential errors, challenge tests should be performed to demonstrate that mistake proofing methods designed to detect or prevent such errors are working. Acceptance sampling plans can be useful in optimizing the number of samples to be tested and to demonstrate conformance to specification.

Medical Device Regulation Consulting and Training – www.Procenius.com

A.2 Primer on statistics and process validation

Each unit of product differs to some small degree from all other units of product. These differences, no matter how small, are referred to as variation. Variation can be characterized by measuring a sample of the product and drawing a histogram. For example, one operation involves cutting wire into 100 m lengths. The tolerance is 100 ± 5 m. A sample of 12 wires is selected at random and the following results obtained:

98.7 99.3   100.4 97.6   101.4 102.0

100.2 96.4   103.4 102.0   98.0   100.5

A histogram of this data is shown below. The width of the histogram represents the variation.

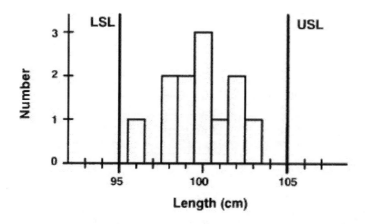

FIGURE 67: HISTOGRAM OF DATA

Of special interest is whether the histogram is properly centered and whether the histogram is narrow enough to easily fit within the specification limits. The center of the histogram is estimated by calculating the average of the 12 readings. The average is 99.99 m. The width of the histogram is estimated by calculating either the range or standard deviation. The range of the above readings is 7.0 m. The standard deviation is 2.06 m. The standard deviation represents the typical distance a unit is from the average. Approximately half of the units are within ±1 standard deviation of the average and about half of the units are more than one standard deviation away from the average. On the other hand, the range represents an interval containing all the units. The range is typically 3 to 6 times the standard deviation.

Medical Device Regulation Consulting and Training – www.Procenius.com

Frequently, histograms take on a bell-shaped appearance that is referred to as the normal curve as shown below. For the normal curve, 99.73% of the units fall within± 3 standard deviations of the average.

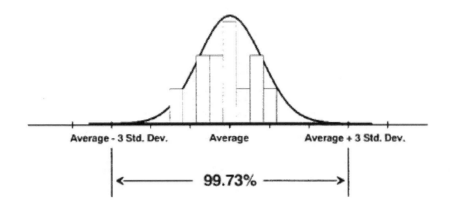

FIGURE 68: NORMAL CURVE APPLIED TO HISTOGRAM

For measurable characteristics like wire length, fill volume, and seal strength, the goal is to optimize the average and reduce the variation. Optimization of the average may mean to center the process as in the case of fill volumes, to maximize the average as is the case with seal strengths, or to minimize the average as is the case with harmful emissions. In all cases, variation reduction is also required to ensure all units are within specifications. Reducing variation requires the achievement of stable and capable processes. Figure 69 shows an unstable process. The process is constantly changing. The average shifts up and down. The variation increases and decreases. The total variation increases due to the shifting.

Medical Device Regulation Consulting and Training – www.Procenius.com

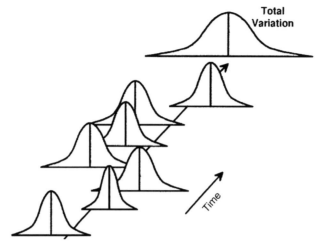

FIGURE 69: UNSTABLE
PROCESS

Instead, stable processes are desired as shown in Figure 70. Stable processes produce a consistent level of performance. The total variation is reduced. The process is more predictable.

STABLE PROCESS

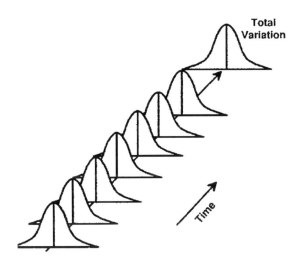

FIGURE 70: STABLE PROCESS

However, stability is not the only thing required. Once a consistent performance has been achieved, the remaining variation must be made to safely fit within the upper and lower specification limits. Such a process is then said to be stable and capable. Such a process can be relied on to consistently produce good product as illustrated in Figure 71.

PROCESS CAPABILITY

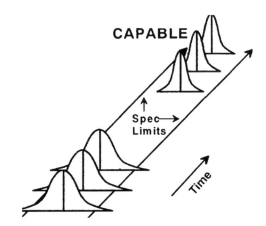

FIGURE 71: PROCESS CAPABILITY

Medical Device Regulation Consulting and Training – www.Procenius.com

A **capability study** is used to determine whether a process is stable and capable. It involves collecting samples over a period of time. The average and standard deviation of each time period is estimated and these estimates plotted in the form of a **control chart.** These control **charts** are used to determine if the process is stable. **If** it is, the data can be combined into a single histogram to determine its capability. To help determine if the process is capable, several capability indices are used to measure how well the histogram fits within the specification limits. One index called CP is used to evaluate the variation. Another index Cpk is used to evaluate the centering of the process.

Together these two indices are used to decide whether the process meets its requirements. The values required to pass depend on the severity of the defect (major, minor, critical) that the manufacturer considers acceptable.

While capability studies evaluate the ability of a process to consistently produce good product, these studies do little to help achieve such processes. Reducing variation and the achievement of stable processes requires the use of numerous variation reduction tools. Variation of the output is caused by variation of the inputs. Consider the example of a simple system, such as a pump for moving fluids:

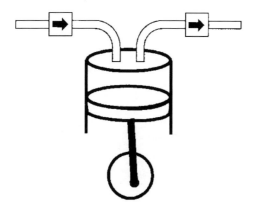

FIGURE 72: THE PUMP

An output is flow rate. The pump uses a piston to draw a fluid into a chamber through one opening and then pushes it back out another opening. Valves are used to keep the fluid moving in the right direction. Flow rate will be affected by piston radius, stroke length, motor speed and valve backflow to name a few. The target flow rate is achieved by designing the piston radius, stroke length, motor speed, etc. The actual flow rate will vary due to variation in wear of the piston, wear of the bearings, wear of the valves, variation of the motor speed, temperature/viscosity of the fluid, etc. Variation of the inputs is transmitted to the output as shown below.

Medical Device Regulation Consulting and Training – www.Procenius.com

TRANSMISSION OF VARIATION

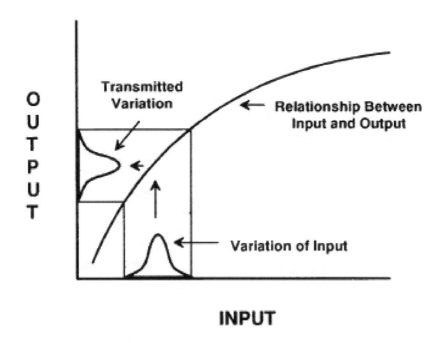

FIGURE 73: TRANSMISSION OF
VARIATION

Medical Device Regulation Consulting and Training – www.Procenius.com

Reducing variation requires identifying the key input variables affecting the outputs, designing the process to take advantage of relative input sensitivities (the relationships between cylinder radius, stroke length, motor speed and output) and establishing controls on input variation (wear, motor speed, temperature/viscosity, etc.) to ensure that the outputs conform to their established specifications. In general one should, identify the key input variables, understand the effect of these inputs on the output, understand how the inputs behave and finally, use this information to establish targets (nominals) and tolerances (windows) for the inputs. Various techniques can be used.

One type of designed experiment called a screening experiment can be used to identify the key inputs. Another type of designed experiment called a response surface study can be used to obtain a detailed understanding of the effects of the key inputs on the outputs. Capability studies can be used to understand the behavior of the key inputs. Armed with this knowledge, robust design methods can be used to identify optimal targets for the inputs and tolerance analysis can be used to establish operating windows or control schemes that ensure the output consistently conforms to requirements.

The obvious approach to reducing variation is to tighten tolerances on the inputs. This improves quality but generally drives up costs. The robust design methods provide an alternative. Robust design works by selecting targets for the inputs that make the outputs less sensitive (more robust) to the variation of the inputs as shown below. The result is less variation and higher quality but without the added costs. Several approaches to robust design exist including Taguchi methods, dual response approach and robust tolerance analysis.

ROBUST DESIGN

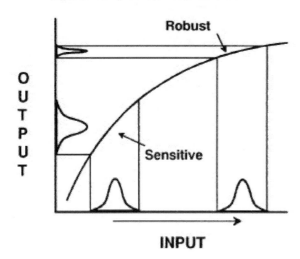

FIGURE 74: ROBUST DESIGN

Medical Device Regulation Consulting and Training – www.Procenius.com

Another important tool is a **control chart.**

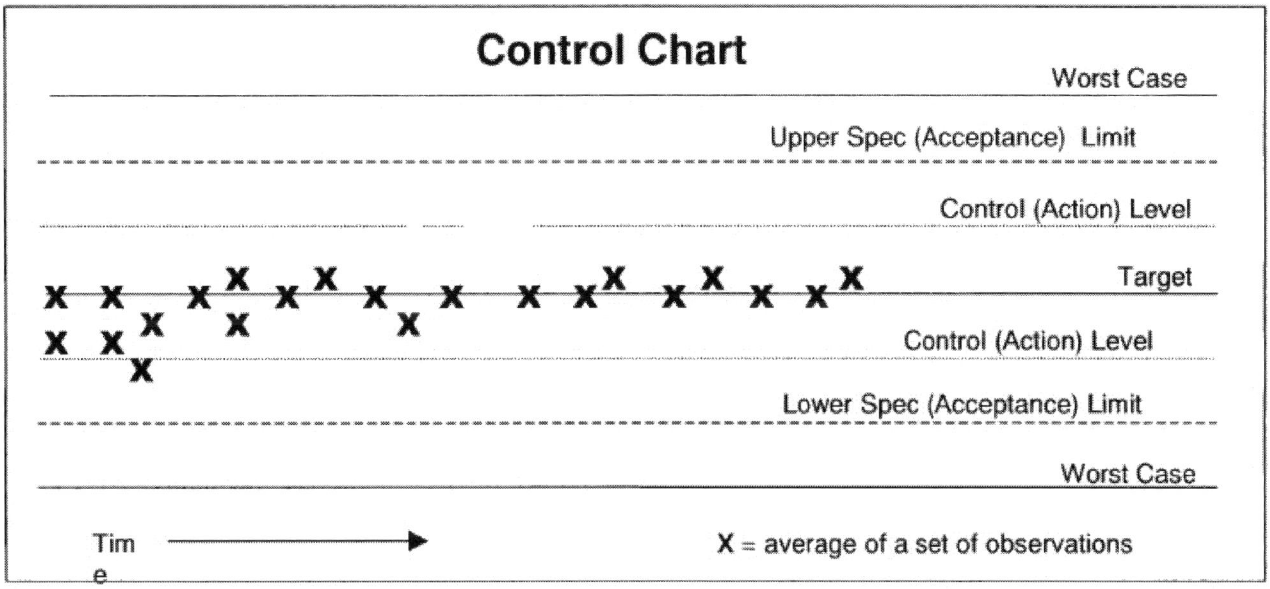

FIGURE 75: CONTROL CHART

Medical Device Regulation Consulting and Training – www.Procenius.com

By monitoring the results of changes of inputs through control charting, the resultant variation in output can be determined and inherent variation of the process identified. Ultimately, control charting may be used to continuously monitor the process and assure a state of validated control. Control or action levels can be determined to adjust the process and maintain the process within the control limits.

Many other tools also exist for identifying key inputs and sources of variation including component swapping studies, multi-variable charts, analysis of means (ANOM), and variance components analysis, and analysis of variance (ANOVA).

When studying variation, good measurements are required. Many times an evaluation of the measurement system should be performed using a gauge R&R or similar study.

B.3 Descriptions of the tools

A brief description of each of the cited tools follows:

Acceptance Sampling Plan - An acceptance sampling plan takes a sample of product and uses this sample to make an accept or reject decision. Acceptance sampling plans are commonly used in manufacturing to decide whether to accept (release) or to reject (hold) lots of product. However, they can also be used during validation to accept (pass) or to reject (fail) the process. Following the acceptance by a sampling plan, one can make a confidence statement such as: "With 95% confidence, the defect rate is below 1% defective."

Analysis of Means (ANOM)-Statistical study for determining if significant differences exist between cavities, instruments, etc. It has many uses including determining if a measurement device is reproducible with respect to operators and determining if differences exists between fill heads, etc. Simpler and more graphical alternative to Analysis of Variance (ANOVA).

Analysis of Variance (ANOVA) – Statistical study for determining if significant differences exist between cavities, instruments, etc. Statistically, this is defined as a methodology for evaluating the results of factorial experiments designed to determine the relative influence of the factors and interactions which cause variation in a process. Alternative to Analysis of Means (ANOM).

Capability Study - Capability studies are performed to evaluate the ability of a process to consistently meet a specification. A capability study is performed by selecting a small number of units periodically over time. Each period of time is called a subgroup. For each subgroup, the average and range is calculated. The averages and ranges are plotted over time using a control chart to determine if the process is stable or consistent over time. If so, the samples are then combined to determine whether the process is adequately centered and the variation is sufficiently small. This is accomplished by

Medical Device Regulation Consulting and Training – www.Procenius.com

calculating capability indexes. The most commonly used capability indices are CP and C_{pk}. If acceptable values are obtained, the process consistently produces product that

meets the specification limits. Capability studies are frequently used towards the end of the validation to demonstrate that the outputs consistently meet the specifications. However, they can also be used to study the behavior of the inputs in order to perform a tolerance analysis.

Challenge Test – A challenge test is a test or check performed to demonstrate that a feature or function is working. For example, to demonstrate that the power backup is functioning, power could be cut to the process. To demonstrate that a sensor designed to detect bubbles in a line works, bubbles could be purposely introduced.

Component Swapping Study - Study to isolate the cause of a difference between two units of product or two pieces of equipment. Requires the ability to disassemble units and swap components in order to determine if the difference remains with original units or moves with the swapped components.

Control Chart - Control charts are used to detect changes in the process. A sample, typically consisting of 5 consecutive units, is selected periodically. The average and range of each sample is calculated and plotted. The plot of the averages is used to determine if the process average changes. The plot of the ranges is used to determine if the process variation changes. To aid in determining if a change has occurred, control limits are calculated and added to the plots. The control limits represent the maximum amount that the average or range should vary if the process does not change. A point outside the control limits indicates that the process has changed. When a change is identified by the control chart, an investigation should be made as to the cause of the change. Control charts help to identify key input variables causing the process to shift and aid in the reduction of the variation. Control charts are also used as part of a capability study to demonstrate that the process is stable or consistent.

Designed Experiment (Design of Experiments or DOE) –The term designed experiment is a general term that encompasses screening experiments, response surface studies, and analysis of variance. In general, a designed experiment involves purposely changing one or more inputs and measuring resulting effect on one or more outputs.

Dual Response Approach to Robust Design – One of three approaches to robust design. Involves running response surface studies to model the average and variation of the outputs separately. The results are then used to select targets for the inputs that minimize the variation while centering the average on the target. Requires that the variation during the study be representative of long term manufacturing. Alternatives are Taguchi methods and robust tolerance analysis.

Failure Modes and Effects Analysis (FMEA) - An FMEA is systematic analysis of the potential failure modes. It includes the identification of possible failure modes, determination of the potential causes and consequences and an analysis of the associated risk. It also includes a record of corrective actions or controls implemented resulting in a detailed control plan. FMEAs can be performed on both the product and the process. Typically an FMEA is performed at the component level, starting with potential failures and then tracing up to the consequences. This is a bottom up approach. A variation is a Fault

Tree Analysis, which starts with possible consequences and traces down to the potential causes. This is the top down approach. An FMEA tends to be more detailed and better at identifying potential problems. However, a fault tree analysis can be performed earlier in the design process before the design has been resolved down to individual components.

Fault Tree Analysis (FTA) - A variation of a failure analysis. See FMEA for a comparison.

Gauge R&R Study – Study for evaluating the precision and accuracy of a measurement device and the reproducibility of the device with respect to operators.

Mistake Proofing Methods – Mistake proofing refers to the broad array of methods used to either make the occurrence of a defect impossible or to ensure that the defect does not pass undetected. The Japanese refer to mistake proofing as Poka-Yoke. The general strategy is to first attempt to make it impossible for the defect to occur. For example, to make it impossible for a part to be assembled backwards, make the ends of the part different sizes or shapes so that the part only fits one way. If this is not possible, attempt to ensure the defect is detected. This might involve mounting a bar above a chute that will stop any parts that are too high from continuing down the line. Other possibilities include mitigating the effect of a defect (seat belts in cars) and to lessen the chance of human errors by implementing self-checks.

Multi-Vari Chart – Graphical procedure for isolating the largest source of variation so that further efforts concentrate on the largest source of variation.

Response Surface Study – A response surface study is a special type of designed experiment whose purpose is to model the relationship between the key input variables and the outputs. Performing a response surface study involves running the process at different settings for the inputs, called trials, and measuring the resulting outputs. An equation can then be fit to the data to model the effects of the inputs on the outputs. This equation can then be used to find optimal targets using robust design methods and to establish targets or operating windows using a tolerance analysis. The number of trials required by a response surface study increases exponentially with the number of inputs. It is desirable to keep the number of inputs studied to a minimum. However, failure to include a key input can compromise the results. To ensure that only the key input variables are included in the study, a screening experiment is frequently performed first.

Robust Design Methods – Robust design methods refers collectively to the different methods of selecting optimal targets for the inputs. Generally, when one thinks of reducing variation, tightening tolerances comes to mind. However, as demonstrated by Taguchi, variation can also be reduced by the careful selection of targets. When nonlinear relationships exist between the inputs and the outputs, one can select targets for the inputs that make the outputs less sensitive to the inputs. The result is that while the inputs continue to vary, less of this variation is transmitted to the output. The result is that the output varies less. Reducing variation by adjusting targets is called robust design. In robust design the objective is to select targets for the inputs that result in on-target performance with minimum variation. Several methods of obtaining robust designs exist including robust tolerance analysis, dual response approach and Taguchi methods.

Robust Tolerance Analysis – One of three approaches to robust design. Involves running a designed experiment to model the output's average and then using the statistical approach to tolerance analysis to predict the output's variation. Requires estimates of the amounts that the inputs will vary during long-term manufacturing. Alternatives are Taguchi methods and robust tolerance analysis.

Screening Experiment –A screening experiment is a special type of designed experiment whose primary purpose is to identify the key input variables. Screening experiments are also referred to as fractional factorial experiments or Taguchi L-arrays. Performing a screening experiment involves running the process at different settings for the inputs, called trials, and measuring the resulting outputs. From this, it can be determined which inputs affect the outputs. Screening experiments typically require twice as many trials as input variables. For example, 8 variables can be studied in 16 trials. This makes it possible to study a large number of inputs in a reasonable amount of time. Starting with a larger number of variables reduces the chances of missing an important variable. Frequently a response surface study is performed following a screening experiment to gain further understanding of the effects of the key input variables on the outputs.

Taguchi Methods – One of three approaches to robust design. Involves running a designed experiment to get a rough understanding of the effects of the input targets on the average and variation. The results are then used to select targets for the inputs that minimize the variation while centering the average on the target. Similar to the dual response approach except that while the study is being performed, the inputs are purposely adjusted by small amounts to mimic long-term manufacturing variation. Alternatives are the dual response approach and robust tolerance analysis.

Tolerance Analysis- Using tolerance analysis, operating windows can be set for the inputs that ensure the outputs will conform to requirements. Performing a tolerance analysis requires an equation describing the effects of the inputs on the output. If such an equation is not available, a response surface study can be performed to obtain one. To help ensure manufacturability, tolerances for the inputs should initially be based on the plants and suppliers ability to control them. Capability studies can be used to estimate the ranges that the inputs currently vary over. If this does not result in an acceptable range for the output, the tolerance of at least one input must be tightened. However, tightening a tolerance beyond the current capability of the plant or supplier requires that improvements be made or that a new plant or supplier be selected. Before tightening any tolerances, robust design methods should be considered.

Medical Device Regulation Consulting and Training – www.Procenius.com

Variance Components Analysis – Statistical study used to estimate the relative contributions of several sources of variation. For example, variation on a multi-head filler could be the result of shifting of the process average over time, filling head differences and short-term variation within a fill head. A variance components analysis can be used to estimate the amount of variation contributed by each source.

Heat Sealing Example

Foreword

Heat sealing processes, as described in this example, use equipment to seal plastic pouches which perform as sterility barriers for disposable medical devices. Seal integrity is crucial for maintenance of sterility. Testing of seal integrity is usually destructive testing, and the process therefor is a special process which requires validation.

This example is presented only to give a simple and brief example of the nature of a process validation. The heat seal process described should not be considered a model for all heat seal validations. Additionally, this example may be modified according to different quality management systems, documentation methods and cultures of regions and/or countries which use this guidance.

There are many other circumstances and variables that might be considered when validating an actual heat seal process. This example uses only three simple input variables: time, temperature and pressure. There may be many more input variables, such as operator training, material thickness and melt indexes of the plastic pouches. Additionally, all the details surrounding the rationale for specific sample sizes, control limits, etc. are not given.

Medical Device Regulation Consulting and Training – www.Procenius.com

ABC Medical Device Company
Process Validation Protocol PVP
98-101

Title: Heat Sealer Validation

Products to be covered: Sterile Gizmos- Codes 12345 through 1278

Equipment/Process to be Validated: Supplier Co., Model xyz, ABC Manufacturing Equipment

Register: MER 98-1248 / Heat Sealing Process: SOP 20-12-14

Process/Product Change Control Number: PPCN 98-364

Objective:

Supplier Co. has developed a new and improved heat sealer, which should improve process flow and reduce setup time. The heat sealer will be validated to assure it performs with existing sterile barrier pouch materials and existing process procedure SOP 20-12-14.   SOP 20-12-14 identifies a design requirement for a seal strength of 2 to 4 kg and a target of 3 kg. The most difficult pouches to seal are the smallest (PN 96-122) and the largest (PN 88-010). The target process capability is a C_{pk} of >1.

Reference Documents:

1.   Heat Seal Process Procedure, SOP 20-12-14

2.   Statistical Methodologies, SOP 3-8-51, SOP 3-9-12, SOP 3-13-81

3.   Master Device Records, Codes 12xxx

4.   Manufacturing Equipment Register, MER 98-1248

5.   Supplier Co. Model xyz Heat Sealer Operating Manual

6.   Process Validation Master Plan: PVP-98001

7.   Lab Processes and Calibration: SOP 9-2-5

8.   Production Processes and Calibration: SOP 20-1-2

9.   Clean Room Procedures: SOP 1-12-77

Medical Device Regulation Consulting and Training – www.Procenius.com

<u>Validation Plan:</u>

The Supplier Co. Model xyz Heat Sealer will be subjected to the Installation Qualification, Operational Qualification and Performance Qualification procedures outlined in the Master Validation Plan: PVP-98001. Statistical methods in SOP 3-x-x will be used as appropriate.

The Installation Qualification will utilize the heat sealer operating manual to define requirements for electrical and air pressure requirements. The heat sealer will be installed, checked and calibrated in Clean Room 3 during a weekend, before the weekend scrub-down. Particular attention will be paid to the exhaust of pressurized air into the clean room, so that the requirement for integrity of the environment is not compromised. A checklist of requirements will be completed and results approved.

Operational Qualification will be completed in three phases. First, during production down time, the heat sealer will be subjected to an initial burn-in to observe the stability of the measurements of clamp closure time, temperature build and pressures. Pouches will be sealed, but detailed assessments of seal integrity will not be completed. Data for clamp closure time, temperature build and pressures will be recorded. Variations in these measures will be subjected to a screening experiment (SOP 3-8-51) to determine possible worst case situations and the risk of weak seals or overturning of the pouches. Initial optimal heat seal settings will also be established.

The second phase of operational qualification will center the process and determine initial process capability. The process will be conducted off line, but during production, in the clean room and with production personnel. Production personnel will be trained on the use of the new heat sealer. Heat seals will be completed for pouches PN 96-122 and PN 88-010. Heat sealer settings for the time, temperature and pressure will be used which were determined to be optimal during the initial phase of operational qualification. Accelerated sampling plan 1-A from SOP 3-9-12 will be used and the results control charted. The seal strength target result will be 3 kg and the variation monitored. The number of runs, samples and evaluations will continue until it is determined that the CP is >1 per SOP 3-13-81. Optimal heat sealer settings will be determined for the next phase.

The third phase of operational qualification will determine the sensitivity of the process to variations in time, temperature and pressure. The normal production process will be used. Production personnel will be trained on the use of the new heat sealer. Worst case combinations of time, temperature and pressure will be evaluated. Runs will be completed 1) with the optimal settings, 2) with a short dwell time, low temperature and low pressure; and 3) long dwell time, high temperature and high pressure. Action levels for adjustment of the heat sealer will be determined as a result of this phase.

Performance qualification will commence after satisfactory completion of operational qualification. Optimal settings for the heat sealer will be used and the heat seal action levels for adjustment of time, temperature and pressure will be used. Accelerated sampling plan 2-C from SOP 3-9-12 will be used and the results control charted.

Variations in seal strength will be investigated and root causes determined. When process stability is demonstrated, and the process variation demonstrates a value of Cpk > 1 per SOP 3-13-81, the process will be considered validated and SOP 20-12-14 will be used to control the process.

Measurement / Testing Equipment and Calibration:

1. Stopwatch, Process Development Lab, Calibrated per SOP 9-2-5

2. Remote IR Thermometer RST-12, Process Dev. Lab, Calibrated per SOP 9-2-5

3. Pressure gauge, 0–500kPa, Process Development Lab, Calibrated per SOP 9-2-5

4. VAR meter, ID 683, Process Development Lab, Calibrated per SOP 9-2-5

5. Heat Seal Pull Tester, PE 8167, Production, Calibrated per SOP 20-1-2

Equipment Maintenance:

During validation the heat sealer will be maintained per the Supplier Co. Operating Manual. Upon completion of the validation, Manufacturing Equipment Register, MER 98-1248 will be updated to include maintenance and calibration of the heat sealer.

Revalidation:

Upon completion of the validation, the Process Validation Master Plan: PVP-98001 will be updated to include the heat sealer in the master validation schedule.

Validation Team Protocol Approval

Title	Name	Signature	Date
Process Engineer			
Quality Engineer			
Project Leader			
Production Supervisor			

Installation Qualification Results

PVP 98-101

Installation Checklist

Requirements were established from the heat sealer operating manual, clean room procedures (SOP 1-12-77) and heat seal process procedure (SOP 20-12-14).

Requirement	Source	Status
Electrical supply	Heat sealer operating manual	Conforms
Air pressure	Heat sealer operating manual	Conforms
Ergonomic positioning	Heat sealer operating manual	Conforms
Spare parts	Heat sealer operating manual	Conforms
Clean air exhaust	SOP 1-12-77	Conforms
Cleanability around equipment	SOP 1-12-77	Conforms
Accessibility for maintenance	SOP 20-12-14	Conforms
Capability for sizes of pouches	SOP 20-12-14	Conforms

<u>Initial Burn-in</u>

The heat sealer operated as described in the heat sealer operating manual and as required by SOP 20-12-14.

<u>Calibration</u>

All gauges and measuring devices on the heat sealer were successfully calibrated per SOP 20-1-2. <u>Lab Notebook Reference</u>

Quality Engineering Lab Notebook, JWS, 98-4, pages 46-62. <u>Issues / Commentary</u>

No new issues were identified.

The environmental challenge of the air exhaust was met by adding an oil based air filter to the exhaust line of the heat sealer. The particulate matter was monitored per SOP 9-15-84 and no changes from normal levels were detected.

<u>Conclusion</u>

The heat sealer installation was successful.

<u>Validation Team IQ Results Approval</u>

Title	Name	Signature	Date
Process Engineer			
Quality Engineer			
Project Leader			
Production Supervisor			

Medical Device Regulation Consulting and Training – www.Procenius.com

Operational Qualification Results

PVP 98-101

<u>Phase One</u>

Clamp closure time, temperature build and pressures were measured over a four-hour time frame with initial heat seal settings for time, temperature and pressure. Control charts were completed as follows:

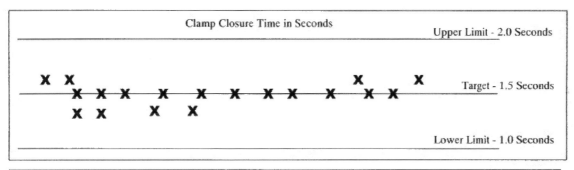

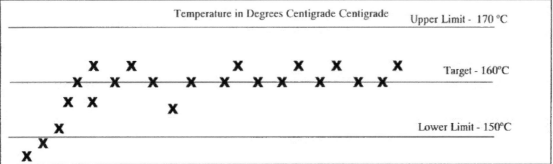

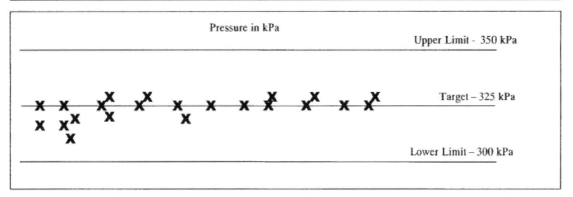

From this analysis, it is apparent that the temperature is the most variable within the lower and upper limits for temperature. Also, temperatures were under the limit for the first fifteen to twenty minutes, as the sealer requires this time to warm up. This screening experiment demonstrated that temperature might be the primary factor influencing heat seal integrity.

Medical Device Regulation Consulting and Training – www.Procenius.com

Initial optimal heat sealer settings were established: temperature controller setting of 7.5, closure time setting of 1.5 seconds and pressure setting of 325 kPa.

Phase Two

Response surface studies were conducted to determine the effects of key inputs on seal strength. Variations in settings were used and the resultant seal strength for ten pouches was calculated. The following table summarizes the results:

Trial Run	Pouch Size	Time	Temperature	Pressure	Seal Strength
1	Small	1.0	150	300	Average 2.1, 6σ 1.2
2	Large	1.0	150	300	Average 2.3, 6σ 1.8
3	Small	1.5	150	300	Average 2.2, 6σ 1.6
4	Large	1.5	150	300	Average 2.5, 6σ 1.3
5	Small	2.0	150	300	Average 2.4, 6σ 1.5
6	Large	2.0	150	300	Average 2.8, 6σ 1.0
7	Small	1.0	160	300	Average 3.0, 6σ 0.4
8	Large	1.0	160	300	Average 3.1, 6σ 0.6
9	Small	1.5	160	300	Average 3.3, 6σ 0.5
10	Large	1.5	160	300	Average 3.4, 6σ 0.6
11	Small	2.0	160	300	Average 2.9, 6σ 0.3
12	Large	2.0	160	300	Average 2.8, 6σ 0.4
13	Small	1.0	170	300	Average 3.1, 6σ 0.6
14	Large	1.0	170	300	Average 3.2, 6σ 0.5
15	Small	1.5	170	300	Average 2.7, 6σ 0.6
16	Large	1.5	170	300	Average 2.9, 6σ 0.4
17	Small	2.0	170	300	Average 2.8, 6σ 0.6
18	Large	2.0	170	300	Average 3.0, 6σ 0.7
19	Small	1.0	150	325	Average 2.2, 6σ 1.7
20	Large	1.0	150	325	Average 2.3, 6σ 1.5
21	Small	1.5	150	325	Average 2.2, 6σ 1.3
22	Large	1.5	150	325	Average 2.5, 6σ 1.4
23	Small	2.0	150	325	Average 2.4, 6σ 1.7
24	Large	2.0	150	325	Average 2.8, 6σ 1.2
25	Small	1.0	160	325	Average 3.0, 6σ 0.3
26	Large	1.0	160	325	Average 3.1, 6σ 0.5
27	Small	1.5	160	325	Average 3.3, 6σ 0.4

Medical Device Regulation Consulting and Training – www.Procenius.com

28	Large	1.5	160	325	Average 3.4, 6σ 0.3
29	Small	2.0	160	325	Average 2.9, 6σ 0.2
30	Large	2.0	160	325	Average 2.8, 6σ 0.3
31	Small	1.0	170	325	Average 3.1, 6σ 0.5
32	Large	1.0	170	325	Average 3.2, 6σ 0.4
38	Large	1.0	150	350	Average 2.3, 6σ 1.8
39	Small	1.5	150	350	Average 2.2, 6σ 1.6
40	Large	1.5	150	350	Average 2.5, 6σ 1.3
41	Small	2.0	150	350	Average 2.4, 6σ 1.5
42	Large	2.0	150	350	Average 2.8, 6σ 1.0
43	Small	1.0	160	350	Average 3.0, 6σ 0.4
44	Large	1.0	160	350	Average 3.1, 6σ 0.6
45	Small	1.5	160	350	Average 3.3, 6σ 0.5
46	Large	1.5	160	350	Average 3.4, 6σ 0.6
47	Small	2.0	160	350	Average 2.9, 6σ 0.3
48	Large	2.0	160	350	Average 2.8, 6σ 0.4
49	Small	1.0	170	350	Average 3.1, 6σ 0.6
50	Large	1.0	170	350	Average 3.2, 6σ 0.5
51	Small	1.5	170	350	Average 2.7, 6σ 0.6
52	Large	1.5	170	350	Average 2.9, 6σ 0.4
53	Small	2.0	170	350	Average 2.8, 6σ 0.6
54	Large	2.0	170	350	Average 3.0, 6σ 0.7

Based on these results it is apparent that the lower temperature limit of 150 oc will result in unacceptable variations in seal strength (overall average of 2.38 kg 6σ of 1.42). Variations in time and pressure within specified limits have little to do with seal strength.

An additional 36 runs were repeated with a lower temperature limit of 155 oc and variations of time and pressure similar to the first 54 runs. The data is not included in this report, but is available in the lab notebook referenced below. The results of these runs demonstrated an overall average of 2.92 kg,

6σ of 0.5. The CP for these runs had a value of 1.8. Optimal heat sealer settings were determined to be a temperature controller setting of 8.2, a time of 1.5 seconds and pressure of 325 kPa.

Phase Three

Normal production processes were used to seal pouches with product and heat seal settings at 1) optimal levels; 2) low temperature, low pressure and short time, and 3) high temperature, high pressure and long time. 190 products were produced at each combination of settings.

Results:

The run with optimal levels resulted in an average seal strength of 3.08 kg, 6o of 0.3, the run with low settings resulted in an average seal strength of 2.8 kg, 6o of 0.5, and the run with high settings resulted in an average seal strength of 2.9 kg, 6o of 0.6.

Lab Notebook Reference

Quality Engineering Lab Notebook, JWS, 98-4, pages 63-98. Issues / Commentary

The input which transmits the most variation to the heat sealing process is temperature. The lower limit of temperature was adjusted to 155 °C from 150 °C.

The heat sealer must have a warm-up time period of at least twenty minutes with normal cycling to have stable temperature control.

Based on these results, when the process is run within input limits, the seal strength target of 3.0 kg should be met with a Cpk of 1.8 per SOP 3-13-81. Initial action levels for adjustment of the heat sealer should be seal strengths of 2.6 kg and 3.2 kg, which should be 3σ variation from the average of 2.9 during operational qualification.

The heat sealer Operational Qualification was successful. Validation Team OQ Results Approval

Title	Name	Signature	Date
Process Engineer			
Quality Engineer			
Project Leader			
Production Supervisor			

Medical Device Regulation Consulting and Training – www.Procenius.com

Performance Qualification Results

PVP 98-101

Normal production of codes 12345 and 12789 were run utilizing pouches PN 96-122 and PN 88-010. Optimal heat sealer settings were used. The heat sealer was allowed to warm-up with normal cycling for one half-hour prior to use. A week of production was completed for each code. Accelerated sampling plan 2-C from SOP 3-9-12 was used and the results control charted. Following is a typical control chart:

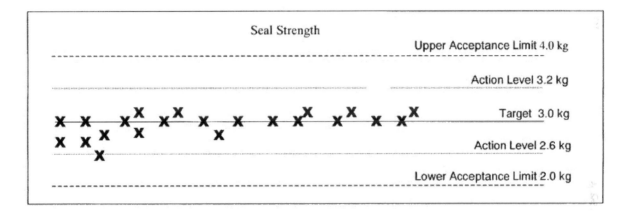

The resultant C_{pk} was 1.75 for the overall process during this performance qualification. The comparison of the CP results for each day demonstrated that the process was both stable and capable. The following CP values were calculated:

> PN 96-122: 1.8, 1.9, 1.7, 1.6, 1.7;
>
> PN 88-010: 1.6, 1.8, 1.7, 1.9, 2.0.

The centering of results about the target was very close: overall average seal strength was 2.93 kg with a target of 3.0 kg

The action levels were never reached, and therefore no adjustments were made and no root causes identified.

Medical Device Regulation Consulting and Training – www.Procenius.com

<u>Lab Notebook Reference:</u>

Quality Engineering Lab Notebook, JWS, 99-1, pages
1-48. <u>Issues / Commentary</u>

The process has demonstrated stability and capability.

The Manufacturing Equipment Register, MER 98-1248, has been updated to include maintenance and calibration of the new heat sealer.

The Process Validation Master Plan, PVP-98001 has been updated to include the new heat sealer in the revalidation process.

Medical Device Regulation Consulting and Training – www.Procenius.com

The Heat Seal Process Procedure, SOP 20-12-14, has been updated to include the new heat sealer and the revised operating procedure for temperature warm-up and lower temperature control limit has been changed from 150 °C to 155 °C.

All production and QA employees have been trained and the training schedule in SOP 20-12-14 has been revised accordingly.

Validation Team PO Results Approval

Title	Name	Signature	Date
Process Engineer			
Quality Engineer			
Project Leader			
Production Supervisor			

Final Report

PVP 98-101

We have reviewed the requirements of the protocol; the IQ, QQ and PQ reports and compared these to the requirements of the reference documents. All requirements have been met and the process is validated.

Medical Device Regulation Consulting and Training – www.Procenius.com

Validation Team Final Report Approval

Title	Name	Signature	Date
Process Engineer			
Quality Engineer			
Project Leader			
Production Supervisor			

Annex B: Quality Systems Preamble
(Design Controls Only)

QSR Preamble

[Federal Register: October 7, 1996 (Volume 61, Number 195)]

[Rules and Regulations]

[Page 52601-52662]

From the Federal Register Online via GPO Access [wais.access.gpo.gov]

[[Page 52601]]

Part VII

Department of Health and Human Services

Food and Drug Administration

---

21 CFR Parts 808, 812, and 820

Medical Devices; Current Good

Manufacturing Practice (CGMP); Final Rule

DEPARTMENT OF HEALTH AND HUMAN SERVICES

Food and Drug Administration

21 CFR Parts 808, 812, and 820

[Docket No. 90N-0172]

RIN 0910-AA09

Medical Devices; Current Good Manufacturing Practice (CGMP) Final

Rule; Quality System Regulation

AGENCY: Food and Drug Administration, HHS.

ACTION: Final rule.

C. Design Controls (Subpart C)

Since early 1984, FDA has identified lack of design controls as one of the major causes of device recalls. The intrinsic quality of devices, including their safety and effectiveness, is established during the design phase. Thus, FDA believes that unless appropriate design controls are observed during preproduction stages of development, a finished device may be neither safe nor effective for its intended use. The SMDA provided FDA with the authority to add preproduction design controls to the device CGMP regulation. Based on its experience with administering the original CGMP regulation, which did not include preproduction design controls, the agency was concerned that the original regulation provided less than an adequate level of assurance that devices would be safe and effective. Therefore, FDA has added general requirements for design controls to the device CGMP regulation for all class III and II devices and certain class I devices. FDA is not subjecting the majority of class I devices to design controls because FDA does not believe that such controls are necessary to ensure that such devices are safe and effective and otherwise in compliance with the act. However, all devices, including class I devices exempt from design controls, must be properly transferred to production in order to comply with Sec. 820.181, as well as other applicable requirements. For most class I devices, FDA believes that the production and other controls in the new quality system regulation and other general controls of the act will be sufficient, as they have been in the past, to ensure safety and effectiveness.

Medical Device Regulation Consulting and Training – www.Procenius.com

62. Many comments were submitted in response to the addition of design control requirements in general, many questioning how these new requirements would be implemented and enforced. For instance, several comments stated that the design control requirements do not reflect how medical devices are actually developed, because the concept of a design rarely originates with the manufacturer, who may not become involved until relatively late in the design evolution. Others expressed concern that FDA investigators will second-guess design issues in which they are not educated or trained, and stated that investigators should not debate whether medical device designs are ``safe and effective."

FDA agrees in part with the comments. The design control requirements are not intended to apply to the development of concepts and feasibility studies. However, once it is decided that a design will be developed, a plan must be established to determine the adequacy of the design requirements and to ensure that the design that will eventually be released to production meets the approved requirements.

Those who design medical devices must be aware of the design control requirements in the regulation and comply with them. Unsafe and ineffective devices are often the result of informal development that does not ensure the proper establishment and assessment of design requirements which are necessary to develop a medical device that is safe and effective for the intended use of the device and that meets the needs of the user.

However, FDA investigators will not inspect a device under the design control requirements to determine whether the design is appropriate or ``safe and effective." Section 520(f)(1)(a) of the act precludes FDA from evaluating the ``safety or effectiveness of a device" through preproduction design control procedures. FDA investigators will evaluate the process, the methods, and the procedures that a manufacturer has established to implement the requirements for design controls. If, based on any information gained during an inspection, an investigator believes that distributed devices are unsafe or ineffective, the investigator has an obligation to report the observations to the Center for Devices and Radiological Health (CDRH).

63. Several comments expressed concern that the application of design controls would severely restrict the creativity and innovation of the design process and suggested that design controls should not apply too early in the design development process.

FDA disagrees with the comments. It is not the intent of FDA to interfere with creativity and innovation, and it is not the intent of FDA to apply the design control requirements to the research phase. Instead, the regulation requires the establishment of procedures to ensure that whatever design is ultimately transferred to production is, in fact, a design that will translate into a device that properly performs according to its intended use and user needs.

To assist FDA in applying the regulation, manufacturers should document the flow of the design process so that it is clear to the FDA investigator where research is ending and development of the design is beginning.

64. A few comments stated that design controls should not be retroactive and that ongoing design development should be exempted. FDA agrees in part with the comments. FDA did not

intend the design requirements to be retroactive, and Sec. 820.30 Design controls will not require the manufacturer to apply such requirements to already distributed devices. When the regulation becomes effective on June 1, 1997, it will apply to designs that are in the design and development phase, and manufacturers will be expected to have the design and development plan established. The manufacturer should identify what stage a design is in for each device and will be expected to comply with the established design and development plan and the applicable paragraphs of Sec. 820.30 from that point forward to completion. If a manufacturer had a design in the development stage before June 1, 1997, and cannot comply with any particular paragraph of Sec. 820.30, the manufacturer must provide a detailed justification as to why such compliance is not possible. However, designs will not have to be recycled through previous phases that have been completed. Manufacturers will be expected to comply in full by June 1, 1998. As stated earlier, FDA wants to emphasize that it expects manufacturers to be in a reasonable state of compliance with the design control requirements from June 1, 1997, to June 1, 1998, because extra time was given to the industry for implementing design controls before the final regulation became effective.

When changes are made to new or existing designs, the design controls of Sec. 820.30 must be followed to ensure that the changes are appropriate and that the device will continue to perform as intended. FDA notes that the original CGMP regulation contained requirements for specification controls and controls for specification or design changes under Sec. 820.100(a).

65. One comment asked how the proposed design controls would apply to investigational device exemption (IDE) devices, since devices under approved IDE's have been exempt from the CGMP regulation. Some comments suggested that any changes to the IDE regulation should be done in a separate rulemaking. Other comments stated that any change to the IDE regulation should be worded so that all of Sec. 820.30 applies since the IDE process is supplying information in support of the design validation requirements but that all design requirements need not be completed prior to the start of the IDE because the clinical evaluation process often brings valuable information to the design project which may need to be incorporated into the design before design transfer.

The IDE regulation was published in 1976 and last updated in 1978, and has been in effect since that time. Devices being evaluated under IDE's were exempted from the original CGMP regulation because it was believed that it was not reasonable to expect sponsors of clinical investigations to ensure compliance with CGMP's for devices that may never be approved for commercial distribution. However, sponsors of IDE studies were required to ensure that investigational devices were manufactured under a state of control.

With respect to the new regulation, FDA believes that it is reasonable to expect manufacturers who design medical devices to develop the designs in conformance with design control requirements and that adhering to such requirements is necessary to adequately protect the public from potentially harmful devices. The design control requirements are basic controls needed to ensure that the device being designed will perform as intended when produced for commercial distribution. Clinical evaluation is an important aspect of the design verification and validation process during the design and development of the device. Because some of the device design occurs during the IDE stage, it is logical that manufacturers who intend to commercially produce the device follow design control procedures. Were a manufacturer to wait until all the IDE studies were complete, it would be too late to take advantage of the design control process, and the manufacturer would not be able to fulfill the requirements of the quality system regulation for that device.

Therefore, FDA has concurrently amended the IDE regulation, 812.1 Scope to state:

(a) * * * An IDE approved under Sec. 812.30 or considered approved under Sec. 812.2(b) exempts a device from the requirements of the following sections of the Federal Food, Drug, and Cosmetic Act (the act) and regulations issued thereunder: * * * good manufacturing practice requirements under section 520(f) except for the requirements found in Sec. 820.30, if applicable (unless the sponsor states an intention to comply with these requirements under Sec. 812.20(b)(3) or Sec. 812.140(b)(4)(v)) and color additive requirements under section 721. (Emphasis added.)

FDA does not expect any new information in IDE applications as a result of this amendment, nor will FDA inspect design controls during bioresearch monitoring inspections. FDA is simply making a conforming amendment to the IDE regulation to make clear that design controls must be followed when design functions are undertaken by manufacturers, including design activity which occurs under an approved IDE. FDA will evaluate the adequacy of manufacturers' compliance with design control requirements in routine CGMP inspections, including preapproval inspections for premarket approval applications (PMA's).

66. Many written comments and oral comments at the August and September 1995 meetings recommended that, because design controls are a major addition to the regulation, the effective date for design controls should be delayed until 18 months after publication of the final rule.

FDA has addressed these comments by extending the effective date of the regulation until June 1, 1997, and by the inspectional strategy described earlier.

67. A couple of comments suggested that FDA lacked the authority to establish the design control requirements. FDA disagrees with the comments. The act and its legislative history make clear that FDA has the authority to impose those controls necessary to ensure that devices are safe and effective. The SMDA gave FDA explicit authority to promulgate design controls, including a process to assess the performance of a device (see section 520(f)(1)(A) of the act). The legislative history of the SMDA supports a ``comprehensive device design validation regulation.'' H. Rept. 808, 101st Cong., 2d sess. 23 (emphasis added). Congress stated that the amendment to the statute was necessary because almost half of all device recalls over a 5-year period were ``related to a problem with product design.'' Id. There is a thorough discussion on the evolution of and need for the design controls in the preamble to the November 23, 1993 (58 FR 61952), proposal.

68. A few comments objected to FDA requiring design controls for any class I devices in Sec. 820.30(a). FDA believes that, for the class I devices listed, design controls are necessary and has retained the requirements. Those relatively few devices, while class I, require close control

of the design process to ensure that the devices perform as intended, given the serious consequences that could occur if their designs were flawed and the devices were to fail to meet their intended uses. In fact, some of the devices included on the list have experienced failures due to design related problems that have resulted in health hazards, injuries, or death. Further, verification, or even validation, cannot provide the assurance of proper design for some devices, especially those containing extensive software. Thus, all automated devices must be developed under the design control requirements.

69. Several comments stated that FDA has underestimated the complexity of a design project in requiring that the plans identify ``persons responsible for each activity'' in proposed Sec.820.30(b). One comment stated that ``define responsibility for implementation'' and ``activities shall be assigned'' were basically redundant requirements. A few other comments stated that ISO 9001:1994 does not call for the design plans to be ``approved'' and that this requirement should be deleted because it would be burdensome. FDA agrees in part with the comments and has revised Sec. 820.30(b) to require the plan to describe or reference design activities and define responsibility for implementing the activities, rather than requiring that the plan identify each person responsible for carrying out each activity. In making this change, FDA notes that Sec. 820.20(b)(1) requires manufacturers to establish the appropriate responsibility for activities affecting quality, and emphasizes that the assignment of specific responsibility is important to the success of the design control program and to achieving compliance with the regulation. Also, the design and development activities should be assigned to qualified personnel equipped with adequate resources as required under Sec. 820.20(b)(2). The requirements under Sec. 820.30(b) were rewritten to be very similar to the requirements in ISO 9001:1994, sections 4.4.2 and 4.4.3. FDA does not agree that the design plan should not be ``approved.'' ISO 9001:1994, section 4.4.2 requires that the plan be ``updated,'' and section 4.4.3 requires that the plan be ``regularly reviewed.'' Therefore, the approval is consistent with ISO 9001:1994 and would not be unduly burdensome since the FDA does not dictate how or by whom the plan must be approved. The regulation gives the manufacturer the necessary flexibility to have the same person(s) who is responsible for the review also be responsible for the approval of the plan if appropriate.

70. A few comments stated that the proposed requirement to describe ``any interaction between or among different organizational and technical groups'' in Sec. 820.30(b) for the design and development plan should be deleted because it is overly broad, unnecessary, and burdensome. One comment said that the communication expected between these groups should be clarified.

In response, FDA has amended the requirement as suggested by one comment so that the plan shall identify and describe the interfaces with different groups or activities that provide, or result in, input to the design process. Many organization functions, both inside and outside the design group, may contribute to the design process. For example, interfaces with marketing, purchasing, regulatory affairs, manufacturing, service groups, or information systems may be necessary during the design development phase. To function effectively, the design plan must establish the roles of these groups in the design process and describe the information that should be received and transmitted.

71. One comment stated that the requirement in Sec. 820.30(b) that manufacturers establish a design plan completely ignores the creative and dynamic process of designing by requiring a plan to have complete design and testing criteria established, with specifications, before the design process is started. FDA disagrees with the comment. Section 820.30(b) does not require manufacturers to complete design and testing criteria before the design process begins. This section has been revised to state that ``plans shall be reviewed, updated, and approved as design and development evolves,'' indicating that changes to the design plan are expected. A design plan typically includes at least proposed quality practices, assessment methodology, recordkeeping and documentation requirements, and resources, as well as a sequence of events related to a particular design or design category. These may be modified and refined as the design evolves. However, the design process can become a lengthy and costly process if the design activity is not properly defined and planned. The more specifically the activities are defined up front, the less need there will be for changes as the design evolves.

72. One comment stated that the language contained in proposed Sec. 820.30(c) should more closely match that of ISO 9001. Many other comments stated that the provision should not require the input requirements to ``completely'' address the intended use of the device because inputs could never ``completely'' address the intended use. Several comments stated that the requirement of ISO 9001 that ``incomplete, ambiguous or conflicting requirements shall be resolved with those responsible for imposing these requirements'' should be added to Sec. 820.30(c), ``Design input,'' because it is important that the regulation identify the method of resolving conflicting information. FDA agrees with the harmonization comment and has revised the language to incorporate the requirement of section 4.4.4, ``Design input,'' of ISO 9001:1994. FDA does not believe that it is necessary to have identical language to harmonize quality system requirements. ISO 9001:1994, section 4.4.1, ``General,'' requires that the manufacturer ``establish and maintain documented procedures to control and verify the design of the product in order to ensure that the specified requirements are met.'' FDA's regulation, under Sec. 820.30(a), imposes the same requirements.

Regarding the comments that input requirements cannot completely address the intended use of the device, FDA recognizes that the provision could be interpreted to impose a burden that may not always be possible to meet and has deleted the word ``completely.'' FDA did not intend the provision to suggest that a manufacturer must foresee every possible event.

FDA emphasizes, however, that the section requires the manufacturer to ensure that the design input requirements are appropriate so the device will perform to meet its intended use and the needs of the user. In doing this, the manufacturer must define the performance characteristics, safety and reliability requirements, environmental requirements and limitations, physical characteristics, applicable standards and regulatory requirements, and labeling and packaging requirements, among other things, and refine the design requirements as verification and validation results are established. For example, when designing a device, the manufacturer should conduct appropriate human factors studies, analyses, and tests from the early stages of

Medical Device Regulation Consulting and Training – www.Procenius.com

the design process until that point in development at which the interfaces with the medical professional and the patient are fixed. The human interface includes both the hardware and software characteristics that affect device use, and good design is crucial to logical, straightforward, and safe device operation. The human factors methods used (for instance, task/function analyses, user studies, prototype tests, mock-up reviews, etc.) should ensure that the characteristics of the user population and operating environment are considered. In addition, the compatibility of system components should be assessed. Finally, labeling (e.g., instructions for use) should be tested for usability.

FDA agrees with the comments, in that it is important that incomplete, ambiguous, or conflicting requirements be resolved with those responsible for imposing these requirements. Therefore, FDA has added the requirement that the procedures shall include a mechanism for addressing incomplete, ambiguous, or conflicting requirements. FDA notes that this must be done to ``ensure that the design requirements are appropriate and address the intended use of the device,'' as required under Sec. 820.30(c).

73. A few other comments stated that ISO 9001:1994 does not call for the design input to be ``approved'' and therefore, this requirement should be deleted because it would be burdensome.

FDA does not agree that the ``approval'' of design input requirements should be deleted, nor that the requirement is inconsistent with ISO. ISO 9001:1994, section 4.4.4, ``Design Input,'' requires that the design input requirements be ``reviewed by the supplier for adequacy.'' Therefore, the approval would not add any additional burden because FDA does not dictate how or by whom the design input requirements must be approved, thus giving the manufacturer the necessary flexibility to have the same person(s) who is responsible for the ``review for adequacy'' also be responsible for the approval, if appropriate. Further, it is important that the design input be assessed as early as possible in the development process, making this an ideal time in the device's design development to have a design review to ``approve'' the design input.

74. A few comments stated that the proposed requirement under Sec. 820.30(c) that ``design input shall be reviewed and approved by a designated qualified individual'' should be deleted as it implies that one person must be designated to review and approve a design, and that there may not be one person who is qualified to assess all of the design input requirements. Addressing the same point, several comments suggested that the provision be revised to allow for more than one person to review and approve the design. One comment said that the FDA's requirement appears to be at odds with the team approach.

FDA agrees with the concern expressed by the comments and has modified the requirement to allow more than one individual to review and approve the design input. FDA endorses the team approach and believes that designs should be reviewed and evaluated by all disciplines necessary to ensure the design input requirements are appropriate.

75. Two comments stated that proposed Sec. 820.30(c) should be reworded to focus on systems for assuring adequate design input, not on the input itself. One additional comment on

this section said that the design input requirements should include not only the device's intended use and needs of the user, but the environmental limits of where it will be used.

FDA agrees that procedures for ensuring appropriate design controls are of the utmost importance and has modified the section to clarify that the manufacturer must establish and maintain procedures to ensure that the design requirements are properly addressed. FDA made this change to the other paragraphs as well, but notes that Sec. 820.30(a), ``General,'' requires the manufacturer to establish and maintain procedures to control the design of the device in order to ensure that specified design requirements are met. The sections that follow set forth some of the requirements for which procedures must be established. It should be emphasized that the input itself must also be appropriate; the requirement is for the procedures to be defined, documented, and implemented. Thus, if the input requirements related to a device fail to address the intended use of the device, for example, the manufacturer has failed to comply with the provision.

FDA also agrees with the additional comment but believes that identifying and establishing the environmental limits for safe and effective device operation is inherent in the requirements for ensuring that a device is appropriate for its intended use. Some factors that must be considered when establishing inputs include, where applicable, a determination of energy (e.g., electrical, heat, and electromagnetic fields), biological effects (e.g., toxicity and biocompatibility) and environmental effects (e.g., electromagnetic interference and electrostatic discharge).

76. Several comments stated that proposed Sec. 820.30(f), ``Design output,'' should be rewritten or deleted because many of the requirements were already stated in proposed Secs. 820.30(d), ``Design verification,'' and 820.30(e), ``Design review,'' and, if retained, should be reordered similar to ISO 9001.

FDA agrees in part with the comments and has rewritten the requirements of design output to be consistent with ISO 9001:1994, section 4.4.5, ``Design output,'' and reordered the sections to be consistent with ISO 9001:1994. FDA retained the provision, however, because it does not agree that the section is redundant with the sections on design verification, design validation, or design review. Design output are the design specifications which should meet design input requirements, as confirmed during design verification and validation and ensured during design review. The output includes the device, its labeling and packaging, associated specifications and drawings, and production and quality assurance specifications and procedures. These documents are the basis for the DMR. The total finished design output consists of the device, its labeling and packaging, and the DMR.

77. One comment stated that the sentence ``Design output procedures shall ensure that design output meets the design input requirements'' is redundant with the requirement under design verification. Another comment asked what is meant by ``release.''

FDA agrees with the first comment and has deleted that sentence in

Sec. 820.30(d) but notes that the design output must be documented and expressed in terms that can be verified against the design input requirements.

Design output can be ``released" or transferred to the next design phase at various stages in the design process, as defined in the design and development plan. The design output is reviewed and approved before release or transfer to the next design phase or production. The design output requirements are intended to apply to all such stages of the design process.

78. One small manufacturer commented that the problems that Sec. 820.30(e), ``Design review," is meant to reveal involve coordination, cooperation, or communication difficulties among the members of an organization and that these difficulties do not exist in a small company. Therefore, the comment stated that the design review requirements should not apply to small manufacturers.

The purpose of conducting design reviews during the design phase is to ensure that the design satisfies the design input requirements for the intended use of the device and the needs of the user. Design review includes the review of design verification data to determine whether the design outputs meet functional and operational requirements, the design is compatible with components and other accessories, the safety requirements are achieved, the reliability and maintenance requirements are met, the labeling and other regulatory requirements are met, and the manufacturing, installation, and servicing requirements are compatible with the design specifications. Design reviews should be conducted at major decision points during the design phase.

For a large manufacturer, design review provides an opportunity for all those who may have an impact on the quality of the device to provide input, including manufacturing, quality assurance, purchasing, sales, and servicing divisions. While small manufacturers may not have the broad range of disciplines found in a large company, and the need to coordinate and control technical interfaces may be lessened, the principles of design review still apply. The requirements under Sec. 820.30(e) allow small manufacturers to tailor a design review that is appropriate to their individual needs.

79. One comment stated that the wording of proposed Sec. 820.30(e) implies that only one design review is expected, and that design review should be conducted at several stages of product development. Several comments stated that to demand that every design review be conducted by individuals who do not have direct responsibility for design development is impractical, especially for small companies.

FDA agrees with the first comment and has rewritten the requirement to make clear that design reviews must be conducted at appropriate stages of design development, which must be defined in the established design and development plan. The number of design reviews will depend on the plan and the complexity of the device. FDA also amended the requirements so that the results of a design review include identification of the design, the date, and the individual(s) performing the review. Thus, multiple reviews can occur and the manufacturer must document what is being reviewed, when, and by whom.

FDA never intended to mandate that an individual without design responsibility conduct the design reviews and, to clarify its position, has rewritten the requirement. The requirement now states that the procedures shall ensure that each design review includes an individual(s) who does not have direct responsibility for the design stage being reviewed. This requirement will

Medical Device Regulation Consulting and Training – www.Procenius.com

provide an ``objective view'' from someone not working directly on that particular part of the design project, to ensure that the requirements are met. In making this change, FDA also notes that it was not FDA's intention to prohibit those directly responsible for the design from participating in the design review.

80. One comment stated that as part of the systematic review of the adequacy of the device design, it is occasionally necessary to produce a prototype device and have it evaluated by a physician who is an expert in the area of the device's intended use. Thus, the comment stated that the regulation should be revised to allow a means for a manufacturer to ship a prototype device to a physician for evaluation. One comment questioned whether design verification and can be conducted using prototypes or machine shop models.

FDA regulations do not prohibit the shipment of prototypes for clinical or other studies. Prototypes used in clinical studies involving humans may be shipped in accordance with the IDE provisions in part 812 (21 CFR part 812).

FDA understands that it is not always practical to conduct clinical studies on finished production units and, therefore, the use of prototypes in clinical studies is acceptable. When prototype devices are used on humans they must be verified as safe to the maximum extent feasible. Final design validation, however, cannot be done on prototypes because the actual devices produced and distributed are seldom the same as the research and development prototypes. The final verification and validation, therefore, must include the testing of actual production devices under actual or simulated use conditions.

81. A few comments stated that Sec. 820.30(d), ``Design verification,'' should be rewritten and reordered similar to ISO 9001.

FDA agrees with the comments and has rewritten and reordered this section to be consistent with ISO 9001:1994. The language in revised Sec. 820.30(f) and (g) incorporates the requirement of ISO 9001:1994, sections 4.4.7, ``Design verification,'' and 4.4.8, ``Design validation,'' respectively.

Under the revised provisions, the design must be verified and validated. It is important to note that design validation follows successful design verification. Certain aspects of design validation can be accomplished during the design verification, but design verification is not a substitute for design validation. Design validation should be performed under defined operating conditions and on the initial production units, lots, or batches, or their equivalents to ensure proper overall design control and proper design transfer. When equivalent devices are used in the final design validation, the manufacturer must document in detail how the device was manufactured and how the manufacturing is similar to and possibly different from initial production. Where there are differences, the manufacturer must justify why design validation results are valid for the production units, lots, or batches. Manufacturers should not use prototypes developed in the laboratory or machine shop as test units to meet these requirements. Prototypes may differ from the finished production devices. During research and development, conditions for building prototypes are typically better controlled and personnel more knowledgeable about what needs to be done and how to do it than are regular production personnel. When going from laboratory to scale-up production, standards, methods, and procedures may not be properly transferred, or additional manufacturing processes may be added. Often, changes not reflected in the prototype are made in the device to facilitate the manufacturing process, and these may adversely affect device functioning and user interface characteristics. Proper testing of devices that are produced using the same methods and procedures as those to be used in routine production will prevent the distribution and subsequent recall of many unacceptable medical devices.

In addition, finished devices must be tested for performance under actual conditions of use or simulated use conditions in the actual or simulated environment in which the device is expected to be used. The simulated use testing provision no longer requires that the testing be performed on the first three production runs. However, samples must be taken from units, lots, or batches that were produced using the same specifications, production and quality system methods, procedures, and equipment that will be used for routine production. FDA considers this a critical element of the design validation. The requirement to conduct simulated use testing of finished devices is found in the original CGMP in Sec. 820.160, as part of finished device inspection. This requirement has been moved to Sec. 820.30(g) because FDA believes that simulated use testing at this point is more effective in ensuring that only safe and effective devices are produced. Manufacturers must also conduct such tests when they make changes in the device design or the manufacturing process that could affect safety or effectiveness as required in the original CGMP in Sec. 820.100(a)(2). The extent of testing conducted should be governed by the risk(s) the device will present if it fails. FDA considers these activities essential for ensuring that the manufacturing process does not adversely affect the device.

Design validation may also be necessary in earlier stages, prior to product completion, and multiple validations may need to be performed if there are different intended uses. Proper design validation cannot occur without following all the requirements set forth in the design control section of the regulation.

82. Several comments stated that adequate controls for verification of design output are contained in proposed Sec. 820.30(d), ``Design verification,'' and repeated in proposed Sec. 820.30(f), ``Design output.'' One comment stated that this section will place undue burden on designers and require additional documentation which will add little value to a device's safety and effectiveness.

FDA disagrees with the comments. Revised Sec. 820.30(f), ``Design verification,'' and Sec. 820.30(g), ``Design validation,'' require verification and validation of the design output. Section 820.30(d),

``Design output,'' requires that the output be documented in a fashion that will allow for verification and validation. These sections thus contain different requirements that are basic to establishing that the design output meets the approved design requirements or inputs, including user needs and intended uses. All the requirements are essential to assuring the safety and effectiveness of devices. FDA does not believe that these requirements place undue burden on designers or require additional documentation with no value added. These basic requirements are necessary to assure the proper device performance, and, therefore, the production of safe and effective devices, and are acknowledged and accepted as such throughout the world.

83. Several comments stated that the term ``hazard analysis'' should be defined in reference to design verification. A couple of comments stated that the proposed requirement for design verification, to include software validation and hazard analysis, where applicable, was ambiguous, and may lead an FDA investigator to require software validation and hazard analysis for devices in cases where it is not needed. One comment stated that FDA should provide additional guidance regarding software validation and hazard analysis and what investigators will expect to see. Another comment stated that by explicitly mentioning only software validation and hazard analysis, FDA was missing the opportunity to introduce manufacturers to some powerful and beneficial tools for better device designs and problem avoidance.

FDA has deleted the term ``hazard analysis'' and replaced it with the term ``risk analysis.'' FDA's involvement with the ISO TC 210 made it clear that ``risk analysis'' is the comprehensive and appropriate term. When conducting a risk analysis, manufacturers are expected to identify possible hazards associated with the design in both normal and fault conditions. The risks associated with the hazards, including those resulting from user error, should then be calculated in both normal and fault conditions. If any risk is judged unacceptable, it should be reduced to acceptable levels by the appropriate means, for example, by redesign or warnings. An important part of risk analysis is ensuring that changes made to eliminate or minimize hazards do not introduce new hazards. Tools for conducting such analyses include Failure Mode Effect Analysis and Fault Tree Analysis, among others.

FDA disagrees with the comments that state the requirement is ambiguous. Software must be validated when it is a part of the finished device. FDA believes that this control is always needed, given the unique nature of software, to assure that software will perform as intended and will not impede safe operation by the user. Risk analysis must be conducted for the majority of devices subject to design controls and is considered to be an essential requirement for medical devices under this regulation, as well as under ISO/CD 13485 and EN 46001. FDA has replaced the phrase ``where applicable'' with ``where appropriate'' for consistency with the rest of the regulation.

FDA believes that sufficient domestic and international guidelines are available to provide assistance to manufacturers for the validation of software and risk analysis. For example, ``Reviewer Guidance for Computer Controlled Medical Devices Undergoing 510(k) Review,'' August 1991; ``A Technical Report, Software Development Activities,'' July 1987; and ISO-9000-3 contain computer validation guidance. Further, FDA is preparing a new ``CDRH Guidance for the Scientific Review of Pre-Market Medical Device Software Submissions.'' Regarding guidance on ``risk analysis,'' manufacturers can reference the draft EN (prEN) 1441, ``Medical Devices--Risk Analysis'' standard and the work resulting from ISO TC 210 working group No. 4 to include ISO/CD 14971, ``Medical Devices--Risk Management--Application of Risk Analysis to Medical Devices.''

FDA disagrees that it is missing the opportunity to introduce manufacturers to some powerful and beneficial tools for better device designs and problem avoidance because the manufacturer must apply current methods and procedures that are appropriate for the device, to verify and validate the device design under the regulation. Therefore, FDA need not list all known methods for meeting the requirements. A tool that may be required to adequately verify and validate one design may be unnecessary to verify and validate another design.

84. One comment stated that for some design elements it may be more appropriate to reference data from another prior experimentation rather than conduct new testing, and that the requirement to list verification methods should be modified.

FDA agrees in part with the comment. The revised language of Sec. 820.30(f) will permit the use of data from prior experimentation when applicable. When using data from previous experimentation, manufacturers must ensure that it is adequate for the current application.

85. ``Design transfer,'' now Sec. 820.30(h), has been revised in response to the many comments objecting to the requirements in the proposed section on ``Design transfer.'' Specifically, the proposed requirement for testing production units under actual or simulated use conditions was rewritten and moved to current Sec. 820.30(g), ``Design validation.''

FDA again emphasizes that testing production units under actual or simulated use conditions prior to distribution is crucial for ensuring that only safe and effective devices are distributed and FDA has therefore retained the requirement. ISO 9001:1994 discusses this concept in notes 12 and 13. As noted above, it is not always possible to determine the adequacy of the design by successfully building and testing prototypes or models produced in a laboratory setting.

The requirement for testing from the first three production lots or batches has been deleted. While FDA believes that three production runs during process validation (process validation may be initiated before or during design transfer) is the accepted standard, FDA recognizes that all processes may not be defined in terms of lots or batches. The number three is, however, currently considered to be the acceptable standard. Therefore, although the number requirement is deleted, FDA expects validation to be carried out properly in accordance with accepted standards, and will inspect for compliance accordingly.

Revised Sec. 820.30(h) now contains a general requirement for the establishment of procedures to ensure that the design basis for the device is correctly translated into production methods and procedures. This is the same requirement that is contained in Sec. 820.100(a) of the original CGMP regulation.

86. A few comments stated that the proposed requirements for ``Design release'' would prohibit the release of components, partial designs, and production methods before the design was final because the requirements mandate a review of all drawings, analysis, and production methods before allowing the product to go into production. Several comments stated that the proposed section on ``Design release'' was a duplication of requirements in other paragraphs of Sec. 820.30 and should be deleted.

FDA did not intend the requirements for ``Design release'' to prohibit manufacturers from beginning the production process until all design activities were completed. The intent of the requirement was to ensure that all design specifications released to production have been approved, verified, and validated before they are implemented as part of the production process. This requirement is now explicitly contained in Sec. 820.30(d).

Medical Device Regulation Consulting and Training – www.Procenius.com

FDA agrees in part with the second set of comments and has moved the requirement that design output be reviewed and approved to current Sec. 820.30(d), ``Design output.'' The remainder of the requirements have been deleted.

87. Several comments on Sec. 820.30(i), ``Design changes,'' stated that it is unnecessary to control all design changes and to do so would inhibit change and innovation.

FDA disagrees with the comments. Manufacturers are not expected to maintain records of all changes proposed during the very early stages of the design process. However, all design changes made after the design review that approves the initial design inputs for incorporation into the design, and those changes made to correct design deficiencies once the design has been released to production, must be documented.

The records of these changes create a history of the evolution of the design, which can be invaluable for failure investigation and for facilitating the design of future similar products. Such records can prevent the repetition of errors and the development of unsafe or ineffective designs. The evaluation and documentation should be in direct proportion to the significance of the change. Procedures must ensure that after the design requirements are established and approved, changes to the design, both pre- production and post-production are also reviewed, validated (or verified where appropriate), and approved.

Otherwise, a device may be rendered unable to properly perform, and unsafe and ineffective. ISO 9001:1994, section 4.4.9, similarly provides that ``all design changes and modifications shall be identified, documented, reviewed, and approved by authorized personnel before their implementation.''

Note that when a change is made to a specification, method, or procedure, each manufacturer should evaluate the change in accordance with an established procedure to determine if the submission of a premarket notification (510(k)) under Sec. 807.81(a)(3) (21 CFR 807.81(a)(3)), or the submission of a supplement to a PMA under Sec. 814.39(a) (21 CFR 814.39) is required. Records of this evaluation and its results should be maintained.

88. Several comments recommended that only changes after design validation and design transfer to full-scale production need to be documented.

FDA disagrees with the comments. The safety and effectiveness of devices cannot be proven by final inspection or testing. Product development is inherently an evolutionary process. While change is a healthy and necessary part of product development, quality can be ensured only if change is controlled and documented in the development process, as well as the production process. Again, manufacturers are not expected to maintain records of changes made during the very early stages of product development; only those design changes made after the approval of the design inputs need be documented. Each manufacturer must establish criteria for evaluating changes to ensure that the changes are appropriate for its designs.

89. One comment on proposed Sec. 820.30(i), ``Design changes,'' stated that validation of design changes is not always necessary and the regulation should provide for other methods to be used. FDA agrees with the comments and has amended the requirement to permit

verification where appropriate. For example, a change in the sterilization process of a catheter will require validation of the new process, but the addition of more chromium to a stainless steel surgical instrument may only require verification through chemical analysis. Where a design change cannot be verified by subsequent inspection and test, it must be validated.

90. Many comments noted that the acronym for proposed design history record (DHR) was the same as that of ``device history record'' (DHR), and suggested that the name of the ``design history record'' be changed. Several comments stated that the requirements of the ``design history record'' should be deleted because they were redundant with the requirements of the ``device master record.'' FDA agrees with the first set of comments and has changed the name to ``design history file.''

FDA disagrees with the second set of comments. The DMR contains the documentation necessary to produce a device. The final design output from the design phase, which is maintained or referenced in the DHF, will form the basis or starting point for the DMR. Thus, those outputs must be referred to or placed in the DMR. The total finished design output includes the final device, its labeling and packaging, and the DMR that includes device specifications and drawings, as well as all instructions and procedures for production, installation, maintenance, and servicing. The DHF, in contrast, contains or references all the records necessary to establish compliance with the design plan and the regulation, including the design control procedures. The DHF illustrates the history of the design, and is necessary so that manufacturers can exercise control over and be accountable for the design process, thereby maximizing the probability that the finished design conforms to the design specifications.

91. A few comments stated that the proposed requirements in Sec. 820.30(j) for the design history record should allow a single design history record for each device family or group having common design characteristics.

FDA agrees with the comments. The intent of the DHF is to document, or reference the documentation of, the activities carried out to meet the design plan and requirements of Sec. 820.30. A DHF is, therefore, necessary for each type of device developed. The DHF must provide documentation showing the actions taken with regard to each type of device designed, not generically link devices together with different design characteristics and give a general overview of how the output was reached.

92. Some comments stated that the requirement that the DHF contain ``all'' records necessary to demonstrate that the requirements are met should be deleted because not ``all'' efforts need documentation.

FDA received similar comments on almost every section of the regulation that had the word ``all.'' The proposed requirement does not state that all records must be contained in the DHF, but that all records necessary to demonstrate that the requirements were met must be contained in the file. FDA has deleted the word ``all'' but cautions manufacturers that the complete history of the design process should be documented in the DHF. Such records are necessary to ensure that the final design conforms to the design specifications. Depending on the design, that may be relatively few records. Manufacturers who do not document all their efforts may lose the information and experience of those efforts, thereby possibly requiring activities to be duplicated.

Medical Device Regulation Consulting and Training – www.Procenius.com

REFERENCES

CDRH. (2015). *www.fda.yorkcast.com*. Retrieved from Quality System Regulation, 21 CFR 820, Basic
    Introduction: http://fda.yorkcast.com/webcast/Play/dd2d4823b14a4e4ca6d60eae43c5ac9c.

FDA 510k. (2014, July 28). Retrieved from The 510k Program: Evaluating Substantial Equivalence In
    Premarket Notifications (510k).

FDA CGMP. (2014, June 30). *Quality System Regulation/Medical Device Good Manufacturing Practices*.
    Retrieved from www.fda.gov:
    http://www.fda.gov/MedicalDevices/DeviceRegulationandGuidance/PostmarketRequirements/
    QualitySystemsRegulations/

FDA Class I/II Exemptions. (2014, 6 26). *Class I/II Exemptions*. Retrieved from www.FDA.gov:
    http://www.fda.gov/MedicalDevices/DeviceRegulationandGuidance/Overview/ClassifyYourDevi
    ce/ucm051549.htm

FDA D.C. Guidance. (2015, May 28). *Design Control Guidance for Medical Device Manufacturers*.
    Retrieved from www.FDA.gov:
    http://www.fda.gov/RegulatoryInformation/Guidances/ucm070627.htm#_Toc382720779

FDA Devcie Classification. (2014, 7 29). *Classify Your Medical Device*. Retrieved from www.FDA.gov:
    http://www.fda.gov/MedicalDevices/DeviceRegulationandGuidance/Overview/ClassifyYourDevi
    ce/default.htm

FDA Device Determination. (2014, 9 12). *Is the Product a Medical Device*. Retrieved from www.FDA.gov:
    http://www.fda.gov/MedicalDevices/DeviceRegulationandGuidance/Overview/ClassifyYourDevi
    ce/ucm051512.htm

FDA Human Factors. (2011, June 22). *Draft Guidance for Industry and Food and Drug Administration
    Staff - Applying Human Factors and Usability Engineering to Optimize Medical Device Design*.
    Retrieved from www.fda.gov:
    http://www.fda.gov/RegulatoryInformation/Guidances/ucm259748.htm#3

FDA Medical Device Classes Define. (2014, 6 4). *Learn if Medical Device has been Cleared by FDA for
    Marketing*. Retrieved from www.FDA.gov:
    http://www.fda.gov/MedicalDevices/ResourcesforYou/Consumers/ucm142523.htm

FDA Preamble. (2015, May 1). *Medical Devices, Current Good Manufacturing Practices (CGMP) Final Rule
    (QSR Preamble)*. Retrieved from www.fda.gov:
    http://www.fda.gov/MedicalDevices/DeviceRegulationandGuidance/PostmarketRequirements/
    QualitySystemsRegulations/ucm230127.htm

FDA QS Manual. (2013, December 12). *Medical Device Quality Systems Manual: A Small Entity
    Compliance Guide, First Edition, CDRH (Withdrawn)*. Retrieved from www.FDA.gov.

FDA QS Regulation. (2015, April 1). *Quality System Regulation, 21 CFR Part 820.30, Regulation*. Retrieved
    from www.FDA.gov:

Medical Device Regulation Consulting and Training – www.Procenius.com

http://www.accessdata.fda.gov/scripts/cdrh/cfdocs/cfcfr/CFRSearch.cfm?CFRPart=820&showFR=1

FDA QSR . (2014, September 1). *Quality System Regulation, 21 CFR Part 820.3, Definitions*. Retrieved from www.FDA.gov: http://www.accessdata.fda.gov/scripts/cdrh/cfdocs/cfcfr/cfrsearch.cfm?cfrpart=820&showfr=1

FDA SW Validation. (2012, January 11). *General Principals of Software Validation.* Retrieved from www.FDA.gov: http://www.fda.gov/RegulatoryInformation/Guidances/ucm085281.htm#_Toc517237928

GHTF. (2004, January). *Quality Management Systems - Process Validation Guidance.* Retrieved from www.imdrf.org : http://www.imdrf.org/docs/ghtf/final/sg3/technical-docs/ghtf-sg3-n99-10-2004-qms-process-guidance-04010.pdf

Hirning, D. a. (2013, May). *FDA Human Factor Requirements Change the Landscape of Medical Device Development.* Retrieved from MedsMagazine.com: http://medsmagazine.com/2013/05/fda-human-factor-requirements-change-the-landscape-of-medical-device-development/

Hooten, W. F. (1996, May 1). *A Brief History of FDA Good Manufacturing Practices.* Retrieved from www.mddionline.com: http://www.mddionline.com/article/brief-history-fda-good-manufacturing-practices.

Investopedia LLC. (2015). *www.investopedia.com.* Retrieved from Investopedia: http://www.investopedia.com/terms/g/groupthink.asp

ISO 13485. (2007). Medical Devices - Quality Managment Systems , 2nd Edition. *ISO/IEC 13485:2007.* Geneva, Switzerland: International Organization for Standardization.

ISO 14969. (2004). Medical Devices - Quality Managment Systems - Guidance on the Application of 13485:2003 , 2nd Edition. *ISO/TR 14969:2004.* Geneva, Switzerland: International Organization for Standardization.

ISO 14971. (2007). Application of Risk Management to Medical Devices, 2nd Edition. *ISO/IEC 14971:2007.* Geneva, Switzerland: International Organization for Standardization.

Med Dev QS Manual. (2014, 11 26). *(Withdrawn) Medical Device Quality System Manual.* Retrieved from FDA.gov: http://www.fda.gov/MedicalDevices/DeviceRegulationandGuidance/PostmarketRequirements/QualitySystemsRegulations/MedicalDeviceQualitySystemsManual/default.htm

Ong, K. (2012, March 28). *What are Design Controls and Why are they Important.* Retrieved from www.medmarc.com: http://www.medmarc.com/Life-Sciences-News-and-Resources/Ask-An-Expert/Pages/Why-are-design-controls-important.aspx

Manufactured by Amazon.ca
Bolton, ON

18460815R00243